Divot Dogs:

The Adventures of 'The Grip' and 'The Street'

Tom Hoch

By Tom Hoch

© 2014 Tom Hoch
All Rights Reserved.

No part of this publication may be reproduced, stored in a retrieval system, or transmitted, in any form or by any means, electronic, mechanical, photocopying, recording, or otherwise, without the written permission of the author.

First published by Dog Ear Publishing
4010 W. 86th Street, Ste H
Indianapolis, IN 46268
www.dogearpublishing.net

ISBN: 978-1-4575-2970-2

Library of Congress Control Number: has been applied for

This book is printed on acid-free paper.

This book is a work of fiction. Places, events, and situations in this book are purely fictional and any resemblance to actual persons, living or dead, is coincidental.

Printed in the United States of America

To Everett, Marian, Emil and Rose

Acknowledgements

Without a supportive family, writing a worthwhile story would be much more difficult than it already is. I am grateful to my wife, Louann, and my daughters, Abby and Jessie, for providing valuable feedback as I presented characters and scenarios to them. Abby was my content editor on this venture, and she was downright brutal. On multiple occasions she steered me back to the right path, especially when I began to pontificate, which I am prone to do at times.

I owe a special thank you to Dave Bischoff, manuscript coach and copy editor. Through Dave's efforts and tremendous patience, the story was strengthened in several areas.

Kathy Kelsey Holmes did the bulldog sketches. She did a spectacular job on my second novel, *Discovering Balance*, and she came through again on this project. She is an awesome artist, and I love the way she draws people and now dogs too. Thanks, Kathy.

A huge thank you goes out to my manuscript readers, Randy Steinbach and Tina Wilkinson. Their constructive criticism and advice was usually spot on and very instrumental to the story.

I would also like to thank the personnel at the following golf courses: Gull Lake View, Stonehedge, Bedford Valley, Cedar Creek and Riverside. They were all very accommodating. These are all great tracks, and if you are ever in the Battle Creek/Gull Lake area, I strongly suggest that you give yourself enough time to play them all.

Preface

This is a book that I've wanted to write for some time. Eddie and Ronnie were constantly messing around in my head, and I decided that writing their story would be the only way to get them out of there. My manuscript coach was worried about the story's lack of a traditional plot. After some deliberation, I decided to stick with my original plan which consisted of a series of sub plots (hence the secondary title of: *The Adventures of 'The Grip' and 'The Street'*).

I'm hoping that my characters are strong enough which will, in turn, cause the reader to overlook the usual: solve the mystery, figure out who killed who, or uncover the motive for some sort of insane behavior, before the author unveils the truth and shocks everyone but the savviest of readers.

Here's my thinking on the whole standard plot thing. If I were to ask you if you wanted to go see the new James Bond movie, would you ask me what the movie is about? No you wouldn't. It's Bond, man! What are you thinking? It's cool gadgets, spectacular chase scenes, really evil dudes and sexy women. Duh. I believe the Bond persona supersedes all other concerns. Besides, F. Scott Fitzgerald once said, "Character is plot." I figure if a man with his literary status believed that, then it's good enough for me. I hope you will agree.

Tom Hoch
March 2014

PROLOGUE

The scenery in the United States is one of the most diversified and among the most beautiful on the face of the earth. The snowcapped mountains are nothing short of majestic—silent sentinels standing guard over the landscape below. The oceans can be the source of relentless destruction one day, and on the next, incredibly soothing. Fields of corn and beans have their own unique beauty, especially if you're the hard working farmer that has been fretting over the health of his plants for the past several months. Our rivers seem to have their own distinct personalities. It's amazing how they wind their way to their destination through overhanging foliage or high cliffs, flowing tranquilly or rushing madly like a herd of stampeding horses. Valleys can be a world unto themselves. With hills on two sides, they seem to be independent of outside activities. A nice quiet place for you and a friend to sit on the back porch with a lemonade, leisurely watching the sun dip below the crest of the surrounding hills.

However, there are places that were not made by the Creator.

These settings were made by man, and they rival the natural beauty that humans were given when the planet was formed. In the early days, man toiled long and hard with shovel and pick to create these masterpieces. In modern times, huge earth moving equipment is used. Shovels and picks are still needed, but their role has been relegated to do the fine-tuning or the ever-present task of cleaning up the messes made by the big boys.

A century ago or a year ago, the result is the same; a beautiful outdoor venue that often takes one's breath away.

A golf course!

There's sand to catch wayward shots and creeks that wind across or alongside fairways and mounds that seem to reach out and snatch a shot that the author swore was enough to clear it. Beautiful, majestic and awe-inspiring, all in one package—the source of giddy accomplishment one day and miserable failure the next.

Some men do bad things on golf courses, which usually results in a litany of bad words. These men cannot escape the curse that accompanies the gem. But there are a few that have transcended the masses to a loftier place, looking down on those who are merely competent players.

Warning! If you want more on mountains, seashores, crop-laden fields or sneaky little rivers, this story is not for you.

This story is about golf, golf courses and, most of all, two very unique golfers.

Now if our main characters were duffers it wouldn't be much of a story, would it? If they played like whiney little wimps it would remind you too much of your usual Saturday morning foursome. Not much of a story there.

The fact is, these guys can play, and they are willing to put up large amounts of cash to back their position.

Got some scratch you'd like to wager? They will be glad to tee it up with you. Although, it might be difficult to find them because, in this era of constant hype, our guys have gone somewhat underground, picking and choosing their spots more carefully than they did in years past.

Today, with all the technology and the exposure that quality players get at a young age, it's difficult to avoid the spotlight. Shoot a couple of good rounds and your buddies start talking. A couple more good rounds, and maybe a course record, and you will draw attention like a low-class celebrity doing another tasteless self-promo. It's tough to fly under the radar and still make some decent coin. It can be done, but you must be incredibly talented and you must have a flair for the game.

Golfers that play only a couple of rounds a year are few and far between. Future golf fanatics are usually hooked their first time out, before the last putt drops on number eighteen. The particular skill set needed, combined with the outdoor venue, draws drooling golfers like bugs to a porch light in midsummer. But not all are attracted to golf's bright light. It's like the first time you heard a Janis Joplin recording—you either fell in love with her soulful growl or you covered your ears and ran from the room.

The beauty of a golf course cannot be described by mere words.

The smell of freshly cut grass causes most golfers to hyperventilate before their clubs are even out of the car. It is a wonderful smell that brings back fond memories to old men and women that are now too frail to draw the club back. Die-hard golfers daydream about striking precise 7-irons to incredibly tight pins or carrying a hazard that requires everything they've got. They often design golf holes on note pads during business meetings. Unbeknownst to them, the boss is sitting two chairs away doing exactly the same thing.

Yes, golf is an incredible game—a game like no other. How many other sports are there where you call your own fouls? The U. S. Open and the NBA finals are played at about the same time each year—mid June. There's a lot of money on the line, along with a multitude of endorsement opportunities. How far would the ten millionaires on the court get if they had to police themselves? For sure, it would be an interesting spectacle. The Vegas over/under line on how long the game would last would make for some exciting bets. "I'll take the under five minutes with a bench clearing brawl for a grand."

Golf has its own language, known only to other practitioners of the sport. Ask a non-golfer what "rub of the green" means and you will get an open-mouthed stare. How about a "waste bunker" or a "chilidip"?

Recently, a golfer at a local bar was explaining his round to his non-golfing buddy who was sitting to his left. He described all the beautiful shots he had struck until he hit an "elephant's butt" off the tee and into the water on seventeen. When asked what an "elephant's butt" was, the golfer turned to the three fellows sitting to his right. They said in unison, "It's high and it stinks". Spellcheck must not be a golfer or a fan, because it doesn't recognize the above terms. Spellcheck is probably not Janis fan either. Go figure. If you've finished your chores at home or the clock tells you the workday is over—grab your sticks and let's go play some small-ball. But first, we have to get the wagers straight. Don't worry if it seems a little confusing. 'The Grip' and 'The Street' will help you with the math. These two characters are usually up to something. Let's look in on them….

PART ONE

The Hustle

CHAPTER ONE

Old School Hustlers

Yeah, I remember Eddie. Now there was one of the sweetest swings that I ever had on my team. I had to suspend him twice for betting with the opposition during matches.

—Clancy Butler, high school golf coach

Ronnie 'The Grip' Costas stood on the ninth hole at the Gull Lake View West course.

The sun was high in the sky, beaming down with sweet approval as the humans below scurried about in their attempts to accomplish something worthwhile. The air had a fresh outdoorsy smell, as a bird chirped his approval in a nearby tree. Off in the distance the sound of a boat motor could be heard, throttle opened wide, as it raced across Gull Lake.

Ronnie looked over at Eddie 'The Street' Ferguson. He gave Eddie his trademark grin.

"I got a live one at Maywood tonight, Street. This horse is ripe for victory. He's in a tough field, so I'm thinking he should go off at around five-to-one. Nothing to get rich on, but a nice pay-off nonetheless."

"Is that so?" asked Eddie. "Is this horse anything like that turtle that you laid down three Franklins on two weeks ago? You know, the one that finished sixth in a seven-horse field."

"Hey," hollered Ronnie, pointing his wedge at his playing partner. "That race was messed up from the start. Horses breakin' stride all over the place. That usually happens with trotters, not pacers. I have a policy on trots—I don't bet 'em. They're too unpredictable. I put that race out of my mind as soon as they crossed the finish line." He paused thoughtfully and used the wedge to knock some grass off a shoe. "My problem tonight is I'm a little short. In fact, I need another hundred to make a decent bet. So, I'm about forty yards out. A hundred says I get it within ten feet."

Eddie came back with, "Fifty inside ten feet and another fifty if you make the putt. I'm not throwing my money away here. I need to see some skill. It's not that hard of a shot. And, if I get mine up and down, it washes yours out." He barked out a laugh. "And the only place you are a little short is in your drawers."

"Done," said Ronnie, ignoring the personal jab.

The ninth hole on the West course at Gull Lake View was a long par five to a slightly elevated green. The putting surface had substantial slope, so staying underneath the hole was key if you wanted to have a putt where you could actually go at the hole. Both players were well aware of that. They had been playing here together for the past three years. When it was just the two of them, they threw a few hundred back and forth. When others were involved the stakes were often much higher.

'The Grip' and 'The Street' were both old school hustlers.

They were semi-retired when it came to hustling other golfers, but they still loved the thrill of a well-crafted gig. A gig to them was when all the pieces were in place. It was chance to dig deep into some other guy's pocket.

Ronnie took half a practice swing, and then hit a sweet little knock-down wedge about seven feet below the hole. Eddie clapped twice in appreciation and walked over to his ball. His wedge settled in about ten feet below the hole, just outside of Ronnie's.

"Damn, caught it a little heavy," said Eddie, picking up the cigar that he had thrown down.

Ronnie smiled and jumped behind the wheel of the cart. After Eddie missed his putt, Ronnie ran his into the heart of the cup.

Sweet! Another hundred to put on *Cryin' Shame* in the fifth at Maywood tonight.

Not that Ronnie needed the money. He and Eddie were both flush. Money was something they seldom worried about. Expenses had to be covered, but other than that, they viewed money only as a way to keep score.

The two golfers climbed into their cart and headed back to the bar and grill.

Once inside, they sat at their usual table and waited for their usual drinks—Johnnie Walker Red for 'The Street' and Jameson for 'The Grip'. Off the course they were very predictable—same table, same drinks, same waitress. Pam had their drinks ready for them even before they walked in.

Pam Strong was one of the best looking girls in her high school class. She had teased blonde hair, a button nose and long dark eyelashes that the high school boys often dreamed about. She always smelled good too, just a splash of perfume. She usually wore an earthy musk scent. It was one of Eddie's favorites. The waitress still possessed an attractive figure, but now, seven years after graduation, her teenage smile was replaced by a somewhat tired look. This, in fact, was an expression that indicated the passage of several rough years and dreams that went unrealized. She knew what time the guys would finish their round, and she always took care of her two best tippers. The assistant behind the counter in the pro shop informed her that the guys were only playing nine today, so she was ready for them.

The conversation between her and the two regulars usually centered around the guys hitting on her, but Pam didn't mind. She knew it was all in good fun and the twenty-five year old waitress usually gave as good as she got. All three saw it as harmless banter, chiefly because Eddie and Ronnie were both about thirty years older than she was.

"Hey, Pammie," said Ronnie in a low voice, as she sat their drinks down. "Why don't you ditch that boyfriend of yours and let me take you out for an evening you won't forget? I'm telling you, it would be an experience of a lifetime."

"Don't listen to him, doll," said Eddie. "He's still trying to make up for his first roll in the hay. It haunts him to this day. That's why he acts the way he does around the opposite sex."

"That sounds about right," said Pam. "I pegged you both for sexual bumblers the first time you walked through the door."

"Ha," laughed Eddie. "Maybe him, but not me. Don't judge a guy by the crowd he runs with. I've got technique, babe. It would be a shame for you to go through life without ever going to the top of the mountain, with someone who knows what they're doing."

"Give her a break, Eddie," said Ronnie. He watched his playing partner slide the folded hundred-dollar bill that he had just lost across the table. "You two would fall off half way up and end up in the emergency room. You with broken bones and Pammie with split sides from laughing so hard."

"Hey, I saw that," exclaimed Pam, referring to the money that had just exchanged hands. "You didn't lose another sleazy bet that involved me, did you?"

"What do you mean?" asked Ronnie feigning concern.

Her pretty eyes narrowed. "What I mean, stud, is like the time you bet on my bra size."

Ronnie tried to look innocent.

Hands on hips, Pam said, "Oh yeah, I know about that little wager."

"I can't believe you would accuse us of something so disgusting," said Eddie. "That's just despicable. It hurts our feelings that you would think so little of us."

Ronnie nodded in agreement.

"Just the same, you'll never know who won that one," said Pam, as she turned and headed back toward the bar.

Eddie leaned toward his playing partner and whispered, "Who won that bet anyway?"

"That one's still on the grill," responded Ronnie. "She's not going to offer that little tidbit, so one of us has to get some first-hand information. And so far, you are striking out big time. You better leave it to me for verification on that one."

Eddie exclaimed, "Okay, I'll believe whatever you tell me on that subject. How about when turtles climb trees?"

"And can back up an 8-iron on asphalt," the guys said in unison, as they clinked their glasses together. The toast was followed by a loud guffaw and a high nasal laugh.

Fifteen minutes later Pam came strolling back with their second, and last, round. "I've been thinking," she said. "You two are my biggest tippers, and I've seen you slide a few hundred across the table now and then. Are you trying to impress me with a show of green, hoping something more will come of it? If so, you are wasting your money and your time. I like you two, but you're both old enough to be my father. I'm not denying that I need the money, but I don't want to give you any false hopes." Worrying that she might have gone too far with her last comment, she added, "I'm not out of line saying that, am I?"

"Babe," said Ronnie. "I've never stooped to paying for it. That would be demeaning for both parties. It ain't our style, is it, Eddie?"

Eddie nodded in agreement.

Pam hoped she hadn't crossed the line with her two best customers. She just wanted to be honest with them. She needed a quick comeback to lighten the mood.

"Well, if you're not doing it for show, and you are somewhat wealthy, maybe I'll sue you for sexual harassment or something."

"I'm old," wailed Eddie, looking around feigning confusion. "Where am I? Isn't this the grocery store? Why are you serving us liquor at the store?"

"I think I just wet my britches," added Ronnie, looking down at his lap. "I can't find my social security check. Did this young lady con it out of me?"

"All right, you two. I was just messin' with you. Don't have an aneurysm. Besides that hundred you pass back and forth, neither of you probably has enough to pay for decent health insurance."

As she walked away shaking her head, Pam was treated with Eddie's guffaw and Ronnie's squeaky laugh one more time.

Ronnie watched with satisfaction as Eddie threw two twenties on the table—one for the drinks and one for Pam.

The tip was huge, but, truth be known, both men had about a grand in their pocket and another five large tucked away in secret compartments in their golf bags.

And, due to the nature of their business, where preparation was paramount, each golf bag also had a compartment that housed a nine-millimeter hand gun.

* * *

Behind the wheel of his '85 Monte Carlo, Eddie drove home from the course in a reflective mood.

He thought back to his first few months at his new home in southwest Michigan. Three years earlier, at fifty-two years of age, he had moved west to Battle Creek from Detroit. He was looking for a new life—something simple and not too stressful. He had dealt with seedy types for most of his adult life, and he decided that he needed a change of scenery. People with higher moral standards and a sense of ethics would be a refreshing change.

I've done a few things that I'd like to forget, but that was back when I was just a stupid kid. Tall, stately elms on the side of the road seemed to nod in agreement.

As an adult, Eddie always tried to do the right thing, the honorable thing. Had he sacrificed his honor, he would be a lot richer today, but he would have had a hard time living with himself. Eddie was a rarity in more ways than one. He was an honest man working in a field that drew all sorts of sleaze bags and other unsavory types. He was also filled with compassion for his fellow man. On more than one occasion he had donated his winnings to a good cause. That kind of move assuaged his conscience and helped him keep his sanity in a world where greed and narcissism were more often the norm than the exception.

'The Street' stood 5'11" and had jet-black hair that he kept meticulously groomed. He was a slender man with smiling brown eyes and a dark complexion from spending so much time in the sun, playing the game that he loved. His grip on his golf club was like his grip on reality—gentle, but under control. Sam Snead had once told him to hold the club just firm enough so it wouldn't fly out of his hands. He took Sam's advice and applied it to more than just golf. Most of the time he was in complete control of his environment. If a situation appeared to be a little too dicey, he would tactfully extract himself and live to play another day. His philosophy was to deal from a position of strength whenever possible and not to anger people that were potentially dangerous. It was a philosophy that had served him well throughout his adult life.

After contemplating his surroundings in Detroit, a city that wasn't nearly what it used to be, Eddie decided to leave the world of full-time golf hustling in search of a more laid-back lifestyle. He was looking forward to a few social rounds a week with some new friends and a few cocktails afterward. There was a time when it was more than just a few drinks, but he was older now and much wiser. It was the wisdom that grew out of a few past mistakes, some inconsequential and a couple that were life-changing. He knew if he was going to persevere, he had to get back up and not let bad decisions get the best of him. In his new surroundings he looked forward to playing a few twenty-dollar Nassaus. Besides, he could easily earn his "walkin' around money" playing poker at the Firekeeper's Casino east of Battle Creek.

Everything was going as planned, until 'The Grip' came into his life.

Three years prior, Eddie was reading a book under the pavilion that sat by the first tee of the West course at GLV, his nickname for the two courses that were just across the highway from Gull Lake.

He had grown accustomed to his new surroundings, and he liked the whole set-up. The pavilion sat where the original clubhouse was built in the 60's. That facility had been torn down in the mid 90's and a more modern clubhouse with a spacious bar and grill and some banquet rooms were built across the street. It was a beautiful June day with the temperature somewhere in the mid-seventies. A few clouds drifted lazily above him on their way to an undisclosed location somewhere to the east of where he was sitting. Eddie had just finished a two-hour chipping and putting practice session and was pleased with how it went. He was about to get up and head across the highway and down the hill to the Bayview Market for a soda, when he heard a strange high-pitched laugh. The first tee was only about thirty yards from where he was sitting, and a foursome was standing there hitting their tee shots. The laugh came from the man who was about to hit. His posture and his grip on the club complimented each other—they were both atrocious. Just looking at him as he addressed the ball would inspire an accomplished player to hurl on the spot, hopefully off to the side of the tee. There was nothing pretty or poetic about this guy's approach to clubbing a golf ball. The slouching man with the strange laugh aimed way left and hit a big slice that eventually came back to the middle of the fairway. Two of the men exchanged sly grins as his ball came to rest about twenty-five yards short of their drives. They were obviously playing against the slicer and his partner. Eddie knew the two guys that were grinning. They liked to play for some serious dough if the situation was right. He usually avoided them. In his former life he would have set them up for a big kill, and he would have had no problem holding some of their cash at the end of the match. The whole situation, money players versus caveman golfer and partner, piqued Eddie's curiosity. Something wasn't right about this guy with the goofy laugh and horrible swing. His intuition told him that somebody was going to get skinned before the round was over.

Eddie walked over to his car and took out a small pair of binoculars from his golf bag. He went back to his reading spot and discreetly watched the group play the first hole. The first hole on the West course was an easy par four—straight, with little trouble. When they got to the green the laugher made a putt and his partner threw his arms in the air. From the body language of both teams, it was obvious who had won the hole. The second hole was a short par three that ran perpendicular to the first. Eddie strolled down the left side of the first hole acting like he was hawking balls where trees met the rough. He had to walk about two hundred yards so he could get a good look at the second green. He stood out of sight at the edge of the tree line and watched through his binoculars. It was a repeat of the first hole—partner's arms in the air followed by dejected opponents. Who was this guy? He had a hacker's grip and his stance was even worse, but he had apparently just birdied the first two holes. And, he was undoubtedly playing for more than pocket change. Hustlers were usually good at spotting each other, like little kids when they passed each other in their momma's carts at the supermarket. There was just something about the other guy that drew your attention to him. Eddie walked across the road and into the pro shop. The assistant pro was behind the counter and he smiled as Eddie came in.

"Hey, Chris," said Eddie to the a. p. "Who just went off on the front side on the West course? I know Weaver and Jensen, but I've never seen the other two."

"I think those two are from Chicago," said the young man, looking up from his magazine. "They're staying in one of the condos."

"Thanks, man," said Eddie, turning around and heading back toward the door. He paused with his hand on the door and looked back over his shoulder. "Hey, what did you shoot yesterday?"

"Seventy-one on the East," said the young man, with a patronizing look on his face. "Not quite in your league, big guy, but I'm getting there."

The employees and the regulars at the course thought Eddie was about a seven handicapper. That's the way he wanted it. In reality, he would have had no problem handling the assistant pro's seventy-one. Plus, with a few hundred on the line, the kid's seventy-one could have easily turned into a seventy-five. Street walked across the highway and down toward the lake. He needed a soda, and he needed to find out who the guy with the terrible grip and swing was. There's one thing a hustler knows—be leery of a player with a bad grip and a bad swing that plays at higher level than he should be playing. A player in this category was an unknown. He was an unpredictable player that an experienced hustler would avoid at all costs. Nothing was more deflating than getting beat at your own game. It had happened to him in the past and it was always followed by an intense soul-searching session. As one who was always interested in improving his craft, he knew he should learn from it and then let it go. But that was easier said than done.

Eddie bought a soda from the little grocery store that sat at the southern end of Gull Lake. He walked across the narrow road and sat on a bench by the ice cream store. This little bay was one of his favorite spots. He happened on it as he was driving around the area a few months earlier. This spot, and the pavilion by the West course, were his favorite reading places. When he put his ear-buds in it also became a perfect place to nap. It only took two days of scouting to decide that the Gull Lake View complex, between Battle Creek and Kalamazoo, was going to be his new golf home. There were five beautiful courses to play, all owned by the Scott family, and because of the challenging layouts and immaculate conditions, they attracted a lot of traffic from the bigger cities. Big city guys usually had more scratch in their pockets and some were not opposed to playing for more than a couple of bucks. And, unlike the locals, tourists went home after a while, to be replaced by an influx of new golfers. Two of the courses were right behind him across the highway and two more, Stonehedge North and South, were only a few miles away. The fifth, Bedford Valley, was about twenty-five minutes away. It was a sweet set-up for a hustler, or a semi-retired one like him. A guy with his past just couldn't quit cold turkey anyway.

From his position up on the bank, Eddie watched a couple boats move around the bay. They had to maneuver their way through the sailboats that were anchored here and there. He thought about pulling out his mp3 player to block out the occasional car noise that passed close behind his bench, but he decided against it. He had a lot on his mind and wanted to focus on the topic at hand. Below him, a small pontoon boat full of little kids with life jackets on pulled into the dock. The teenage girl that was driving jumped out and secured the lines. *Must be babysitting*, he thought. *This would be an awesome place to grow up—lakes, golf courses, and decent summer weather. Kids that grow up on the water probably learn to swim before they can walk.* The girl ushered her charges up the stairs and into the ice cream store. They waved at Eddie and he waved back.

Who was that guy?

Eddie decided to make a few phone calls when he got back to his place. He used to have a few connections in Chicago. Hopefully they were still around and still breathing. It wasn't a big deal, and he didn't consider this guy a threat. He just wanted to know who he was and what he was up to. It never hurt to know what was going on, especially when an unknown showed up on your turf. The boaters came out of the ice cream shop licking on cones.

"How's the ice cream?" asked Eddie.

"Great," came the response from one little red-haired girl. The ice cream was already dripping down her cone and on to her hand.

"If they get too messy," said Eddie, looking at the older girl, "you can just dip them in the lake to clean them up."

"I've done that before," laughed the babysitter. "It works great."

"See ya," said Eddie waving.

"Bye, mister," came the response, as the troop headed down the steps and back to their boat.

Yep, this is going to be a nice place to live, thought Eddie. *And it will be a lot nicer as soon as I find out who the hustler on the West course is.*

Eddie walked back up the path and across the highway toward the course parking lot. He had important business to take care of. Hopefully, he could dig up the laugher's identity with a few phone calls.

It took only two calls for Eddie to get the information he was looking for. Ronnie 'The Grip' Green, a.k.a. Ronnie Costas—what kinda name was that? It's obvious where it came from. The man held a club like a thirty handicapper. So, Eddie surmised, Ronnie's plan of attack was to come off as a duffer and then, when he collected his winnings, claim that he had never played that well in his life. It sounded like the approach of a second-rate hustler. Eddie got up from the kitchen table and headed for the door. It was time to show some locals how to play poker. This Grip guy was apparently not going to be a problem.

The man never crossed his mind again until that day in early September.

CHAPTER TWO

Introductions

Eddie Ferguson? Don't know the guy. And if I ever see that son of a bitch again, I still don't know him!

—Claude Worthy, disgruntled investor

"Heard it through the grapevine. No longer would you be mine!"
"Tell me about it, Marvin!" said Eddie, to no one in particular.
He loved Motown! It was easy, being from Detroit.
Eddie was practicing long putts on the East course putting green. He loved this particular green. It was huge with a lot of undulations. He had his ear buds in and was listening to music from the 60's. He was partial to the old stuff: In addition to *The Four Tops* and *The Temptations*, he liked *Credence Clearwater Revival, The Animals,* and the sweetest voice he had ever heard, Roy Orbison.
He made a smooth stroke, then straightened up and looked out over the course. The scenery around him reminded him of a huge green carpet that was expertly fitted to the terrain. His attention was drawn back to the putting surface as his ball tracked straight into the hole. He had read the putt perfectly. He should have. This was his third attempt from this particular spot.
Eddie was also partial to the blues, but he liked to hear that genre at live shows, preferably with a nice looking lady at his side. In his golf and poker travels he had gotten to know a few blues musicians. In some ways, their lives had paralleled his.
Eddie had had his ups and downs in his younger years. He almost lost his two young daughters to a "nut case" of a wife, as he and most anybody else that knew her, would describe the woman. Drinking had almost got the better of him too, but he persevered and did right by his daughters. One of his girls now lived in Florida and the other in Texas. Both were married with careers and kids of their own. He walked back to his car in the lot thinking about how fortunate he was to find this golfers' paradise without having to leave the Midwest.

* * *

The transplanted Detroit native was settled in to his new surroundings and had made several friends. He was now a regular at the Monday morning game and usually played in the Thursday afternoon game. On a whim he had also volunteered to play on couples' night if they were a man short. On most days about twenty guys showed up to play and the buy-in was twenty bucks for the Monday and Thursday games. Moe Stadler ran both of them and he kept everything on the up and up. Eddie was in the black with these two games, but not by much. He knew enough not to tip his hand. He messed around a lot just having fun, playing little games with himself. Aiming at traps and water hazards and mishitting several irons that kept his scores around 80. He was getting pretty creative at appearing mediocre. Golf was now mostly a recreational activity with him anyway—except for the time he took the St. Louis loudmouth for a couple grand a month earlier. That guy was the most obnoxious person he had ever come across, and he knew a lot of obnoxious people. Taking that guy's dough was the most fun he had had since moving to the Battle Creek area.

* * *

Eddie had hooked up with the loudmouth and another guy on the first tee of the West course. One was a non-stop chatterbox while his friend rarely spoke. On the second tee box, Clint, the guy that thought he was the life of the party, suggested they play a little twenty dollar skins game. The Detroit hustler agreed just to see where this was all headed. It looked like the two out-of-towners were going for the old "two brothers and a stranger" gig. If Eddie had it figured right, the quiet guy, Glen, was the better golfer. At the turn, he would have won the most holes, then Eddie, then Clint. Clint would complain about how bad he was playing and would try to get the other two to up the bet, so he could recoup his losses. Eddie was supposed to go along out of sympathy for Clint, who was losing the most. Once the stakes got to a decent amount, Glen would really turn it on. When it was all over Clint and Glen would split the money that Eddie lost. Eddie was supposed to walk away feeling somewhat good about his losses, because he wasn't the big loser. Sure enough, after finishing the front nine, Glen had four skins, Eddie had two, and Clint had not won a hole. The deal was only the top guy collected, so Eddie was down forty bucks and Clint was down eighty.

Eddie had a hard time keeping a straight face, as his two opponents were putting on some great theatre. If they would have pulled this type of stunt back in Detroit they would have been laughed right off the course and maybe right out of town. He gave Glen two holes outright by hitting into traps and then taking two to get out. On the tenth tee Clint quietly told Eddie that if they were playing for some real money, Glen would fold like a cheap card table. He'd seen his friend do it before back in St. Louis. At this point, Eddie decided to make his move.

"Okay, fellas," said Eddie, bringing the situation out into the open. "I think I know where you're heading with this. I like to play for a little dough from time to time too. I will tell you that I'm usually better than what I showed you on the front, and I bet that Glen didn't show me his best game either. Clint, I got no idea what you're capable off, except for trying to talk the ears off of a guy. How about this—Glen gives me half a stroke a hole for the first five, and if I'm winning, I'll give him a half a stroke for the last four. That way no one gets burned too bad. We'll play for fifty bucks a hole. The same deal for you, Clint, but we play for a little more."

"I aint giving you any strokes, Eddie, full or half," wailed Clint. "You saw how bad I played on the front. If anything, you should give me half a shot on all nine."

"All right, let's play the first five even, and whoever is ahead will give the other guy half a pop on the last four. That gives the loser a decent chance to make up his losses. With the half stroke you win all ties. That's all it's good for. Now, how much do you want to play for? You name it." Eddied looked Clint straight in the eye. The posing and jockeying was over. It was time to get to the gettin'.

"Two hundred a hole," said Clint, puffing his chest out and sticking out his hand. He was hoping that a wager like that would make Eddie a little nervous, and maybe throw him off his game.

Eddie came back with, "Two fifty and you've got a bet. I'll even give you some advice on how to play the holes, 'cause I've played here more than you." The poker player in him said to raise when he felt he had the advantage.

Clint looked at Glen who just shrugged his shoulders. Maybe their little plan would backfire on them. They shook hands and the game was on. The back nine on the West course was nothing like the front. The difference in nines would definitely play to Eddie's advantage. There were elevation changes and some of the holes were just plain devious, like ten, eleven, and twelve. Eddie figured if he got out to a good lead, the St. Louis natives would lose confidence and the pressure might affect their swings. He had seen this happen too many times to count.

Number ten went down a big hill with a left-to-right slope. Eddie hit a small fade down the left side that ended up in the middle of the fairway. Both of his opponents misjudged the slope and went too far right, ending up with bogeys. 'The Street' put down the scores and two little marks next to his name on the card. Eleven was the toughest par three on the course, front or back. The green was elevated with a big trap guarding it. The players could barely see the putting surface from the tee, which made it even tougher. Eddie said that after he hit he would then tell them if his shot was good, bad, or average. When his ball landed softly over the front trap, he said, "That's the ticket, right there."

Clint was intimidated by the front trap and hit his tee shot too hard, flying it over the green and into a small stand of trees. Glen hit a shot similar to Eddie's, but neither of them made their putt. With his half stroke from Glen, and Clint's bogey, Eddie made two more marks on the card. Hole number twelve was a nightmare for a lot of people. It was a par four with a second shot that had to be played up what some of the locals called "heart attack hill". The three competitors hit nice drives out into a soft fairway. When it was Eddie's turn to hit, Clint made a lot of noise messing around in his bag, unzipping zippers and rattling his clubs around. Eddie looked up and smiled.

"Clint, you can do anything but piss on my ball while I'm hitting. It doesn't bother me in the least. I once had a guy fart in my backswing on every shot for sixteen holes. He must have loaded up on tacos before the match. He finally ran out of gas with two holes to go."

"Sorry, man," said Clint. "I was just looking for my cigar cutter. I didn't mean to distract you."

"No worries," said Eddie, as he hit a beautiful four-hybrid onto the green.

After five holes, Eddie had ten marks next to his name and his opponents had none. Glen had three pars and two bogeys, but the half stroke he had to give hurt him dearly. Eddie had parred every hole. Since Glen was now getting the half stroke, if he could tie Eddie on three of the next four, he could walk away losing less than a hundred. At this point, he figured the education was worth it. It didn't dawn on Glen until the fourteenth hole that he was playing against the guy known as 'The Street'. He had heard some of his golf buddies back home talk about famous golf hustlers past and present, and Eddie's name was mentioned more than once. He chuckled to himself and decided not to let Clint know until they were in the car on their way home. The way he figured it, it was somewhat of an honor to lose to a living legend. Hell, he even liked the guy. Didn't Eddie tell them his name on the first tee? He thought 'The Street's' last name was Davis, but the guy probably used several aliases.

Glen and Eddie were standing next to each other in the middle of the fourteenth fairway, a beautiful par four that made a 90-degree left turn to an elevated green. Clint was over on the right side looking for his ball. They both told him they saw it splash in the little pond, but he said he wanted to make sure it wasn't playable before he took a drop.

Eddie stood there calmly smoking a Macanudo. It was like old times again, and he was enjoying himself immensely. Eddie fell in love with golf the first time he walked onto a golf course. He was with ten other boys taking a short class on how to caddy at a private club in Detroit. The caddiemaster and his number one caddy played the first hole and then played back up eighteen, giving instruction as they went. Being outdoors, the smell of the grass, and even the smell of the leather grips on the clubs, all drew Eddie into a world that he had never known in his twelve short years. He was hooked from that first day. From that moment on, he decided to learn everything he could about caddying and playing the game.

Eddie had seen a lot of changes to a game that had given him the opportunity to live a comfortable lifestyle over the years. The old saying, "the one thing that never changes is that things will always change," definitely applies to golf. The grips are now simulated leather or some other synthetic material, and caddies are a thing of the past at most clubs. *The equipment has changed the game more than anything,* thought Eddie. *Back in those days we would have never dreamed that a tour pro could hit a 5-iron 225 yards. Modern golf clubs and balls were now juiced up in an attempt to hit the ball much farther. Commercialism—it's everywhere. When will golfers figure out that the only way you can buy a golf game is through lessons from a competent teacher? And if you don't have the skills, there's only so far you can go. It's a good thing that golf is one of the only sports that you do not have to play well to have a good time. Imagine how frustrating it would be to attempt to play tennis without being able to sustain a three or four shot volley. Golf was different. A guy could shoot a hundred and still enjoy himself out here.*

"Hey, Street," said Glen, releasing Eddie from his thoughts and, at the same time, informing Eddie that he knew who he was. "Did you really skip a ball over a pond and onto the green for fifty grand?"

"Yep," said Eddie, without looking over at his opponent. "It cost me twenty thousand just to set the shot up. They gave me three tries, and I did it on the third one. There was a lot of pressure on that last shot. If they would have raked the pond for balls, they would have found about half of the pro's range balls in there. I told him about it afterward and sent him fifty dozen new ones. Do me a favor, man. Keep 'The Street' thing to yourself. The locals around here don't know about me, and I like to keep it that way. I don't play with them for more than twenty or thirty bucks anyway. This is a nice place, and I'd like to stick around a while."

"No problem," said Glen, patting Eddie on the back. "Just so you know, I aint gonna lay down on the last four when I get my half a shot—on account of you being a legend and everything. Just thought you'd like to know that." Glen proceeded to stick his second shot about ten feet under the cup. Eddie followed with a shot that settled in three feet closer. They both lipped out their putts and had to settle for pars. Eddie got another mark, but now he had to give Glen a half stroke on the remaining four holes.

When the round was over, Clint had lost every hole. Eddie considered letting him win the last one, but decided against it. He had a fifteen-footer for a birdie and the shutout on eighteen green. He looked over at Glen and winked, then he calmly rolled the ball into the cup.

"Sumbitch," said Clint. "I owe you $2250. You were layin' in the weeds all the time. What did you shoot, about two under?"

"Yeah," said Eddie. "To be honest, I would have been happy with the original game, scheme and all. I figured I'd win a few bucks on the back, and I'd have a good story to tell down the road. I guess I wanted to see if I still had it."

The bets were paid and the St. Louis travelers packed up and headed for home. When they crossed over the state line into Indiana, Glen told his buddy whom they had lost their money to. Clint said he had never heard of Eddie 'The Street' Ferguson or Davis, or whatever the guy called himself. Glen chuckled and leaned back to take a nap. That's just the way Eddie would have wanted it. Just before he fell asleep, Glen heard the radio play a catchy tune that had been around for a while. He thought the name of it was *The Gambler's Run* or something like that.

* * *

Eddie, dressed in his usual tan cargo shorts and white golf shirt, was lagging forty footers and was on his last ball when a pair of white golf shoes stepped into his field of vision. He looked up in surprise to see Ronnie Costas grinning at him. Ronnie was a few inches shorter than Eddie's 5'11", and he was mostly bald under his Chicago White Sox ball cap. He was wearing white cargo shorts, but his choice of shirts was not something Eddie had hanging in his closet. It was the pinkest shirt that he had ever seen. Only at a golf course could a guy get away with wearing something that would normally send onlookers into fits of hysterical laughter. White shorts and a pink shirt were no problem at a golf course, but if he walked into a neighborhood bar back home in Chicago wearing that ensemble, it would be an even money bet that someone was going to get clocked. Ronnie looked like a man that would be more at home driving a truck or working at a place where guys went home with sore backs every day. His huge hands and bulging forearms complimented the rest of his stout body. He stuck out his paw and said, "Hello, Street."

Eddie took the offering and said, "How ya doin', Grip?"

It was obvious that 'The Grip' had also done his homework.

That moment was the start of a close friendship that so far had lasted three years. They couldn't believe how similar their lives were. In addition to being golf hustlers, they both had night "jobs". Eddie played poker and Ronnie was a horseplayer. Eddie had played serious cards since he was ten. He regularly took his fellow caddies for a few bucks until he got greedy one day. It cost him a severe beating and his pockets were emptied. After that, he was much more selective about how much he won and whom he took it from. Ronnie came across his handicapping and wagering skills purely by chance. On a whim, he went to a seminar one day held by the great horseplayer, Al Stanley. After class, Al and his students went to Maywood Park to put what they had learned in to practice. Ronnie lost every race he had bet on, but it was a learning experience. He sat up late that night and replayed the five races he had wagered on in his head. Before he fell asleep, he had a good idea why he had lost and what he needed to do to be a successful horseplayer. The "secret," if you could call it that, was to know horses, races, and money. He had vowed to himself to become an expert on all three.

CHAPTER THREE

Pam's Dilemma

I played this dude named Ronnie something a few years ago. He looked like he worked construction or some other physical job. Then he took my rent money from me. When he found out that I was hurtin' for dough, he offered to play me again and lost it all back, plus a couple a hundred. The man's a prince in my book.

—"Cadillac Joe", truck driver/low handicapper

It has been said that the strong in our society have the greater responsibility.

How much different would the world be if the majority of the dictators throughout history had their citizens' best interests at heart? What would the United States be like if federal and state politicians decided to put serving the public at the top of their list instead of their re-election campaigns? On a smaller scale, if an individual or a group comes across an opportunity to help out their fellow man, why not take the time to enhance the quality of someone else's life? Quite often, even the smallest gesture can make a huge difference to the recipient. The United States gets poor marks in this area and we are undoubtedly heading in the wrong direction. The "me generation" appears to have expanded into the "me era". This "I always vote my pocketbook" or "stick it to the other guy before he sticks it to you" attitude is frustrating to those who really care about their fellow man and the planet that we call home.

Sadly, this narcissistic attitude has found its way to the game of golf. Out on the course, nothing is more frustrating than to see a green full of ball marks. It only takes a few seconds to fix one, but bending over does require some effort.

Hey, if your back is that bad, maybe you should be home playing bridge or dominoes instead of golf! A huge hunk of sod lying in the middle of the fairway, in the vicinity of the hole where it came from, is a close second on the frustration scale. How about multiple divots lying there side-by-side, indicating that the guys ahead were playing some sort of scramble?

Really?

Not one of the guys in the group thought it would be prudent to repair the damage they did to the course? They're probably the same guys that spit sunflower shells all over the greens—inconsiderate imbeciles, one and all.

On the other hand, it's always refreshing to be paired with someone that does care about the course and his fellow golfers. The guy that picks up trash along the way, or the guy who will repair eight to ten ball marks on a given green and not make a big deal about it. This is the type of guy that the legendary Harvey Penick would definitely call his friend. There seems to be a shortage of these types, but they're still out there. They're not necessarily purists or throwbacks from a different age. They're just golfers who believe in showing an appreciation for the game and for the work that the grounds crew does to keep the course in the best condition they can, given the manpower and resources available to them. These are the type of golfers that will go over to the guy on a mower and compliment him on the work that he does for the betterment of the grounds. It doesn't cost anything to pay that compliment and it's usually worth its weight in gold.

Helping your fellow humans and nature out.

What a novel concept!

But, there are always cynics. "It's gonna hurt, right? And how much is it going to cost me? Don't they pay guys to fix the course up after the golfers are through with it? Let them do the grunt work. If I'm expected to fix things out here, then I want to be on the payroll. I'm just here for a good time (a favorite yuppie saying). Help others out? Man, I've got my own problems to deal with".

These are the guys that a real golfer would like to slap upside the head. It probably wouldn't change their attitude, but it would give the slapper a small sense of vindication.

* * *

Our heroes had just finished playing the front nine on the East course and decided to have a quick lunch before playing the back.

Normally golfers don't stop between nines, but the assistant pro behind the counter said they would have no problem getting back out. When he asked how they played, they both answered with their usual, "the course record is safe and nobody got hurt." Eddie was actually two under, but he was still ten bucks down to Ronnie. When it was just the two of them, they let it all hang out.

Pam brought them their ice tea and turned without saying anything. Ronnie looked over at Eddie and raised an eyebrow. Eddie responded with a shoulder shrug. When Pam brought back their sandwiches, and sat them down without making eye contact, they both sensed something was up.

"Hey, are you sick?" asked Eddie. "If you are, you shouldn't be serving food."

"No, I'm not sick," said a red-eyed Pam. "If you must know, I'm having a miserable day. And stop being so nosey. Why don't you two get jobs?"

"I had a real job once," said Ronnie, looking over at his partner. "I didn't like it much. What about you, Str—-, uh Eddie? You ever have a real job?"

"Yeah, back in high school. It didn't last long. I decided that hard work was for big strong dudes. Good-looking guys like me should be able to get by without breaking their backs. So far, it's worked out pretty good."

"I don't know about that," quipped Pam. "I've seen the cars that you two are driving around in. I bet you both pick up a lot of girls with those fine pieces of machinery."

Ronnie leaned over and whispered to Eddie as if Pam wasn't standing there. "I think she's feeling better. She's got her sass back."

Pam just turned and stalked away.

Pam Strong was not just having a miserable day—she was having a terrible day.

Her ex-boyfriend was back in town, and he was a walking nightmare. He had given her an early Christmas gift when he moved away two years earlier. Their relationship had been rocky from the start, and when she decided to terminate it, he got ugly. Most of his threats were verbal, but he had slapped her a couple of times. Her problem was she had no one to turn to. She dated a couple of guys on and off after the breakup, but it was nothing serious. And besides, neither of them would have been able to stand up to a jerk like Jeff. He was an adult bully. She found that out a little too late. In the beginning he was a real charmer, and she fell for his act like a high school girl. How could she have been so stupid? Now he was back expecting to take up as if nothing had happened. She was in dire need of a knight in shining armor.

Pam walked out to her car after her shift was over. It was a league night, so she had been too busy to think much about Jeff's return. She knew she needed some help, but had no idea where it was going to come from. Maybe she could hire some big, mean biker type to scare him off. For a price they could act like they were a couple. It was a great plan, if the guy's fee was five bucks. That's about all she had to spend on a knight's fee. Pam started her car and was just about to put it in gear when a blue and white '57 Chevy convertible pulled directly in front of her, blocking her way. She shut her engine off and got out. Walking over to the gorgeous classic convertible, she saw Eddie Ferguson behind the wheel and Ronnie Costas sitting on the passenger side. Ronnie got out of the car and swung his arm toward Eddie.

"Get in, babe," said Ronnie. "Eddie and I are going to cruise around the lake and we'd like some female company."

"Have you two been drinking?" asked Pam. "I'm not getting in if you have."

"Define drinking," chuckled Ronnie. When Pam refused to move he added, "Not if you count one whiskey each. That's not drinking—that's just sampling. C'mon, it's a beautiful night. We're harmless. You know that."

"You better be," said Pam, as she got in and slid over to the middle of the bench seat.

Eddie immediately put his arm around her and winked at Ronnie. "Hey, Potsy, how about you drive so my date and I can sit in the back?"

Pam removed his arm and put his hand on the wheel. "Two hands on the wheel, Romeo. And watch the road. I would like to get back in one piece. Whose car is this, anyway?"

Ronnie got in and Eddie steered the Chevy out of the lot. He turned right towards the lake and gunned the powerful engine. Both back tires broke loose and let out a loud screech.

Eddie looked at Ronnie and proudly exclaimed, "Girls just love it when a guy peels out."

Ronnie chuckled and nodded in agreement. Pam just stared ahead and smiled. Actually she did like nice cars with powerful engines, and this was the nicest car she had ever been in.

"Is this your car or did you steal it?" she asked. "I'm not going to be a part of any grand theft auto plan, if that's what you two are up to."

"Relax and enjoy the ride," said Eddie. "It's a beautiful evening."

Eddie crossed the highway and proceeded down the hill to Gull Lake. At the bottom of the hill he turned left and drove around the bay. Just past the marina he turned into a small lot that afforded a nice view of the water. The lights across the way sparkled on the dark waters of the bay. He shut the engine off and looked over at Pam. She stared nervously at the two men seated next to her.

"To answer your question, yes, this is my car. We're in it because Ronnie's cruiser is only a two-seater."

Pam looked at Ronnie and asked, "I suppose you have a really cool car too?"

"Yup. A '61 Vette. And it's got a bigger engine than this one's got."

Pam looked back at Eddie and saw him looking at her with a serious face. "What's going on?" she asked with a hint of fear in her voice.

"Look, Pam," said Eddie. "We just want to help. We know there's something going on with you and you don't have any kind of support group to turn to. You live alone and don't have a lot of friends. We also know you have taken a couple of classes at Kellogg Community College in Battle Creek and would like to be a nurse some day."

"Your parents live in Arizona," continued Ronnie, "and you don't talk to them as much as you should."

"Have you been spying on me?" asked Pam, on the verge of tears. They were making it sound like she was a major loser. She knew she wasn't a loser or a bad person. Bad luck and poor timing had been her life story ever since she graduated high school, eight years ago. Things had not worked out the way she had planned, that's all. "I think I want to go back to my car."

"In a few minutes," said Eddie putting a gentle hand on her shoulder. "Hear us out first, okay?"

It didn't take much for Pam to tell them everything, culminating with the return of her abusive boyfriend. She finally broke into tears, which she rarely did. She had always tried to handle her problems herself in a way that lived up to her last name, Strong. But there was something about these two that made her open up. She could sense by their demeanor that they just wanted to help, asking nothing in return. She had never met even one guy who showed that sort of no-strings-attached compassion. Up until this point in her adult life, the men she had been associated with always had ulterior motives. When she was done explaining her situation with Jeff, they offered to take her home so she could get enough personal things for a week. They also agreed to put her up at the motel next to the golf course. That should be enough time to come up with a plan. Pam knew she needed help, and so far, Eddie and Ronnie were the only ones to offer any sort of assistance. Besides that, there was something about these two that intrigued here. There appeared to be more to them than just a couple of recently retired guys that had nothing better to do than to play golf every day. Hopefully they weren't some sort of lawbreakers hiding out from the authorities, or worse, from other criminals.

"What's taking her so long?" said Eddie.

"No worries, my man. We can deal with this scumbag if we have to," said Ronnie.

"Yeah, I forgot. You're from the south side of Chicago. Well, if he shows up he's all yours, tough guy."

Eddie and Ronnie sat outside of Pam's house as she gathered her things. They had driven around the block twice before stopping. There was no sign of Jeff, or his car, so they pulled up to the curb and told Pam to hurry. She wasn't sure that this was the way to solve her boyfriend problem, but the two old guys appeared to know what they were doing. Maybe two not-so-young "knights" were just as good as the one young one she was hoping for.

After she packed her suitcase they drove her back to the course and checked her in to a room. They decided to park her car out of sight, way back in one of the parking lots among the condos. If Jeff came snooping around, which was highly unlikely, it would still be tough for him to put two and two together. She had done one smart thing when it came to Jeff. He knew she was a waitress, but she never mentioned to him where she worked.

Eddie drove Ronnie west to his place in Richland. They were both lost in their own thoughts. A simple steak dinner together had turned into a mini-adventure. If forced to admit it, both of them would readily attest to the importance of their relationship. A guy should have a few mates, male or female. Loneliness is an affliction that too many people suffer from. The sad part is—it's totally avoidable. An observant eye and a little compassion would make the world a better place for untold millions that suffer from simply having no one to spend some quality time with.

Eddie pulled in to Ronnie's drive and looked over at his friend. "Well, what's your plan?"

Ronnie's grin was hard to make out in the darkness. He took out a bill and laid it on the seat.

"Twenty bucks says my plan is better than yours."

Eddie laid his twenty on top of Ronnie's. "You've got a guy, right?"

"I got a guy, and I'm sure he's better than your guy. Private Dick. Will take jobs like this for certain people. We go way back. He owes me a little more than I owe him, but it will still cost us."

"What figure do you have in mind?"

"I'm thinking six large will do it, plus expenses," said Ronnie. "You've got to pay top dollar if you don't want any complications."

"Six large," whispered Eddie. "You're right. You've got to pay quality to get quality. Think he can get here in a few days?"

"I'll give him a call," said Ronnie, pulling out his phone and pushing just one number.

"You've got him on speed dial?" asked Eddie.

Ronnie nodded in the affirmative, as he listened for his guy to answer. "Herman, Grip. How you doin? Hey, turn down the music. I've got a situation to pass by you." The conversation lasted only two minutes. Herman would meet them at the golf course grill for lunch in two days. There was no mention of any money.

"Well?" asked Ronnie, as he closed his phone and looked down at the money on the seat.

"Pick it up," said Eddie. "That was quick. Are you sure this guy is what we're looking for?"

"He's more than what we're looking for. Did I mention that he's ex-Special Forces? Who's your guy? A retired security guard at Dairy Queen?"

"Not hardly, but your guy will have to do. I'll get you my end tomorrow. I'll have to make a withdrawal."

"Right. How about you just withdraw it from your golf bag when we play tomorrow?"

"What?" hollered Eddie. "How do you know what I'm carrying in my bag?"

"Dude, we might as well be brothers, twins in fact. You don't think I know what kinda cash you carry around? No self-respecting player would have any less than five grand in their bag. Excuse me, sir, will you take a check for the three grand I just lost to you? Give me a break. By the way, is your piece loaded with the safety on or is the clip in another compartment?"

"The clip is in the little bag where I keep my tees and stuff," admitted Eddie. "Yours?"

"I'm from Chicago, not a little burg like Detroit. Mine's always loaded."

CHAPTER FOUR

Herman

Herman, the Private Dick? Stay away from him, man. When provoked he's got more attitude than Cuck Norris and Rambo put together. I think Huey Lewis was thinking about him when he wrote the song, "Bad is Bad". I'm serious. Don't walk. Run away and run fast.

—Walt Cummins, bookie/pimp/frequent lawbreaker

The two hustlers sat at their regular table sipping on their usual refreshments. They had just finished the Monday morning game, each dropping fifteen bucks. A loss was always chalked up as insurance money—money invested to lead the normal life of a retired accountant and an insurance man. At least that's what they claimed to be when asked. The nature of their business, at times, caused them to be somewhat liberal with the truth unless they were talking about golf. They never lied about golf. That would be just plain dishonest.

From his vantage point, Street was the first to see the tall black man that had been watching them through the glass that separated the grill and the hallway. The big man moved gracefully into the room and came up behind Ronnie. In one smooth motion he had him in a light choke hold.

"You the white boy that's been messin' with my woman?" whispered the man in Ronnie's ear. Eddie's eyes went wide, but Ronnie never even flinched.

"Sit down, Herm," he said with his fork half way to his mouth. "I want you to meet a friend of mine. Say hello to Eddie Ferguson."

Eddie stood up and shook hands with the big man as the rest of the people in the room relaxed. A 6'4" muscular black man was not a normal sight at the Gull Lake View Bar and Grill—even if he was dressed like a golfer. Herman was the kind of guy that drew people's attention when he walked into a room. He had a body and an air of confidence that tended to make people take a second look. Strangers would often approach him for an autograph, thinking he was a professional athlete. He always smiled and signed for them—a fictitious name.

Ronnie smiled to himself as he thought of Herman's favorite signature. The big guy usually wrote, Reg Guyford, which stood for "regular guy".

It took the two golfers about fifteen minutes to lay out the situation to Herman, who scribbled down Pam's address and a few other pertinent details.

The plan was simple. Herman would scare Jeff away from the area, without any bloodshed or broken bones, if possible. And he would impress upon him the unhealthy ramifications of returning to the area. They walked outside together to their golf cart, casually talking as if they were setting up a normal business deal. Ronnie reached in to his golf bag so Eddie did the same. Herman took the two brown paper bags from the guys, each containing three grand, and stuffed them into his pockets. Ronnie handed him an extra three hundred for miscellaneous expenses. Herman said he would call when the plan had been properly executed.

"Everything up front," observed Eddie, as Herman retreated to his car. "I like that. It shows respect. You knew he was in the clubhouse?"

"Yeah, I saw his feet in one of the restroom stalls when I went in to wash up. Those big dogs were hard to miss. He must have seen us coming and ducked in there to hide."

"Slick," said Eddie. "I could tell by the way you two talked that you are, or were, good friends."

"You noticed that, did ya? Herm and my son, Robbie, served in the same unit. Rob actually saved Herm's life during an intense firefight."

"You've got a son? You never mentioned him."

"He was killed in the early days of the Iraq war," said Ronnie, choking back the emotions he felt whenever he talked about his son.

Eddie grasped his friend by the shoulder. "I'm sorry, Grip, it's gotta be tough for you."

"Yeah, I really miss him. He was a great kid and a dynamite athlete. He was a natural at just about any sport. Couldn't hit a golf ball to save his life though."

"Hey," said Eddie, reaching into his pocket. "Let me help out with the expense money."

"No way," said Ronnie. "I'll probably win that back from you in a couple of days anyway. And don't worry about Herman. He knows his stuff, and he can be extremely resourceful if the situation calls for it."

They both threw their bags into their cars and waved to each other. The thought, *was Pam worth it*, never crossed their minds. They both had their reasons for helping out a person in need.

Finding a dirt bag like Jeff was easy. Herman sat down the street from Pam's house and waited for him to show up. It didn't take long. Finding the door locked, Jeff pounded on it for a couple of minutes. When he got no response he tried to look through the front window. He was clearly upset when no one answered. In a fit of rage, he tore her mailbox off the house and threw it into the bushes. Before getting back in his beat up Ford Escort he looked up and down the street. Maybe Pam had parked down the street and was hiding inside. Whatever, he'd catch up with her sooner or later. Herman followed his man to a sports bar over by the interstate. He parked in the back of the lot and waited.

Three hours later Jeff came out with a female companion. She didn't look like the kind of girl that one would consider taking home to meet mom and dad—a lot of make-up and a real short skirt. Jeff and his new friend were both staggering a little as they walked to his car. They got into Jeff's junker and headed out of the lot. Herman looked up from the book he was reading. He had one of those nifty little lights that connected to the steering wheel. *I can't believe this idiot picked up a girl*, thought Herman. *He must be paying her. And now he's going to drive. He can barely walk.* Jeff surprised him by driving less than a block before he pulled into a motel parking lot. The ex-Ranger just smiled. This was going to be easier than he thought.

Tap tap.
Jeff's arm was underneath Shelly or Tracie and it was starting to go numb.
Tap TAP!
And a woodpecker was pecking at his head. Why would a bird mistake his head for a tree?
TAP TAP TAP!
Jeff opened his eyes and saw a large black man sitting next to him on the bed. The man had been tapping on his forehead with his index finger. Jeff tried to move but the intruder put a large hand on his chest and held him down. When he jerked his arm out from underneath his "date" she woke with a start.

"Sit tight," ordered Herman. "We've got some business to discuss." Brandi had enough sense to lie there and be quiet. "Here's what's going to happen, Sport. In a few hours the sun will be up, and you will pack up your few possessions. You will then leave town—never to return. If you decide to come back, for any reason, a few of my associates will place your feet into two small tubs. Quick drying cement will be added. Then you go for a boat ride. Lake Michigan isn't the deepest of the great lakes, but it'll do. Do you know which one is the deepest? No? I didn't think so. Anyway, where was I?"

"Something about a boat ride," said Brandi in a soft voice. "Listen, mister, I barely know this guy."

"I know," said Herman. "He picked you up at a bar up the street. What would your mama think?"

Brandi looked down and started to sob.

"Hey, man," said Jeff, finally finding his voice.

Herman flicked him in the head with a finger.

"Ow," screamed Jeff. "C'mon, what did I ever do to you?"

"A piece of shit like you will never be in a position to do anything to me. The only thing I need to hear you say is, 'I understand'. Do you know that drowning is one of the most horrific ways to die? People that have nearly drowned, and then have been brought back, say it's just awful. Before you take that last big gulp of water you have a few seconds to think about all the rotten stuff you've done to other people. You might even have time enough to find Jesus if you're good at holding your breath."

"Who put you up to this?" wailed Jeff. He was rewarded by another head thumping.

"The only thing I need to hear you say is, 'I understand and will comply with your instructions'."

"Okay, okay. I understand, and I'll do what you say."

"See, that wasn't so tough, was it? Now, let's review. You come back to this area, for any reason, disguised or not, you get a new pair of boots. A classy guy like you probably won't even be missed. Just like in that old country song, *Goodbye Earl*. You'll be a missing person that wasn't missed at all. Do I need to break a few bones to make my point?"

"No," exclaimed Jeff. "You look like a guy that means what he says. I ain't got any reason to stick around here anyway. Guess I'll just head back to … that's probably something I should keep to myself, huh?"

Herman stood up and stared thoughtfully at the two of them. He had another decision to make. The problem solved itself when Brandi opened her mouth.

"Wow," she said softly. "You must have ticked somebody off real good."

"Shut up, Traci," sneered Jeff.

"Brandi."

"Whatever."

"Okay, Brandi," said Herman. "Get up and get dressed. I'm taking you home."

"But, I'm naked under here," said the blond.

"This is no time for modesty," replied the big guy. "Get dressed, we're leaving."

Brandi slid out from under the sheets and went over to the chair where her clothes were. Jeff looked at Herman and gave him a sly grin as Brandi started to dress. He was rewarded with another finger flick to the head. When Brandi was ready, Herman took her by the shoulder and guided her to the door. He looked over his shoulder at Jeff.

"You've got two hours. If you're not completely gone, I will come looking for you. Even if you could swim like Michael Phelps it still wouldn't save you."

Jeff just stared at the two of them. What a way to end an otherwise swell night! And it was all Pam's fault. If she had been home he wouldn't be leaving town this way.

The day had started off dark and smelling like rain, but the skies cleared up toward noon. A robin serenaded the opening of the clouds as the sun made its first appearance of the day.

Possible rain notwithstanding, sunshine found Ronnie and Eddie considering hole number two at the North course at Stonehedge.

It was a short par three with a big green. Today it was playing about 140 yards. Ronnie looked over at his playing partner and proposed a little wager.

"Fifty bucks says I can hit my driver and hold the green."

Eddie looked at the shorter man suspiciously.

Careful, make sure you know exactly what the bet is, he thought.

The wording on any bet was always crucial. A lot of money had changed hands because one side wasn't completely clear on what was being wagered. In this business it paid to be overly cautious. It was absolutely necessary to know exactly what was being proposed before any wager was agreed upon.

Eddie remembered of a scene from an old movie where a guy bet a thousand dollars that he could cut the ace of spades from a normal deck of cards. The guy he bet should have asked him to define "cut". As soon as the bet was agreed upon, the first guy took out a huge cleaver and slammed it into the deck. He didn't get all fifty-two of them, but the ace in question was one of the ones he did get.

"I assume you mean you will fly the ball to the green and hold it?" asked Eddie, seeking clarification.

"Exactly. If I don't fly it to the surface, I lose, regardless if it stays on the green or not."

"All right, let's see it."

Ronnie took an extra long novelty tee out of his bag and stuck it into the ground. With the ball teed up about six inches above the turf, he took a couple of smooth practice swings. He had the ball positioned way out in front of his left foot. Ronnie held the club like a tour pro. No need to use the hacker's grip on this shot. Eddie stared intently at the shorter man. It was obvious what Ronnie intended to do. With the ball way out in front of him, Ronnie was going to open the driver's face a little and hit it on the upswing. The ball flight would look like he hit it with a wedge. The lack of backspin would be the only problem. Ronnie figured if he landed the ball on the front third of the green, it should stop before it ran off the back. Normally he only attempted this shot into a green that had a lot of back-to-front slope, but today he was feeling it.

The Chicago hustler took the club back about half way and made a smooth stroke. The ball flew high and true toward the green, cleared the fringe, and landed about twelve feet onto the putting surface. The first green was soft and wet, due to the overnight watering and lack of morning sun, and Ronnie was counting on the second green being similar to the first. Sure enough, the ball landed softly and came to rest ten feet short of the back edge.

Eddie whistled with appreciation. "Nice. How long have you been practicing that little number?"

"I started doing it about ten years ago. It just came to me one day in the park where I always practiced. I was way down one day and decided it would be my equalizer. Hit it on number seventeen at Medinah one day for ten grand. He gave me 10 to 1 odds, so all I had to put up was a grand. Man was that dude ever pissed. I had to land it in the perfect spot—left front with a little fade. I was never asked back after that. Trust fund babies, they're all over. It's not like he actually worked for his dough."

"Tell you what," offered Eddie, as they pulled up next to the green. "Fifty says you can't get it down in two using that driver."

Ronnie looked the forty-foot putt over from all sides. He acted like it was the winning stroke in the U. S. Open.

"Quit stalling," said Eddie. "This aint my first dance. You think that by taking so long that I'll think you're nervous and might offer to raise the bet. Just slap it up there."

Ronnie grinned at his playing partner. "You've seen that ploy before, huh? You Detroit guys are smarter than the Windy City boys give you credit for." Ronnie stepped up to his putt and promptly left it seven feet short of the hole. Eddie didn't say a word. The remaining putt was relatively straight, so Ronnie might have left it short on purpose, hoping for some additional action. Hearing nothing from his partner, Ronnie positioned himself for the money stroke. His second putt rolled up to the edge of the cup and hung there peering over the edge.

"Aggh," hollered Ronnie in disgust. "Stinking raised cups. The guy that cut this hole just cost me a hundred."

Eddie grinned and lit up a Macanudo. "Dude, I got an idea on that baby driver that you hit back there." The hustler from Detroit was always thinking about new angles. His nickname was well deserved. In addition to maintaining his cool under pressure, he was considered a man of vision among the people that knew him well.

For the next three holes the two ex-hustlers conjured up a plan to capitalize on Grip's finesse driver. After a lot of creative discussion, they decided how the gig would develop. They would stand on the tee, hopefully on a crowded day, and wait for the group behind to catch them. Then they would banter back and forth in an attempt to draw the guys behind them into putting some of their own money down on what sounded like a ridiculous shot. The crafting of the bet was every bit as important as the execution of the shot. A seventy-five percent success rate would be acceptable, especially if they could get their marks to give three-to-two or even two-to-one odds. They decided to target only tourists on their last day of play before they headed home. It wouldn't take much detective work to gather the data that they needed. Gary, in the Stonehedge pro shop, could be counted on to supply that information. It was a simple scenario with very few things that could go wrong.

* * *

Everything had transpired as smooth as a vanilla malt at Steak and Shake. Herman met the guys for breakfast the next day. He told them that Jeff got the message and it was highly doubtful that he would be returning to the area.

"I've dealt with low-lifes like Jeff before," explained Herman.

He went on to say that no class and no brains was a bad combination. It was doubly bad when the subject thought he possessed both brains and class. Not knowing what you're doing isn't necessarily dangerous. Not knowing and thinking you do know, can lead to disastrous consequences.

"Look, fellas. The job was a no-brainer, so I'd like to give you half of what you gave me back."

"Nonsense," said Ronnie.

"I agree with Grip," said Eddie.

They both just sat there grinning.

"Alright then," said Herman.

The big man stood and shook hands with Eddie and gave Ronnie a big hug. He reminded them that his services came with a guarantee. If Jeff ever showed up again, they should call him immediately. His initial plan was to scare Jeff off. If that didn't work there was always plan 'B'. Up until this point, as a civilian, he had never put anybody in the hospital for more than a couple days, but a guy in his business obviously knew someone who would.

* * *

"I don't believe it!" exclaimed Pam hugging both of them with an appreciative look in her eyes. "Thank you guys so much."

Pam was extremely grateful. She now saw the two "old guys" in a totally different light. She offered to do anything for them, except the obvious. They told her she could cook dinner for them some night, but it would have to be at her place. Neither of them wanted her to know where they lived. With their attempts at keeping a low profile, it wouldn't behoove them to let their guard down. Eddie had been to Ronnie's place and vice versa, but that was about it. Their occasional dates were the only other people in the area that knew where they lived. Eddie had a lawyer "friend" that he met when he volunteered to play on couples night a year ago. She was divorced and very career oriented, and she could swing the club without making a fool of herself. The relationship was convenient for the both of them. Ronnie was seeing a grocery store manager that he had met a few months after moving to the area. 'The Street' and 'The Grip' both knew about each other's love life, but neither had seen the other's woman yet. Both would have been surprised at the beauty and intelligence of the women in question. Apparently their discerning taste wasn't limited to just cars and whiskey.

Ronnie felt good about the favor he and Eddie had done for a lady in need. He had always been the kind of guy who would help someone else out, and he got the impression that Eddie was that way too. He didn't volunteer the information to Eddie that he was the one who lent Herman the money to start his practice as a private investigator. They both respected the fact that their relationship would only be complicated if they shared too much information about themselves.

Ronnie pulled up in front of his small country home just north of Richland. His set-up was a little out of the ordinary.

The house was a small, fairly new prefab job. On the outside it wouldn't cause a passerby to give it a second look. The inside was an entirely different story. When Ronnie turned the lights on, the room in front of him lit up with soft blue recessed lights. He could change the color to blue, red, or green just by tapping the rheostat. Recessed canister lights were also there to brighten the room, but he rarely used them. The furnishings and the rest of the décor indicated that the owner knew something about style. In addition to a plush recliner, two comfortable-looking brown leather sofas sat in front of a large flat screen television. The kitchen was off to the right and it was loaded with every kind of culinary gadget known to man. Ronnie prided himself on his ability to put a first-class meal on the table. His study was in the back part of the house. He had several windows put in so he could look out at the trees and the occasional wildlife that wandered into his yard. The room was paneled with expensive walnut and there was the best carpet money could buy on the floor. Ronnie usually wore his "house shoes" (he refused to call them slippers) in this room. There were three computers and four monitors in what he called the "horse room". The room was also equipped with a printer, a fax machine, and a paper shredder. This is where he spent Thursday, Friday, and Saturday evenings, analyzing the racing form and placing a few wagers. The better horses ran at the end of the week and these were the races he focused on. Once in a while a Sunday afternoon card would catch his eye, but he mostly only played on the three previous nights.

Looking out the back window of the "horse room", Ronnie could see a large patio with a fire pit. He spent a lot of time out here and with the cool Michigan nights a fire was usually burning in the pit. He and Eddie had often sat on the patio drinking too much whiskey and trading stories. On those nights, Eddie made use of the second bedroom. Ronnie had done the same at Eddie's place.

He went through the house, as he always did, checking to make sure nothing was amiss. Then he went out the back door across the patio and into the large pole barn. The barn was about two and a half times as big as the house. His toys sat quietly in the barn, waiting for him.

The boat was right in front of him and the Corvette was over by the far wall. The four-wheeler sat between them. He had taken Kathy, the restaurant manager, for a ride on some of the country trails close to his house the last time they had been together, and she absolutely loved it. He was thinking about giving her a call and maybe going out to dinner. A sleepover wouldn't be bad either. He felt he deserved it after his recent good deed.

Before he went back inside, Grip walked over to the boat and leaned over the edge resting on his elbows.

It was a sixteen-foot runabout with a fifty horse Mercury on the back. That was enough motor for him, as he didn't ski or fish. He usually took the boat over to Sherman Lake, just south the golf course. Gull Lake was bigger, but too busy for his tastes, and you had to know somebody to even be able to put your boat in the water there. Sherman Lake was open to the boating public.

When he was on the water, he was looking for two things—serenity and solitude.

The perfect environment for remembering.

CHAPTER FIVE

Tub Buddies

A classy woman is like a guy's favorite driver. Once you get a hold of one, I'd advise you to hold it close. Some other dude is bound to be looking at what you're holding, and he might just decide that the object in question would be better off if it was in his possession.

—Shelly "The Shaft" Martin, avid golfer/full time gigolo

Taking a bath with someone can be an uplifting experience.
With your mate, it can be relaxing or exciting, depending on your intentions at the outset.
With your children or grandchildren, it can be quality time and
sometimes downright hilarious. Sitting in a tub with a one-year-old and some toys is a truly wonderful experience. Add some bubbles and watch the joy on their little faces!
A tub is great place to read or to soothe a sore back. It's also an ideal environment to come up with new ideas or to just contemplate the ways of the world. If you plan on doing some serious tub time, then you need to get a big one. One that you can stretch out in so you don't feel cramped, like you did when you were two years old and your mom still gave you a bath in the kitchen sink. A few high-powered jets and some mellow tunes will enhance the experience. Truth be known, a lot of innovative ideas probably came to a bather who was languishing away in a big tub—either solo or with a tub buddy.
What, though, do tubs have to do with 'The Grip' and 'The Street'? Eddie knows what he is doing when it comes to tub activities, but Ronnie is still a novice. However, he is very observant, and he is a quick study.

* * *

Ronnie was napping quietly in the late afternoon sun on his patio when he heard an engine revving in his driveway. He quietly walked around the far side of the house to get a look at the car. Always cautious, he wanted to see them before they saw him. He didn't get many visitors out in the country and it paid to be on guard at all times. Discreetly peering around the corner he saw Eddie in is '57 Chevy convertible, with a very attractive female sitting beside him. Eddie saw him peeking around the corner of the house and hollered, "Hey, Potsy, let's go out to dinner."

Ronnie walked around the corner of the house and up to the car. "Is this the bartender you've been raving about? It's nice to meet you, Ginger." Ronnie extended his hand to the pretty lady.

"Dude, ixnay on the Ginger thing," said Eddie. "It's Tuesday night, remember? Ginger works Tuesdays."

"It's nice to meet you," said Suzanne, extending her hand. "Eddie has told me a lot about you, but he failed to mention your sense of humor. You were trying to be funny, right?"

Suzanne appeared to be around fifty. She wore a light blue summer dress with thin straps coming over her shoulders. Her brownish blond hair was cut shoulder length, and her shoulders and arms had an athletic look about them.

She had a Detroit Tigers baseball cap on to keep her hair from blowing all over the place. Intelligent eyes and an ingratiating smile told Ronnie that this lady could hold her own in a conversation. He decided to test her.

"Nice hat, Suzie. It looks like a throwback from the sixties. You know, the style they wore when Clemente played for the Tigers."

"Well," said the attorney, "if Clemente would have played for the Tigers, he would have been their left fielder, because Kaline was camped in right, and I doubt that even Roberto could have moved Al out of his regular spot."

"So she knows her baseball, Eddie. It's nice to meet a female with her priorities straight."

"So, what do you say?" asked Eddie. "Shall we treat the ladies to a night on the town?"

"I'll give Kathy a call," said Ronnie. "Come on back to the patio and relax for a few minutes. Help yourself to some drinks. You know where the fridge is in the barn."

Ronnie went in to the house and called Kathy, then he jumped in the shower. When he came out he saw the door open to the barn. He went in to investigate. 'The Street' and Suzanne were sitting in his Vette sipping on bottles of Guinness.

"Hey, Grip," said Eddie. "This car must have magical qualities. Suzanne started breathing hard as soon as she sat down. Want to trade for a week?"

"Trade cars or trade women?" asked Ronnie.

"What the hell," said Eddie looking at Suzanne. "Let's do both." He received a punch in the arm for his comment.

"You better not spill any beer in there," cautioned Ronnie. "Kathy will be ready by the time we get to her place. She lives on the north side of Kalamazoo, so it's not far. All I need to do is get my hat."

"Don't wear that pork pie thing that you wear on the golf course. I don't want to get into any fights defending your right to wear something so ridiculous."

Ronnie waved at them as he headed back to the house. "Lock up when you're done in my babe-mobile."

"Why did you call him Grip?" asked Suzanne. "Is that some sort of nickname?"

"Yeah," said Eddie covering up his gaff. "Did you see those huge paws on the guy? I think he got the name in high school. I don't think he likes it, so don't call him that. It just slipped out."

"Funny, he doesn't look like a retired accountant. I picture him as more of an outdoor type."

"Well, you also said that I don't look like an insurance agent. Looks can be deceiving, babe. We're just a couple of old Divot Dogs with great looking women and really cool cars."

"Divot Dogs? What's a Divot Dog?"

"You know. A guy that has nothing better to do than to play golf all day."

"Living the dream, huh?" With that she gave a soft kiss on the lips. "Thanks for calling me this afternoon. I really needed a night out. My job has been a real bear lately."

"Don't say 'bear' around Ronnie, unless you want an in-depth report on the Chicago Bears' chances of getting to the playoffs this year."

"I'll remember that," said Suzanne, opening her door. "Now, what's it going to take for you two dullards to show a couple of girls a good time tonight?"

"I think you know the answer to that, counselor."

"I should have known. With men, that's always the answer."

"We're simple creatures," said Eddie taking her arm. "There's nothing more to us than what you see."

Kathy was sitting on her front porch when the convertible pulled up to her house. She was dressed in a black summer dress similar to Suzanne's. Her red hair cascaded over her shoulders as she walked out
to the car. Eddie wasn't surprised at the similarities between the two women—same height, same sexy build and a smile that said they weren't intimated by the opposite sex. Ronnie made the introductions and then Kathy turned and ran back into the house. She came out with a Chicago Cubs hat on.

Ronnie lit up with a big smile. The Cubs hat was a gift had given her on their second date!

Kathy suggested a steak house downtown that had great seafood too.

The evening turned out to be a very relaxing one. The two women immediately took to each other and the conversation ran the gamut from sports, to current events, to history. Kathy prided herself with her knowledge of U. S. history and she impressed them all with her knowledge of World War II.

"I was recently reading," she said, swirling the wine in her glass, "that the captain of the U. S. S. Indianapolis was the only U. S. captain to be court martialed for losing his ship in the war. Even when the Japanese sub commander testified at his trial, that there was no way the sinking of the ship could have been avoided. Years later the Indianapolis captain couldn't take it any more and committed suicide. It was all very tragic. Excuse me, I'm going to freshen up."

"I'm coming too," said Suzanne, getting up and following.

The two women stepped into the restroom and looked at each other. It was time to talk.

"Let's compare notes on our two gallant escorts," said Kathy with a grin. "You first."

"Okay," said Suzanne, leaning against the sink. "Eddie is a great guy that I met playing couples golf at Gull Lake. He's quite sophisticated, and we share a lot of the same values. And he's always been a real gentleman around me. Most of the time he's pretty laid back. I really enjoy spending time with him, which isn't all that often. My job has me working a lot of hours lately."

"That sounds pretty much like Ronnie. I met him at the store that I manage. He was actually asking some intelligent questions about some hard to find vegetables. But there are some facts that just don't seem right."

"Like?"

"Well, Ronnie said he has worked with numbers his whole life, like an accountant or something, but I watched him add up a bill once and he took way too long for a guy that's supposed to know them forward and backward. He is good with numbers when it comes to betting horses, though. Did you see all the computers in his house? When I first saw them I thought he was a day trader. You know, one of those guys that stays glued to the computer all day buying and selling stocks when they move a few pennies one way or another. But all he said was he likes to bet on a race once in a while as a hobby."

"No, I didn't see his computers. Eddie and I never went inside the house. Ronnie does have some cool toys though. I love that Corvette. I'm hoping we can borrow it some evening and just cruise around for a few hours. I wouldn't mind driving it myself. Eddie's also a lot of fun to be with, but you're right, some things don't add up. He says he's a retired insurance man, but he doesn't seem to know all that much about insurance. I've tried a few cases that involved insurance companies, so I know a little about the business. And it appears that I know more than he does. It is rather peculiar. Was Ronnie ever married?"

"Yes, his wife died about ten years ago of cancer. If that wasn't bad enough, his only son died about the same time. He was a soldier, and he was killed in Iraq. It must have been incredibly tough on him. He doesn't talk about them much. How about Eddie?"

"Eddie was divorced about twenty years ago. He raised two daughters that now live down south, one in Dallas and the other in Venice, Florida. He visits them every winter and on special occasions during the summer. I've seen pictures of them and they are both beautiful young ladies."

"So what do you think?" asked Kathy. "Are they retired government agents or maybe spies? Does Eddie always pay cash for stuff? I've never seen Ronnie use a credit card. I'm not even sure if he has one."

"Yeah, Eddie always pays with cash too. Their pasts are somewhat ambiguous, but I don't think Eddie is hiding anything nefarious. They both just seem to be old-school types. There's nothing wrong with that. I'm happy having a great guy like him that I can also call a friend."

"You're right. I guess I'm just a little too nosey. You know what they say—'if a situation is too good to be true, it usually is'. And once you figure that out, it all begins to fall apart."

"I wouldn't worry about these guys," said Suzanne. "I think they're both keepers. They're just two retired dandies that like to play a lot of golf. Eddie said they were Divot Dogs. I've played golf ever since I was in law school, but I've never heard that term before."

She didn't add that she had her law office run background checks on the both of them. There was more than one Ed Ferguson in the Detroit area and a multitude of guys named Ron Costas in Chicago—however, accountant and insurance agent was not mentioned in either report. One thing she had not considered was that maybe Ferguson wasn't really Eddie's last name. "I think I'll go back to the table, have a little more wine, then go back to my guy's place for a while. That would cap off a perfect evening."

"Sounds good to me," said Kathy. "I don't know about the last part, though. I have to get up early. It's inventory time, and I have to be at the store to resolve all the issues that will come up. Ronnie will understand. How about we split another glass of wine?"

* * *

Eddie dropped Kathy and Ronnie off at their respective places, and then they cruised the south end of Gull Lake. He and Suzanne stopped for an ice cream cone across from the Bay View Market. They sat on Eddie's favorite bench watching the lights from the surrounding homes reflect off the water. Neither of them felt the need to speak. Talking would have ruined the specialness of the moment. When the cool air made Suzanne shiver, Eddie offered her his hand and they walked back to the convertible. She asked him to leave the top down and to crank the heat up. All the way home, she kept her hand on top of his as he worked the gearshift. Up to this point, the hustler had never given much thought to the role that luck had played in his life. But at this moment, he didn't think he could be any luckier, even if he had won the lottery.

When they got back to Eddie's place, he went through the door first and looked around his house, asking her to wait at the entrance. Suzanne wasn't surprised when he did this, as she had seen him do it before. He lived in a nice neighborhood by the airport at the west end of Battle Creek, but he was always on his guard. She figured that it came from living in a bigger city most of his life.

"Well, what do you want to do, babe?" asked Eddie, hoping for a romantic answer.

"You know what I want to do, Ed," came the sexy reply. "I've been sitting in your car for a while, and now I want to sit in that big old tub of yours."

Eddie had a huge tub that was equipped with ten high-powered jets. It was a state-of-the-art relaxation machine. There was also a flat screen built into the wall above the faucets with four speakers placed strategically around the room.

"Those controls are pretty complicated," he said. "Need some company to help you figure them out?"

"Absolutely," said Suzanne, stepping out of her dress on the way to the bathroom.

* * *

Eddie leaned back against the sloping edge of his tub. The hot water had almost a hypnotic effect. Suzanne sat between his legs leaning back against his chest. His arms were around her with his hands resting on her belly. Neither of them said much for a while. They were just taking in the atmosphere and enjoying the physical contact. The flat screen on the wall in front of them was playing mellow songs from the seventies.

"So," said the beautiful naked lady with her soft hair resting on his shoulder, "you spent most of your career in insurance?"

"It was more like investments," said Eddie, wondering where this was going. It's not that he was ashamed of his past, he just wanted to keep things simple. He knew he would open up to her some day, but he had to do it when he was ready. He told a small fib about his past when he was introduced to her at the golf course and, up to now, he hadn't decided to correct it. Besides, he was just trying to live the life of a retired businessman. What did it matter what sort of business he was in, as long as it was legal and didn't harm anyone? As far as he knew, a friendly wager between two golfers wasn't a prisonable offense. Once they started seeing each other more often, he knew he had made a mistake. Maybe it was time to take her in to his confidence. If he did, it would mean Ronnie's "cover" would be blown also. He was about to give her a glimpse of his past when he heard a noise coming from inside the house. He had a gun close by, but not close enough. It was in one of those fake picture frames out in the living room. It wouldn't do them much good from where they were sitting. He stiffened up trying to hear, which alerted his companion.

"What was that?" she whispered.

"Someone is in the house," he whispered back. "Sit up quietly so I can get out."

Suzanne leaned forward so Eddie could maneuver himself into a standing position.

"Yo, Street, are you all right?"

Ronnie's voice was a relief.

"In here," hollered Eddie. "I'm in the tub."

"Why didn't you answer your phone?" asked Ronnie, approaching the door. "And why was your front door unlocked? Man, I thought something happened to you."

The door started to open when Suzanne cried out, "Stay out, I'm in here too!"

"Well, cover up, Sweet Cheeks, 'cause I'm coming in. We've got important business to discuss."

Eddie grabbed a towel and threw it over Suzanne. She couldn't believe it! He had no objection to his friend seeing them in the tub together. There was definitely something different about these two.

"C'mon in," said Eddie, as he reached for his drink that was sitting on the side of the tub.

Ronnie stepped into the room and checked them out. The towel was already wet and left little to the imagination where her figure was concerned.

"Tub buddies, huh? What's up with the front door? Is this neighborhood on the honor system now?"

"I'm sorry," said Suzanne, finding her voice. "I was the last one through the door, and I was so excited about this wonderful tub that I forgot to lock it."

"What's so important, that you drove all the way over here at this time of night?" asked Eddie. "And, to answer your question, my phone is in my pants pocket out in the other room."

"What did you guys do, drop your laundry as soon as you closed the front door? You're getting sloppy, my man. I think I'll just peek under this towel." Ronnie made like he was going to lift the edge of Suzanne's cover.

"Stop that, pervert," said Suzanne, slapping his hand. "Eddie, do something."

Eddie just laughed at her predicament. "Sorry, babe. He's got us at a huge disadvantage. What is it, Ronnie, Herman?"

"Yeah, but not what you think. He called me about forty-five minutes ago and informed me of a situation. It's made for us, man. I can smell the money in the wind, blowing all the way from Chicago. Uh, can we talk here, with your counselor slash bathing beauty present? We're working with a deadline here. We need to let Herman know if we're in or out."

Eddie made a snap decision on letting Suzanne in on his true nature. "Yeah, go ahead. If it gets too intense, we can claim lawyer/client privilege."

"Hey," objected Suzanne. "I am an officer of the court. You're not going to talk about something that I shouldn't be hearing are you?"

"We're not mafia, doll," said Eddie. "We're golfers."

"Now I am confused," said Suzanne. "I know you are both golfers. You and I met on the golf course, remember?"

"Dude," said Ronnie, "we've got about a fifteen-minute window to call Herman back with an answer. Lawyer lady, you need to just listen. I'm sure your fellow bather will fill in all the details after I leave. Here's the gig. Some big Chicago money came up with this to add some excitement to their dull, dreary lives. They are putting together a little competition. Eight guys over fifty and eight under. Each player puts up one stack. They'll play as a team against the other three teams in their age group. Low score for the three days takes all. The format will be interesting. The three matches against your opponents will be played in what the locals call a 'devil's card'. You know, six holes best ball, six holes alternate shot, and six holes scramble. Before you tee off you declare what format you will be playing on what holes that day. That means that strategy will play an important part. And here's the kicker—we're going to play Medinah, Butler, and Cog Hill. I know those tracks forward and backward. What do you say? It's on in two weeks. Oh, one more thing. The competitors cannot have any tour history. If you've played even one hole at a tour event, any tour, you're not eligible. And they will check on that."

"I don't know," said Eddie, reaching for his drink. "Let me think about it for a bit." He took a big swallow and smacked his lips appreciatively. "I'm in. Do me a favor will you? Hand me the pad and pen on the counter over there."

Ronnie handed the pad and pen to Eddie and the Detroit hustler scribbled something on it. Ronnie glanced at the pad and broke out into a big grin.

"Good thinking. I'll see you at Cedar Creek tomorrow. We'll hit some balls and talk strategy. Suzanne, did you know that your wet towel isn't hiding much? I just want to say, partner, you're mediocre taste in whiskey is trumped by your taste in women. Carry on with whatever you were doing. Oh yeah, I'll lock the door on my way out."

"Wait," said Suzanne. "Can we borrow your car sometime?"

Ronnie gave her a quizzical look.

"She wants to drive it," explained Eddie.

"It's not an automatic," said Ronnie, "And the gears are a little tricky."

"She knows her way around a stick," said Eddie, playfully squeezing Suzanne's hips.

"We'll see," said Ronnie, as he backed out and closed the bathroom door. Suzanne was somewhat mystified as to what just transpired.

"Okay, Street. That's what he called you, right? What is going on? I mean, I know you're going to Chicago to play golf, or was that some sort of code for something a little more sinister?"

"No, just golf talk. To be honest, this type of competition is a new one on me. I assume the guys that are putting it together are going to be betting on the contestants. They're probably the type that just loves to gamble and are always looking for a new way to throw their money away. And heaven help them if any of the players don't go out and play it legit. It should be fun and it could get real interesting."

"How much is one stack?"

"Ten grand."

"Are you serious? You're going to play for ten thousand dollars?"

"Yeah, but that's just for starters. We'll have side money on every match. It's what we do, sweetie. I mean, it's what we used to do, sort of."

"You sound awful blasé about this whole thing. And a little bit cocky I might add. Do you think you two have a chance to win? Remember we've played together on a few couples' nights, and I have to be honest, your game isn't bad, but it doesn't appear to be anything out of the ordinary. There are a lot of guys playing on couples night that look like they're better than you are."

"Appear is the key word here. I'm just trying to get along and not draw any attention to myself. So far it's worked out just fine. I'll admit it was tough to lose to that Maynard creep a few weeks back. He and his wife talked smack for the whole round. The ball I hit into the water on seventeen was a work of art. I was trying to hit it one groove thin and I swung that stick like da Vinci wielding his brush. That should give you an indication of my commitment to living the simple life here. And to answer your question—yes I think we will win. The tournament share ill be thirty grand each, and we should be able to take a few grand more in sides. Not bad for a few days work."

They were both silent for a while, thinking. Suzanne was trying to figure out how much of this episode was just talk and how much was reality. Eddie was trying to remember what he knew about Medinah #3. He had played it years ago and could walk through most of the course in his mind. Non-golfers were usually amazed at how a player can go over his round in detail shot by shot after finishing eighteen holes. Some guys could tell you how their round went on a particular course even years later. Eddie remembered bogeying number two, a tough par three. He'd hit a 6-iron over the green and almost chipped it back into the pond that guarded the front.

"I have to ask this, so please don't be offended," said Suzanne, breaking their silence. "You two aren't going to cheat, are you? And if not, how can you possibly pull this off?"

"No," answered Eddie chuckling, "We're not going to cheat. Cheating guys like these is definitely asking for a few broken bones or maybe something worse. We're going to pull it off because Ronnie and I can hold our own against any golfer playing the senior tour today."

"If you two are that good, why haven't you played on the tour?"

"We had our reasons. Mine was all about raising two girls. I wanted to be there for them and traveling around from tour stop to tour stop was no way for a single father to raise his daughters. I told you about my ridiculous ex-wife. I just didn't want to risk losing them."

"Well, I guess that makes sense. You sure had me fooled on your golf abilities. What if I wanted to put down something on you? Say, the paltry sum of five hundred dollars."

"Just give it to me and I'll have Herman handle it."

"Herman. Who is Herman?"

"Just a guy. He's one of Ronnie's."

"Just a guy? I suppose you have a guy too?"

"Sweetheart, everybody in our business has a guy," said Eddie moving his hands further up her body. "Some have more than one, depending on the situation. Now what did we have in mind when we got into this tub about an hour ago?"

"Are you referring to my excellent 'stick handling skills'?"

"Yeah, that crossed my mind once or twice."

* * *

Walking back to his car Ronnie looked again at what Eddie had scribbled on the sheet of paper.

"Son of a bitch," he exclaimed. "I've known the guy for a few years and he never bothered to tell me his real name. Like I didn't know it when I walked up to him on the putting green way back then. Even money says he knows my name aint really Costas. Like I said, we could be brothers."

* * *

It was another sunny day with puffy piles of clouds in the sky. They were the type of clouds that, with a little imagination, resembled whatever the viewer wanted them to. Psychotics would see disturbing images, while hippie types would envision peace and love images, and maybe a huge bong next to something that resembled Jimi's or Ozzy's profile.

Eddie pulled up next to the range at Cedar Creek and opened the passenger door of his white 1985 Monte Carlo. The Monte had a lot of miles on it, but it was still a smooth running piece of machinery. In its day it was one of the most popular cars around. Cedar Creek was just west of Battle Creek. It had a first class practice facility where the two of them could work on their games away from prying eyes. He took his bag out and sat it on the ground, inspecting the pockets for the equipment he needed. He never put his clubs in the trunk. Trunks could get extremely hot in the summer and it could affect the epoxy that held his clubs together. Today's modern epoxy was a lot better quality than what club makers used even fifteen years ago, but he didn't want to take the chance of it softening on him. It was hard to believe that only a few decades ago a shaft was pounded into the hosel and then secured in place with a pin or a screw. It amazed Eddie that a guy like Bobby Jones, back in the twenties, could hit the ball so pure with such shoddy equipment. The sticks he used back then, when compared to today's hi-tech wizardry, were no more than a crude piece of metal stuck on the end of a switch.

Ronnie was already at the far end of the practice tee hitting short irons. His natural swing looked like it should come from another man's body. His muscular arms and shoulders shouldn't have been able to swing a club with that exquisite tempo. Watching him reminded Eddie of Bob Murphy, a silky smooth tour player from years ago. Ronnie was definitely a technician when it came to the golf swing. Eddie was more of a "feel" player. They played a little game once in a while to sharpen their skills. Eddie called it "no look" golf. The passenger in the cart had to keep his eyes closed until the driver stopped. With his eyes still closed, the passenger got out and was then allowed to look at the ground only. He was told all the information he would need to make the shot: distance to front of green and pin, wind and anything else that might come in to play. He would then ask for his club and would attempt the shot—without ever looking at the target. Eddie told him that this little exercise would improve his feel. It had to do with trusting your swing mechanics. It frustrated Ronnie that Eddie always beat him at this little game.

"How long have you been here?" asked Eddie, as he sat his bag on the rack.

"About a half hour," answered Ronnie, rolling another ball over from the huge pile. "How did the rest of the evening go?"

"Wouldn't you like to know?"

"I meant, did you fess up about your questionable past? All the schmucks that you've fleeced over the years?"

"They weren't schmucks," said Eddie. "I prefer to think of them as guys that thought they could play better than me on a given day and were willing to put up a little dough to back their opinion. That's what America is all about—backing your ideas with cash."

"What about specialty bets? You ever bet you could skip a ball across the water as if you've never tried it before? Or how about banking the ball off a tree or a port-a-potty when your opponent says there's no way you can get the ball on the green?"

"Ha. Yeah, I've done the water thing, and I once hit a shot off this dude's garage and on to the green for two hundred bucks. I got the idea a couple of weeks earlier while standing on the next tee. The guys behind us hit one off the building, and we all ducked thinking someone was firing his piece at us. I went out there the next day and set a couple of balls down behind a tree on the other side of the green. I was totally blocked from the putting surface. I hit two low 4-irons off the garage, and from that angle, both of them bounced back and ended up on the green."

"Weren't you worried about tearing up his building?"

"Are you kidding? There must have been a couple a hundred dents on the back of that thing. He obviously built right on the edge of his property line on purpose. He had a huge back yard, so all I could figure out was that he put the garage there to keep balls off his lawn. I don't think he cared about the dents."

"Sweet," said Ronnie. "Okay, I stayed up late last night planning our strategy. Besides, I would have had a hard time getting to sleep after seeing your woman in the tub like that. How did you get so lucky?"

"It aint luck, my man. And you should talk. Kathy is a real sweetheart. If a guy didn't know any better, he'd think those two were sisters."

"Yeah, she is a doll—and with a good head on her shoulders. I guess I shouldn't be looking at another man's back yard, or in this case, tub. Here's what I'm thinking. We scramble the middle six at Butler, because there's two par fives in that stretch and the last six at Medinah, because sixteen and seventeen are real bears, and by that time we should be protecting our lead. I'll explain the rest of it to you on the drive there. Pard, I think we can cash in on this action. I asked Herman to check into letting us play under assumed names. The organizers will do a background check, because of the 'no tour players' stipulation. Other than that, we can make up a couple of nicknames and just use them."

"How about I call you Spike or Chopper?" asked Eddie.

"Not cartoon names. You look like a 'Desert Jack'. Come up with something a little more sophisticated for me."

"I like 'Numb Nuts' Norman."

"Never mind. We'll work on that later. Watch me hit a couple and tell me what you see."

Ronnie hit half a dozen balls with his driver and striped every one of them. His hacker's grip was replaced with the grip of someone who knew what he was doing.

"Nice," was all Eddie said. "Let's go get a sandwich and hit the rest later. And to answer your question, I told Suzanne pretty much everything—at least the golf end of things. You know, I actually feel better about it. I didn't like keeping things from her. She already knew something was different about us. I'd lay down a hundred that she did a background check on me, and probably on you too. I'm sure she didn't get far using Ferguson. She never mentioned it, but she is a woman, and she has the resources to do it. Plus, women can't be too careful these days. There are a lot of sickos out there."

"Yeah, don't I know it," said Ronnie, as he put his driver in the bag. "Let's get that sandwich. You're buying for the security check I did on your place last night. I could have robbed you blind while you were frolicking in the tub. How would you explain that to the police? So, what happened after I left?"

"None of your business. Your uninvited appearance almost wrecked our evening. Oh yeah, she wants to put five bones on us next week."

"Really, what did you tell her?"

"I said she should just make it a hundred. I'm a little worried about your ball striking lately."

"You better be kidding. We're going to clean up on this thing. I'm hoping it will be an annual deal. You know, once we win, there will be a bunch of guys lined up to knock us off. We need to keep it close, though. We don't want to scare away the competition. Did I mention that they're going to have a pari-mutuel board going too? We'll get Herman to watch the board for us. I'll show him how to look for the best value. He can get Suzanne's money down for her."

"Let's not get too excited," said Eddie, as he opened the door to the grill. "We do need to come up with some creative side bets. I'd love to get my hands on some of that old Chicago money. Takin' it from you all the time, Mr. Green, is getting old."

"How long have you known my name isn't Costas?"

"Probably as long as you've known my last name aint really Ferguson."

CHAPTER SIX

The Blues

The blues takes you to a different place. A place where you feel that it's all worth it, that everything will make sense in the long run.

—'Buggy Whip' Johnson, blues musician

Eddie sat in a lawn chair at the far end of the practice tee at Cedar Creek. He was taking a break between buckets. The sky was a beautiful light blue that almost matched his '57 Chevy. The temperature was a cool 73 degrees with a light breeze. It was the sort of day that would keep a workingman from sweating, if he was a slow mover and took precautions not to exert himself too much. 'The Street' worked his way through the first bucket with no problems. The second one was for situation shots—hooks, slices, high shots and knockdowns.

Eddie favored the low boring shot. It would hold its line into the wind, and if you took enough club, the only problem was gauging your distance correctly. He had won a lot of money watching guys swing harder into the wind, only to have their ball fall yards short of the target. It worked especially well when there were trees involved. If you kept the shot below the treetops, the wind would only be a minor factor. There was no way of telling how hard the wind was blowing up above the trees, so why hit it up there if you didn't have to? A bogey golfer who had never seen an accomplished player would be surprised to watch them hit a pitching wedge. The accomplished player wouldn't normally choose a real high trajectory if the situation didn't call for it. If a shot is struck properly, less airtime means more backspin. It can be confusing to the novice golfer, because he is under the impression that in order to get the ball to stop quickly on the green, it has to be hit way up in the air. Usually, by the time a high shot lands, a lot of the backspin is lost, so it hits and bounces a few times then rolls for a while. Of course, on soft, wet greens, most shots will stop, whether they're hit high or low.

He flipped through a golf magazine, checking out the latest equipment. *Nice new drivers this year. And the prices are going up, as usual. Four hundred bucks for a driver that has about sixty dollars* worth of material in it. Man, somebody is making a killing here. I wonder who is raking in the most— the manufacturer or the Madison Avenue guys that are running the advertising campaigns. And what about the tour guys? They're getting their cut. And here's the rub— two years from now they'll be telling golfers this stuff is all outdated.

"Hey mister!"

The semi-retired hustler looked up.

There was a boy standing by him, maybe fourteen or fifteen years old. He was wearing a t-shirt and cut-off jeans for shorts. The young man's most striking feature was a gap-toothed smile that made his whole face light up—sort of a cross between Tom Watson and Huckleberry Finn. Eddie recognized him as the kid that usually drove the picker that scooped up the range balls.

"Hey, mister," repeated the kid. "I've been watching you hit balls. Could you give me a couple tips? I'm having all sorts of problems."

"Sure, kid," said Eddie getting up and stretching, "but it will cost you. If you'll run down to the grill and have them refill this glass with ice tea, I'll watch you hit a few."

The kid came back with a full glass of tea and handed it to Eddie. The teenager said his name was Mitch, and that his uncle usually mowed the fairways out on the course. Mitch was the range boy, a job that he took seriously. He rode out in his uncle's truck in the morning, then rode back home on his bicycle. It was a great summer job, and he got to hang around the golf course all day. The pay wasn't great, but free golf and range balls were huge perks for a golf fanatic like him.

"Thanks," said Eddie, taking the plastic glass and setting it on the ground in the shade of his golf bag. "All right, let's see what you've got."

'The Street' worked with the kid for an hour. Eddie was a natural teacher, and Mitch soaked up everything the old guy said. When Eddie explained that he might as well stop practicing all together if he could not hold the club properly, Mitch changed his grip to emulate his instructor's. Changing one's grip, even one that you've only been using for a few months, is no small task.

"Mitch, the clubface must be square or relatively square at impact. Look at my hands. You've got to hold it properly at the top end, so it will give you the best chance of squaring everything up at the bottom end."

Eddie went on to say that if he had a bad grip he would have to do something to compensate for it when the club entered the hitting zone. In this case, it would be possible for two wrongs to make a right, but only a guy with incredible skill could pull that off. And when the pressure was on it was just one more variable that you had to deal with. Why make the game tougher than it already is?

Mitch went over to his range picker twice to get more balls. He couldn't believe that an adult that he had just met would spend so much time with him. And the guy seemed to know his stuff. At the end of the session, he asked Eddie to hit a few for him. Eddie looked around and didn't see any observers so he hit about a dozen shots. No two shots were the same—a low draw, a high fade, knockdowns and a 4-iron that looked like a pitching wedge.

Mitch was impressed.

"I've got a buddy that can hit a driver that high," said Eddie after the sky-high 4-iron.

"That was pretty cool," said Mitch. "Thanks a lot, uh…"

"Eddie is fine, Mitch. You practice the stuff we worked on, and we'll hit some again in a few weeks. You've got some skill. Right now you need to work on the fundamentals that we just went over, okay?"

"I'll work on them," said Mitch, as he headed back to his picker. "Thanks again, Eddie."

Eddie smiled and waved as he picked up his bag and headed back to his car. He prided himself on being observant, but he missed the pro shop manager's intense gaze from inside the shop.

The manager had been watching and formulating a plan for the last half of the practice session. Eddie might be a big help getting even with a couple of high rollers that showed up at the course once or twice every summer. He'd have to talk to Eddie the next time he came to hit practice balls.

* * *

Eddie, Ronnie, and their women were heading out for a night on the town. The Chicago gig was four days away, and Eddie promised the other three a night to remember.

'Buggy Whip' Johnson was playing at a little blues club in Battle Creek. The club catered mostly to a black clientele, but Eddie had been there a few times and most of the regulars had accepted him. He was surprised at the talent that frequented the little club. A lot of the bands were traveling from Chicago to Detroit or vice versa, and Big Daddy's Blues Joint was about half way between the two cities. Eddie came by the place in a strange way. A couple of months ago, at the casino poker tables, he had just taken a few hundred off a well-dressed black man named Slick.

When Eddie walked out of the casino, a few hundred on the plus side, Slick was standing out front smoking a cigarette.

"Hey, Eddie," said Slick.

Eddie, always on guard, turned slowly and looked at the smiling man who had just called his name. "You look like a man that might enjoy some quality music. Am I right?"

"I like good music," said Eddie, as he walked back toward Slick. "What have you got in mind?"

"I'm heading for a little blues club in B. C., and I figured you might like to come along. What'ya say?"

Eddie pulled out a Macanudo and lit it. He stared through the rich cigar smoke at the black man's eyes. "You aren't thinking about getting some of your losses back, are you, Slick?"

Slick smiled again and slowly reached into his left front pocket. He drew out a wad of bills that filled his hand. "Three, four hundred aint enough dough to get excited about, my man. What I really want to do is get you drunk, but not too drunk, so I can pick your brain on how you play the game. I used to think I was pretty good, but lately I've been second guessing myself, and that ain't no way to play poker. You, on the other hand, seem to win your fair share of pots. There's something I aint doin' right, and I'm tired of donating. So, I'm askin', can I interest you in some good music and some good whiskey?"

"What do you do for a living, Slick?" asked Eddie, as he tried to get a read on the man.

"Ha, I'm a liquor salesman, and I don't mind tellin' you, business is good. People like their booze, no matter what the economy is doing. One more thing, there aren't too many white dudes that come to this place. So if that's a problem, just tell me now."

"I got no problem with that," said Eddie. "I happen to be a big blues fan. I even know a few pretty good blues musicians. What are you driving? I'll just follow you there."

Eddie followed Slick's maroon Cadillac to Big Daddy's and the two of them hit it off right away. Slick introduced the Detroit hustler to just about everybody in the joint, including Big Daddy Moon, the owner. B. D., as he was known to his friends, made it a point to let Eddie know that he was welcome back any time. The music was good and so was the company. Slick bought most of the rounds, but in the end he felt that he had gotten his money's worth. He asked Eddie about one particular hand. The one where Eddie's three sevens took down Slick's two pair.

"All right, man," explained Eddie, leaning forward, taking on the role of teacher. "As you know, five card draw is easy to play, but it's difficult to play well. Here's how I played that hand. I had the trips from the beginning. When you drew one card ahead of me, I also drew one. Now, what do you think I was thinking when I saw you draw only one card?"

"You figured that I was drawin' to a straight, a flush, or two pair."

"Right, and when you saw me draw one card, you were probably thinkin' the same thing about me. Now, the odds say when you draw one card to improve your hand, most of the time you won't. After the draw, when the guy to your left placed a modest bet, you just bumped it a little. That told me you were drawin' to two pair, or maybe you paired up a face card, tryin' to make your flush or straight. Here's where it gets tricky. There was a decent amount in the pot already, but I still bumped it a little more to see what you would do. Since my raise was minimal, you thought I had two pair just like you. And your 'kings up' looked like top hand. Am I right?"

Slick just nodded. He had quite a few whiskeys in him, but not enough to keep him from focusing. Eddie was laying some good stuff on him. Hopefully, he would still remember it in the morning.

"The guy to your left called, and you decided to press the issue, assuming the one card we both drew didn't make either hand. Your modest raise was what I was hoping for. You were right, the draw didn't help me, but I didn't need it to. I already had my trip sevens. I'll admit I was surprised, and a little nervous, when the other dude stayed in the hand and called. If you remember, he drew three cards. His trip threes was like a bonus to me. I would have been s.o.l. if he would have turned over trip eights or better. My mistake was I was so focused on you that I never even considered him. Live and learn, Slick. Live and learn."

When Eddie and Slick walked out of Big Daddy's it was almost one in the morning. Two big burly dudes fell in behind them. Eddie had just stepped onto the sidewalk when he heard Slick say, "Okay, Ferguson. Hand over them poker winnings." Eddie didn't know what to think. Did Slick string him along all this time just to recoup the few hundred that he lost earlier? He turned around slowly and saw three of the biggest grins imaginable. "Hey, man," said Slick. "Tell me you just fell for my bluff."

"I did," said Eddie, shaking Slick's hand. "I was trying to figure out which pocket I had the least amount of money in. You've got potential, Slick. Thanks for the good time."

* * *

"C'mon, Eddie, tell us where you're taking us?" asked Kathy from the back seat of Eddie's Monte Carlo. They had just left Clara's, a converted railroad depot that served great food.

"We're going to a little blues club to hear a friend of mine play," said Eddie.

"Hey, Suzanne," asked Ronnie. "Taken any long soaks in the tub lately?"

"Wouldn't you like to know," replied Suzanne over her shoulder.

"You know, there's room for three in that big sucker," offered Ronnie.

"I think you've got something there," said the attorney. "Kathy, how would you like to experience the ultimate indoor bathing experience?"

"Alright, alright," said Ronnie. "I was just kidding anyway. Get control of your passenger up there, Eddie. Tell us more about this 'Buggy Whip' guy."

"He's a real blues legend," said Eddie. "I met him playing poker about fifteen years ago. He was down on his luck and I sorta helped him out a little. So far, he's refused the commercial side of music and has gone his own way. He travels the country and plays at the smaller joints. I don't think he makes a lot of money, but he's doin' what he wants to do. You've got to respect him for that. One thing you guys should know is this place we're going to will be mostly black. Actually, we'll probably be the only white people there. I've been there a few times and have gotten to know some of the regulars. There are some real characters there, but they're good people. Anybody have a problem with that?"

"No problemo, here" said Ronnie, looking over at Kathy. She shrugged her shoulders signifying that it was okay with her.

Eddie parked the Monte about a block from Big Daddy's and the four of them walked from there. They got a few strange looks from the people on the street when they turned and went into the little blues club. A big guy named Germaine was tending the door.

"Germaine," said Eddie, shaking the man's hand and slipping him a twenty.

"Edward, the card player" said Germaine. "You're up on the left under the picture of Satchmo."

"Satchmo?" asked Suzanne.

"Louis Armstrong," said Ronnie. "She knows her baseball, Eddie, but her musical knowledge is somewhat suspect."

Eddie led his little group to their table amid several stares from the crowd. A stunning black lady in tight black pants and a silver top showed up as soon as they were seated.

"Jamaica," said Eddie, as the young lady leaned over and kissed him on the cheek. "These are my friends: Suzanne, Kathy and Ronnie. Guys, say hello to Jamaica Moon, psychology student and daughter of the owner."

The group said hello and placed drink orders. When Jamaica brought their drinks back she told them their timing was perfect. 'Whip' would be on stage shortly. Eddie motioned for Jamaica to bend down close and he whispered something in her ear. He also tucked a folded bill into her hand. She shook her head in the affirmative and went back to the bar.

"How did he get the nickname?" asked Ronnie, as he sipped on his Jameson.

"When he was a kid his dad would chase him and his brothers around the house whacking them with a buggy whip when they did something wrong," explained Eddie. "His big brother was huge, and consequently the slowest of the bunch, so he usually took the brunt of it."

"You would think that would be incentive to lose a little weight," observed Suzanne.

"You would," answered Eddie, "but he had another solution. Charles, that's his given name, said that one day his brother just stopped, grabbed the whip from his dad's hand and started beating him with it. That would have been something to see."

The lights went down and four musicians walked on to the small stage. 'Buggy Whip' Johnson appeared a minute later to a huge ovation. He stood there a minute looking the crowd over. Jamaica walked up to the stage and sat two bottles of Chivas Regal in front of the blues man. She pointed over toward Eddie's table and said something to him. Charles put his hand above his eyes to shield some of the glare. He spotted Eddie when the golfer raised his glass in salute.

'Whip' leaned into the mike and said, "I see my good friend Eddie D is in the house this evening. Keep calm people. Maybe he'll sign a few autographs later."

Eddie's group turned and stared at him, wondering what the musician was talking about. Most of the rest of the people in the room craned their necks to get a look at the guy that 'Whip' was referring to. Eddie calmly took a sip and pointed to the man on stage. 'Whip' grinned and went right into his first number.

The music was more than Eddie's companions expected. They were sitting in a small blues club in southern Michigan, and they were listening to some of the finest blues ever played. Johnson was a master guitar player and his vocals ranged from the froggy delta sound to what could almost be described as elegant. Every number received a loud ovation from the audience. Johnson waited for the room to quiet down, then he addressed the crowd.

"Before we take a break, we'd like to do a little tribute. Although he was born in Arkansas, he loved this area and is now buried right here in Battle Creek. You know who I'm talking about, Jr. Walker." Once more he waited for the crowd to settle. "I'm told that Jr. Walker and the All-Stars have performed right here on this very stage. I'd like to say it is an honor and a privilege to tread the same floor that he walked on. The best way to pay tribute to him is to play a couple of his songs. Man, that cat could play."

The saxophone player moved to center stage and the band did "What Does It Take" and "Shotgun". The crowd went nuts. As the band got up to take a break, 'Whip' motioned for Eddie to join them in a little roped off area next to the stage.

Eddie gave Johnson a big hug and then introduced his friends. Ronnie stuck out his hand and introduced himself as Ronnie Green. It was obvious that Charles 'Buggy Whip' Johnson and Eddie Davis went way back. They laughed and talked about old times. Charles explained how a lecture from Eddie had helped to get him off the heavy drinking and back to doing what he did so well—playing the blues. He didn't mention that Eddie had also recently kicked the booze habit.

The second set was as good as the first. The band had just finished their third song when a very large man came up and stood behind Eddie's table. It was obvious that he wasn't real happy with the white people in the club. He had been sitting and stewing about this fact ever since they walked in. Alcohol was also a huge factor in his decision to act on his feelings. He had quite a few drinks in him and now he stood there with fists clenched at his sides staring at them. The group had their backs to him and didn't notice him standing there. From the stage, Whip saw what was transpiring. He looked out at the big guy and spoke to him through the mike.

"Hey, my man. Yeah, you, the big guy in the green shirt. You look a little distraught, if you know what I mean."

The club chatter in the background slowly died down, sensing something serious was about to go down. Germaine had walked up and was now standing a few paces off to the man's left and behind him.

"Let me ask you this," continued Johnson in an unbelievably calm voice. "Have you ever had a song written about you? No? I didn't think so. Well, that man in front of you has had a song written about him. So, until your song is written, why don't you chill out, have a drink and just relax. The rest of the people here are expecting their entertainment to be of a musical nature."

There were a few murmurs going through the club. People that couldn't see were asking what was going on. Ronnie and Eddie both turned to look at the big guy standing behind them. The girls also turned with concerned looks on their faces. Ronnie saw Germaine with what looked like a small nightstick in is hand.

After a couple of tense moments, the big guy had a change of heart and went back to where he was sitting. The chatter started up again. The band was collecting themselves and sipping on their drinks when a guy from the audience hollered, "What's the song, Whip?"

Charles Johnson turned to his band and said a few words.

He turned back and looked straight at Eddie and began to play. His guitar was the only thing the audience heard for the first minute. Then the rest of the band joined in. It wasn't the type of music that they usually played, but a group of guys this talented could pretty much play anything. The hard driving guitar sounded like something Stevie Ray Vaughn or Kim Simmonds from Savoy Brown would play. Most of the bar inhabitants recognized the melody. Whip leaned into the mike and sang the beginning vocals:

Now The Gambler came from the Motor City,
Made a mistake and married for pretty.
He was thinkin' with parts that weren't made for thinkin',
Had trouble copin' so he turned to drinkin'.

The people at Eddie's table looked over at him. Eddie just sat motionless and stared at the guitar player on the stage. He couldn't remember the last time he had heard his song played live. It brought back bittersweet memories from his earlier days. Ronnie had heard *The Gambler's Run* by the band, Gambler's Folly. He couldn't believe that the song was actually written about his good friend and fellow hustler.

The band played the main melody again and then faded into silence. The crowd screamed and hollered for more. Charles Johnson stood and bowed toward Eddie's table. Eddie nodded his head slightly toward Johnson, then he saluted the rest of the band with an open hand. Whip sat down and went right in to their next number. Three songs later, Eddie motioned that it was time to go. As they wound their way through the crowd Eddie was fist bumped several times. He smiled and didn't let go of Suzanne's hand until they were back out on the street. Suzanne was looking at the side of his face the same way Kathy was looking at Ronnie. They both let loose as soon as they got in the car. Suzanne went first.

"Eddie D. Who the hell is Eddie D? I got the impression that my guy's name is Eddie Ferguson. Song or no song, what are you trying to pull?"

Eddie reached into his pocket and took his driver's license out of his money clip. He handed it to the fuming little lady sitting next to him. "Look, sweetheart. Ferguson is my middle name. I'm here for a fresh start, and I sorta like my middle name more than my last name. Davis is kinda boring. I wasn't trying to deceive you or anything like that. Are we okay?"

"**We** are not okay," said Kathy, as she sat in the back seat staring at Ronnie in the dark. "I suppose Costas is your middle name?"

"Uh, no it isn't," stammered Ronnie. "Look, I was going to tell you, babe. I went by a different name for the same reason Eddie did. We were trying not to draw attention to ourselves. It's probably a little harder for a guy that's a big celebrity. He's the bigger jerk here. He's got a song named after him for Christ's sake."

"Ah," said Eddie, holding back a snicker. "The last refuge of a desperate man. Divert the attention to someone else."

"You're both jerks," said Kathy, softening her tone a little. "Where did you come up with the name Costas anyway?"

"I took it from the sports announcer guy. You know, Bob Costas. I think it's a cool name."

"I always liked Wolf Blitzer," said Eddie, turning west onto Columbia Avenue.

That was all it took to lighten the mood.

"You guys are jerks," said Suzanne. "What are we going to do with them, Kathy?"

"The question is, what are they going to do for us, now that they are busted?" she asked.

"Besides the name thing, didn't you enjoy the evening?" asked Ronnie. "C'mon, it was memorable. How many ladies got to hear one of the finest blues guitarists in the business tonight? And you got to meet him, thanks to Mr. Ed here. That makes Eddie and me heroes—sort of."

"What did the song mean when it said you were thinking with parts that weren't made for thinking?" asked Suzanne.

"Those are just lyrics in a song, babe. You know, making a big deal out of something small. The song wouldn't be interesting if they didn't embellish a little."

"I don't know," said Suzanne. "This all sounds very sinister—like you two are hiding something more from us."

"All right," said Eddie in a serious tone. "Here's the deal. The little whiner back there and I are undercover FBI agents and you two are both busted. Kathy for changing the expiration dates on food in her store. And you, attorney lady, for jury tampering."

"Oh, yeah," said Suzanne. "What case was that?"

"A couple of years back," explained Eddie. "It had to do with a fast food joint. The case where the guy wanted money from the restaurant because some kid changed the message on his receipt."

"My firm never handled a case like that," responded Suzanne, suppressing a smile.

"According to our records, you did. And you offered favors to a jury member for his vote."

"That is ridiculous," said Suzanne. "What kind of favors?"

"Is it?" asked Eddie. "Cuff 'em both, Ronnie. We'll figure it out on the way to the airport."

"All right, everyone," said Kathy. "Let's not get carried away here. No harm was really done, and it was an incredible evening. Suzanne, we can't send these two off to Chicago feeling guilty about the way they tried to deceive us. I'm told that golfers have to have clear heads to play their best."

"Okay, you two get a pass on your sleazy behavior," agreed Suzanne. "But you better come up with an incredible way to make it up to us. Right, Kathy?"

"Sounds good to me. So you know a lot about undercover work, do you Ronnie?"

"What I don't know, I make up. And I get very few complaints."

"Home, Mr. Legendary Gambler Man," ordered Kathy. "The skills of your partner in crime are about to be tested."

"You should drink more often," said Ronnie. "You get all feisty when you go past your limit."

Eddie got out and walked Suzanne to her door. As he did with his own home, he went through her house to check it out while she waited at the entrance. He never explained to her why he did this. Years ago, Eddie was working in the pro shop of a private club. He had won a considerable sum off a disgruntled club member, and the guy was waiting for him just inside his front door when he got home. The intruder was on him before he could turn on an inside light. Luckily for Eddie, he had a couple of clubs leaning against the entrance wall. A pitching wedge to the kneecap sent the guy limping and howling down the street. His face was covered, but Eddie had a good idea who he was. The next day Eddie heard that the guy had quit the club and he was relocating somewhere down south.

"I don't want there to be hard feelings between us when I'm in Chicago," said Eddie, as he slipped his arms around Suzanne's slender waist. "My life has been somewhat complicated, but I want you to know that, besides the name thing and, uh, what I did for a living, I have never lied to you."

"What about pretending to be a hacker on the golf course?" asked Suzanne, as she put her arms around his neck and gave him a gentle kiss.

"That wasn't lying," whispered Eddie, as he kissed her back. "I was just having a bad day."

"Why don't you tell Ronnie and Kathy to cruise around for a while?" suggested Suzanne, heading for the bathroom.

"They've had too much to drink and shouldn't be driving," said Eddie. "I'll take them home and then I'll be back. It'll be about an hour. Ronnie can pick up his car at the restaurant tomorrow. Will you wait up for me?"

"If I'm asleep, just wake me, Mr. Gambler Man."

"Hey, that legendary gambler stuff is all blown way out of proportion. Let's just keep that to ourselves, okay?"

"I won't blow your cover, so to speak. But you better come up with something to get back into my good graces."

"I'm working on it," said Eddie as he locked and closed the door. When he got back to the car, it appeared that Ronnie and Kathy had gotten out for a little fresh air. He looked up and down the street, but didn't see them. Then he looked through the rear window and was surprised to see them lying in the back seat like two teenagers.

"What the hell?" was all he could come up with, as he slid behind the wheel. Ronnie reached up over the seat with a twenty-dollar bill.

"Just drive, dude. And you didn't see nuthin' back here."

"All right, boss."

He took the twenty and put the Chevy in gear.

CHAPTER SEVEN

Chicago Money

Chicago used to be a town full of action. Sports or politics, it didn't matter. There was always something you could bet on. Now it's pretty much dried up. Even Ronnie Green, the golfer, left town. I heard he's down in Florida fleecing rich retired dudes. Good for him. I always liked the guy. He sold me my first house.

—Detective Harry Krone

Chicago is more than a huge metropolitan area—it's an experience totally unto itself.

There is so much to see: the museums, the buildings, the elevated trains, the ballparks and, of course, the lake. Al Capone ran his illegal empire from the Windy City. Cicero was actually his headquarters, but it was close enough to the city proper. Unable to pin anything more serious on him, the Feds finally put the guy away for income tax evasion.

He died from a venereal disease while doing time at Alcatraz, right? Nope, he died while living in Florida, at his home by the beach. He was too sick for the prison to care for him, so they kicked him out.

The Windy City is known for many things, good and bad (see shootings per day). The average person could probably recite the above list of landmarks, but, unless you're an avid golfer, the golf courses around the Chicago area would probably not come to mind.

This would be a huge oversight.

Chicago has a plethora of championship golf courses that have hosted a long list of major tournaments. The rest of this page does not afford enough room to list them all, even if size ten font is used.

Several of the layouts of these courses are just plain brutal. Only accomplished golfers and masochists tend to tread these fairways. Playing the forward tees at one of these venues is certainly no disgrace.

Besides, a round of golf is supposed to be an enjoyable experience. You're not supposed to walk off the eighteenth green foaming at the mouth and in convulsions.

Only a true fanatic would put himself through such misery day after day. But golf has its share of fanatics and that's what keeps these terrific layouts in business.

* * *

The two accomplished golfers were looking forward to the next few days. They headed west on I-94 with their clubs in the back seat of Eddie's '85 Monte Carlo. Ronnie talked strategy all the way to the Indiana state line.

It appeared that he had everything covered. They were going to stay at Herman's house, and his wife was a great cook. Ronnie had suggested that she make meals with very little spice in them. Stomach problems were one variable that they wanted out of the equation. Eddie was impressed with Ronnie's preparation. The man had thought of everything—even a few things that never entered Eddie's mind. But, it was Ronnie's city, so he deferred to him on all matters.

Herman and his two house guests sat around the big guy's dinner table and discussed their itinerary for the next few days. They only had two days before their matches started, so they were going to play Medinah and Butler the following day. Cog Hill was on their schedule for the day after that. After playing the number four course at Cog Hill, affectionately known as Dubsdread, they would rest in the afternoon. No whiskey—this was serious business and there would be a lot of money changing hands. Herman would handle security for their team. Eddie thought this was going a little overboard, but as things progressed, he would be grateful for Herman's expertise and for Ronnie's attention to detail.

The guys cruised around Medinah #3 in the morning. It was impossible not to be in awe of the layout. In addition to the P. G. A. and the Ryder Cup matches, the historic venue had also held both the regular and senior U. S. Opens. They played with two members. It was very rare, except for during a tournament, that someone could play here without a member in the group. The two members seemed nice enough, but it didn't take long to figure out that they were listening a little too closely to their guests' conversation. They were taking discreet notes, while Eddie and Ronnie made theirs openly.

"Let's mess with these spies a little," whispered Ronnie. "It might pay dividends down the road."

"What did you have in mind?" asked Eddie.

"Just follow my lead. I need you to hit a bad one. Don't shank it or anything. Just push it into the trees. Let's see how this plays out."

Eddie pushed his next shot into the trees on the right and Ronnie started in on him.

"Damn it, Eddie," said his partner. "I thought you got that out of your system. When the pressure is on you get about half way through the ball, then you quit on it. C'mon, man, we've got a lot of money at stake here."

"Don't worry," countered Eddie. "When the time comes, I'll be there. You need to worry about your game and quit freakin' out about mine."

"Look, partner," said Ronnie, easing up a little. "I'm not freakin' out here. I just need your best game. Are you going to be able to deliver or not?"

"If you'll get off my ass, I'll deliver, all right?"

The two club members watched the show with interest. When the boys weren't looking they each hastily scribbled something in their little notebooks. On the next hole Eddie duck hooked one into the trees on the left.

He got in the cart and glared at his partner. "I got through that one, didn't I?" Neither one of them talked to each other for the last three holes.

On the way back to Herman's for lunch, Ronnie explained that there was going to be a pari-mutuel board, where anyone could bet on the contestants. Their little show back there might help drive their odds up, if word got out that they didn't handle the pressure all that well. Eddie just grinned in response. This was Ronnie's gig and he was trying to cover all the bases.

In the afternoon, the two hustlers were going to drive over to Oakbrook and play Butler National. Over lunch with Herman, they talked about using their little act on their opponents to up their side bet on the back nine. They decided that a ploy like that was making things a little too complicated. Keeping it simple had worked for them in the past and there was no reason to veer from this strategy. Eddie surprised both of them when he told them he saw the two Medinah members scribbling in their notebooks.

"How did you see that?" asked Ronnie. "I couldn't look at them for fear of busting out laughing."

Eddie pulled a little mirror out of his pocket and laid it on the table. "You've got to be careful when you use it," explained Eddie. "If the sun reflects off of it, and somebody sees it, it could cause problems."

"Man, Eddie," said Herman. "You ever thought about going into private investigation? I could use a guy with some street smarts."

"Naw, that sounds a lot like work to me," said Eddie. "Besides, it's way too dangerous. A guy's got to play to his strengths. You private dicks get into too many brawls to suit me."

* * *

The practice rounds at Butler National and Cog Hill went as planned.

Eddie and Ronnie both took copious notes and hit several shots from different positions on the course. At each course they had two club members/observers in their group. It was obvious that the members' job was to report back to someone on what they saw. On the other hand, if the members were planning on "investing" in this little tournament, it wouldn't hurt to have some inside information on these two. Later that evening, they planned on getting together with their fellow observers to compare notes. It wouldn't be that big of a deal if they were planning on betting a couple of hundred bucks. However, guys that could afford the dues at the three venues hosting the competition were obviously capable of laying down more than cigar and whiskey money.

When they were done, Eddie totally agreed with Ronnie's strategy of what format they should play for each course. The Detroit hustler was impressed with his partner's knowledge of the three layouts. They both went to bed feeling confident that the next three days would go their way.

* * *

The main dining room at Butler National was full the next morning. The sixteen competitors sat at the front tables so the rest in attendance could get a good look at them. Eddie recognized a guy that he had played against in Venice, Florida. The Detroit hustler had won fifty bucks from the guy and they agreed to meet the next day for another game. Eddie figured his win the first day was set-up money. He had shot seventy-seven, throwing away maybe six strokes to keep it close. It was obvious that his opponent was throwing away shots also. It was rather comical to watch the two golfers posturing and trying to convince the other guy that this was the best they had to offer.

The second match never took place, because Brian, at least that's what he told Eddie his name was, didn't show the next day. Eddie figured he probably had something else a little more profitable going. As it was, Eddie never saw Brian's best game. That didn't matter much now, as Brian was only about thirty, so he was playing in the younger division.

The M. C. for the tournament stood and addressed the crowded room.

"I would like to welcome our competitors, and their, uh sponsors, for the inaugural Arbor Day Tree Fund Tournament."

There were a few chuckles around the room. Even though it wasn't even close to Arbor Day, the creators of the tournament needed to cloak the competition with a worthy cause. Who would object to an event that intended to raise several thousand dollars for trees to be planted around the three clubs involved? The tree money would come from the pari-mutuel win and place pools.

After explaining this, the M. C. went over the rules of the competition. It was just as Ronnie described it to Eddie that night in the tub. They would play each course against a different team in their age bracket. Before the match started, the players would give their scorecard to their opponents. It would be clearly marked as to what format they would be playing on each block of six holes.

Ronnie leaned over and whispered to his partner, "I hope these hacks know the difference between a best ball and a scramble. I've seen flyers at clubs advertising a "Best Ball Scramble Tournament". You can't play two different formats at the same time. I don't know where they got the idea that in a best ball you hit your tee shots and then played the best shot. Duh."

"I know what you mean," answered Eddie. "I guess they never saw any of the old episodes of Shell's Wonderful World of Golf. That was always a two-man best ball format. If Hogan and Snead were partners and Snead made his twenty-footer for a birdie, Hogan would just pick up his fifteen-footer. Snead already had the best ball for the team."

"It's really pretty simple," added Ronnie. "Even if they hadn't seen any of those old shows, if you thought a best ball and a scramble were the same, how would you explain playing the three best balls out of four—or best two out of three? I guess if there weren't a lot of confused golfers out there, it would have been tougher for us to earn a living, huh?"

When the M. C. was done answering questions, the pairing sheets were handed out. 'The Grip' and 'The Street' studied the names on their sheet. They each knew one of the six guys they would be playing against.

"Poole is a real long hitter from Texas," said Eddie, as they walked outside and sat in a cart. "I've never seen him play, but I've been told he can flat crush it. That's not a problem for us, 'cause we won't be getting into a driving contest with him. He'll do his thing and we'll do ours."

"Jenkins is from right here in Chicago," observed Ronnie. "He's forty-five or six and has played in a lot of amateur tournaments. He owns his own business, so he's never had to worry about getting off work to play. I played with him once. He's pretty solid all the way around. I'd be surprised if he was putting up his own dough. I think he just likes the competition. I expect he will play well, 'cause there's not a lot of pressure on him. These other guys don't look familiar. That one dude's name looks like he's from Europe somewhere. There is going to be some serious coin changing hands before this thing is over."

"As long as some of it finds its way into our hands, I don't care where these guys are from," said Eddie. "Let's wander over to the pari-mutuel table and check on our odds and get some money down. I gave Suzanne's money to Herman. How is he going to get his bets down?"

"Some of the public courses in the area are taking action too," said Ronnie. "It's all very hush-hush. Don't worry. He knows what he's doing. By the way, we'll have to settle up with him on his security services when this is all over. I don't want to put any extra pressure on you, but if we don't win, it could get expensive."

"Gee, Grip," said Eddie in a whiny voice, "just when I was getting my confidence back, you have to go and say something like that."

Ronnie slapped his partner on the back. "Cut it out, man. You live for this shit as much as I do. Hey, do you have twenty bucks on you? I'm a little short right now."

"Can you believe those odds?" asked Eddie, as they walked away from the pari-mutuel area. "They've got us at five-to-one to win and five-to-two to place."

"Most of the win money is going down on Poole and his partner," added Ronnie. "We couldn't have asked for a better situation. The guy ahead of me bet twenty thousand on them. That's the reason our numbers look so good. I overheard two dudes talkin' about Poole's long drives and his partner's ability to hit the ball low. They think that's the winning ticket. We've got them on the last day at Medinah. I like that because we'll be able to keep an eye on them. I'm assuming that this tourney is on the up and up, but you know how crazy people can get when there's money involved."

"Yeah," said Eddie. "Especially money that they don't have to work for. Let's get over to the range and hit a few. You gonna wow them with that big slice or are you gonna play it legit?"

"Maybe off the first tee," answered Ronnie, as they reached their cart. "After we all hit our first tee shots, we'll approach them for a little side money. Seeing that banana might loosen their pockets up."

"Let's not get too greedy," warned Eddie. "Remember the old saying, 'pigs get fed, hogs get slaughtered'. These other guys can play or they wouldn't be here. Hit your banjo on one, and then we'll offer them a little side action. How about a grand each?"

"Sounds good to me. I'm ready to get out there and spank a few."

* * *

The sixteen competitors were allowed a half-hour on the practice tee, then they were all called to the practice green.

The tournament director went over the basics again. There would be some spectators following the golfers, so a volunteer marshal was assigned to each group. There was also a scorekeeper with a headset on. He would relay the scores to the clubhouse after every hole. Some of the bettors wanted to watch the action first hand, while others would rather sit in the air conditioning with a beverage of their choice. There would also be course security roaming the area in John Deere Gators. The Gators were all-terrain utility vehicles used by the grounds crew. Today, the grounds crew was on the course at sun-up getting things ready. Once the play started, except for the security guys, they were to be nowhere near the golfers.

Grip and Street were in the last group. Their opponents introduced themselves by their last names only. Crisp and Rivera were not from the Chicago area. The two Gull Lake hustlers gave their real last names. They figured if word of their involvement in this thing got back to Michigan, the names Ferguson and Costas would be tougher to connect to the Chicago action.

Poole and Maun were just ahead of them. They watched Poole unleash a 300-yard drive down number one. The crowd cheered their approval. Eddie looked at his partner and mouthed, "Game on". Ronnie was grinning from ear to ear. When the group ahead was clear the two teams exchanged cards and confirmed what format they would be playing on what holes. The marshal also wrote this information down on a pad, while the scorekeeper relayed the information back to the clubhouse via his cell phone. Then he held out two flat sticks, and Eddie drew the one with number two on it. Crisp stepped up and hit a respectable drive about 260 down the middle. Rivera hit a carbon copy of his partner's drive. He walked over and fist bumped his partner. Eddie walked over and stood by his opponents as Ronnie strolled onto the tee. He messed around more than he needed to, teeing on the left side, then picking up and moving over to the right side. He seemed nervous, gripping the club like he was going to split some wood. His big slice went down the left side, then curved back into the fairway and settled about twenty-five yards behind his opponents' tee shots.

Eddie took a couple of steps toward the tee markers. He turned toward Crisp and Rivera and walked back to them. He asked in a low voice, "You gentlemen wouldn't want to put a little on the side would you? Say a thousand each on today's score?"

Rivera and Crisp both glanced over at a pale, skinny man in plaid Bermuda shorts. He had the look of a guy that rarely ventured out when the sun was shining. He was what serious gamblers called a 'hairy leg'—the money man behind the operation. Bermuda shorts nodded, and Eddie headed to the tee. The Detroit hustler's ball took off low down the right side of the fairway. Once velocity stopped being the primary factor and spin took over, the ball curved back toward the middle of the fairway. It landed about ten yards short of the two balls lying there and bounced right over the top of them, coming to a stop fifteen yards closer to the green.

The first six holes went pretty much the way the guys had it scripted. They played best ball for the first six. That way they could both play their own game and get a feel for how the day was going to go. Their opponents, surprisingly, decided to play a scramble right off the bat. It was obvious that they wanted to get off to a fast start.

The investors back in the clubhouse were impressed when Crisp and Rivera birdied three out of the first six. 'The Street' and 'The Grip' played respectably, finishing the first leg at one under. They each missed two greens, but not the same ones, so they had a putt for birdie on all six. Eddie almost chipped in on number five, but settled for a tap-in par.

The second leg was where Eddie and Ronnie expected to rack up some birdies. They were a little disappointed when they only birdied the two par fives. Eddie hit driver off the fairway for his second shot on both of them after Ronnie had played solid three-woods. Their opponents surprised them when they played alternate shot on the middle six holes. The middle six at Butler starts out with a bending par five that requires a conservative tee shot. It was definitely an advantage to be able to hit two drives on that hole. Crisp and Rivera's strategy backfired when they didn't pick up any strokes on the fives and gave two back on the par threes. As a result, they went into the last six holes only one under. This appeared to shake them up a little, as they played the last leg in one over, ending up at even for the day. They both gave Eddie and Ronnie a brief handshake on the last green and headed for the parking lot. Their backer walked over and discreetly handed each of them a roll of ten hundreds. He didn't appear to be very happy about the whole situation.

The two Michigan hustlers had stood three under on the eighteenth green when Ronnie ran in a thirty-footer for birdie. It was an excellent way to end the day. Four under put them in second place behind Poole and Maun's sixty-seven. So far, things were looking good. They decided that one drink each wasn't going to hurt anything. Being experienced money players, they decided to have that drink at Herman's place where they knew what was coming out of the bottle.

In this business, one could never be too cautious.

* * *

"What did you think of those greens today, pardner?" asked Ronnie.

The Michigan contingent sat on Herman's back deck sipping drinks and discussing the day's events.

"I liked the way they rolled, except for some of those pin placements," replied Eddie. "You would have thought we were playing the U. S. Open out there. I gotta admit, after playing a few holes I figured one or two under would be low for the day."

"You should have seen us on eighteen, Herm," said Ronnie. "We were playing alternate shot and I hit a good drive, right down the water line. Eddie here, chunks a four-iron for our second, about thirty feet short of the flag. I actually heard Crisp grunt when I stepped up and rolled it in."

"I saw it," said Herman.

"You saw it?" questioned Eddie.

"Yeah, I was at the back of your small following. I think one guy actually clapped for you two on that hole."

"I never saw you out there," remarked Eddie. "Did you see him, Grip?"

"Nope, and that's what we're paying him for. Lay low and step up when we need him and his team. How many guys are assisting, Herm?"

"I've got two people working with me on this. One is an ex-Ranger and the other is very capable. We've worked together before, and they have my complete trust. When this is over we'll meet back here. I'll introduce you guys, and we can settle the finances. What did you take off your opponents today?"

"A grand each," said Ronnie. "Their 'hairy leg' was there and he didn't seem all too pleased about settling up. You know, a legitimate gambling man expects to be paid when he wins and doesn't complain when he loses. It's the way of the world, man. If it bothers you that much, you probably shouldn't be in the game. What's the number one rule of gambling, Street?"

Eddie lifted his glass in salute to his partner. He knew there was a reason he liked this guy, other than just his golf skills. They both had a similar outlook on the whole scheme of things. There is no substitute for the right attitude coupled with a decent amount of skill. If they didn't win this thing, he was confident they would take second. They both had enough on their team to place in the pari-mutuel pool to pay Herman and his guys. Losing ten grand was not what they came for, but it was better than dropping a huge bundle. Besides, he got to play three awesome golf courses with his buddy in a high-pressure situation. Ronnie was right—he did live for this shit.

"Never bet money you can't afford to lose," responded Eddie. "If you put yourself in a do or die situation, be prepared for the worst. I don't mind the pressure, but I'm a man who likes to sleep at night."

"Yeah, and you should see who he's sleeping with, Herm," said Ronnie.

"You aren't doing too bad in that department yourself," said Eddie.

Herman chuckled and got up to check with his wife on supper. When he came back, Ronnie had gone in to use the restroom.

"Can I ask you something, Herman?" asked Eddie in a hushed voice.

The private eye sensed that the conversation was about to turn serious, so he nodded slowly, not sure where Eddie was going with this.

"What can you tell me about Ronnie's boy?"

Herman took a deep breath and looked off into the distance. "You know who Pat Tillman was?" he asked wistfully. Eddie nodded that he knew about the famous NFL player that quit pro football and enlisted in the Army Rangers. "Well Robbie was pretty much a carbon copy, except he didn't play college or professional football, like Tillman did. He enlisted right out of high school. That guy could do it all, strong safety and tailback in football, great basketball and baseball player. Probably would have won the state championship in wrestling if they had let him wrestle and play basketball at the same time. Our unit was very close, like most Ranger outfits. Robbie saved my life a few weeks before he was killed. An IED exploded by the side of the road we were walking, and I caught some shrapnel in the leg and was bleeding pretty bad. Seconds after the explosion, we started taking small arms fire. Robbie sprinted to my position, threw me over his shoulder and carried me to cover. I was a little lighter back then, but I was still a big guy. The dude was running with me up there like he was carrying a twenty-pound sack of potatoes. I've never seen another man like him. He was killed walking on that same road a few weeks later. Some dumb-ass sniper got off a lucky shot. We got him, but there wasn't anything we could do for Robbie."

Herman looked through the glass and saw Ronnie talking to his wife, Charise, so he leaned forward and added, "I think meeting you was good for him. Before he moved to Michigan he was drinking too much and hanging out at the track more than he really needed to. There's a real unscrupulous element that hangs around Maywood and Balmoral, and he was running way too much with those boys. With him the horses are an adventure in math, logic and psychology. At least that's what he told me one time. He doesn't do it for the excitement. To him it's another game to be mastered. Before the move, it was getting to be more like one big party. You gotta have a reason to get up in the morning, and partying and having a good time shouldn't be your main motivation. He does have a grandson, but the mother, Robbie's widow, won't have anything to do with Ronnie. She even moved away and changed their last names. Ronnie and her never got along. She blames him for Robbie's enlistment and for backing him when he re-upped. He could have played professional ball. He was that good. Robbie was the kind of guy that books are written about. You know, a real patriot. He felt that he was needed the most in the military, so that's where he wanted to be."

"Does he know where his grandson lives?" asked Eddie.

Herman was about to answer when Ronnie opened the sliding door and announced that dinner was ready. After dinner, the schedule for the rest of the evening was to relax and watch a ball game in the basement. Herman sat with his five-year-old son in his lap until he fell asleep. Eddie and Ronnie stuck to their plan of one drink each.

At eleven, they all headed to bed.

Herman slipped into bed beside Charise.

She looked at him with raised eyebrows, "So they did good today? What are their chances?"

"Damn, babe," said Herman. "Those two old guys can play. Eddie bent a shot around a bunch of trees and right up on the green like it was nothing. He just lit a cigar and walked back and sat in the cart. I still can't figure out why they haven't tried to play the professional tour? I know Ronnie hates to travel. He wouldn't get on a plane if his life depended on it. But, there are other ways to get from city to city. I don't know what Eddie's story is. The odds on them to win in the pool are five to one. That's really high considering there are only four teams in each bracket. It's probably because there is an incredible amount of money on this guy named Poole and his partner."

He gave her a hug and a kiss. "Winning this little competition should be no problem for our boys, barring any unforeseen circumstances."

Unforeseen circumstances are my department, thought Herman as he adjusted his covers. *It's just a golf tournament, but we need to be prepared for anything that comes up.*

CHAPTER EIGHT

Goombahs

If Eddie Davis and Ronnie Green teamed up I would bet everything I had on them. Those two can beat any two senior golfers on the planet.

—"Shiftless" Gary, currently doing three-to-five for bilking unsuspecting widows out of their late husband's pension money

"Are you ready for Dubsdread?" asked Ronnie. "It's a public course, so there will probably be a lot of people there."

"I'm ready," answered Eddie. "I've heard a lot about this place, and I'm anxious to see it. It looks tough on TV, and I bet it's even tougher up close."

"Here's our plan of attack for today," explained Ronnie, after closing the door and leaning confidently against it, arms folded. "We'll start out with alternate shot, then scramble the middle six, and then play best ball on the last six. Nine and eleven are both par fives, so I'm counting on birdies there. If we can get by the first six at one over it would be acceptable. Number six is a long par three that will take at least a utility club to get home. You should drive on the odd holes, which includes a par five. I'll get us on the threes. Does that sound like a plan?"

"It's fine with me," agreed Eddie. "You're the brains behind this outfit. I'm just here for my personality and sex appeal."

"I'm glad I'm not betting on either of those qualities. I don't know the guys we're playing today, so it should be interesting. Poole and Maun will be behind us this time. We'll hang tough today and tomorrow it'll all be on the table."

* * *

'The Street' and 'The Grip' introduced themselves to Weber and Springer. Weber was a German that pronounced his name as if it started with a 'V'.

Their first round at Butler National didn't go so well for their opponents.

A seventy-five put them eight shots back of the leaders and seven shots back of Ronnie and Eddie. It didn't take the Michigan entries long to figure out the situation with Weber and Springer. It appeared that they just plain didn't like each other. They were scrambling the first six and started arguing about which ball to play on the second hole. Eddie and Ronnie kept their distance and tried to not let it affect their game. They offered a side bet of a thousand each on the first tee, but Springer balked, so they settled on five hundred. It was obvious that these two were playing on their own dime without a backer.

Everything was clicking for the two hustlers until they bogeyed number six. Ronnie did hit the green on the long par three like he predicted, but his ball flight was too low and it ran into the back left bunker. His partner played a solid shot to eight feet, where Ronnie's subsequent putt did a 360 and hung on the edge. Ronnie's prediction of one over on the opening holes proved to be accurate. With that in mind, they expected to get a few strokes back on the next six. As it was, the team shot five under on the middle six holes, but it wasn't their team.

Springer and Weber pulled off a little magic on the middle six holes, and miraculously, they did it playing alternate shot. On eight, a fairly short par four, Weber holed their second shot for an eagle. The dozen or so people standing around the green acted like the shot had just won the tournament.

"They must have their milk money on these guys," remarked Eddie, as he prepared to hit his second shot. He had to back away twice as some fool was standing on the back of the green directly behind the pin waving his arms. Before one of the observers could get to the guy, a tall black man appeared and escorted him away from the green area. After Herman took care of him, Eddie proceeded hit a smooth wedge to six feet. When they got to the green the spectators told them that their opponent's ball bounced once, hit the flag half way up, and then came straight down into the hole. On nine, a respectable par five, Springer played the team's third shot out of a greenside trap. He caught it thin, and as the people on the far side scrambled for cover, the ball hit the flag stick again and ended up right next to the hole. Springer and Weber appeared to be on speaking terms after their two miracle shots. The two hustlers matched their opponent's eagle on the par five eleventh. Ronnie hit first and his second shot was about thirty yards short of the green in the fairway, so Eddie hit his driver and got it to the front edge of the green. From there, he poured in a thirty-five footer. Not to be outdone, Springer holed his pitch shot from twenty yards out. At the finish of the second leg, the Michigan team had an eagle and a birdie to show for their efforts, while Springer and Weber had two eagles and a birdie.

"They pulled a couple of shots out of their lower anatomy back there," observed Ronnie. "Hopefully that will keep them from squabbling like little kids for the next six holes."

The hustlers stood two under on seventeen green, and their opponents were at minus four. Eddie was looking at a fifteen-footer for birdie, and Ronnie had a six-footer for par on the same line. When it was Eddie's turn to putt he called the marshal over. He explained that when he was away that meant the whole team was away, and either team member could putt. It didn't have to be the one farthest from the hole. Eddie wanted Ronnie to putt for his par first, so he could see the line, and if his partner was in with a four, Eddie could be a little more aggressive with his putt. The marshal knew his rules and agreed. The hustlers had discussed this strategy before, but this was the first time they had both been on the same line in the best ball format. Ronnie putted first and they watched his ball break sharply at the cup as it slid by. Eddie's ball barely got there, but it took the same break and toppled into the hole. As they walked off the green, a spectator asked Eddie what was going on with the putting order. Eddie stopped and graciously explained the rule. The guy expressed his thanks and wished them good luck.

"Dude, did you know who that was?" asked Ronnie.

"No, who was it?"

"It was the governor of Illinois," said Ronnie. "I saw him a few holes back, but didn't want to make a big deal out of it."

"Do you think this guy will end up in prison like most of the other ex-governors?"

"Oh yeah. It's becoming a tradition. Hey, somebody's gotta be number one, right?"

"I can think of a lot of other reasons to be number one," said Eddie, as they walked up to the eighteenth tee.

Ronnie rolled his three-footer in for a par on the eighteenth to give the guys a 69. Weber and Springer played the last stretch respectable and carded a 68. As it was, that was the low round of the day. Poole and Maun shot a 70, tying them with Ronnie and Eddie. The contestants and the spectators expected the scores to be somewhat lower, but the first two courses were set up like the golfers were playing one of the four majors. The guys in charge obviously felt that these type of conditions would favor the players they were betting on.

After they loaded up and headed for Herman's place, they had a serious discussion on what to expect the next day at Medinah. Ronnie informed his partner that there would be goombahs all over the place trying to distract the golfers. Eddie had never heard the term before, so the Chicago native explained the concept of these gangster wannabes. They were guys that didn't really have any appreciable skills to earn a living, so they did whatever somebody or some organization asked them to do. And, they were willing to do almost anything. Ronnie went on to explain that not all goombahs were like that though. Some were just good old city boys from the old neighborhood that still hung around together. Therefore, the term was a generic one that described more than one type of individual.

* * *

"You got a plan for tomorrow?" asked Ronnie, looking over their empty dinner plates.

"I've always got a plan," answered Herman. "Problem is, we've got a lot of variables out there. We'll do what we can, but you two should be prepared for just about anything. So far, this whole thing looks legit, but that doesn't mean it will stay that way. There are a lot of people out there that don't like to lose, and they will go to great lengths to be on the winning side. By the way, the wife and I put five hundred on you guys to win. Just thought you'd like to know that."

"Geez, thanks for adding to the pressure," said Ronnie. "Did you hedge a little and put some down on us to place didn't you? Our final odds to finish second ended up at two-to-one."

"Nope," said Herman, as he grabbed his son and sat him on his lap. "You'll win this thing. We've got faith in you. Did you know that you and Poole's team are one stroke ahead of the guys in the younger division?"

"You're kidding?" said Eddie. "Well, I hope your faith is justified. We dropped five hundred each to those two jokers today. And, by the way, that was money that we had set aside to pay you and your security team. Partner, if it looks like we're going to lose tomorrow, we need a plan to hightail it out of this city."

The next morning was a carbon copy of the first two days. There were only a few clouds in the sky and the high temperature was supposed to top out around eighty. It was a great day to play some golf and to add to their respective retirement funds. Eddie and Ronnie had put up the same money on themselves in the pool—two thousand to win and two thousand to place. With only four teams in their bracket, the pool only offered first and second place. Their thinking was, if they came in second, they would end up clearing two thousand on pool bets, losing two grand on the win bet, but raking in four grand on the place bet. That would hopefully be enough to pay Herman for his security services. Of course, if they took second, the ten large entry fee was going home in someone else's pocket. On the other hand, if they won it all, they would be pocketing forty-four thousand, plus side bet money.

"Dude," said Ronnie, as Eddie pulled out of Herman's drive and steered the Monte Carlo toward Medinah. "This is probably a bad time to tell you this, but I'm into some low-life gamblers for about a quarter mil. If we don't win this I could lose a couple of fingers or even worse."

Eddie knew better than to respond to such a dramatic statement until he had more information. He stared through the windshield and waited for Ronnie, who was looking out the passenger window, to continue.

"I'm just funnin' ya, partner," said Ronnie, suppressing a grin. "I figured a little humor would brighten our day. You gotta admit I had you thinking for a minute."

"Yeah, I was thinking if it would be easier to make your death look like a suicide or an accident."

"Whoa, that's pretty harsh," said Ronnie. "You wouldn't kill a guy for money, would you?"

"It wouldn't be the first time," answered Eddie, still staring straight ahead. "I didn't want to do it, but I had run out of options. There was a lot of money involved. I'm not talkin' just nickels and dimes either."

Now it was Ronnie's turn to stare. His attempt to be funny had apparently turned serious, and he didn't like where this was heading. So Eddie had killed a guy. Maybe he didn't know him as well as he thought he did. He stared intently at the side of driver's face. It started with a small muscle twitch and then it turned into a huge grin, followed by Eddie's unique laugh. The Detroit poker player turned toward him and raised his eyebrows.

"All right, dammit," exclaimed Ronnie. "You got me on that one. I was just trying to ease the pressure a little and you get all creepy on me. Man, you had me going. Let's focus on the task at hand and forget about losing fingers and people getting killed. Here's today's plan. We play alternate shot on the first six, our own ball on the middle six, and then we scramble on the last leg. The middle leg has two par fives, but I figure if everything is on the line late in the match, we want as many options as we can get. I will admit that sixteen and seventeen scare me a little. What do you think?"

"This is the one course of the three that I've played before," said Eddie. "I like your strategy, and I wouldn't be surprised if Poole and Maun play it the same way. This will be an exciting day one way or another. What about the goombahs? Do you think they will be a problem?"

"Truthfully, yes. Let's hope that Herman and his team can keep their influence to a minimum."

"What's this security thing going to cost us?" asked Eddie.

"Ha," laughed Ronnie. "I don't really know. As always, we didn't discuss his fee, but he knows what he's doing, and I'm sure he's hired top-notch help."

The Michigan team didn't say much for the rest of the trip to the course. Both were lost in their thoughts, going over what they needed to do to walk away with a fistful of dollars. Eddie stopped at the guard shack and showed his competitor's pass. The guard told them where to park and gave them directions to the men's locker room. He also told them to change their shoes in the locker room, not in the parking lot. There were strict rules against that sort of thing at this club. Before the Monte came to rest at the bag drop area two young men appeared ready to assist the players. They took their bags out of the trunk and told them what cart they would be on. Eddie slipped each of the guys a ten, and they seemed grateful. As it was, a ten wasn't nearly enough.

The players walked out of the pre-round meeting shaking their heads. They were informed that the practice range was closed, but they could hit a few drivers down the twelfth hole on the number one course. It was the hole on the other side of the trees that ran parallel with eighteen on the number three course. It was to be drivers only, as the members didn't want a bunch of extra divots on their course. The contestants thought this was a little strange, but there was nothing they could do about it. They got another surprise when they saw the number of spectators milling around. There were several hundred, but most of them were there to follow the younger golfers.

Davis and Green were the last match off, and they were paired with the co-leaders for the over fifty bracket, Poole and Maun. Their group had a substantial crowd of about one hundred followers. The players introduced themselves and exchanged cards marked with the format they were playing. Eddie looked at the card and smiled. Poole and Maun's card mirrored theirs. They were also going to start with alternate shot, then a best ball, followed by a scramble. As it turned out, Poole and Maun were both from Texas, and they were decent guys. Poole told Eddie he was a club pro for a while at a huge resort complex. He quit the golf business when he found out the real estate guys selling lots around the complex were making four or five times as much as he was. He said that real estate had been very good to him, providing loads of money and the time to play golf. Maun looked a little shady, but seemed to be respectable.

After getting a thousand dollar side bet, 'The Street' stepped up and laced one down the middle. Poole followed with a huge drive that stopped thirty yards past Eddie's. The mood of the day was established when Ronnie pulled out a wedge for the team's approach. He was only about 120 out, which was a comfortable distance for him. He looked down at his grip before he put the club in his hands and saw a strange substance on it. He called Eddie over and showed it to him.

"Damn," observed Eddie. "Somebody put Vaseline on your grip, Grip."

"Jerks," said the Chicago hustler, as he vigorously wiped the club with a towel. "So that's how it's going to be today."

Poole walked over to see what was going on. "What's up, guys?"

"Somebody was worried about the calluses on Ronnie's hands," said Eddie, with a hint of sarcasm. "It looks like they put some Vaseline on his wedge to soften them up for him. I had no idea that Chicago was such a caring city."

"That sucks," said Poole. He looked over at his partner and hollered, "Hey, Don, pull your clubs out and check your grips." Then he turned back to his opponents. "Take your time and check the rest of your clubs, guys. This aint no way to play a golf tournament."

The guys took the rest of their clubs out and inspected them. Eddie's wedge was also slicked up. The rest of the players' clubs were fine. It was obvious that somebody with money on Poole and Maun thought they needed a little edge. Ronnie still didn't like the feel of his club, but managed to hit his shot about twenty feet from the hole.

"Do you think Poole was sincere with his comments?" asked Ronnie on the second tee. Before Eddie could answer, Poole told them to bring their wedges over. The hustlers took them out of their bags and walked over to where Poole was standing by the ball washer. The tall Texan told them to hold their clubs out grip first. Then he tilted the ball washer forward and dumped its contents over their wedges.

"There," he said. "Wipe them down. That soapy water in there should get most of that slippery crap off of them. You shouldn't need your wedges for a couple of holes, and they should be dry by then. I'm sorry about this, fellas. When I saw your names on the pairing sheets, I was hoping it would come down to you versus Don and me. I can't wait to tell my son that I played, and beat, Eddie 'The Street' Davis."

"Here we go with that legend stuff again," said Ronnie. "What the hell did you do to get that famous? I can give you two a side and own your ass all day long."

"I'll hold you to that when you we get back home" said Eddie. "Hey, thanks, John. You're a real sportsman, and there aren't too many of us left."

"No worries, Eddie. I just don't want any excuses when we walk up and collect all that cash tonight."

The two teams battled back and forth for the next fourteen holes. Poole's long drives kept his team in the game. Ronnie and Eddie stood on the fifteenth tee one up. They should have been up a few more, but caught a couple of bad breaks. The one that really hurt them was when Ronnie's second shot on eleven, a dog leg left par four, hit a sprinkler head and the ball caromed off into the thick rough. Neither he nor Eddie, who was in the greenside bunker, could get up and down. That reduced their two-stroke lead to just one. The pleasantries between the teams had stopped right about then. It was now a given that whoever won this match would be taking home the big prize.

Ronnie hit first on fifteen, a relatively short par four. His drive split the fairway. Eddie followed suit and hit one about ten yards farther. Poole's drive found the trees, and since Maun was in the fairway, he just walked over and picked up his ball. As Poole walked out of the trees, Ronnie looked over at him and saw a guy half hidden behind a tree. The guy lifted something and aimed it at Ronnie. Before he could figure out what was going on he felt a strange sensation. He put his hands up to cover his face. It took a few seconds to realize what he had just experienced. What Ronnie didn't see was what happened next in the trees. A tall black man with a grounds crew shirt pulled up on a utility vehicle and jumped out. He grabbed the guy with the laser and smashed his head into the tree he was standing behind. Then he dumped the man into the little trailer he was towing and sped off.

"Hey, partner," said Ronnie, as he waved Eddie over. "We need to talk for a second." Eddie walked over and asked his partner what was up. "I can't see, man. Some idiot just shined a laser in my eyes. I can sort of see around the edges, but not directly what I'm looking at."

"Goombahs," mused Eddie, as he guided his partner toward their cart. "All right, man, come over here and sit in the cart for a second. Let's see if this is a short term condition."

Eddie waved Poole and the marshal for their group over and explained what had just happened. The marshal wasn't real sympathetic. He told them they would have to treat it like an injury and to make the decision if Ronnie could continue or not. Since they were playing a scramble for the last six holes, Eddie could obviously finish the round by himself. 'The Street' lit up a Macanudo and went over their options. Then he looked over at Ronnie and smiled.

Oblivious to his partner's smile, 'The Grip' looked up in the vicinity of Eddie's face and said, "Street, we could use some of that legendary stuff right now. I hope Herman got the guy that did this."

"He got the guy," said Eddie. "I saw him haul somebody off in a little trailer. All right, partner, how about we play a little game of no-look?"

Ronnie thought about it for a few seconds before a look of understanding crossed his face. It was a game they played once in a while at Gull Lake to hone their touch. You would stand over your ball and look down. Your partner would tell you the yardage, give you the club you requested, and then line you up. You were not allowed to look at the target. The shot was played trusting the other guy to line you up right, and trusting your own swing. Eddie was better at the game, because he was more of a feel player. The last time they played it though, Ronnie showed a marked improvement. This game was a little different from the one they had played—now Ronnie couldn't see the target or the ball.

Eddie lined his partner up, then moved off to the side. Ronnie made a shaky swing and hit a fat wedge about fifteen yards short of the green. He was not happy, but he knew his role was now that of a supportive teammate. Moping and grousing around wouldn't do either of them any good. Eddie dropped his ball and hit his wedge fifteen feet wide but hole high. Maun's second shot was only ten feet short of the flag. After getting lined up, Ronnie hit the team's first putt. It was too hard, but the roll of the ball told Eddie all that he needed to know. He played for a little more break and snuggled the ball into the right side of the hole. Ronnie didn't see it, but when he heard it fall into the cup he let out a little, "Yeah". Maun putted first and dropped the ten-footer in. 'The Grip' and 'The Street' were still up one with three to go.

The sixteenth hole at Medinah is just plain brutal. It bends right to left and the green is elevated so high that you can't see the bottom of the flagstick. Ronnie slapped an anemic 180-yard drive out to the right. He couldn't bring himself to just swing away and trust his instincts. Eddie followed with a picture perfect drive, down the right side with a little draw. The team's second shot would be 182 playing like it was at least 200. Eddie and Ronnie played first, as Poole's drive was well ahead of theirs. Ronnie was still a little tentative and caught his hybrid a little thin. Maun and Poole did a double take when Eddie told his partner that his ball hit just a little short and bounced up on to the green. They could see it three-quarters of the way up the hill and it appeared to be trickling back down. What Maun and Poole didn't know was that a nickname like 'The Street' wasn't just given out one day on a whim—the name was earned. Eddie was thinking all the time. That's what made him a good poker player and an even better golfer. He might need his partner on one of these last holes, and he needed a guy with a little bit of confidence. One thing they both knew about golf was: if you don't think you can pull a shot off, you will pay for your hesitancy from the top of your backswing right on through the ball.

Eddie cut a three-iron that disappeared over the front edge of the green. It looked real good from where he was standing. Poole hit first for the opponents and his five-iron was a thing of beauty. It ended up dead on line about fifteen feet short of the hole. Eddie's ball ended up on the back edge, but still puttable. Ronnie's effort didn't help much, as it rolled about twenty feet by. The Detroit native took a deep breath and cozied his putt up to about two feet. He marked and stood by as Poole rolled in the fifteen-footer. The match was all square with two holes to go. Poole looked over at Eddie on the next tee and smiled at him. It was obvious that he loved this kind of action too, and he didn't let the money get to him. Eddie decided that he liked the guy, so he tipped his cap in response. Seventeen was the other hole that Ronnie dreaded. It was a medium length par three over water. The green was below the tee and it had a lot of slope. A well-placed tee shot was a must on this hole. Keeping the ball below the pin was easier said than done. Anything hole high or past would be strictly a speed putt, and both teams knew that this would not be a good time to hit something delicate, leaving it up to the golf gods as to when it would stop.

The best Poole and Maun could do was twenty-two feet behind the flag. It wasn't a bad shot, but under the circumstances, they would rather be chipping uphill from off the front of the green. Ronnie and Eddie walked out together on to the tee. The crowd following them had grown to about two hundred. Word had gotten around that the old guys were tied and everything was on the line in this group. Eddie stood on the tee talking calmly to his partner.

"What the hell's the matter with the shorter guy?" asked a spectator.

Poole looked over his shoulder and said, "He can't see very well. He's pretty much blind right now."

"Well, if the guy can barely see, then he shouldn't be playing in something like this," said the guy who was standing next to the man that asked the first question. "Do you think he's faking it?"

"It just happened recently," explained Poole. "And, no, he's not faking it."

"Don't you know who that is?" asked a third man. "That's Ronnie Green. You know, 'The Grip'. He's one of the best senior players in the whole Midwest, maybe even the whole country. He used to live around here, but not any more. My buddy said he moved somewhere down south, like Florida. I'll tell you one thing, he aint no faker, and he aint no choker either."

"Hey, Partner," said Eddie in a low voice. "They're talking about you over there. It sounds like they think you're a helluva player. I guess this is the time to tell you that I think you're a helluva player too. If we don't win this thing, we will definitely take second. We'll lose our entry fee, but we'll take a little more out of the pool than we put in. I got the feeling that you are in the same boat that I'm in. Taking second here won't mean a damn thing when it comes to our lifestyle. When we get back, I'm taking Suzanne out to dinner, and then we're going back to my place. I bet you're going to do the same thing with Kathy. So, I guess what I'm saying is, I'm proud to be playing here with you, and I think we both know who has played the best golf these last three days. You're a good friend, and you came along at a time in my life when I needed a good friend. Now, I want you to hit this 5-iron like you don't have a fucking care in the world. Just you and me standing on number one at Bedford Valley—smoking cigars, talking trash and swinging it smooth."

Ronnie took a few practice swings to feel the weight and length of the club. He barely clipped the grass tops with the last two swings. To an accomplished golfer, the club feels like an extension of their hands. They have a feel for ball striking that can't be explained. They can usually tell, without looking up, exactly how far and how much off-line they had just hit a particular shot. Eddie teed up his partner's ball and told Ronnie when he was lined up to the target. Ronnie bent over the ball with a feeling of pure joy. It had been a long time coming, but at that moment joy had finally crept back into his heart. Most of his banter with Eddie, and the other golfers at the GLV complex, was a cover-up for his real feelings. Losing a wife and a son in the span of twelve months can do that to a guy, even though it was over a decade ago. He had a little smile on his face when he took the club back. At the top of his follow through, 'The Grip' was still smiling. He knew that he had flushed it. The crowd around the tee and green gave him a tremendous ovation. He looked over at Eddie's shadowy figure and saw him holding out his fist. Ronnie only got half of his fist to connect with his partner's. That mattered little, as his 5-iron was two feet left and eight feet below the hole. Poole joined in with the other fans and clapped vigorously. Maun just shook his head and got into the cart. Eddie's attempt was solid, but Ronnie's gave them the best chance at birdie.

"I want you to know," said Ronnie, as he and Eddie road down to the green. "My eyes were watering back there because of my current condition. So don't read anything else into it."

"Yeah, mine too," replied Eddie.

Poole and Maun barely got down in two, as Maun's effort trickled outside of their opponent's mark. Poole got his putt to stop five feet below the cup. They stood and watched Ronnie hit his putt a little too hard. They were in disbelief, as was the rest of the crowd, when the ball smacked into the back of the cup, went airborne for about a foot, then fell back in. Eddie retrieved his partner's ball and they headed to eighteen, one up.

"Hey, Street," said Ronnie, as he got out of the cart on eighteen and took his driver out of the bag. "My eyesight's starting to come back. I saw that last putt as it hit the back of the cup. All we need is a par here. The pressure is on those two. The pin is tucked back left, so it will take some doing to get a three. We're going to need a Brink's truck to cart all of our cash home."

"Let's not get too excited," said Eddie. "You know the old saying: it's never over…"

"You know," interrupted Ronnie, "I never liked that saying. The guys in my old neighborhood knew that it wasn't really over until your momma called you home. That's when it was definitely over. If we didn't come in immediately, we got the switch. Of course, most of the moms in our neighborhood were pretty big, and some of them probably could sing."

"Let's stay focused here," reminded Eddie. "Do I need to line you up or can you see well enough?"

"I've got it," said Ronnie as he walked onto the tee. He stepped up and quickly hit his drive down the right side, short of the fairway bunker. It wasn't great, but it was playable if Eddie totally messed up his drive. Eddie stepped up and hit his drive like a man that was used to playing for high stakes. Poole showed what he was made of when he crushed one twenty-five yards past Eddie's. Eddie marked his ball with a tee and Ronnie placed his within six inches of the mark. The strategy was to play to the right side of the green and go for the two-putt. Ronnie pushed his 5-iron into the right greenside bunker. Eddie had to do better. If they ended up playing Ronnie's ball, it would be a long trap shot, and the odds weren't good even though they would get two chances at it.

Eddie threw down his cigar and looked the shot over. The yardage to the middle of the green was 181. His normal shot was a draw, so this scenario was to his liking. He intended on starting his ball just inside the right trap, and with his draw it would be working its way toward the middle of the green. He gripped his iron and took a long deep breath. It was time to hit the money shot. His partner did his bit on the last hole, and now it was time for him to step up and finish it. He reminded himself to calm down and not grip the club too hard. Squeezing the club would keep the hands from doing their job. He was just about ready to take the club back when there was a commotion directly across from where he was standing. A lady in a straw hat apparently had a confrontation with the guy next to her.

"Start over," said Ronnie in a reassuring tone. "Put a smoothie on it and let's go collect our loot."

Eddie started his routine over. He took the club back and made a rhythmic swing down and through the ball. He knew at impact that he had hit it too far—two yards too far. A non-golfer would have trouble understanding how really good players know how far on a given day, and under certain circumstances, that they can hit each club. Eddie was watching Lee Trevino play a pro-am thirty years ago when Lee hit a shot at a fairway bunker. His playing companions said they thought he had hit it in the bunker. Lee asked how far the bunker was and they told him. He responded that he couldn't hit it that far under the current conditions with the club he had just used. Sure enough, when they got to Lee's ball, he was two strides short of the bunker.

Maun hit his 7-iron in the front left bunker. That left it all up to Poole. He looked over at his opponents and winked. They both tipped their caps to him. They tipped them again when his 8-iron took off right at the pin. When they got to the green they saw that Poole's iron had not held the green. It was about four feet off the back and thirty feet from the hole.

Back down the fairway, at the scene of the team's second shot, a man was still holding his wrist and staring at the lady in the straw hat. When Eddie was about to hit, the man had reached into his pants pocket and had pulled out a miniature air horn. The lady, who was standing behind him, grabbed his wrist and squeezed him so hard that he dropped the noisemaker. He couldn't believe that a woman had that kind of strength. He was still glaring at her when the players moved up to watch Maun and Poole play their second.

"Whatever you pull out next," warned the woman, as he reached into his other pocket, "you better be prepared to use it or lose the hand that's holding it it."

He looked at her muscular arms and decided that she meant what she had said. The lady looked like she had spent some serious time in the weight room. She surprised him a second time when she reached out and took his hand in hers. They strolled up to the green together, his hand in her vise-like grip. They got there just in time to see the contestants' third shots.

After some discussion as to who was away, the marshal stepped it off and determined that Maun and Poole would play first. They both pulled out what looked like 8-irons. A common mistake made by high-handicappers is to use a club with a lot of loft when they are just off the green. The only time to use a lofted club would be if there is a problem stopping the ball or if the grass was too high. A club with less loft has three things going for it: One, less loft means more accuracy. The most accurate club in the bag, the putter, has almost no loft at all. Two, it makes the shot easier by bringing the target back to you. You simply don't have to carry the ball as far, because a less lofted club will roll farther once it's on the ground. Three, it is more forgiving. If you hit the less lofted club a little thin or a little fat, the results will be much more favorable than a miss-hit with a pitching or a sand wedge. Poole and Maun were well aware of this, and had pulled out clubs that would give them the best chance of holing the shot. They motioned for the forecaddie to pull the flag.

Maun's shot looked good off the clubface. It was tracking right up until it was three feet from the hole, then it broke subtly to the right and skirted past. There was a huge groan from the crowd. Hundreds of thousands of dollars were about to change hands here, and unless Poole could hole out his chip, it would not be going into the hands of those that backed the two favorites. The tall Texan stepped up quickly to his ball. There was no reason to look at the line again, as he had just seen his partner's ball veer to the right at the cup. His chip was a couple of inches to the left of Maun's line. Rolling toward the hole, the line looked perfect. The only problem was the speed, and the pace of the ball was going to put a big wad of cash in the Michigan team's pocket. The ball hit squarely at the back of the cup, popped up a few inches, and came to rest two feet beyond the hole. The only difference between Poole's chip and Ronnie's putt back on seventeen was the fact that Poole's chip was going downhill to a cup where the back side was a tad lower than the front. In Ronnie's case, on seventeen, the backside was a little higher than the front.

It has been said many times that golf is a game of inches. It's a safe bet that most golfers don't know that the inches that make the difference are not on the green or anywhere else on the course itself. The inches are on the clubface. One inch one way or another is the real difference in a quality shot versus a mediocre or a disastrous shot. But, there are always exceptions, and this was one of those times where a few inches on the ground made a huge difference. If Poole's shot had landed three or four inches sooner than it did, the additional friction from the grass and gravity's effect, might have been enough to decrease the speed just enough to keep the ball from hopping out of the hole. Poole looked over at his opponents and motioned for them to finish the job.

The lady in the straw hat squeezed her man's hand hard as Ronnie rolled his putt up. It stopped a couple feet short and to the right of the hole. Both players were surprised that the ball did not break more toward the hole. As he had done several times in the past three days, Eddie told Ronnie to leave his ball there and not mark it. He wanted to use it as a guide. If he could roll his about a foot inside of Ronnie's ball at about the same pace, it should stop in the vicinity of the cup. Close was all he was looking for. Only a fool would try to make this putt from this distance when a two-putt was all that was needed to collect first place cash. If you went for it and were a little too aggressive, the ball could roll past the cup and start to trickle down the hill. Coming back up the hill would be nice, but all that pressure can play tricks on even an experienced player's putting stroke. One of the spectators explained to his wife that if Eddie's putt hit Ronnie's ball, it would be a penalty. But, since they were playing a scramble, they obviously would choose not to use Eddie's shot. They would simply put Ronnie's ball back where it was and putt that one. And, if Eddie's putt hit Ronnie's ball it probably wouldn't have ended up any closer anyway, so nothing would be lost. Oblivious to everything except his breathing and his hands, the Detroit hustler rolled his ball inside of his partner's where it eventually stopped six inches short of the hole.

When Poole heard his partner say, "Pick it up," his eyes went wide.

Ronnie chuckled and responded, "Yeah, right." He stepped up and holed the winning shot.

The same guy that explained why Eddie told Ronnie not to mark his ball clarified this new situation to his wife. "That was pretty low. One, there are more than two teams playing so one team can't give a putt to another unless all the contestants in their age division agree on it. And the other guys they're playing against aren't even here. Two, in stroke play, unless you agree at the outset of the competition, you don't give putts. This is a formal match for big money. Giving putts wouldn't make any sense. Everyone has to have a score. If 'The Grip' and 'The Street' would have picked up their ball and walked off the green without holing out, they would have been disqualified, even though one of their opponents said it was okay to do so. But, as you can see, they're too smart for that. That's why we had two hundred bucks riding on them. At five-to-one, we just made a thousand bucks.

"Those are silly names," said his wife. "Why would two grown men have nicknames like that?"

"Sweetheart, if you have to ask, you wouldn't understand," replied her husband. "C'mon, I want to go over and shake their hands."

The lady in the straw hat let go of the goombah's hand as soon as Eddie hit his putt. She wasn't sure if he had anything else in mind to disrupt the competition, so she stayed close. It was a good move, because he was thinking about screaming at Ronnie when he putted, then bolting for the parking lot. That was before some Amazonian woman grabbed hold of him. Now he was worried he would have to give back the two hundred dollars that he had received for his non-existent services. He didn't even think about the beating he was going to get for failing to accomplish such a simple task.

CHAPTER NINE

Mother Hubbard's

Mother Hubbard's? Yeah, I know where it is. It's right down the street from the House of Blues. I saw Robin Trower play there once. Man, the way he held that guitar upright. It was like he was strokin' it instead of playin' it. It was a thing of beauty, like Ronnie Green feathering a wedge into a tight pin placement. Trower and Green. You've got to respect guys that can handle their equipment. I think they're both dead now. That or they're livin' down in Florida somewhere.

—Chad "The Stick" Larose, owner Rosey's Pool Emporium

"Pretty wild stuff," said Herman, chuckling.

Herman, Ronnie and Eddie sat at a little neighborhood bar a short distance from Mother Hubbard's, a sports bar on Hubbard and Dearborn. Their winnings could be picked up at Mother Hubbard's any time after eight o'clock. The private investigator entertained them with incidents from the last three days.

The guy with the laser was dumped in the trees way out on course number two. "Conscious," said Herman, "but his forehead looked like an alligator's after he kissed that tree."

Herman also told them about Tina's incident with the air horn. Tina and Buck were the other two members of the security team. Tina was a veteran, a part time stuntwoman, a competitive body builder, and was as fearless as they come. Buck was an ex-Ranger like Herman. He lived in St. Louis, but was in the Chicago area to assist Herman on another case that he was working on. The Private Eye said his two accomplices were experienced and up to the task.

Before they left the little bar, Herman went over the plan to collect their winnings and exit the establishment without donating to any desperate causes. His apprehension made the two golfers a little nervous. Up until now, they didn't think there would be a problem getting their hands on, and keeping, something they had rightly won.

"One more time," instructed Herman. "You watch for me to pull up in my car. Then you exit the bar quickly and get in. We'll make a quick right and we'll be heading south toward the House of Blues. Buck will be in the area and so will Tina. It'll be better if you don't know what they look like. We will all meet at my place later and settle our finances. Got it? I pull up, and you two walk quickly to the car."

"No worries," said Ronnie. "You're being pretty dramatic here. I'm not questioning your methods, but why do you think there's a chance of us getting robbed? There will be a lot of people there, and a bunch of them will be carrying out large sums of money. I heard one guy put five thousand on us to win. At five-to-one that's twenty-five G's, plus his original five, so he'll be pocketing thirty grand himself."

"And he'll have a plan to get it out of there safely, believe me," said Herman. "Okay, I didn't want to mention this, but you are not Chicago's two favorite sons right now. You're the wild card that they hadn't planned on. The reason your odds were so good was that there was a boatload of cash bet on Poole and Maun. I'm talkin' close to half a million. There was about seventy thou on you two, and at five-to-one, that's a 350 thousand dollar payoff. Through the grapevine I heard that Poole and Maun have left town already. My sources tell me it's not all about the money. While you guys were on the back nine today, the tournament coordinators ran checks on you again. There were a lot of phone calls made, but you were cleared of never playing in any tour event. Obviously, these guys are sore losers. They're the type that usually comes out ahead on their business deals, legal or otherwise. It doesn't make sense for them to get all bent out of shape, 'cause they can afford it. I guess they thought they had a lock on this thing and it backfired on them. I say, fuck 'em if their little plan didn't work. They can afford it."

"How's this thing going to work tonight?" asked Eddie.

"There will be a main table set up at the large area in the back of the place, and some guys will talk about all the money raised for city trees," explained Herman. "Then the winners will be announced, and you guys will get a little bag with forty thousand each in it—your original ten and the thirty from the six guys you beat. It will be too big to put in your pocket, so stuff it under your shirt in your waistband and tuck your shirt back in. There will be private security and city cops all over the place, so the only danger is getting the money outside and into the car. Oh yeah, don't take it into the restroom with you. At another table, the pari-mutuel pay-offs will take place. Those winnings can be collected any time after the official awards are given out. We'll hang for a little while. A lot of people will want to buy you drinks and congratulate you. I don't think I need to tell you about not accepting a drink from anyone. One of the bartenders is an informant of mine, and I know I can trust him. Short guy with black-rimmed glasses. He will mix your drinks. Once we're back safely to my place, we'll chill there for a while, then you need to head back to Michigan, tonight. And, by the way, you are already in for next year if you're interested. This is going to be a yearly thing, and the winners will be automatically invited back."

"What did I tell you, Street?" asked Ronnie. "Is this a happening city or what? This kind of stuff doesn't happen in Detroit, does it?"

"There's not much happening in Detroit at all anymore," said Eddie. "But, if this went down in Detroit, I'm sure it would be similar to what happened here. Everyone likes to win, and most aren't prepared when they lose. Money can do strange things to people. I remember a saying by

Mark Twain, 'Unexpected money is a delight. The same sum is a bitterness when you expected more.' Some people do not handle winning or losing money very well."

"You see why I like this guy, Herm?" asked Ronnie. "He's such a deep thinker."

"And all this time I thought it was because of his golf game," laughed Herman, as he stood up.

"Yeah, that too," admitted Ronnie.

"Gentlemen," said Herman, as they stepped out on to the sidewalk. "Let's go collect our winnings." The two golfers forgot that Herman and Suzanne were both twenty-five hundred richer as a result of their proficiency with their sticks and their minds.

All in all, it was a good five days in the Windy City.

* * *

"Check the guy out directly ahead of us," said Ronnie.

The three of them—Ronnie, Eddie, Herman – were standing in front of Mother Hubbard's Sports Bar and taking in the atmosphere. A man dressed in ragged clothes approached them for spare change. Eddie and Ronnie both handed him a twenty. A big Chicago cop appeared out of nowhere and told the man to beat it or he would run him in.

"Damn, that guy smelled," exclaimed Ronnie as he watched the guy slink away. "It was worth twenty to just have him leave. There but for the grace of a few made putts goes us in ten years, partner."

"Not hardly," chuckled Eddie.

"That guy wasn't legit," said Herman. "The smell and the clothes were part of an act and you two fell for it. Ronnie, you've been away from the city for too long."

The sports bar was packed to the rafters. The contestants had a reserved table and they were all there, except for Poole and Maun. The bettors wanted to talk to the players whether they won or not. Free golf advice was flowing as much as the alcohol was. Eddie and Ronnie met the under fifty winners and were told that they shot the same fifty-four hole score. They invited the Michigan entry to play in the younger division next year. Eddie told them if there was more money in it they would consider it.

The M. C. went through his spiel about raising money for the city tree program, then he turned it over to the money guys. The winners were announced, and they went to the head table and collected their bags, which each contained four hundred one hundred dollar bills. 'The Grip' and 'The Street' sat and talked to well-wishers and guys looking for free swing advice for about another hour. When the area where the pari-mutuel bets were being paid off didn't look too busy, Eddie and Ronnie went over and collected another fifteen thousand. Those envelopes were a little smaller than the bags, so they folded them and shoved the cash into their pockets. Herman collected his winnings as well as Suzanne's.

It was time to vacate the premises.

"Okay, just like we planned," said Herman in a calm voice. "When I pull up in the car, you come directly out. Be leery of anyone that wants you to stop and talk, or take a picture, or anything else."

"Got it," said Eddie and Ronnie at the same time. This was the exciting part. Herman's plan was a good one and they trusted him. They did question their head of security about requesting a cop to see them to the car. Herman explained that it would be too easy for thieves to place a fake cop by the door offering to escort people out. The best plan was a simple one. Ten or twelve steps and they were safely in his vehicle.

Herman went out the door, turned left, and headed down Hubbard Street to retrieve his vehicle. The street was filled with the normal nighttime traffic in the heart of the third largest city in the country. Five minutes later a black Chevy Impala honked its horn. It was three cars away from the front door, but traffic was not moving, so they figured Herman had honked to get their attention. The timing looked good. As soon as the light changed, they would be on their way. The guys cut an impressive sight as they headed toward the Impala. The bulges in their shirts gave them the look of experienced beer drinkers. They were almost there when the smelly panhandler that they met earlier appeared in front of them. He held an Astra nine millimeter close to his body to shield it from anyone looking their way.

"Hand over the bags in your bellies and the envelopes in your pockets," ordered the panhandler. "Do it quickly and don't make a scene. That wouldn't be smart—for you or for me."

"I can't believe this," moaned Ronnie, as he pulled the bag out from underneath his shirt and gave it to the homeless-looking guy. "We give you twenty a piece and now you're robbing us?"

"You probably think I'm ungrateful, huh?" said the thief, as he stuffed their money bags into his waist band. The envelopes were folded and crammed into the lower pockets of his greasy cargo pants. "It's like they say, 'no good deed goes unpunished'. Let's do business again sometime."

With that, the street person pocketed the pistol and took off like a shot up Dearborn Street. He was quite adept at dodging the pedestrians coming his way. Out of nowhere another guy appeared and proceeded to chase the robber. The second guy was fast, but he was no match for the thief. He showed a combination of agility and speed that the hustlers had never seen before. He juked right and left and never even touched the people he was running through.

"Damn, that guy runs like a scared rabbit," observed Eddie. They continued to watch as the first guy made it to the end of the block and then jumped on the back of a waiting motorcycle. The bike disappeared around the corner leaving the guy in pursuit with nothing to show for his valiant effort to catch him.

"It looks like Buck was a day late and we're about fifty-five thousand short," said Ronnie. "Where the hell is Herman?" The car they assumed was his took off up the street when the light changed and the traffic started moving.

"I don't know," said Eddie. "Obviously, something has gone terribly wrong. I hope your buddy is all right."

Before Ronnie could respond to Eddie's last statement, two street toughs walked up to them and demanded their money. The golfers looked at each other and smiled. "Sorry, guys," said Eddie in a calm voice. "Our cash just went sprinting up the street. Some homeless looking guy took it from us. Go ahead and search us. We got nothing."

The two "would be robbers" told the tournament winners to put their arms out so they could be searched. Finding nothing, one of the guys called someone on his cell phone. The voice at the other end must have told his boys to let the golfers go. They voiced insincere apologies to Eddie and Ronnie and told them to have a nice evening.

"This town is nuts, Grip," wailed Eddie, waving his arms. "As soon as we hit the street with our cash, guys are lined up to take it from us. What's next, a gang of little old ladies wandering the neighborhood looking for easy marks. We should have at least taken a few hundred out of our bags and stuffed them in our socks. At least we'd have something to show for the last few days."

"Hey, here comes Herman now," observed Ronnie, as a black Impala rolled up and stopped next to them. The guys got in and stared at the Private Detective. Herman had a determined look on his face. "Are you okay?" asked Ronnie.

"Yeah," said an embarrassed Herman, as the traffic started to move. "How about you two? You still got your cash?"

"Nope," answered Ronnie. "That stink machine took it from us. What an asshole! We throw him forty bucks as we're walking in, then he takes all our winnings as soon as we walk out of the building. We saw a car that looked like yours, and when the driver honked we started to walk towards it. It was hard to tell under these streetlights. He pulled a gun on us when we were half way to the curb. What happened to you?"

"When I got to the car," explained Herman, as he steered through the nighttime traffic, "two guys were waiting in the shadows. They pulled handguns and told me to stay put. It was obvious that they had a plan of their own. They didn't even search me for the five grand I was carrying. I don't know if the car that honked at you was part of the plan or not. If it wasn't, it sure was a convenient coincidence. Anyway, they kept looking at their watches and then just told me I could go. Apparently they had everything planned out."

"That's not all of it," said Eddie. "After Mr. Stink took our dough, two other guys approached us with the same thing in mind. It's getting so you can't tell the thieves without a scorecard around here. They checked us out after we told them they were too late. The speedster that ran by them had the goods. Then, after talking to some guy on the phone, they said we could go—just like that. People were walking by and staring, but no one said anything. Damn, that thief could run. Whoever hired him chose the right man for the job, 'cause Buck was right behind him and would have caught any normal guy."

Herman just drove through the city and didn't say anything more for the next twenty minutes. He appeared to be lost in thought. The guys knew that he felt bad about what had just happened. Security was his area of expertise, and it looked like he and his team had dropped the ball. Herman was the kind of guy that didn't take failure lightly. Maybe he was already hatching a plan to get their money back. Eddie and Ronnie both decided to pay Herman whatever his fee was anyway. There are some things that you just can't plan for. The black Impala turned onto Herman's street. He drove slowly, looking around for anything out of the ordinary. Just because they didn't have their winnings, didn't mean that somebody else didn't have a plan to hit them as they returned home. Chicago can be a crazy city—especially when large sums of money are involved. Herman pulled into his drive and shut the engine off.

"Herm," said Ronnie in a quiet non-accusing way. "What happened to the rest of your team? Did somebody else get a hold of Buck and delay him? He was fast, man, but he should have eaten another bowl of Cheerios this morning, because the guy he was chasing was incredible. Oh yeah, then Mr. Stink-bomb jumps on the back of a motorcycle and poof, he's gone. What was Tina's situation? We didn't see any buff women there, did we Street?"

"Buck was a running back for Georgia Tech before he joined the Rangers," said Herman, as they sat in the driveway. "He is one of the fastest guys I've ever seen. That's one of the reasons I picked him for this job. Tina was stationed outside too. And, you guys are confused on one small detail. Buck wasn't chasing anybody. He was the guy in the lead."

The two hustlers were silent for a few counts as they took in this new information. Then they looked at each other and smiled. Herman had Buck take the money from them! They looked at Herman, waiting for an explanation.

"Let's go inside and get us a drink," grinned the head of security. "You guys are going to love this plan."

"Sumbitch," said Ronnie slapping the big guy on the back, as they walked toward the house. "Didn't I tell you, Street—my guy is better than yours."

"That you did, Grip. That you did."

* * *

"So, let me get this straight," said Ronnie, as they sat in Herman's living room sipping expensive whiskey. "Buck's orders were to take the money from us if he didn't see you parked right across from the door when we came out?"

"Yup," answered Herman. "If we all weren't in the right position, he was to take the cash and bolt. I figured it was our best chance to get it out of there. Tina was waiting at the end of the block on the bike. I didn't tell you two the plan, because I didn't want you to get too cocky thinking everything was covered."

"He pulled a gun on us," protested Ronnie.

"It wasn't loaded," said Herman, as they heard a motorcycle come up the drive. "He had the clip in his pocket. Hey, if this happens again next year, I think we should hire two real cops to accompany us out of the area. I actually did think of that, but the two guys I had in mind were both scheduled to work. If we give them enough advance notice next year they should be able to switch shifts or something. They'll do it for five hundred each. Small price to pay to not have to go through what we had to tonight."

Herman went over to the front door and let in the rest of his team. Herman introduced Tina and Buck. Buck was all cleaned up and was wearing jeans and a golf shirt, while Tina had on shorts and a sleeveless blouse. The old guys couldn't believe the arms on Tina. In their day, women just didn't look like that. Buck dropped their winnings on the table and grinned. Then he quoted Colonel Hannibal Smith from the 'A' Team, "I love it when a plan comes together."

The security team rehashed the last three days.

A lot happened behind the scenes that the golfers never even saw.

Tina said she was hanging around the parking lot at Coghill and overheard two guys talking about disrupting play if the guys they bet on were behind. They were laughing about doing whatever it took to help the team out. She walked up to them and calmly pointed out Herman, who was standing on the other side of the lot. The guys' faces took on a different expression when she described what Herman would do to them if they didn't leave immediately. They got back in their car and left the premises. Then she told them about the guy with the air horn on the eighteenth at Medinah.

Since Ronnie's sight was almost totally recovered, they laughed when Herman told them what the guy with the bark imprint on his forehead said. He thought Herman was going to kill him, so he started crying about his family and what it would be like if his kids had to go through life without a dad. Herman said he pulled the guy out of the trailer, kicked him in the rear, and told him to run for his life. He stood and watched as the guy scampered through the trees on the number two course whimpering like a whipped puppy.

"Let's settle up, guys," announced Herman. "You owe these two a grand each and two hundred for expenses. The motorcycle was borrowed from a friend of mine, so that didn't cost us anything."

Eddie and Ronnie looked at each other and shook their heads. "I don't think so, Herm," said 'The Grip'. The security team wasn't sure what was going on, so they didn't respond. It would be best to wait until the golfers explained themselves. "What do you think, Street?" asked Ronnie.

Eddie rubbed his chin for dramatic effect, and he appeared to be deep in thought. "How about fifteen hundred and two hundred more for expenses?" asked Eddie. "That seems like a fairer price. Any objections, guys?"

Tina and Buck were more than happy to accept the generous offer. They pocketed their earnings and shook hands all around. Ronnie gave Tina a big hug in addition to the handshake. After the security team left, Eddie and Herman gave Ronnie an inquisitive look.

"What? You two were thinking the same thing I was. But I was the only guy smart enough to act on his thoughts. I wanted to know what she felt like."

"How was it?" laughed Eddie.

"She is one solid broad," answered Ronnie. "And don't think she won't tell her friends that she hugged an old guy that had just won about fifty grand in a golf tournament."

"Yeah," added Herman. "I'm surprised she didn't ask you for an autograph. Dude, she makes several hundred thousand a year doing movie stunts. She just took this job for the thrill of it. We've worked together before. You won't believe how many times a situation comes up where I need a strong woman. Tina and I worked with the cops a few years back looking to catch a rapist."

"What happened?" asked Ronnie.

"She picked up a 180 pound man and slammed him to the concrete. I don't know what she would have done if the cops hadn't rushed in. She's quite the combination of beauty and strength."

"Nice call, Herm," said Ronnie. "Now what do we owe the head of security?"

"Nothing," said the big guy, as he dug out his and Suzanne's winnings and waved it at them. "I won twenty-five hundred on you two. That's enough. Oh yeah, Eddie. Here's your girl's share."

* * *

It was midnight.

The Monte Carlo was heading east on I-94, speeding along through the night. The Monte's engine purr was almost hypnotic.

Eddie was listening quietly to an oldies station while Ronnie dozed. *We Gotta Get Outta This Place*, by the Animals, was coming through the speakers.

Eddie grinned.

play on the big circuit. She figured I was her ticket to fame and fortune. When our second daughter turned two, she told me that she was leaving and taking the girls out of state unless I could come up with fifty grand. I wasn't making very much back then, working in a pro shop at a public course and doing a little hustling on the side—a couple of hundred here, a grand there. Anyway, she gave me a month to come up with the dough, so I packed my bags and…."

It was night and the temperature hadn't dropped much after the sun went down—not like it did back home in Michigan. Eddie steered the car through west Texas. It was midnight it was still around 85 degrees. He had the window down, because the air wasn't working, and he didn't want to spring for the repairs—at least not now.

He was on a tight budget and needed every cent. His Texas winnings were around nineteen grand, which was a good start.

After quitting his job at the public course in Detroit, he laid out a plan to earn the fifty grand that was needed to keep his two daughters. He took his wife's threat seriously. He had heard horror stories about what some sleazy lawyers would do to a guy, just for the chance of getting into the woman's pants that he was representing. And knowing his wife the way he did now, it wouldn't surprise him a bit for that little favor to be on the table.

An acquaintance in Dallas got him into a high-stakes match with a couple of stock brokers. He walked away from that one with eight thousand in his pocket. It was a nice start. The next night he lost half of it in a poker game with the wrong kind of people. He was pretty sure he was being cheated, but couldn't prove it.

When things got tense words were exchanged, and one of the guys pulled a pistol out and started waving it around. The barrel ended up in Eddie's mouth. He was proud of one thing after it was all said and done. He didn't piss his pants. When the gun was in his mouth, he could see the lunatic at the other end smiling. Eddie just stared at him, trying to look non-threatening. Somebody made a comment about how everybody needed to just relax. The amount of money involved wasn't enough to kill somebody and maybe end up on death row. After all, they were in Texas and the Lonestar State had a certain reputation with executions. The guy finally came to his senses and withdrew the pistol. As they walked out of the place, one of the guys that Eddie knew told him that his actions showed good "street sense".

For the next couple of days he was referred to as Eddie 'The Street' Davis. The name followed him after he left town.

Fort Worth proved to be a more lucrative environment. He teamed up with a club pro and they took a couple of real estate developers for fifteen grand. In the beginning, it was just straight up golf for a few hundred. It got expensive after a few presses and some serious haggling. After eighteen, Eddie and the club pro were five grand up. Their opponents said they wanted a chance to get their money back. Looking back, the Detroit hustler considered this to be a defining moment in his golf career. He needed to keep the game from getting too complicated. He didn't want to lose any of his morning winnings because their opponents were better with a pencil. So he talked his partner and their opponents into playing a scramble for the afternoon round—for a cool ten grand. The real estate guys wanted an edge, so Eddie agreed to play without woods in his bag. Before they teed off, Eddie went out to his car and replaced his three woods with a one-iron, and two more wedges. 'The Street' and the club pro put together a sweet round shooting eight under. Eddie dazzled them on the twelfth hole, a par five, by hitting a nice little cut with his one-iron onto a small green. He rolled the putt in for an eagle. From then on it was no contest.

With a little under twenty thousand in winnings, Eddie headed for southern California.

It was a good start, but he needed at least thirty thousand more.

Palm Springs and Los Angeles proved to be more than he had ever dreamed of. His Dallas buddy had called ahead and had given a verbal letter of introduction to a Palm Springs pro that loved to take low-handicapped, rich tourists for anything and everything.

'The Street' teamed up with the pro and some other local talent and proceeded to skin anybody and everybody that was willing to play for more than a few dollars. After two weeks of perfect weather and great golf, the money spigot started to dry up. Word got out that a Detroit hustler was taking on all comers and rarely losing. Eddie's skills were not limited to just swinging a golf club. He had to come up with some well-crafted scenarios to keep the money flowing. One of his more creative ventures was to offer to play a short to medium par four in reverse. In a scramble format, he and his partner would hit their wedges off the tee and then their drivers off the deck for their second shots. They would do this on one hole each nine. Their opponents liked this little edge, thinking that they would pick up a stroke—maybe with a par. Eddie spent two weeks in California and only once did he and his partner fail to make at least a par on holes that they reversed their club order. Twice they made birdies, which infuriated their opponents.

Always looking for an edge, Eddie jumped on a chance to take a grand off of a local low-handicapper. The guy was a hard swinger that would occasionally crank a tee shot out to about the 280 range. This was before oversized titanium drivers showed up, so anything over two sixty was considered reasonably long. By tour standards, it wasn't outrageous, but the guy was sixty-years old. He would often brag about his long drives on a given hole in the bar after a round. Usually followed up by, "How many sixty-year-old guys do you know that can hit a driver and a wedge into sixteen?"

Eddie listened to his boasting one evening, then asked the pro, who he had played with that day, what the guy's story was. The pro told him that the guy was long for his age, but erratic. This gave Eddie an idea. The Detroit hustler was up exactly $79,000, more than enough to make sure his girls would grow up with him and not their mother. After gleaning as much information as he could from the club pro, he walked over to the braggart's table and offered him a deal.

"Mr. James," offered Eddie. "I hear you're a big hitter that likes to play for a little now and then." The guys at the table, sensing a dramatic moment, quieted down. "Well, I've got a grand that says I can out-drive you with my 3-iron." Greg James wasn't sure what was going on, so he just sat there speechless. Eddie laid out the bet for him. "We'll hit tee shots on the seven driving holes on the front nine. You hit driver or whatever, and I'll hit my 3-iron. We'll add up the total yards, and the guy with the most distance wins. It's that simple."

Greg found his voice and asked, "And you will hit a standard three-iron? Not some gimmick club that you had made up?"

"The pro can check it out for loft and length before we start," said Eddie, looking at the rest of the guys around the table. "It's just a standard 3-iron. Bring your friends. It should be fun."

Eddie was counting on two things when he proposed the bet. One, was the fact that Greg and his buddies had been drinking. That's why he waited for them to down their fourth round of drinks before approaching them. Two, was the fact that Greg wouldn't think too much about the strategy that was involved. As it was, he didn't even think about the fifth hole, a par four where a lay-up off the tee of about two fifteen was required.

"You're on, young man," said Greg, slapping the table for emphasis. The hustler's slight build gave him no reason to think Eddie could hit his 3-iron any further than 190 yards. He looked over Eddie's shoulder at the pro. "Let's do it tomorrow morning. Okay with you, Bill?"

"No problem, guys," said the pro with a smile. "We'll just start people off the back in the morning. You will have clear sailing."

No one at the table full of drinkers asked why they didn't just go off the back nine for the contest. The grounds crew would probably still be mowing greens, but they wouldn't be using the greens anyway, just the tees and the landing areas. Eddie was thankful when there was no objection to doing it on the front. The pro quizzed him the next morning on his strategy, and Eddie told him to watch and learn. Eddie asked the pro to go along and tabulate the drives, just to make sure the contest stayed fair. Bill said he would bring a tape measure. There were cinderblocks buried in the fairways with two hundred and three hundred painted on them, with an arrow pointing back to the tee. They would use them as a reference point to get the exact yardage.

* * *

The next morning there were about twenty carts around the first tee.

Word had got out that Greg James was going to take some easterner for a thousand bucks. After getting his 3-iron checked out in the pro shop that was packed with Greg's golf buddies, Eddie headed for the practice tee with about a dozen balls. Greg was already there pounding drives. Before they headed for the first tee, they each gave Bill a thousand bucks. The spectators clapped when the contestants walked out on the first tee. They flipped a coin and Eddie hit first. After that, they would alternate. He hooded his Ping 3-iron a little and sent a low hook down the right side of the fairway. It was not Eddie's standard 3-iron shot, as this one was hit strictly for distance. The hustler could hit his irons several different ways, and today there was no reason to hit a shot that was designed to hold the putting surface. Today, it was all about the yardage. Greg followed with a big swing that caught the ball square and propelled it out to about 270 yards. His buddies were high-fiving each other and yukking it up.

Six more shots to go, and Greg was all ready up sixty yards.

The controversy came on the fifth hole.

Greg had hit first and smoked his shot out into the pond. Normally, he would lay up on this hole about 200 yards or so, but he figured he would hit his tee shot out into the pond and would get full credit for the yards it traveled. As it was, Eddie also hit into the pond—about two feet into it. He raked his ball out with his club and showed it to the pro. The pro said he would give Eddie credit for the total distance of his shot. Then Eddie turned and asked Greg where his ball was. Greg pointed out into the pond. When Eddie asked for proof, Greg didn't know what to say. He deferred to his pro.

"I don't have money on either of you, so I'm totally impartial," said Bill. "Greg, the rules of golf say you cannot lose a ball in a hazard if there is a reasonable chance of your ball being in there. I think we all agree that you drove your ball from the tee into this pond. But, how far in we don't know. If someone was to dive in there, and come straight up with your ball, I would give you credit for the distance you hit it."

At this point, Eddie asked a question. "Greg, if someone comes up with it, how will we know it's yours? Did you put an identification mark on it like I did?" Eddie pulled another ball out of his pocket and showed Greg and Bill how he had marked them. It was obvious that Greg had never even thought of putting an ID mark on his ball. He did it regularly when playing in tournaments, but this was a driving contest. They both looked to the pro to settle the dispute.

"We found Eddie's ball about a yard into the pond, so he gets 216. Greg, we know yours crossed the hazard line at 215, but beyond that, we have no more information. You get 215 on this hole. That's my decision and it's a fair one."

Greg's buddies urged him not to argue. The pro's logic made sense and, what the hell, he was up by a bunch of yards anyway. Greg said he was okay with the ruling. They moved on to the next hole.

Number eight was the sixth driving hole on the front nine. It was a tight par five off the tee, then it opened up some the closer you got to the green. Greg knew he was up 141 yards, due to the fact that he had lost eleven yards on the last two holes—one on the number five lay-up hole, then ten on number six where he caught it thin and hit it into the thick rough across from the 200-yard marker. On the advice of his drinking buddies, he decided to play it conservative. A nice little 3-wood down the middle would make it impossible for Eddie to catch him on the last hole. Looking back, Greg should have played it a little more conservative—like with a 5-iron. As it was, he didn't quite square the clubface up, probably because he was trying to be too careful, and his fairway wood started off down the right side with a slight fade. The ball bounced once in the fairway, once in the rough, and then once off the cart path. The group let out a big gasp, as they knew there was only about fifteen feet of course on the other side of the path—after that, you were on somebody's lawn. When they got to the ball it was out of bounds by about five feet. Bill recorded a zero for Greg's drive on number eight. Eddie's 210-yard tee shot put him up by exactly 69 yards with one hole to go.

The drama intensified on the last tee when Eddie went over to Greg and offered him a draw. "Let's just say you hit it 269 and I hit it 200. We'll go in and have a drink and laugh about the whole thing. I was just trying to show you and your buddies that hitting the long ball isn't the only thing there is to playing this game."

Greg looked at his opponent's outstretched hand and froze. If he took the offer he would be the butt of who knows how many jokes around the club for years. Nope, he had to finish it. He told Eddie thanks, but no thanks. Eddie stepped up and smoked his 3-iron down the right side with a little draw. It was a carbon copy of his other tee shots. This one hit in the fairway and took a big hop toward the green. It came to rest 215 yards out from the tee. Greg didn't know the exact number, but he did know that he needed a career drive to keep from losing a grand. As most golfers do when they need to put a little extra something into their shot, Greg squeezed the club harder. The result was a weak fade that got only about ten feet off the ground. The contest followers couldn't believe it. Their man had lost to a skinny guy hitting a 3-iron off the tee. At least this little episode would instill a little humility in Greg. It did—for about a week. It appeared that the sixty year-old had a short memory. He was back to his normal obnoxious self by the next weekend.

The day after Eddie headed back east, the club pro went up to Greg and his cronies at their usual table. He informed them that Greg had been taken by a famous hustler, Eddie 'The Street' Davis from Detroit. The guys looked at each other as if to say, "I've never heard of the guy." From that moment on, Greg's buddies spoke of Eddie 'The Street' Davis in reverent terms. The strange thing about it was, all Eddie had to do to establish his reputation with these guys was hit seven good 3-irons. For a man of his abilities, that was something he could do right after he rolled out of bed in the morning—after only a couple of practice swings.

* * *

Eddie's plan had come together.

Most of his winnings came from the golf course, but he also came out ahead playing poker. He reaped an extra bonus on the trip by greatly enhancing his poker skills. Some of the guys he played against were among the best in the country. He had no idea that poker would become a huge spectator sport in the future. It would become so big that it would even end up on television. He bought a cashier's check for $50,000, made it out to himself, and sent it in a registered letter to a trusted friend back home.

He headed east across California and Arizona with $29,000 in the trunk and a light heart.

He was going home to put the marriage behind him, and his two daughters would now be the main focus of his life. He vowed to be the best dad he could be. The tour was always a thought in the back of his mind, but that would not be possible now. He would tell the judge at the custody hearing that he was a committed dad with a steady source of income. After all he had been through, he wasn't about to abandon his girls for a shot at money and fame. He wanted to see them every day. He wanted to ask them how their school day went and what boys they liked. Working in a pro shop during the summer and sporting goods stores in the winter was just fine with him. Hustling golf and playing a little poker on the side should give them enough money to live comfortably. In addition to that, on the advice of a guy he often played golf with, he had recently made a small investment that might turn out to be a home run. If he had been smart and had married a quality woman, he might have taken a shot at the big time, but as the saying goes, 'you make your bed and then you have to lie in it'.

At this point he had no regrets, just dreams for a quality family life with two wonderful little girls.

* * *

Eddie was somewhere in eastern Arizona, and he was trying to decide if it would be smart to pull over for a short nap. He caught himself nodding a couple of miles back, and was hoping to make it to the next town. The large amount of money he was carrying made him leery of just stopping on the side of the road for twenty minutes or so, but he was reaching the point where it would be dangerous to keep on driving. Even out here in the desert you never knew who would happen by at this time of night, looking for an unexpected windfall. The Detroit native was about to pull over when he saw what looked like a large delivery truck up ahead with its flashers on. When he got closer he saw it was an old step-van. It was the kind that some bakeries used to deliver bread with. He pulled in behind the truck to see if the driver needed any help.

Eddie's headlights revealed a scene that he would remember forever.

Four men were sitting in lawn chairs on the shoulder of the road by the passenger side of their van, while a fifth guy sat on the ground leaning against the van's front tire. A kerosene lantern illuminated the area. Three of them were playing guitars, one was beating on an upside down five-gallon bucket, and the last guy was blowing into a harmonica. The sight of these guys sitting out in the desert playing instruments gave Eddie an idea. The musicians didn't stop playing when they saw the stranger walk up. The drummer pointed to an empty chair with one of his sticks indicating that the new guy should take a seat. Eddie raised a finger to indicate he would be back in a minute. He went back to his car and grabbed a case of Coors beer. It was warm, but that mattered little out here in the middle of nowhere. The band nodded their approval when he came back with the beer and sat it down.

When the song was over the guys introduced themselves.

The band's story was certainly a captivating one. They had just played several jobs out west and were headed back home to Arkansas. The attendance at most of their performances was minimal due to poor advertising and just plain bad timing. Their manager disappeared right after their last job with most of the money they had earned on this trip. They were deciding their next course of action when their van's water pump gave out and here they sat. Two band members were all for throwing in the towel. The drummer was undecided, while the other two wanted to press on. The lead guitar player, Jimmy Smith, was obviously the glue that held the group together. He was excited about some new songs that he had just written and felt that if the guys would tough it out, they were on the edge of a big breakthrough. It only took two songs for Eddie to figure out that Jimmy was an extraordinary talent. The man could flat out play.

"Watch this, Eddie" said the drummer. "Jimmy, let's do Caledonia. Start out like Clapton, then do it the way Stevie Ray Vaughn would, then finish like Buddy Guy."

Jimmy's fingers moved smoothly over his instrument. Eddie could tell when he changed his style of play. It was definitely a performance that people would pay good money to hear. He couldn't figure out why this group of guys wasn't playing the big arenas. They had all the ingredients necessary to make the big time. Their bluesy rock sound had Eddie tapping his foot and grinning like a fool. After half a dozen songs they took a break and opened a round of beers.

"So what's your story, Eddie?" asked Jimmy, as he leaned back and looked up at the stars.

"I'm on my way home," said the hustler. "I've been on what you would call a fund raising tour." Eddie told them more than he normally would, but he was dead tired and he had a few beers in him. When he was done, he had pretty much told them his whole story—his earlier drinking problems, the pending divorce from his crazy wife, and his desperate attempt to keep his two little girls. Jimmy said he had one daughter himself, so he knew how Eddie felt. He sympathized with Eddie and applauded his successful efforts to gain custody.

Somewhere around four a.m. Eddie retired to the front seat of his car. A couple of the guys went into the van and the rest just slept in their chairs. The plan was for Eddie and Jimmy to drive thirty miles to the next town when the sun came up. They needed to find a garage with a tow truck and some breakfast.

Hopefully there was a junkyard in the area that had a water pump for their old van.

* * *

Eddie and the lead guitarist came upon a convenience store only five miles up the road.

They loaded up on coffee and doughnuts for themselves, figuring that they would get food and drink for the rest of the guys on the way back.

"What do you think of our sound?" asked Jimmy.

"You weren't even plugged in and you had me squirming in my chair," responded Eddie. "What is exactly holding you back from making the big time?"

"It's a combination of things—most that are fixable. But I guess the main thing is money. Some equipment needs to be replaced and we need to hire a competent manager that really knows the business. We told you about the last jerk that ran out on us. He was our third, by the way. In some ways music is like writing books or painting pictures. The artist needs to get their name and their work out there where the public can hear it or see it. There are so many people that think they have the ability to be successful, and a lot of them do have what it takes, but I guess it all boils down to that one big break. I feel bad for the really talented ones that never get a decent shot to make it big. Here's the strange thing—I'm not even sure if I want to make it to the big time. There are a lot of sacrifices that go with being famous and some things I'm not willing to give up—like my family.

"I'm with you there," said Eddie. "Family should always come first. Jimmy, since we're just street corner talking here—how much money are you talking? You know, to take a shot at the national music scene."

"I guess somewhere around fifteen thousand," said Jimmy. "That would get our equipment up to date and all the other miscellaneous stuff that a band needs to go out and do it right. Why, do you know some sugar daddy and maybe a manager that is willing to invest that much into a bunch of relative unknowns?"

"Maybe I do," said Eddie. "There's a guy at a club where I used to work that represented some Motown talent years ago. He's and older guy and semi-retired, but I think he's a real straight shooter, and he definitely knows the business, and he's still got some connections. Do you have a demo tape that I could give him?"

"We've got a tape, but you're forgetting about our money problem. Have you got another guy with some dough to invest?"

"Actually I do," said Eddie. "We'll talk about that when we get back to your van."

The garage in town said they could get a water pump and have the band rolling by early afternoon at the latest. The guys were excited when Eddie and Jimmy showed up with breakfast and the good news about a possible manager. When Eddie told them he would be the investor, he was surprised at their reaction.

"I don't know, Eddie," said Jimmy. "You hardly know us and didn't you just tell us you were desperate for cash. Hell, you had to make a gambler's run to save your kids. You might lose your whole investment if this thing goes sour."

Billy Burton, the rhythm guitar player, was the band member that did most of the song writing along with Jimmy. He grabbed his guitar started playing an upbeat blues riff and then just stopped. He looked over at Eddie and sang, "Now Eddie came from the Motor City, made a mistake and married for pretty."

"That's not bad," said Jimmy. "It could be sort of a ballad that tells the story of his run. I like how you totally stopped to do the vocals." Jimmy closed his eyes and hummed to himself for a while then sang the next two lines, "He was thinkin' with parts that weren't made for thinkin', had trouble copin' and started drinkin'."

"C'mon guys, that makes me sound like some sort of major loser," said Eddie.

"Don't worry," said Jimmy. "Billy and I will have you looking like a superstar before the song is over. How about we call it 'The Gambler's Run'? I like the sound of that."

The band watched as Eddie went over to his car and opened the trunk. He opened a shoebox with some ratty looking golf shoes in it. Below the shoes were several bundles of cash. He counted out fifteen thousand dollars and walked back to the guys.

"Here's what I'm thinking. I'll go back to Detroit and talk to the Motown manager. If he likes your demo tape and sees your potential, I will send you a check for fifteen G's. I'll write up some sort of agreement between us for you to look at before you accept the money. I'm showing the cash to you now to let you know how serious I am. It appears that y'all have been treated pretty rotten by some people in the past, and maybe it's time you got your break. All I ask is, if this thing goes, you need to keep things in perspective and don't let the big time change the things you value. What do you say?"

The band stood around and talked for about ten minutes, then they came over to Eddie with outstretched hands. "One more thing," said Billy. "We want to change our name to *Gambler's Folly*. If you're fool enough to back us, we'll give it our best shot. It looks like our van breakdown last night was the best thing that ever happened to the band."

* * *

"So that's the story?" asked Ronnie. "You were their stepping stone to the big time?"

"Yeah, it's a shame that Jimmy was killed in that plane crash. It took about eighteen months for those guys to hit the national scene. And, they did keep things in perspective. They turned down jobs that paid a lot of money to be with their families. Jimmy died almost exactly twenty-two years after that eventful night. We became pretty close. He made me the executor to his daughters' trust funds. His girls are great. Annie, the younger one, is sixteen now. She just moved to Texas with her mom. Margie, the oldest, goes to Northern Arkansas State."

"Do you ever speak to his girls?" asked Ronnie.

"That's the strange part," admitted Eddie. "I was so busy playing the part of single dad and putting food on the table that it left me with almost no time to get away. I worked a lot of hours in the summer, at shops and playing for money, and in the winter the girls were in school. We planned on our families getting together a couple of times when the band played in the Detroit area, but something always came up. I saw Margie once, but she was too little to remember me, and Annie wasn't even born yet. I'm going to watch Annie play ball this spring when I'm visiting my daughter in Texas. I'll introduce myself then. I haven't talked to his widow in a long time. His death was awfully hard on her and I think talking to me just stirs up old memories. Besides, I think she partly blames me for the band hitting it big and, consequently, for all the traveling they had to do. In her mind, if I hadn't loaned them the money and hooked them up with a decent manager, they would have stayed a local band, with real jobs, that just played on weekends."

"I like the song, man. I have heard it before, but I had no idea that it was about a real person."

"It blew things way out of proportion," said Eddie. "I thought they were just messin' around when they made up the first couple of lines that night. About a year later I heard it on the radio. Like I told them, you've got to keep things in perspective. As soon as you think you're something, someone will come along and show you how insignificant you really are. Except for Jimmy dying, I guess things worked out for all of us—the band and my family. They're still playing. You should see them. They're in their mid-forties and they've got these huge grins on their faces like there's nowhere else they'd rather be than on that stage, making music for their fans."

* * *

The guys were approaching Kalamazoo and the Sprinkle Road exit that would lead them to Ronnie's place in Richland. They were both lost in their own thoughts. The dash lights lit the car's interior enough for Eddie to see Ronnie's features.

"We sure took those guys down, didn't we, Grip?" asked Eddie.

"Yeah, it was one sweet little gig. Except for all the extra-curricular events that happened. Can you believe someone would stoop low enough to try to blind me? Bunch of losers."

"Those guys need to get real jobs," said Eddie. "If you can't handle the gambling thing, you need to stay on the sidelines. Anyway, we played as a team, and I wanted to let you know that I meant every word I said back on seventeen at Medinah."

"I appreciate that, man. And I will admit that it was inspiring. It would have been a great scene in a movie. Like I said before, we could be brothers."

"That being said," continued Eddie, "there's something that's been bothering me, and we need to talk about it."

Ronnie sensed a dramatic moment coming up, so he remained silent. Dramatic moments could be good or bad, and if the inflection in Eddie's voice indicated anything, this was going to be a bad one.

"It's my laugh, isn't it?" asked Ronnie. "Sorry, dude. I've always laughed like that. I think I'm too old to change it. I can work on my manners, but the laugh is here for the duration."

"It's not you, it's me," said Eddie.

"Not the 'it's not you, it's me' speech. That's what you tell a woman when you're going to break up with her. What is it? Just come out with it, man. We're adults here—at least most of the time. Hey, you're not IRS are you?"

"No," said Eddie. "I just want to tell you something that I've never told anyone before. It's been bothering me for a long time."

"So you killed somebody," said Ronnie, trying to be funny. "Hey, who hasn't?"

"Partner, I'm being serious here. A while back, I was playing poker with some members at a club that I was working at. Well, to make a long story short, one of the big winners got real drunk and ended up staggering away from the table, leaving his cash there. It was pretty chaotic and no one noticed. One of the guys volunteered to drive him home, leaving us shorthanded, so the game broke up. Since I worked there, I stayed and cleaned up the place. I pocketed the two grand he left behind. If anybody asked, I could have said I was safekeeping it for him, because he was so drunk. But when I showed up for work the next morning, I just kept my mouth shut. I guess I wanted to see if anyone noticed. The bottom line here is, I'm not the person you think I am. I've never stole anything since, but it still bothers me."

"So no one at the game ever mentioned his dough?" asked Ronnie.

"They had other things on their mind," said Eddie. "He died of a heart attack later that night. I even thought about giving it to his widow. They were a rich couple and both were pretty arrogant about it. You know, ordering everyone around like they were some kind of royalty. That might have been part of the reason I took it. I don't know. It still wasn't right."

"I can see that it bothers you," said Ronnie, trying to come up with a justifiable reason why his buddy shouldn't feel so bad. "Let me ask you this. Have you ever given any money to a good cause? Like a charity or just someone in need?"

"Yeah, all the time."

"Well, look at it this way. You took the rich guy's dough, and you gave it to some needy person. You were like the middle man, helping somebody that the rich people should have been helping in the first place."

"What kind of logic is that?" asked Eddie. "I'm no Robin Hood. I'm just a plain thief. You don't take something that doesn't belong to you, if you don't have permission. You learn that in the first grade."

"How long ago did this happen?" asked Ronnie.

"I was seventeen," answered Eddie.

Ronnie stared over at the driver for several seconds. He didn't want to make light of the situation, just in case Eddie was being serious, and not trying to feed him a line.

"And since then, you've been an honest guy?"

"Pretty much," said Eddie. "I told you about the St. Louis guys I took for a few grand a while back. Before we played the back nine for bigger stakes, I told them I was better than what they saw on the front. I didn't say exactly how much better. That was for them to figure out. But I did tell them. I'm not a con man. I'm a golfer that likes to play for more than just pocket change."

"Street, I stole a school bus when I was seventeen," admitted Ronnie. "This other guy and I took it for a joy ride, then we ditched it. When my old man found out, and I still don't know how he did, I caught holy hell. He put the fear in me, I'll tell you that. Look, you were a kid that did a stupid thing. You can't beat yourself up for that one incident. You're 'The Street', man. A legend to a lot of people."

"Yeah, that's what bothers me—all that legend talk. If they knew what I did it would be a different story."

"Do you think you helped the band out that night because you took that guy's dough back when you were seventeen?" asked Ronnie.

"Could be," said Eddie, as he pulled into Ronnie's driveway. "It does sound strange. I meet these guys, listen to them play, and then commit fifteen grand to them the next morning. It sounds like something only a fool would do. I'm glad Suzanne isn't a psychiatrist. She'd have a heyday trying to figure out what makes me tick. Get out, partner. I'm still wide awake so I'm heading home to my relaxation spa."

Ronnie jumped out and grabbed his gear. "By the way, I never killed anybody. I just said that to make you feel better."

"You're a strange dude, Grip," said Eddie extending his hand. "That's why I like hangin' around you. You're not a bad golfer either. See you in a couple of days."

* * *

The next morning, Eddie slept in.

After a quick workout and a late breakfast, he phoned his investment broker. He had two guys managing his money—one back in Detroit and one in Battle Creek. The B. C.

guy didn't know the whole story on his new client. He just knew that Eddie had money and he liked to play golf for a few dollars now and then. Maybe he could talk Eddie into a round and dinner at his club sometime. There were a couple of guys there that liked to play for more than a dollar or two.

"Hey, Murph," said Eddie over the phone. "I want to put twenty-five grand in my account, but it's cash. Is that a problem?"

"Not if it's clean and you can explain where you got it," said Pat Murphy. "It is clean isn't it? You didn't rob a bank or anything?"

"Naw, I quit that line of work years ago. A few guys decided to pay off some debts, that's all."

"Let's do this, to be on the safe side," said Murph. "Put the cash into your checking account. Tell the bank what you just told me—some guys paid off loans that you made to them. Be prepared if they ask you their names. Then send me a check for the $25,000. That way the IRS won't come snooping around your account. If you gave me $25,000 in cash there would be questions and paperwork to fill out. The rules are tighter today on account of all the drug money around. Hey, let's play golf sometime. You ever play the Battle Creek Country Club?"

"Nope, never have. I heard it's a beautiful layout."

"It's gorgeous, man," said Murph. "I'll give you a call soon and give you a chance to win back some of my commission fees."

"That sounds fine. I'll get the check out to you later today. You know what to do with it."

For a guy that's trying to lay low, there sure are a lot of guys that want to get me in a money game, thought Eddie.

It's like I've got a sign on my back or something.

CHAPTER ELEVEN

Cedar Creek

I'm sitting eight feet under the hole with a straight uphill putt. If I make it, I take two large from the famous Ronnie Green. Then the s.o.b. hits his shot. It lands short of mine, hops over my ball, and settles in about two feet from the hole. I was so shook, that I missed my putt. Green acted like it was no big deal and offered to buy me lunch. I hate that guy, but I also respect him. I wouldn't want to go against him on a regular basis.

—Mike Jensen, PGA member

"So here's the deal, Eddie," said Bert, the pro shop manager at Cedar Creek. The two of them were sitting in a cart by the first tee out of earshot.

"I've watched you practice a few times," Bert went on, "and Mitch, my range boy, says you're the best ball striker he's ever seen around here. Normally I would feel insulted, because I've been a scratch golfer for over twenty years. But I think I've got it figured out as to who you are. You're a Detroit hustler called 'The Street'. A friend of mine is a pro in the Detroit area, and when I described you to him he said my description fit you to a tee."

"What's your big mouth friend's name?" asked Eddie, lighting up a Macanudo.

"Herbie Winters," answered Bert.

"Yeah, I know him. Good player. Likes the ladies."

"Ha, that's him. He's had to jump from club to club for that very reason. Once he got caught in the club president's office with the guy's wife. He was lucky to get out of there alive. Anyway, there are two guys on their way here who like to play for money. They e-mailed me to set them up with a few money games. They took me and another guy for about five hundred last year, and I sure would like to get that back. It's not the money; it's the principle of the thing. These guys are real wise asses and a little bit scary. Sometimes they come off as if they've got a screw loose. I'm not sure if it's an act or if that's just their normal way of doing business."

Eddie took a sip of his ice tea and looked at the guy sitting next to him. He'd been around the game long enough to be leery of everyone. Maybe this guy was trying to set him up. He knew he wasn't the best golfer in the world. A top tour pro, slamming drives 300 plus yards played a different game than he did. He wasn't afraid of any senior players, but young guns with hi-tech clubs were guys he'd just as soon not tangle with or donate to.

"How old are these guys?" asked Eddie.

"Mid-thirties," said Bert. "If I had to guess, they're two or three handicappers. They both crush the ball off the tee, but their short games keep them from being scratch players. Since they hit it so far, they make a good scramble team. That's what happened to my partner and me last year. In the first round we played a best ball and were up a couple of hundred, so these shysters asked us for a chance to get their money back. I was two under on my ball and my partner was even. They both shot around 75. We figured, what the heck, so we played eighteen more, only this time we played a scramble. Like I said, we dropped five hundred each to them."

Eddie still wasn't sure about Bert's story. "It's pretty quiet right now," he said. "Let's play a few holes and you can tell me more about these clowns."

The manager went in and retrieved his clubs. Eddie drove the cart up to the range where his sticks were. He was intrigued with Bert's story. How do three-handicappers go around winning money from more accomplished golfers?

As they came up number nine, an easy dogleg par five, Eddie had the answer.

According to Bert, these two were the kind of guys that gave golf a bad name. They did everything but threaten their opponents. Their antics ran the gamut from sophomoric to borderline insane. Bert said he was putting for what appeared to be an easy birdie on number eight when one of his opponents went over to his cart and acted like he was hacking up a lung. Concentrating under those conditions was pretty much impossible. He left his putt a foot short. Afterward, the guy apologized profusely for his "asthma attack". It happened again a few holes later. That, and the constant screaming at each other was incredibly unnerving. Bert said that a couple of times he and his partner had to separate them to keep them from punching each other. He was pretty sure it was an act, but they were good enough to make him wonder. The bottom line was—these two were very strange and they used it to their advantage on the course. Off the course they were very congenial—joking around and buying drinks for everyone.

"I think you're my man," said Bert, as Eddie rolled in a short birdie putt on number nine. "You just shot three under and you've never seen the course before. What do you say? Do you want to make some cash and help me get even with these guys?"

"I tell you what," said Eddie. "You swing a nice stick, but I've got a partner that's used to playing for high stakes. How about my partner and I play these two for say, five grand? For a lot of guys that's enough dough to question themselves at the worst possible time—like at the top of their backswings. You need to craft the bet, though. We don't want to play guys twenty years younger than us straight up. Even though, from what you've told me, we can probably beat them head-to-head—especially if we're playing for more than cigar and whiskey money. If they agree to the format and the size of the bet, you can ask for $250 from each team. It'll be the juice for setting the whole thing up."

"So I need to come up with a scenario that draws them in, but doesn't look like they're being hustled? I think I can do that. How good is your partner, if you don't mind my asking?"

"I'm surprised you haven't seen him on the range," said Eddie. "We practice here a lot. He's shorter than me and looks like he wrestles alligators—broad shoulders with huge hands. There isn't a stroke difference between us."

"I've seen him," said Bert. "But every time I look his way, he's usually talking and not hitting. The few I have seen him hit tend to slice."

"That slice straightens out when the money is right, believe me." Eddie didn't mention that his partner had recently hit a career shot at Medinah for a boatload of cash. And, at the time, he could barely see the ball. "I'll call you in a few days, and you can let me know what you've come up with. Then we'll come over and play the whole layout to get our strategy down."

* * *

Ronnie liked the set-up. He trusted Eddie on Bert's story. Eddie told his partner that he went out and talked to the range boy right after his round with the shop manager. Mitch said Bert was a great guy and had always treated him and his dad well. That was enough for Eddie to think Bert was being straight with him.

Three days later, Eddie was on his way to the casino to play a little poker, so he stopped by the course to see what Bert had come up with.

It was eight in the evening, but still light out.

In early July it stayed light until about 9:30, because Battle Creek was on the far western edge of the Eastern Time Zone. It was the same time there as it was in New York City. If you played fast, you could tee off at 8:00 p.m. and still get nine holes in. The shop manager was standing behind the counter when Eddie walked in.

"What did you come up with, Bert?" asked Eddie.

"I think you're going to like this," said Bert, as he came around the counter and stood close so they could speak without being overheard. "I knew they wouldn't give you any strokes, so I used the format as the equalizer. The original deal was that you and your partner would play a scramble for the whole eighteen. Greer and Donaldson, those are the names that I know them by, would play a best ball on the front nine, and then a scramble on the back. I didn't think I could get that, but that was my opening offer. We finally settled, if you two agree, on them playing a best ball for the first six holes, then scrambling the last twelve. I told them you two were almost sixty and didn't hit it over 270, so they would have a big advantage on the holes where they could cut it loose. One other thing—they only want to play for three grand. That tells me the stakes were just a little too high for them, and they might be out of their comfort zone playing for five. And here's what clinched it; after nine holes, either side can pony up 250 bucks each and walk away. Meaning, if one team was too far ahead, they didn't have to risk losing three large."

"Nice," said Eddie. "So, if we were more than two holes ahead, they would probably give us the 250 and walk. But that's not in our best interest."

"That's exactly what I was thinking. So, best-case scenario is, you guys are up only one or two holes at the turn, but it has to be ugly. Make them think you are lucky to be ahead, and they will have no problem making it up on the back. I'm sure you've done a little acting yourself if the situation warrants it."

"Not as much as you might think," said Eddie, reaching into his pocket for his money clip. "I like to get the bet right and then just go out and beat people. I have used the 'if you don't think things are on the level, you can buy your way out of it' deal before. And you're right. Sometimes it is the clincher. A lot of guys don't mind being beaten, but they don't like to feel they've been cheated or lied to. Here's our 250 for making book. Did they have a problem with their side of it?"

"Surprisingly, no," said Bert. "I hope you are ready for their theatrics. You are going to see some strange things out there."

"Nothing would surprise us unless one of them strips down and plays a couple of holes naked. We'd be laughing so hard it would be difficult to take the club back. Don't worry, we'll handle them."

Four days later the two teams met on the tenth tee and listened as Bert went over the ground rules. Ronnie and Eddie were playing a scramble for the entire round, so they could pick up and place their ball all over the golf course. Bert had to explain the pick and place rule to Jim Greer and Greg Donaldson, because they seemed confused. It was simple: if the ball you decided to play had a bad lie, you would simply mark your ball and the other guy would play first. He would place his ball approximately six inches from the mark, no nearer the hole. After his partner hit, the guy who hit the original shot, would then place his ball within six inches and play away. You did not have to put the original ball back exactly where it was. It just had to be within six inches. Since you are placing your ball, you can set it down nice and easy, even if you're in a hazard, which pretty much guarantees a good lie to hit from. One thing you couldn't do was wipe your ball off. If it had mud or dirt on it, you had to be careful not to dislodge it. Greer and Donaldson were playing a best ball for the first six holes, so they just played regular golf. The low score on a given hole was their best ball. They were playing summer rules, which meant they couldn't touch their ball until they got to the green.

There was no one on the back nine yet, so the group had clear sailing. When they made the turn to play the front, Bert said he would have the first two holes open in front of them. He would simply monitor their pace and keep the first tee open once the guys hit the seventeenth hole. He knew exactly when they would be on seventeen, because the sixteenth was a par three that could be seen from the clubhouse. Club pros and pro shop managers were usually magicians when it came to traffic control on their golf course and the Cedar Creek manager was no different.

The two experienced hustlers had no idea about the adventure they were about to embark on.

* * *

The match started off simply enough.

Both teams birdied number ten, a fairly easy par five. The next hole, a 195-yard par three, set the tone for the rest of the round. Greer hit it way left and Donaldson hit it way right. Since Eddie's 4-iron was twelve feet right of the hole, Ronnie, wanting to keep it ugly, also hit his way right. He walked over to get his ball and saw Donaldson fluff his up into a good lie. It was only the second hole and their opponents were already cheating! Ronnie couldn't believe it. The guy had some stones. He decided to wait and see what Donaldson did with his pitch shot. If he left himself with an easy putt, he would call him on it. Donaldson hit his wedge on, but it was about thirty feet away. Ronnie kept quiet about the rules infringement, but he mentioned to Eddie on the next tee that they should keep a closer eye on these two. The situation reminded Ronnie of a time when a major league baseball player was using a corked bat, which his opponents were well aware of. There was no reason to point it out to the umpire until the guy actually got a hit with it.

Greer didn't even get his second shot on.

When their opponents didn't make par, the two hustlers conveniently missed their birdie putt. The whole idea was to be up one or two holes at the turn, but it had to appear they were lucky to be leading by that much. They wanted their opponents to play for the full three grand and not pay $250 each to walk away.

On their way to the twelfth tee, a 530-yard par five, Greer and Donaldson started arguing about their poor play on the last hole. Eddie and Ronnie tried to ignore them, but it was tough when two grown men were screaming face to face. The guys knew it was a show, but still had a tough time to keep from busting out laughing. Eddie was down the middle, so Ronnie sliced his drive over onto the adjacent number three fairway. Greer was long down the middle and had the best chance at getting home in two. When Ronnie settled over the ball for his second shot, Donaldson started farting. He apologized, saying something about his chronic digestive problems. He farted again at the top of Eddie's backswing. They halved the hole with pars.

Things got crazy on the next tee.

The thirteenth was a short par four with a sharp dogleg to the right. Donaldson was still doing his farting routine while Ronnie and Eddie teed off, but when it was his turn to hit, he was standing over by the ball washer with his pants off. All three asked him what the hell he was doing and his response was, "I just shit my pants." Eddie had trouble keeping his composure. He remembered remarking to Bert that they were prepared for anything, unless one of them stripped down and attempted to play naked. His remark proved to be somewhat prophetic, as Donaldson was now standing there holding his pants. He calmly threw his underwear into the trash receptacle and unhooked the little towel that hung from the ball washer. He got it wet by cranking the ball washer around real fast so soapy water would spill out the top. The rest of the group just stood there and stared. After cleaning himself up, he proceeded to hook the towel back up to the washer.

"I wouldn't do that," said Eddie. "Just throw it away. People already complain too much about the shitty conditions on the courses they play. We don't want them to complain about the shitty towels too."

Donaldson threw the towel away and put his pants back on, sans underwear.

"See what happens when you try too hard," said Ronnie, with a smirk on his face.

Donaldson just glared at him.

Two holes later, Greer put his fingers in his mouth and whistled just before Eddie made contact. He apologized and said he thought he saw the cart girl a couple of holes away. He explained he had to have something to drink because his stomach felt queasy.

The hustlers were up two holes standing on the eighteenth green, which was their ninth hole, because they started on the back. They had a fairly straight ten-foot birdie putt to win the hole. Their opponents didn't know it, but they had no intention of making it. Two up with nine to go was exactly where they wanted to be. They both had taken turns hitting erratic shots at opportune times, leading their opponents to believe that they were the type that might fold under pressure on the second nine. Ronnie had hit two slices that resulted in lost balls and Eddie duck-hooked one across two fairways. It was so far over, they didn't even bother to look for it.

They thought they had seen it all when Donaldson messed his pants a few holes back, but the next trick was beyond description. Greer was walking up to tap in their par putt when he stopped, put his hands on his knees and started retching right there on the green. Eddie and Ronnie looked at each other in astonishment. The guy had just puked right in their line!

"Sorry, guys," said Greer, wiping his mouth with the back of his hand. "I told you I had a nervous stomach. Man I sure could use a 7-up or something. Hey, just move your ball over so you don't have to putt through that mess."

When they moved their ball over to clear Donaldson's leavings, their straight putt turned into one with a six to twelve inch break. They both left the putt underneath the hole.

The boys gave Bert a subtle thumbs up when they went inside for refreshments and to use the restroom. They were sitting in their cart waiting for the shysters to come out of the clubhouse when Ronnie had an idea. He took out his phone and snapped off a couple discreet pictures of their opponents when they came out of the building. After a quick phone call, he sent the pictures to Chicago, where Herman was waiting for them.

"Hey, Greg, are you guys okay?" asked Eddie. "You can quit here according to our agreement. I'd hate to have to call an ambulance out there."

"Yeah, we're good," said Greg. "We're two down, but I feel this will be our nine. Let's get on with it."

When they got to number four Greer and Donaldson were only one down. Their antics continued when Greer hollered and fell back into the greenside trap retrieving his ball. Donaldson was on the green about a foot inside Eddie and Ronnie's ball, so they were going to play his anyway. The fall came at an opportune time—just as Ronnie was putting. He flinched and pushed the putt to the right. Ronnie shook his head and gave his partner a concerned look. One of those lunatics was going to pop a blood vessel or have a heart attack before this thing was over.

After a birdie on six for a win, Eddie and Ronnie were two up sitting on the next tee. The seventh at Cedar Creek is a tricky little par four. The hole doglegs right over a small stream that runs across the fairway. To the right of the fairway is a small pond. In a scramble, it's worth taking a shot at from the tee as long as you've got a ball in play. Ronnie looked over to see both of their opponents holding their drivers. His experience told him that just because they had them out, it didn't mean they were going to hit them. He walked to the tee and hit a nice little hybrid fade short of the creek. Eddie stood up and hit his driver right at the green. It looked good when it left the clubface, but they couldn't see where it landed. Greer and Donaldson both bombed their drivers in the same general direction as Eddie's shot.

Ronnie was about to get into the cart when his pocket started to vibrate. He pulled out his phone and read the text message.

"Damn, Street," whispered Ronnie. "We've got trouble. Herman just got back with me on the two photos I sent him at the turn. These guys are seriously connected. They're from a big crime family in New York City. Herman says they're very unstable and to stay the hell away from them. They've got a real violent history."

"I figured as much," said Eddie, as he steered the cart down the fairway. "A few holes back, when Greer was looking in his bag, I got a glimpse at what looked like an automatic weapon. These dudes shouldn't be on the golf course. They should be locked up somewhere. All we have to do is draw two and lose one on these last three holes and we walk away with three grand each. Your info from Herman has shed a whole different light on the situation." Eddie slowed down and looked over at his partner. "You know what we have to do now, don't you?"

"Hell yes, I know what we have to do," barked Ronnie. "But I don't have to like it, do I?"

"It's agreed then," said Eddie, holding out a fist so Ronnie could bump it. "We dump. Let's make it look good so these two crazies don't take offense and do something irrational."

* * *

Bert was in shock when he handed Greer and Donaldson their winnings. After the two mobsters left with their six grand, he went over and sat at the hustler's table. They were both smiling and drinking a beer. As he walked up he caught part of their conversation. Eddie was explaining why the Tigers were twice the team that the Cubs were this year. They certainly didn't have the demeanor of two guys that just dropped a wad on the course.

"What happened?" asked a shocked Bert, as he sat down.

"We were right where we wanted to be, two up with three to play," explained Eddie. "Then we dumped. Do you know who those two guys are?"

"Nope. They're just two off-the-wall golfers who happen to be able to crush a golf ball. Why, who are they?"

"They're guys you don't want to take any dough from," said Eddie, staring seriously into Bert's eyes. "They're dangerous lunatics. My advice is, the next time they call you for a game, tell them that after our match, word got out, and their reputation is so established around here that no one will play them. Hopefully, they will go away and never come back. Believe me, you don't want to mess with those two."

* * *

Bert watched Eddie and Ronnie throw their bags into their car and drive off.

He felt bad about the whole situation.

Later that night, he thought about what went down on the course that afternoon. *Those two old boys made the right move today*, he thought. *I guess that's how you get famous nicknames. Forty years from now, I'll be telling my grandchildren how 'The Grip' and 'The Street' threw a big money match that I had set up for them. And it was definitely the smart play at the time.*

* * *

"You won't believe this," said Eddie, as he was describing their match to Suzanne and Kathy. The guys decided to take the girls out to a nice restaurant, then to a movie. Normally, they weren't the movie type, but they knew it was one the girls wanted to see. "So, after one of them messes his pants, the other one barfs right on the green, between our ball and the hole."

"You're making that up," said Kathy. "No sane person would do something like that."

"Sane is the key word there, sweetheart," said Ronnie, as he was slapping the table trying to keep his laughter under control. "Those two must have come straight from the asylum. I never had so much fun losing a bet in my life."

"So we lose number seven," continued Eddie, "which is actually our sixteenth, and these guys are all hyped up. They're strutting around like they're about to win the U. S. Open, and they're still one down. On the next to last hole Ronnie is putting first from about twenty feet, so I tell him loudly not to leave it short. He then proceeds to rip it six feet by. I follow with a feeble attempt that ends up four feet short. We're making like we're real nervous and both of us miss the four-footer. Now we're tied, and they have all the momentum. Donaldson steps up and smokes it about 300 yards right down the middle. We're about forty yards back and leave our second shot on the front fringe. Greer hits it to twelve feet and they make the uphill putt. We were hoping they would, because we ended up making birdie. Our strategy was, if they didn't make the eagle putt, we would lose to them on the first playoff hole."

"I would have loved to hear their conversation in the car as they left the course," said Ronnie. "I'm sure they thought they were world beaters. Those are two guys that I never want to see again."

"You two should be more selective on who you play with," said Suzanne. "It's too bad you didn't have the info on them before the match. Then you could have said you were sick or injured and wouldn't be able to play."

"I don't know, babe," said Eddie. "That wouldn't be the honorable thing to do after we agreed to play them."

"What's more important?" asked the lawyer. "Your honor or your life? Don't answer that. Anyway, I'm going to the restroom. Coming, Kathy?"

"Why do women always go in pairs?" asked Ronnie. "Is it some kind of herd mentality?"

"Safety in numbers, sweetie," answered Kathy, giving him a kiss on the cheek.

"Don't run out on us," said Eddie, as the girls walked away. "Due to a recent financial misfortune, we're not sure we can cover the check."

"Do you believe everything they were telling us?" asked Kathy, as the two of them stood in front of the restroom mirrors.

"Yeah, no one in their right mind would make up a story like that," said Suzanne. "And I thought golf was supposed to be a gentlemen's game. Those guys they played against were disgusting." When Suzanne opened her purse to put her makeup away she exposed an expensive jewelry box.

"Wow," said Kathy. "What's in the classy box?"

Suzanne reluctantly opened the box for Kathy to view the contents. Inside was an elegant pearl necklace.

"Those are beautiful. Why aren't you wearing them? They would definitely compliment the dress you are wearing."

"Please don't take this wrong," explained Suzanne. "But Eddie told me not to wear them because he thought it might look like he was trying to one-up Ronnie. He gave them to me when he came back from Chicago. I was going to put them on later."

"So your man bought you something expensive with his winnings, did he?" asked Kathy feigning jealousy. "And he thought Ronnie was too, shall we say frugal, to buy me something?"

"I really wish you hadn't seen the box, Kathy."

"I'm glad I did," said Kathy, smiling and reaching into her purse. "Because now I can show you the little bauble that my guy bought me." Kathy pulled out a similar box containing a diamond pendant and held it up for Suzanne to inspect.

When their two dates came back to the table wearing their recent gifts, the guys were speechless. So that's what women did when they went to the restroom together—they compared notes. Neither of them knew about the other's purchase. They looked at each other and raised their glasses in salute.

Like they had said on numerous occasions—they could be brothers.

PART TWO

The Kid

CHAPTER TWELVE

Young Entrepreneur

Will and I are in the same grade and we've been friends ever since he moved here. The guy loves golf, even though he can't play for shit.

—Billy Kaminski, high school classmate

Eddie's stroke was smooth and measured. He watched with pleasure as the ball soared up, arced over the reed-filled edge of a pond, and then sailed on, descending smoothly onto the fairway, avoiding a trap and then landing sweetly just short of the 100 yard marker.

"Jeez, Eddie," said Ronnie, looking around nervously. "Tone it down, will ya? You don't want any possible marks to see that piece of artistry. You'll scare them all away."

It was the last week in July and things were going smoothly. Eddie had flown to Florida and then to Texas to visit his daughters and their families. July wasn't exactly the best time to head south, but there were birthday parties and a dance recital to attend. The devotion that Eddie showed to his girls when they were growing up didn't just dry up like a summer puddle when they got older. He talked to them frequently on the phone and his computer was filled with pictures of his two daughters and their childrens' activities.

Ronnie had gone back to Chicago to visit Herman and some old golf buddies. He was surprised that he and Eddie were still a hot item around the Chicago golf scene. As always, the stories that were told about him and his partner were exaggerated beyond belief. Getting a serious money game in that city would be out of the question for a while. It's not that he couldn't get a game. The problem was arranging something where he actually had a chance to win. Possible opponents asked for too much of an advantage, and throwing his hard earned money away wasn't his style. One scratch golfer offered to play Ronnie for ten grand if he could replay six shots of his choosing during the match. Ronnie was impressed with the guy's ingenuity, but it was a losing gig from his point of view. The guy could hit again if he went O. B. or if he buried one under the lip of the trap. He could also replay a six-foot missed putt after he saw the first one roll toward the hole. Ronnie countered with the guy replaying one shot a side and Ronnie could choose the course. The scratch golfer declined.

On Eddie's first day back the guys were playing a leisurely afternoon round on the East course at GLV.

Playing sub par golf while solving all the world's problems is no easy task. They did agree that the government was too big and it would take a radical overhaul to make it smaller. Eddie surprised his playing partner when he suggested that half of Washington D. C. should be relocated to the center of the country.

"I'd leave the monuments and the Capitol Building and the White House where they are," he explained, as he bent over to read his birdie putt on the eleventh hole. "But a lot of other offices, like the Treasury, the IRS, and the Department of Defense, I'd relocate to Kansas or Nebraska. Washington is too crowded as it is, and the middle of the country would be a safer location than sitting out on the east coast."

"How would people that were doing business with multiple departments get back and forth?" asked Ronnie. He wasn't buying in to Eddie's radical notion of ripping up half of the nation's capitol and moving it out to farm country.

"With today's technology you don't need to travel that much," explained Eddie. "If you had to meet face to face, then high-speed rail would be the answer. Did you know that the rail system is the most efficient way to move freight across the country? It should be the same way with people. The trains just need to go faster, because of all the stops they have to make. People get on and off, while freight just waits to be unloaded at the finish line."

"It sounds like you've put a lot of thought into this," said Ronnie, as they walked off the green after making their birdies.

"Hey, my life is more than playing golf and poker and running with fast women. We could get a city planner to design a super hi-tech city for the new half-Capitol. How about this: Electric trains run around the outside of the entire city twenty-four hours a day. The tracks also go into the city's interior, to the stores and anywhere else the people need to go. The only vehicles allowed are for emergencies or the delivery of goods and services. The kids even ride the train to school. No more buses. And another thing—no more DUI's, because the drunks are riding the train."

"Okay, now you're starting to scare me," said Ronnie, with a concerned look on his face.

"And," continued Eddie, undaunted, "there would be huge electronic information billboards all around town. They would give info on events, the weather, and any other information that would be beneficial to the people. It would be a cool place to live. That's all I'm saying. We've got the technology, so why not use it?"

"I've got one question," said Ronnie.

"What's that? Who's going to pay for it all?"

"No, not that. What did you mean when you said you run with fast women? I didn't think Suzanne was that type. Is there something you'd like to share with me?"

"Dude, how old are you? Anything I told you would go straight to Kathy, and then straight back to Suzanne. That's aggravation I don't need."

"Alright, alright," said Ronnie, as he teed his ball up on number twelve, a short par four with trees left and right. "All this talk about moving the Capitol and futuristic cities is out of my league. I will admit, I didn't know you were such a deep thinker. Hey, what's that kid doing over there?"

A young boy was standing about 175 yards out on the left. He was mostly hidden by a small tree, but they could see his head as he leaned sideways to watch them hit their tee shots. When the guys got to their balls, the kid walked over to them. He was wearing a baseball cap, a t-shirt and ratty-looking shorts that should have been thrown away months ago. He appeared to be about thirteen or fourteen years old. He was about 5' 8" tall with a slender built. Black curly hair spilled out under the sides of his faded hat. The boy had a big smile on his face, and he was carrying what looked like a plastic grocery bag full of golf balls.

"Gentlemen," said the boy. "By the looks of your smooth golf swings, and the position of your tee shots, I'd say you were low handicappers. Any chance you would like to buy some premium, slightly used golf balls? The good shots in them haven't been used up. Otherwise I wouldn't have them in my possession."

"Kid," said Eddie, "you picked the worst hole to sell balls. The mosquitoes back here are terrible."

"I'm covered with special bug juice," said the boy, as he looked around for any course workers. "Besides, the bugs keep the grounds crew from sticking around on this hole and the next one. Apparently, the stuff they wear isn't as good as mine."

"Let's see what you've got," said Ronnie.

The boy opened his bag and showed them about fifteen assorted balls. He was right about them being premium balls. Most of them were Titleists, with a couple of other high-priced brands.

"What are you asking for these?" asked Ronnie.

"A buck a piece," answered the boy. "If you buy them all, I'll throw the bag in at no charge."

"Such a deal," said Eddie. "My partner here hits a lot of balls into the trees. I bet he would give you twenty bucks for the whole lot."

Ronnie looked at Eddie and rolled his eyes. He reached into his pocket and pulled out his money clip. The clip was full to the point where it couldn't hold any more. The kid was impressed by all the bills that Ronnie was carrying. He pealed of a twenty and gave it to the boy.

"What's your name, son?" asked Ronnie.

"My name's Wilson," said the boy, extending his hand.

"My friends call me Grip and this is Street," said Ronnie, as he shook the youngster's hand.

"Well, Wilson," said Eddie. "You're quite a salesman. You got some of that special bug juice left? The stuff we're wearing seems to attract them."

Wilson pulled a small prescription bottle out of his pocket. "I keep it in this pill bottle because it doesn't leak," he explained. "My mom makes it up. It's like an old family recipe."

"How about you sell me that bottle for ten bucks?" asked Eddie, reaching into his front left pocket.

Wilson handed the bottle over and pocketed Eddie's ten. "Thanks, gentlemen. Please do me a favor and don't tell the pro shop that I'm selling balls out here. I'm sort of trespassing."

"No worries," said Eddie. "I suppose we'll be in the market for some more of these, as soon as Grip here deposits them back where you found them. We should put a special mark on them so you know which ones were his. You could probably turn them over three or four times until they get too scuffed up."

Wilson waved and headed back into the woods to look for more balls.

"You're a funny guy," said Ronnie. "Why didn't you give him a twenty for the bug juice? By the looks of the holes in his shorts, he could probably use the dough."

"Yeah, I don't think those holes were for fashion purposes," said Eddie. "I only gave him a ten because he looked sharp enough to figure out his juice wasn't worth more than that and would have seen it as a charity thing. I liked that kid. He's a lot different than most of the young people I see around. You've got to give him credit for being resourceful."

* * *

It was a good day for Wilson as he made his way back to where he had hidden his bicycle. He had forty dollars in his pocket and it was only mid afternoon. As he rode the five miles to his home in the little village of Hickory Corners, he planned the rest of his day. He had enough time to mow two lawns for his regular customers, then he planned on fixing the railing next to the back steps at the house where he and his mother lived. What little daylight was left was for hitting golf balls. There was a small field close to his house and the owner didn't mind him hitting balls there as long as he picked them up. As many times as Wilson had been on the Gull Lake View course, he had never played it. At his house, there was no extra money for golf. He was going to keep ten dollars from his day's earnings, and the rest would go to his mom. Her job at the restaurant didn't pay much, so every dollar counted.

* * *

Wilson exchanged his sneakers for his work boots and headed out the door to get his mowing and trimming equipment. He thought about his last two customers back at the course. It must be nice to have that kind of money. Both of them had money clips that looked like they were about to burst.

Grip and Street—what kind of names were those?

They were probably big city gangsters or maybe something even worse, like politicians. He was surprised when Grip said he would buy the whole bag of balls. He hoped the two old guys were legit and not crooks. They seemed pretty nice. No matter, with no father around he had to do everything he could to help out with chores and expenses. He saw the guys looking at his worn shorts and decided that he needed a new pair. In three weeks he would officially be a freshman in high school. One thing that stuck in the back of his mind was the way the two old guys swung the golf club. Their tee shots on number twelve came to rest about six feet apart. He had lingered just long enough to watch Grip play his second shot, and it looked like he had knocked it stiff. If he saw them again, maybe he would ask them for a swing tip or two. He didn't believe it when Street said Grip would lose the balls he bought. Something told him that these two guys usually finished their round with the same ball they started with.

* * *

Wilson had ten balls left and it was getting dark. He took his golf game seriously, even though he rarely got a chance to play. Maple Hills was the first and only course he had ever played. It was a little nine-hole layout a few miles east of Stonehedge. The owner was a nice guy that would let him play as many holes as he wanted for one fee. His mom would drop him off on her way to Battle Creek and would pick him up on the way back. He read everything he could about the game and was familiar with the rules and the strategy involved. His problem was, his shots started out fine, but then they would slice off to the right. The harder he tried to fix it, the worse it got. He could hit the ball flush almost every time, but he had seen enough good golf shots to know that the better golfers didn't hit a big slice unless the shot called for it.

He hit his last ball in the semi-darkness and decided to come back early the next morning to pick them up. The young entrepreneur hustled home to put on his favorite movie and to wait for his mom to get home. He grabbed a soda out of the fridge and made himself a peanut butter sandwich.

He settled down on the couch to watch *The Legend of Bagger Vance.*

Wilson had seen the video several times, but never got tired of it. Every time he watched it he learned something new. As usual, when his mom got home from work, he was asleep on the couch with the movie still playing. Once the tape hit the end of the old VCR, it would rewind and start all over again. Carol Randall smiled down at her sleeping son. She was extremely proud of him. They had lost his dad when Wilson was only two, so the boy didn't remember him at all. Wilson was a very independent young man, and once he was old enough, he did everything he could to help out.

His dad would have been just as proud of him.

* * *

Pam served the guys their regular drinks after their round. She now saw them in a different light, but the banter was still there.

"So, are you two party animals going to spend another quiet evening at home all by yourself?" she asked, hoping to get a rise out of them.

Eddie looked over at Ronnie and winked. "What time do you get off, doll?" he asked. "Ronnie and I are willing to show you the town if you can handle it."

His answer wasn't the one she had expected. "I get off at nine. Why, what did you have in mind? Nothing kinky, I hope. I'm not really in to that weird stuff."

"How about a late dinner at a classy place and then a little live entertainment?" asked Eddie.

"I don't know. A girl can't be too cautious these days. I do trust you two, especially after all you've done for me. Okay, let's do it."

* * *

The three of them stood outside of Big Daddy's Blues Bar.

The guys were surprised at Pam's command of current events, as she had held her own all through the dinner conversation. Ronnie and Eddie both had an arm around her as they stepped through the door.

As usual, Germaine was sitting a few feet inside on his usual stool.

"Germaine," said Eddie, shaking the bouncer's hand and slipping him the customary twenty. "You remember Ronnie don't you? And this is Pam. She's slumming tonight, hanging out with a couple of old guys while her millionaire boyfriend is out of town."

"Good to see you, Mr. D," said Germaine, as he shook Eddie's hand, then Ronnie's. "You and Ronnie Green are welcome any time. This is one fine lady you are escorting tonight. I'm surprised she's got only one millionaire boyfriend. Grab a table. I'll send Jamaica over to take your order. The band is taking their first break. They should be back on stage by the time you get your drinks."

Jamaica, the owner's daughter, showed up as soon as the three of them sat down. She was dressed in tight black pants with a bright red blouse. Black boots rose almost to her knees and an expensive gold necklace caressed her neck. She bent over and gave Eddie a kiss on the cheek, and when Ronnie gave her an exasperated look, she gave him the same.

"Where have you two been?' she asked in a stern voice. "You've missed out on some killer entertainment lately. We had a guy from Florida in here last week that you would have loved. His name is Tony Vegas and he had this place hopping. He played a few cover songs, but mostly his own stuff. I know what you two are drinking. What can I get for your lady friend?"

Eddie introduced Pam and she ordered a screwdriver. Pam looked at her two escorts as Jamaica headed to the bar to fill their order. She raised an eyebrow insinuating that something wasn't kosher.

"What?" asked Ronnie. "You think we just stay at home every night? I'll have you know that Eddie and I are famous partiers."

"Right," said Pam. "She's beautiful. How much did you have to pay her for those kisses? And what's up with the different names?"

"That hurt," said Ronnie, as he watched Jamaica return with their drinks. "Watch this. Hey, Jamaica, the last time we were in here, who were we with?"

"You were with a red-haired hottie and Mr. D had a dark blond, beautiful executive type on his arm. If I remember, you two almost started a fight when you showed up."

"That wasn't our fault," said Eddie, as he handed her a twenty and motioning for her to keep the change. "How's school going?"

"I just finished my only summer class and I aced it."

"Good for you, babe," exclaimed Eddie. "Keep it up. Hey, I've got a question for you. Who said, 'education is what's left after you've forgotten everything you've learned'?"

"That sounds like something Einstein would have said," she answered confidently.

"I'm surprised you've heard of that one," said Eddie. "It's one of my favorites."

"Not only have I heard of it," said Jamaica with a smile, as she walked away, "I wrote a five-page paper on that very quote."

"I wish I had a college degree," said Pam. "I think I'm smart enough, but something always gets in the way."

"Having a degree just proves that you found a way to get through college," said Eddie, leaning forward in his chair. "Some people learn a lot, while others are there for the social experience, if you know what I mean. A lot of successful people didn't go to college."

"Does your definition of success include the word money, as in lots of it?" asked Ronnie.

"Surprisingly, no," answered Eddie. "I think a person is successful if they're doing something that they want to do and it's a worthwhile venture. As long as their time is spent doing something productive, I consider them successful."

"I agree," said Ronnie, lifting his glass.

"Wow," said Pam. "I think I'm out with a couple of philosopher types tonight. There's obviously more to you two than just playing golf and drinking whiskey, and doing favors for girls in distress. I haven't heard from Jeff since you two took care of him. He hasn't called or anything. You didn't have him killed, did you? I hope not. He was an incredible jerk but he didn't deserve to die."

"As far as you know, we didn't," said Ronnie, as they turned their attention toward the stage. The band had just walked out for their second set of the evening.

"You're just kidding, right? Please tell me you're just kidding."

"He was told what would happen to him if he ever came back to this area," explained Eddie. "Trust us, you don't have to worry about him any more."

* * *

Three days later Eddie was heading east on the highway toward Battle Creek when he saw a boy on a bicycle coming towards him in the opposite direction. The rider turned right on to a side road and immediately crashed into the ditch. Eddie slowed down and made the turn coming to a stop next to the boy who was now standing and looking at his bike.

"Hey, Wilson, are you all right?" hollered Eddie out the passenger window.

"Yeah," said the young man. "I was hustling to get off the highway and my front tire just blew out."

Eddie got out and came around the car to look at the bike. "Your wheel looks alright. It shouldn't cost you too much to get a new tire or maybe just a tube. Let's throw it in my trunk and I'll take you home."

They put the bike in the trunk and Eddie hooked up a couple of bungee cords to keep the lid down. By the time they had driven the five miles to Hickory Corners, a small village northeast of GLV, Eddie had learned a lot about Wilson. He lived with his mother who worked at a restaurant on the west side of Battle Creek. He was going to be a freshman at Gull Lake High School, and he was a little nervous about his first day, which was coming up fast. Eddie told him not to worry, as he seemed the type of kid that would be able to adapt to a change in his environment. As they pulled into Wilson's driveway, Eddie saw a woman taking clothes off the clothesline.

Carol Randall was a short Hispanic woman with black hair that was kept up off her shoulders with bobby pins. She had the look of a woman that worked a lot and worried a lot. She frowned as she walked over to the car and looked at the bike that Wilson was unloading. One knee was skinned up and he had scratches on his hands.

"What happened, Willy?" she asked in a concerned motherly voice.

"Crashed, Mom. Blew a tire. Hey, this is Stree…"

"Eddie Ferguson, Ma'am," said Eddie, sticking his hand out. "I met Wilson on the golf course a few days ago."

"Thank you for bringing him home, Mr. Ferguson. Willy, we need to get you inside to clean up those scrapes. We don't want them to get infected. Thanks again, Mr. Ferguson."

"No problem," said Eddie, as he got back into his car. "See you around the course, Wilson."

"Thanks, Street," said Wilson, as he and his mother headed toward the back door.

Eddie didn't back out of the drive right away. He sat there and looked over the Randall place. The back yard was a fairly good size and the grass was mowed and neatly trimmed. The garage was old with several boards on the sides that didn't match the original ones. Inside the garage door, leaning on a sawhorse, was a ratty-looking golf bag with a few clubs in it. Next to the bag were two plastic grocery bags full of balls. So Wilson was a golfer. Eddie backed the car out of the drive and headed back the way they had come. What was it he said about being successful if you were doing something worthwhile? Well, his mind started to work out a plan to fit that description.

* * *

"So here's what I think we should do," said Eddie, as he and Ronnie were about to tee off on the back side at Bedford Valley. "I'd like to take the kid over to Stonehedge and have the pro fit him for a set of clubs. And I think you and I should foot the bill."

"The kid's only fourteen," said Ronnie. "What if he shoots up three or four inches over the winter? Then the lie on his sticks might be too flat for him. And what about the length?"

"We get him a set of forged blades so the lie can be adjusted. Adding some length to a club isn't a problem either. You just cut the grip off and add an extension."

"You sound like you know a little bit about the club building business," said Ronnie.

"I did some alterations and some club building at several of the pro shops that I've worked in. I actually got pretty good at it. I could fit the kid, but the Stonehedge pro's got all the gadgets to do it right. How about you? You ever work on clubs?"

"Nope, I just swing them. I had a pro fit me for a set one time, and every club felt great, except for the four-iron. It just felt like a piece of metal in my hands. We put it on the swing weight machine and it matched the other clubs. Then the guy turned it to get the total weight and it was way out of sync. You know, a lot heavier than it should have been. That night he took it apart and found about an inch of lead cord in the hosel. He said the manufacturer put it in there because the head was too light and it needed more weight to get the desired swing weight. The problem was, when you load up the hosel with weight the sweet spot isn't in the center of the clubface anymore. It actually moves toward the hosel. That's why the club just didn't feel right to me. When I asked why they didn't just put a heavier four-iron head on the shaft, he just shrugged his shoulders. To this day, I refuse to even look at a club made by that company."

"What company was that?" asked Eddie, as they rode down the tenth fairway.

"Ha," said Ronnie with a huge grin. "The company that makes the clubs you're playing."

* * *

Two days later the four of them stood on the practice tee at Stonehedge. Wilson was incredibly excited when he told his mom that Eddie and his friend Grip were going to work with him on his golf swing. Carol wasn't too keen on the idea, but her son was such a hard worker, and he loved the game so much. When Eddie came over to make the offer he was very convincing. She decided if two old guys wanted to help her son out, then it was fine with her.

The pro had Wilson hit several balls with a bunch of demo clubs that he used for fitting. Then he put the kid on a plywood board and had him hit balls off of that. On the bottom of the clubs was a special kind of tape to see exactly where the club was making contact with the board when it impacted the ball. He explained to the three of them that there were more modern tools to check the proper lie for a golfer's swing, but he liked the old method. It had always worked for him, and he trusted the results. When he had all the information he needed, he shook hands with the three of them and headed back to the pro shop. He told them he would have Wilson's new sticks in a couple of weeks.

"What did he mean when he said my new sticks?" asked Wilson.

"You were just fitted for a set of clubs," said Eddie.

"But I can't afford something like that," protested Wilson.

"Don't worry, kid, Eddie's loaded," said Ronnie. "He could buy this whole course if he wanted to."

"He's kidding," said Eddie, as Wilson looked at him with wide eyes. "We're both going to set you up. If a guy's going to learn this game, he can't do it with mismatched equipment. Tell you what, you can buy your own bag. I think you can even get an employee discount at the Stonehedge or Gull Lake View pro shop."

"How can I do that?" asked the kid, as he tried to process what was being said.

"One more thing," said Grip. "The pro wants you to run the range for the rest of the year. Usually the grounds crew takes care of it, but they will be doing some major improvements on the course this fall, and they won't have the time. Eddie and I told him that we had just the guy for the job. You report to the pro shop tomorrow at eight in the morning. He'll tell you what your duties are. Once school starts, you can work after school and on weekends."

"And here's the good part," added Eddie. "The range won't be that busy during the week, because things slow down around here once September rolls around. That means you will have time to practice if you get all your work done. So what do you say? You want to go for it?"

Wilson had tears in his eyes when he gave the two hustlers a hug. This was more than he could have ever hoped for. His mom had always told him that if he worked hard and kept a good head on his shoulders, then things would work out for the best. When the hugging was over the guys noticed someone standing close by. Mitch, the Cedar Creek range manager, had walked up to the range with his clubs. Eddie had invited Mitch over to "The Hedge" for another practice session. His mother had just dropped him off on her way to Kalamazoo to do some shopping.

"Hey, Mitch," said Eddie. "This is Wilson. Shake hands guys and let's spank some white boys. I'll work with Mitch, and Grip, you got the kid."

For the next hour and a half, the two high schoolers were put through the paces. The hustlers drilled them on the fundamentals, but nothing too complicated. When Mitch's mother drove up and waved at him, he gave her the signal that he would be right there. Mitch and Eddie walked over to see what Ronnie and Wilson were working on. They caught the last bit of Ronnie's explanation on how to hold the club.

"So, holding it in this position will give you the best chance of squaring the face up at impact," explained Ronnie, as he modeled a neutral grip. "If you hold it differently, you have to do something unnatural to make up for it. If your grip's too strong, you have to hold off through impact or you're going to hook everything. If it's too weak, you will have to compensate by flipping your hands through real aggressive. The goal is to give yourself the best chance to hit it almost exactly the same every time. There are some great golfers out there that can do something unnatural almost every time to make up for a faulty grip, but they are rare. Remember, the swing should be as simple and as natural as you can make it. The simple approach will be a huge advantage when it comes to hitting that crucial shot in the round. Hold the club differently if you want to hit something other than your basic shot. Understand?"

"I think I do," said Wilson. "Holding it square at this end gives me the best chance of keeping it square at the other end."

"Exactly," said Ronnie, as he looked up at Eddie and Mitch.

They both laughed, because Ronnie had just given Will the exact same advice that Eddie had given Mitch on his first lesson.

"What do you think about the kid?" asked Eddie, after their two students had left for home.

"You saw that swing, right?" asked Ronnie.

"I did," answered Eddie, pulling out a cigar. "It looks like the kid's got some talent."

"He did everything I asked him to do and in short order. He can't hit it straight yet, but it looks like he's a natural. He's a great kid. I'm glad you came up with the club idea."

"It was teamwork," said Eddie. "You got him the job."

* * *

Wilson explained to his mom about the job and his new clubs that were coming. She was suspicious of the two older guys that wanted to help her son out.

"Tell me again why these guys, that were complete strangers two weeks ago, want to help out a kid they had just met. It sounds fishy to me."

"Mom," said Wilson. "They're great guys that just want to help out another golfer. Eddie also works with a kid named Mitch that runs the Cedar Creek range. He goes to Lakeview High School and I think he's on the golf team. He's a year older than me, so he's going to be a sophomore. You know how much we need the money. This range job will be perfect for me. I can work that job and still mow my lawns. And I get to hit balls if I've got all my work done."

"I've met Eddie," said Carol. "What's the other guy's name?"

"Eddie calls him, Grip, but I think that's just a nickname. He calls Eddie 'Street' most of the time. I did hear another man call him Mr. Costas. Why, do you think he's some kind of escaped criminal or something?"

"Don't be silly. I just think we should be careful. Guys doing nice things for no reason makes me a little nervous."

"Mom, if either of these guys says or does anything weird, I'll stay away from them, okay?"

"Just keep your wits about yourself. That's all I'm saying. Maybe they are legit, but these days it pays to be on your guard. How about this, since you're an employee now, why don't you ask around a little. You know, get some other peoples' opinions on these two."

CHAPTER THIRTEEN

Melissa

There's an old saying that describes my situation to a tee, "Life can be pretty simple until you throw a good-looking woman into the equation. Then logic and reason are out the window and all bets are off."

—Quincy St. James, amateur philosopher/convenience store owner

Swing thoughts are the images that go through a golfer's mind from the time he takes the club back until he makes contact:
- Release the clubhead so you square the face up as you come in to the ball
- Pull down hard with the left hand (the right hand for lefties)
- Throw your right knee at the target
- Pause at the top of your backswing
- Fire the right side
- The lower body should lead the downswing so you don't come over the top
- Think tempo—don't worry, be happy

Once you've got the basics down, it all should be second nature and you won't have to think about it so much.

When a golfer addresses the ball, he inadvertently goes through a checklist in his mind:
1. Grip club in a fairly neutral position
2. Bend at the waist
3. Knees should be flexed but not bent
4. Make sure ball is positioned correctly for the type of shot you are about to hit
5. Align yourself to the target
6. Feet a little wider apart
7. Ease off on the grip pressure and tilt hands slightly forward
8. Arms hanging loose and close to your body

Surprisingly, the above list only takes a couple of seconds to accomplish. An experienced golfer doesn't worry about all the little things—he just does them. But, it takes a while to get to this point. At her first lesson a beginning golfer told her pro that she wanted to take up the sport because it looked so easy on television. He reminded her that she was watching some of the best players in the world. Making what they do look easy is the mark of an accomplished athlete. A sign of greatness is to be able to perform at the highest level time and time again under tremendous pressure (see Nelson, Hogan, Nicklaus, etc.).

The bottom line on all the above is; the game was not designed to be mastered. There are too many variables to be controlled. It would be a sad day indeed if one individual would unequivocally, without question, conquer the sport. If this miracle ever came to pass, there would be a huge influx of used clubs for sale on E-bay and at garage sales across the country.

Wilson showed up at the Stonehedge clubhouse a little before eight a.m. the next day. The pro took him out to the range and explained his duties. His main job was to pick up the balls, run them through the washer, and keep the ball dispenser full. Driving the ball picker was easy, but he also had to take a couple of shag bags to get the ones around the edges and in the trees. He was also supposed to fill the divots on the tee area with a mixture of sand and grass seed. About once a week he was expected to mow the landing area. One of the grounds crew would come by to mow the tee, so he didn't have to worry about that. The pro showed him how to run the range mower. It wasn't in very good shape, but it ran smooth enough to get the job done. Wilson impressed the pro with his knowledge of mowers. It looked like Ferguson and Costas knew what they were talking about when they recommended this kid.

He was at the range all day for the first week. When school started he rode as fast as he could to the course, as soon as he got off the bus. He would work for about three hours, then hit balls for the last hour. He didn't have time for much else—school, work, chores and homework made for a full day. He was an 'A' and 'B' student in middle school, and his mom expected him to keep up his high marks now that he was in high school. The pro had told him to stay home if the weather was bad. No one would be out there hitting, so he might as well take a break.

On Friday afternoon, after his first full week of school, Will showed up for work at five o'clock. The day was windy, but there was some sort of tournament the next day, so he wanted to be prepared for a lot of golfers. There were only two golfers hitting balls, and he recognized their swings right away. Ronnie saw him ride up on his bike and motioned him over. There, leaning on the bag rack, was a full set of clubs. Three Taylor Made "woods" and nine irons—three through sand wedge. Wilson just stood there and stared.

"You got a bag, kid?" asked Eddie.

He went inside the storage building and came out with the bag and head covers that he had bought a week earlier in the pro shop. Finally, he was going to swing real clubs—clubs that were ordered especially for him. These clubs were the nicest things he had ever owned. He had a look of pure joy on his face as he put them one by one in his bag. Eddie and Grip just stood there silently and watched.

"Okay, let's get to work," said Eddie. "Grip's got an idea on how you can get rid of that slice, so you can hit these things the way they were meant to be hit."

"Take out the 6-iron and swing it a few times to get warmed up," instructed Grip.

Wilson swung the club several times, starting slow, then increasing the clubhead speed. The full cord grips felt great. They were the same kind Street and Grip had on their clubs. He rolled a ball over and made an awkward pass at it. This club definitely felt different in his hands. It would take some time to get used to it. He hit the fourth ball flush and watched it start at the target, then it curved to the right, as most of his shots did. He looked up at Grip and Eddie, hoping for a solution.

"Time for some magic, little man," said Grip, as he knelt down in front of Wilson and put his hands over the boy's hands. "One of the main reasons a guy slices is because he squeezes the club too hard, which keeps his hands from working the way they are supposed to. Your shots start out on a good line, so your swing plane is fine. The problem is in your hands. Do you feel that you are gripping too hard?"

Wilson shook his head indicating that he didn't think he was doing that.

"Alright," continued Grip in a soft voice. "Here's your swing thought. I want you to hit the ball with the toe of the club."

When the kid gave him a questionable look, Grip explained himself.

"I don't mean **off** the toe. I mean **with** the toe. In your mind I want you to think you are rolling the club over so far that the toe of the club is the only thing that will make contact with the ball. Go ahead. Try it. You'll be surprised."

The kid wasn't too sure about this kind of advice, but he gave it his best effort. The first two balls just rolled off the tee. Then it happened. He flushed the next one and it exploded off the clubface. He looked at Grip with surprised eyes. He had never hit a ball like that before. It started straight, then moved a little right-to-left—a beautiful draw.

Grip held up his gloved left hand, making a fist. He hit it with an open right hand a few times, sliding the open hand across his fist.

"Your clubhead, because it's open at impact, has been striking the ball sort of a glancing blow, like my right hand is doing to my fist. A lot of the clubhead energy is going toward spin instead of velocity. Now, watch this."

Grip squared up his right hand and smacked his left fist again. His glove was still on, but this time it gave off a loud "crack" when he made contact.

"Now that you have the clubface squared, or a little past square on that last shot, the energy from the club is transferred more efficiently to the ball. Pretty cool feeling, huh? I didn't hit my fist any harder than before—I just squared up my hand that time."

The kid was all smiles. "I really smoked that thing."

"Don't worry about the distance. Concentrate on doing the same thing every time. You're hitting it hard enough and far enough with the swing you just made. As soon as you start thinking about hitting it farther, you will lose your consistency. It won't be long before you will know, right down to a couple of yards, how far you hit each club. Watch this."

Grip looked down the tee where Eddie was now hitting low seven irons into the wind.

"Hey, Street. How far do you hit that club normally?"

"I hit my seven 155 to 158 on a normal day," replied Eddie.

"Can you hit it 170?"

"Yeah, but I might hurt myself, and my shot pattern would suffer. It won't be nearly as tight as my 155-yard normal swing. If I have to hit it farther, I take a longer club. This game is about technique first, then power. If you don't have the technique, all that power is just going to get you into trouble. You don't get bonus points for hitting less club out there. This is a thinking man's game."

"Okay," said Grip. "We're out of here, kid. Now you know what it feels like to square up the clubface. Work on it, and don't squeeze the club too hard. Hold it like you're holding your girlfriend's...."

"Time to go," interrupted Eddie, as he picked up his bag and headed for the car.

When Grip climbed into the passenger seat, Eddie was staring at him.

"What?"

"Like you're holding your girl's… He's only fourteen, dude. What were you thinking?"

"That's all I could think of, man. I hope he doesn't tell his mom about that. She'll think were perverts."

"Not we, you. Watch your mouth next time. Hey, is he a great kid, or what?"

"He's a great kid, Street," said Grip wistfully, as he looked out his window. "And he's going to be a fine golfer someday."

* * *

Wilson hit every club in his bag, but had to quit when it got too dark to see. While a lot of his classmates were hanging out and having a good time on a Friday night, he was pedaling furiously home to get his household chores done before his mom got off of work. His new clubs and bag were locked in the range equipment building with an old tarp thrown over them. One couldn't be too careful with equipment like that. The next morning he showed up at 7:00 and the range was already full with a few golfers in the wings waiting for an open spot. The kid went back and forth, picking up baskets and filling divots with sand. On Eddie's suggestion, he kept a wet towel handy to clean off the golfer's clubs when they were done hitting. A few of them even tipped him. One guy stayed on the range after the others left for their shotgun start. Wilson walked down and watched him hit.

"Damn, kid," said the guy, looking over at Wilson. "I'm supposed to be playing in this scramble today, but I won't be any help to my team with this big banana ball. I don't play much, but this is embarrassing. You got any advice for an old duffer?"

"Well," explained Wilson. "A really good golfer once told me that you need to feel like you're going to hit the ball with the toe of the club. You won't really hit it with the toe, but sometimes you have to exaggerate to get the results you're looking for. When the ball slices it means you're not squaring the clubface up. That little tip really helped me."

Wilson walked away to let the man work on what he just told him. He checked the gas in the cart that pushed the ball picker and saw that it was about empty. He unhooked the picker and headed over to the gas tank to fill up. When he got back the man was gone. He wondered if Grip's tip helped the guy out as much as it did with his own ball striking.

Around 1:00, Wilson was sitting in the grill eating lunch, when the guy he gave the tip to on the range walked up to him.

"Son, your tip worked wonders for me today. I'm no scratch golfer, but I didn't embarrass myself out there, either. Only lost three balls, which is pretty good for me. Thanks again. Lunch is on me." The man dropped a ten-dollar bill on the table and walked away.

Wilson was about to say something when the Stonehedge pro called his name and motioned for him to come over.

"Giving lessons out there, I see," said the pro. "We have a policy here that whenever a staff member gets paid for a golf tip, they have to split it with the pro."

Wilson wasn't sure if the pro was kidding or not. It was only ten bucks. He started to reach into his pocket, when the pro grabbed his arm.

"I was just kidding, man," said the pro laughing. "Word has gotten back to me that you're doing a great job out there. The range is looking good and the golfers tell me you are polite and you take your job seriously. If you're ready to take on a little more responsibility, I'll tell the course superintendent that you are available to do some mowing out on the course. He needs to pull some of his guys off their mowers to get some other stuff done. It'll probably just be the roughs. That's where the new guys usually start. By the way, you'll make more money when you're mowing. Okay?"

"Sounds good to me," said Will, beaming.

* * *

"C'mon, kid," hollered Street from his cart. "Jump in, Grip's waiting for us on the tenth tee."

It was mid October and the range at Stonehedge was doing very little business. Will's time spent mowing roughs was also way down, as the grass wasn't growing very fast this time of year. This meant that he had a lot of time to practice. His progress was nothing short of remarkable. Grip told him that by the end of the season he should be able to hit five out of ten practice shots the way he wanted to. He was up to seven when the two hustlers turned teachers showed up that afternoon.

Wilson grabbed his clubs and joined Street in the cart. Eddie drove through the tunnel that ran under the highway and over to the tenth tee on the North course. Wilson had played the South course a few times, but had never played the north layout. As an employee, he could play for nothing, but he really didn't have time during the week, and the busy weekend play kept him occupied at the range.

His heart was pumping when he hit his tee shot on number ten. He made solid contact and was only about thirty yards behind Street's low draw and Grip's straight as an arrow tee shot.

The kid was having the time of his life. He was playing golf on a beautiful course with a couple of great golfers that also happened to be real characters. They talked smack all the way around and offered course management tips to their young protégé. The last hole made a real impression on Wilson. Before they hit, Street explained how he and Grip were going to play the hole. He would hit his tee shot, and if he had a good lie in the fairway, he would probably hit his driver off the short grass, trying to get as close to the green as he could. Grip would play the hole differently. He would hit whatever he had to hit to have a third shot of about 100 yards. He had a lot of confidence in his wedges and from 100 yards out he was almost unbeatable.

"You need to play your tee shot here a little farther right than normal," explained Eddie. "That left-hand trap is no place to be. Then, depending on your lie, hit your 5-wood or a medium iron down the fairway. Hopefully, you will then be about 150 or so from the green. A smooth 6-iron should put you on the front edge. You can try to crush it when your timing gets better. Right now, just play it smart. Do you know how you stand, scorewise?"

"Not really," answered Wilson. "I'm not doing too bad. I made a triple and a double, but I've also made a few pars."

"You're two over bogey," said Grip. "What kind of scores have you been shooting on the south course?"

"Low to mid-fifties. I keep making too many mistakes, and then I get mad at myself, and that just makes it worse. How do you guys keep your cool when things are falling apart?"

"You'll get better at handling your emotions," said Grip. "It will come with experience. You just have to take a couple of deep breaths and focus on the next shot. Do what you can do and don't try to do more than that. Stay in your comfort zone."

Wilson was all smiles as they walked off the eighteenth green. His playing partners made birdies and he was pretty sure they both had broken par. He had just bogeyed eighteen for a 48. It was by far the lowest score he had ever shot. When they got to their carts the two old guys messed around in their bags for a while, then they came out with two boxes. They handed them to Wilson with big grins on their faces.

"Happy birthday, kid," said Grip, handing him his box.

Wilson opened up Grip's box and saw three shirts with the club logo on them. Eddie's box had two windshirts in it.

"How did you know it was my birthday?" asked Wilson.

"Grip found out," said Street. "He's got connections."

"You guys have done so much for me," said Wilson, trying hard to keep his composure. "I can't thank you enough."

"You're a good kid," said Street. "A hard worker like you deserves a break now and then. Keep it up. You're making great progress. Next year at this time, you should be breaking 40. Then it gets a lot tougher and a lot more fun."

"He's right," added Grip. "Next year we'll play at least once a week together. Before you know it, you'll be giving us strokes."

"Not hardly," said Wilson. "You two are the best golfers I've ever seen."

"Well, you're not going to see us for a while," said Street. "I'm heading to Florida and then to Texas for a good part of the winter. My daughters live there. Grip spends most of his winter in Chicago hanging around with unsavory types at the race track."

"He's exaggerating," said Grip. "I'll be going back and forth from my home in Richland to Chicago, and I usually spend about six weeks around San Diego. The weather is always great there. I'm going to give you my cell phone number if there's anything I can do for you. You know what you need to do? Find a place where you can hit balls this winter. If you have a big enough room, you can hang blankets over a clothesline. That should keep you from breaking any windows."

The guys dropped the kid back off at the driving range and shook hands with him. Street was a little surprised when Grip also hugged the kid. It even looked like he got a little misty. He figured it must be because Grip had lost his only son and being around the kid brought back memories when his son, Rob, was that age.

* * *

Wilson wore one of his new golf shirts to school a few days later and wasn't prepared for the reception he got.

"What do we have here?" asked Troy Feltner, sophomore and number one player on the high school team. "The range boy is dressing like a real golfer. Little missy, you have to be able to actually hit the ball if you're going to wear a cool shirt like that. Did the guy at the pro shop know that you were going to wear this thing in public?" A few of the guys standing around snickered at Troy's comments. "Just because you pick up and wash our practice balls, does not make you a golfer."

The golf team hit practice balls at least once a week at the Stonehedge range. Wilson usually made himself scarce when they showed up. He would take a couple of shag bags and walk the perimeter picking up balls that the picker couldn't get. On more than one occasion he thought Troy and a couple of his close buddies were hitting at him when their coach wasn't looking. For guys that were supposed to be decent golfers, they sure seemed to be wild at times. Wilson didn't have any classes with Troy, but their lockers were fairly close together, making it hard to avoid him entirely.

Melissa Perkins, fellow freshman and the best female golfer in school, was standing nearby. She went over to Troy after he made his comments and appeared to be chastising him. Wilson felt a surge of gratitude until he saw her walk away with Troy holding his hand. The life of a high school student definitely had its ups and downs.

On the upside, Wilson's neighbor said he could hit balls out of his pole barn into the large grassy area behind it. It was the same field that Wilson used when it was warm. All he had to do was slide the door open wide enough to hit out into the field. He now had about 500 balls in his arsenal, so he went out in the snow about once a week to pick them up. It was a lot better than hitting into hanging blankets, as Grip had suggested. He could actually see the flight of the ball this way. A propane heater kept the temperature tolerable. The ball didn't go as far in the cold, but that wasn't a problem. On his last trip to Kalamazoo to go shopping with his mom, he stopped at Bobick's Golf Discount store and bought one of those mats with artificial grass on it. It had simulated fairway grass and taller stuff to make it feel like you were hitting out of the rough. When he wasn't studying or doing his chores he devoured as many instruction books that he could get his hands on. He loved hitting balls by himself and listening to music on an old radio that he had salvaged from one of the trash cans out on the course. Some of the guys liked to listen to baseball or football games while they played in the afternoon, and they probably pitched the radio when it stopped working. Upon inspection, the contacts for the batteries were all corroded, but the power cord was still in a little side compartment. He took it home and plugged it in and it worked just fine. For some reason, listening to tunes made him feel like someone else was there with him as he practiced. One thing was certain; the guys were going to be surprised when they got back in the spring.

* * *

Melissa was the most beautiful girl that Will had ever seen. Well, at least the most beautiful one that he had ever talked to. She always seemed to be in a great mood. He couldn't ever remember a time when she appeared to be grumpy or moody.

Wilson was the first man to come off the bench on the fresh/soph basketball team. He used to love basketball, but now it was just something to do until the weather warmed up and he could play golf again. After a home game in late January, he headed for the boys' locker room to get a notebook that he had left in his locker.

Melissa was standing outside the locker room looking impatient. She was her normal gorgeous self. She had on a white sweater and a dark blue skirt. Her hair was pulled back in a ponytail and held in place with a matching blue hair tie. His heart rate started to speed up as he got nearer. She must be waiting for Troy. He was a varsity starter on a sub .500 team. If you asked him, he would tell you that he was major college material. He had a better chance playing big time golf. He carried about a five handicap, which meant he normally shot any where from 75 to 80. Not bad for this area, but it wouldn't get him a scholarship at Michigan State. Wilson had heard that Western Michigan University, in Kalamazoo, was interested in him.

"Hi, Wilson," said Melissa in a voice that made the kid's knees wobble. "If you're going in there would you tell Troy that I'm out here waiting for him?"

"Sure, Melissa," responded Wilson, as he opened the locker room door. Once he was inside he smelled something like leaves burning. Wilson had never smoked anything, but he knew what that smell was.

"Hey, Troy," hollered Wilson, "if you're in here, Melissa is waiting outside."

"Stall her, dude," hollered Troy from the shower area. His giggle was cut short by a round of coughing. "Tell her I'll be out in a couple of minutes. Thanks, man."

Wilson got his notebook from his locker and headed back out to face Melissa. Troy was incredibly stupid. If he got caught smoking weed on school grounds, he would be expelled. Goodbye rest of basketball season and goodbye high school golf—maybe goodbye scholarship.

"Uh, he said he'd be out in a couple of minutes," was all Wilson could come up with.

"What's he doing in there?" asked Melissa. "We're supposed to go out for pizza with some friends, and we're already late."

Wilson shook his head and started to walk away. Troy was such a jerk. He decided to do something that he might regret later. He walked back to Melissa and looked her right in the eyes.

"Melissa, it's none of my business, but I think you could do a whole lot better. I'm just saying."

Before she could answer, and before Troy came out, he turned and walked briskly away.

Melissa just stood there and stared at his back as he disappeared around the corner.

CHAPTER FOURTEEN

Vacation Action

Ronnie Green can take care of himself. He's not a brawler by any sense of the imagination, but I showed him a few moves and he took to them real quick. Besides, if he gets into real trouble, he can just come to me. I owe the guy.

—Tyrell Franklin, heavyweight contender/part-time enforcer

Spring always shows up on its own terms in the Midwest. If it was up to Wilson, spring would closely follow Christmas.

Wilson had thoughts about trying out for the golf team. Melissa's season was already over, as the girls played in the fall. He thought her best round was a 43, which wasn't too bad for a high school freshman. He remembered her swing as being somewhat loose with a lot of unnecessary action. *She scores better than me,* he thought, *but I'm already critiquing her swing. On the downside, if I went out for the team I wouldn't be able to keep my range job, at least during the season, and I'd have to put up with three years of humiliation from Troy. Grip and Street said they'd play at least once a week with me next year. I like hanging around those two old guys, and I'd learn a whole lot more from them anyway. Hey, maybe I'll become a hustler, like them. That would be a cool way to make a living—stressful, but cool. I'm sure mom would be all for it—not!*

Money continued to be tight at the Randall household. Business at the restaurant where his mom worked was down. She said it was the economy. Not as many people were eating out like they used to. Wilson helped out by shoveling walks and doing odd jobs around Hickory Corners. Once it warmed up he could start making some real money again at the practice range and working out on the course. Basketball season had just ended when Wilson got a call from the pro at Gull Lake View. The pro asked him if he wanted to work a couple of nights a week babysitting. Apparently there were two card clubs that played at the GLV clubhouse, and their regular sitter had come down with mono. It was easier for the moms just to bring their kids along. All the sitter had to do was watch and play with about eight kids that ranged from three to nine years-old in one of the banquet rooms that was adjacent to the bar and grill. Wilson wasn't sure until the pro mentioned he would make about thirty-five to forty dollars for the three hours he would be there. Each parent would throw in five bucks for the sitter. The deal clincher was that transportation would be provided. Some of the card players lived at Fine Lake and they had to come through Hickory Corners to get to the GLV clubhouse.

The babysitting job was only going to last five more weeks, but the money was greatly appreciated. Everything was going fine until Troy got wind of what Wilson was up to.

"You've got to be kidding me," said Troy, as he walked up behind Wilson in the hallway. "You wash golf balls in the summer and now you wash baby's butts in the winter. Don't you have any pride? It must be hell to be poor."

Before Wilson could answer, Melissa walked up, smiling at both of them.

"Hi guys," she said in her normal perky voice. She was a little too late to hear Troy's latest putdown. "Wilson, did you know that you can go to prom if a junior or senior girl asks you? If you're interested, I can mention your name to a couple of girls that haven't decided what they're going to do yet. Troy's friend, Shawn, and his girlfriend are juniors, so they each asked us to go. Pretty slick, huh? It was Troy's idea."

"Uh, I'll think about it, okay? I'm not much of a dancer."

"Yeah, stud," snarled Troy. "You think about it. I'm sure there are lots of girls that would be honored to have you as a date." His sarcastic sneer disappeared as Melissa stormed off. "Now see what you've done, range boy? She's pissed, and it's your fault. Way to go."

Wilson watched as Troy hurried off to catch up with Melissa. He couldn't figure out why she liked such an obnoxious jerk. So his dad was a big cement contractor and they had lots of money. In his book, character and honor were more important than money any old day. Now Wilson had an extra incentive to become an accomplished golfer. Some day he was going to beat Troy Feltner and that was going to be one sweet day. He would trounce the superstar, and then Melissa would come up and throw her arms around him…

"Willy," said one of his freshman classmates, snapping his fingers in Wilson's face. "What did I tell you about spending too much time in your happy place? Besides, if you're doing something illegal in there, you could be arrested. These security cameras do more than just record images."

"Yeah," said the guy next to him. "These cameras can read your thoughts, man. And you might have just been busted for thinking nasty thoughts about Melissa Perkins. Get her out of your head. She's poisoning your mind. It aint gonna happen. Not now, not ever."

"You dorks sure know how to bust a guy's bubble," said Wilson as they headed down the hall. "C'mon, let's get to class."

* * *

Eddie sat in the clubhouse at a municipal course in Dallas, Texas where he was visiting his daughter and her family. Eddie knew he was welcome at her home, but he didn't want to be a nuisance, so he spent a lot of time practicing or playing if the weather was decent. Several guys at the course knew who he was, and they were always on the lookout to get him into a money match with some unsuspecting guys who weren't aware of Eddie's skills. The Detroit hustler was drinking a beer with some buddies after a nice sociable round where only a few bucks changed hands. His game was a little rough when he showed up, but after some serious practice, he was back to his old self. He had just shot 67 and, even though he had to give a boatload of strokes to these yahoos, he ended up fifteen bucks to the good.

The talk at his table now ran the gamut of subjects, from sports, to politics, to cars. It was hard to hear each other. It wasn't because they were drinking and everybody was talking louder than normal. It was because one guy at the next table was dominating the conversation, and he wasn't using his inside voice.

"Ya'll would have a decent course here," said the loudmouth, "if you built some more traps and moved several of your tees back. Hell, I drive number six about half the time when I'm here. That should be a par three and a half. You've got a lot of nerve calling it a par four. I own that hole, boys."

Eddie's eyes narrowed to slits, as he motioned for Cleon to give him the pencil that he had just used to tally the bets. Cleon smiled and rolled the pencil over. The gambler scribbled a bunch of figures down and, after a bit, broke into a grin. The guys at his table were looking at him, anticipating that something was up. They sensed that things were about to get interesting. Eddie gave his buddies a "watch this" look and went over to the guy.

"Excuse me, sir," said Eddie, putting on a nervous front. His group was elbowing themselves back at their table. "I couldn't help but overhearing your assessment of hole number six and I…"

"I don't believe I caught your name," said the loudmouth, extending his hand.

"I'm sorry," responded the hustler, as he gave the man a limp handshake. "Name's Eddie. I come down from Michigan in the winter to play with some of these jokers."

"A Yankee, huh?" asked the guy that introduced himself as Ken.

Eddie gave the guy a sheepish grin. "Yeah, I guess I am. I've got some relatives around here, though."

"So what, does that make you, what, a three-quarter Yankee? Buddy, if you're not a southerner, then you're a Yankee. What do you want, anyway?"

"Well, I've got a proposition for you."

"Really? What kind of proposition?"

"Well, I heard you say that you own number six and you drive it about half of the time," continued Eddie, as he dangled his hook.

"Yeah, I said that, and it's true. It aint that hard of a hole if you're a big hitter like me."

Eddie brought a chair over from the next table and sat down. "Tell you what, Ken," said the hustler, changing his tone and his demeanor. "I don't think you can hit that green from the tee half of the time, and I'm willing to put up some dough to back my opinion."

"Is this some kind of joke that those hacks put you up to?" asked Ken, nodding toward the guys at Eddie's table.

"No, man," said Eddie. "I just figured you were the type of guy that would back up what he said he could do. You know, some guys are all talk. What's that saying that Texans like to use, 'big hat, no cattle'? How about this—you give me ten bucks a ball, hit 100 balls, and I'll give you twenty-five bucks for every ball you hit on the green. If you hit half of the balls on, like you claim, I'll have to give you $1250 back. Do better than fifty percent, and you can really get into my pockets. Heck, I'd be willing to pay to see a guy put on a driving exhibition like that."

The rest of the guys at Ken's table sat quietly, trying to verify Eddie's math. Ken looked like he was deep in thought. Did this guy have some angle that he couldn't see?

"I don't know," said Ken, minus the bravado that he was exhibiting earlier. He was tempted, but he wanted a bigger edge.

Eddie was ready for him and when Ken hesitated he sweetened the pot.

"Thirty bucks for every ball you hit on. You hit half of them on and I'll be giving you back 1500 bucks. You in, or was that just talk that we were hearing over at our table?"

"Do it, Ken," said one of the guys at his table. "You drove that green today and almost made a deuce. You can make some cash off of this guy."

"It's supposed to be a fairly calm day tomorrow," said Eddie. "What do you say? Tomorrow around noon would be a good time. We put one of your guys and one of my guys by the green with a radio to verify the results. You give me the grand, and I'll pay up after every ball you hit on the green."

"Let's do it," hollered Ken, slamming his hand on the table. "Yankee, you better bring a ton of cash tomorrow. I'm going to need a wheelbarrow to cart it off. Tomorrow at noon. I'll go talk to the pro, so he can give us the hole for about an hour. It aint that busy around here at noontime during the week. He can squeeze people off the back if he has to."

Ken went over to the pro shop to talk to the pro. Eddie went back to his table and sat down. He could have wandered over to the shop to make sure there was no funny business going on. Sure enough, after getting permission to hold the contest, Ken slipped the pro a twenty and asked him to tell the course superintendent not to mow the sixth green. That might keep a few balls from rolling off the back. The pro looked over Ken's shoulder and met Eddie's gaze. He and Street went way back. Eddie gave him a slight nod. Let the guy think he had an advantage.

"All right," said one of Eddie's buddies, after Ken's table cleared out. "What are you thinkin'? We know you've got some kind of angle here. You always do. That guy hits a long ball. I don't think they were lyin' when they said he drove number six today."

"He might have and he might not have," said Eddie. When he got no response he sat back with a smug look on his face. "Let's say I hit my tee shot on six on to the fringe—hole high. Then I sink the putt for a deuce. What would I say when you asked me how I played that hole today?"

"I get it," came the response. "You would say you drove the green and made the putt for an eagle. But, you really didn't drive the green. You drove the fringe."

"Exactly. In my mind I drove the green, but technically, I drove the short grass next to the green. You'll notice I always said, 'drive the green' when I was laying things out for Ken. It would have made him think a little more if I would have said, 'drive the putting surface'. There's a huge difference. Also, don't you think after he hits about fifty balls he won't be tired and start pressing? He's not that big of a guy, which means he's swinging hard all the time. On a normal day, when he gets to that hole during his round he's probably pretty fresh, 'cause he's only played five holes up to then, and because of the par three, he's only swung the driver four times. Tomorrow will be different. I guarantee his shirt will be soaked before we're done."

* * *

Everyone was in place at noon the next day. There were about twenty guys hanging around the sixth tee when Eddie and one of his buddies pulled up in a cart. The weather was as predicted, calm and sunny. Ken had foolishly hit half a large bucket warming up on the practice range. He walked over to Eddie and handed him ten one hundred dollar bills. Obviously Ken hadn't thought of how Eddie was going to pay him back when he hit one on the green. Eddie just smiled and shook his head. The poker player in him had read Ken perfectly. Always thinking, Eddie had stopped at the bank earlier and was now carrying 400 in tens and twenties. He figured that would be more than enough. Several of the guys on the tee were placing their own bets. One even offered a smaller version of Eddie's creation—a dollar for every ball hit and then three back if it ended up on the green. The spotters down by the green radioed back that they were ready.

Ken hit four balls out of the first ten onto the green and had received $120 for his efforts. He was loose and all smiles, kidding with his buddies on the tee. He told them to pay attention, because he was just getting warmed up. Eddie sat silently in his cart and smoked a cigar. Ken hit ball number eleven, and it looked good too.

"Hole high, but a foot off the green," came the response over the radio. "Two feet off the back and about six feet short," was the report on the next two balls.

Ken started to press and matters got worse. After he hit ball number thirty, he said he wanted to take a break. He had not scored on even one ball in the last twenty drives. After a brief rest, he hit twenty more. Only one found the putting surface, giving him a half way total of five out of fifty. The reports coming back on the radio described several shots that were close to the green, but not on the actual putting surface. He fared a little better on the second fifty, getting home twelve times. Out of the $1000 dollars that he gave Eddie at the beginning, only $510 found its way back into his pocket. Eddie was now holding $490 of Ken's money. Ken was soaking wet after taking 100 full out swipes at the ball. His last twenty swings were painful. His back and shoulders were aching and he had a terrific headache. Most guys would have been somewhat humbled, but not Ken. He was upset that a Yankee had played him for a fool.

"That's better than you could have done, Yankee," he said, pointing his driver at Eddie. "Even if you were twenty years younger."

"I never was a long ball hitter like you, so you're probably right," commented the Detroit hustler. "However, I am a reasonable man. What do you say we play a round tomorrow for a hundred? I'll give you four-to-one odds. It'll give you a chance to get most of your money back."

"I was heading back home to Houston tonight," said Ken, as he considered Eddie's offer. "Okay, I'll stick around another day, but only if you give me a stroke a side. I hear you're pretty good for a Yan…a northerner."

"See you here at ten tomorrow," said Eddie, as he motioned for his buddy to drive off.

A day and a half later, Ken headed back to Houston $590 lighter. His 77 was no match for Eddie's 69. The hustler headed back to his daughter's house after his match with Ken. He had decided to give each of his grandkids $100 from his winnings and then take them all out to dinner. But before they went out to eat, he had a softball game to catch. Right after Jimmy Smith died, Eddie found out that his friend had made him executor of his two daughters' trust funds. Jimmy's oldest daughter, Margie, was now over twenty-one, so she had full control of her portion. His youngest, Annie, was only seventeen, so she still had four years until it would be hers to do what she wanted with it. He had taken in several of Annie's games and was impressed with her athletic abilities. She was a junior in high school and she appeared to be a girl with a good head on her shoulders. After today's game, he planned on introducing himself. He figured it would be tearful event for both of them, but he wanted to talk to her and tell her how proud her dad was of her. She was getting a check for $300 every month with his signature on it. Now it was time to meet her, and if he had to admit it, he would say he was a little apprehensive.

On the drive to Reston, a small town north of Fort Worth where Annie lived, he thought about what he was going to say to her.

* * *

Eddie sat in the bleachers behind home plate and came to the conclusion that Jimmy Smith's youngest daughter was one of the best softball players he had ever seen. He was amazed by her skills, as she appeared to have no weaknesses on offense or defense. A couple of her teammates looked like they knew what they were doing also. With one more inning to go, his phone started to vibrate in his front pocket. He got up and walked over to a spot where he wouldn't bother anyone and took the call. His daughter was on the other end and she needed him to come home immediately. Eddie's two-year-old granddaughter was running a fever and, since her husband was out of town, she wanted him to watch the four-year-old while she took the younger one to the doctor. Eddie said he would hustle back. As he left he saw a good-sized high school kid staring at him. From the few games he had attended, he knew that the kid was the shortstop's boyfriend. The little shortstop and the first baseman appeared to be Annie's best friends. His meeting with Jimmy's daughter would have to wait for another day.

* * *

Ronnie sat on the beach near San Diego and looked out at the Pacific Ocean. He rated the white crest of waves against an azure sea a close second to a few of the gorgeous courses he had experienced back in Chicago and Michigan. The white sand and the cobalt sky up above with its breezes and fresh smells was nature at its finest. Everything seemed so peaceful at this time of day. It was easy to understand why the people visiting and living in Key West would stop what they were doing just to watch the sun take its leave at the end of another day. He came to this particular spot often. Thoughts of his late wife and son filled his head. He had never taken Rob to the ocean, but they had spent a great deal of time together on the beaches of Lake Michigan. Throwing a Frisbee on the beach with his wife, Lois, and Rob was one of his favorite things to do. It was a simple activity, but they all got a big kick out of it.

Ronnie thought back a few months earlier when Eddie asked Wilson where his dad was. Wilson looked down at the ground and said he was a soldier and he was killed in the Middle East somewhere. Ronnie had to turn away so they couldn't see the anguish in his eyes. Even though it was dozen years ago, it still hurt when he thought about his son, Robbie.

He thought seriously about calling his daughter-in-law to see if her feelings toward him had changed. The woman flat out hated him, and in her mind, she had a good reason to. Rob knew that his dad didn't think his wife was good enough for him, but he figured he would change his mind when Ronnie saw what type of person she really was. Rob's wife had a police record, because of a shoplifting charge when she was sixteen, and he hoped Ronnie would let that go over time. Ronnie's biggest problem was that Carol had lied to Rob about being on the pill when they were both seniors in high school. Ronnie saw this as the old, 'I'm going to get pregnant so he will have to marry me,' ploy that has been used to some degree of success over the years. He felt his son deserved better and told him so, on numerous occasions. Looking back, he wished he had acted differently. He just wanted the best for his son. Now it really didn't matter.

Ronnie's sobs were muffled by the waves as they crashed onto the beach. The ache in his heart seemed to be with him constantly. Most of the time he did a good job of covering it up, but the worst of it was when he was alone, and for some reason, by the water. He looked up and saw a lady about his age standing in front of him. He wondered how long she had been standing there. There was a huge black Lab on the other end of the leash in her hand.

"Are you all right, sir?" asked the woman in a concerned voice.

Ronnie wiped his eyes with the back of his hands and stood. The woman in front of him had medium length blond hair and a warm smile. Under her loose fitting white shirt was a one-piece swimsuit. Her dog came over to check Ronnie out when he stood up. He reached down and scratched him behind the ears. The dog tilted his head to show his approval.

"I'm fine," said Ronnie. "Just doing some reminiscing and it got to me for a minute. Thanks for asking…"

"Marilyn," said the lady extending her hand. "Marilyn De Salvo."

"I'm Ronnie Costas," said Ronnie, taking her smaller hand in his. She had a firm handshake for a woman.

"Let me guess, a lost family member?"

"Yeah," he answered, looking out at the ocean. "Wife and son. It's been over ten years, but I still miss them. Some things just don't go away over time. They say they do, but not in my case."

"I know what you mean," said Marilyn. "I lost my husband five years ago, but it seems like only yesterday. Would you like to walk a bit, Ronnie? Reggie and I would enjoy your company."

"I have a friend back in Chicago named Reggie," said Ronnie as they walked along the beach. "Good golfer and an even better bowler. He's quite a character." *And that s.o.b. still owes me fifty bucks if I remember correctly*, thought Ronnie.

"So what do you do, Ron?" asked Marilyn. "You're much too young to be retired."

"I'm a semi-retired golfer," answered Ronnie, a little surprised at her straightforwardness.

"So, you're like a tour pro?"

"No, never played the tour. I just play for a little cash now and then. It's what I've always done."

They walked down the beach and made small talk. Marilyn let Reggie go and he bounded in and out of the water. They both laughed when a wave toppled him and he came up sputtering with a confused look on his face. Ronnie decided that she was getting a feel for him by asking some personal questions. These days a woman couldn't be too careful. He could be a serial killer wandering the beach looking for fresh victims.

Marilyn decided that Ronnie didn't look like a serial killer. She also decided that he didn't look like a golfer either. He did, however, appear to be a successful guy—maybe a guy with some money in his pockets. When they were opposite a large house with an immense patio, Reggie ran through the open gate and jumped up on a couch.

"Hey," hollered Ronnie. "Give me his leash and I'll go get him, Marilyn."

She laughed and said it was okay. It was the only piece of outdoor furniture that he was allowed on. Marilyn went through the gate and motioned for Ronnie to follow. Now he was thinking maybe she was a serial killer and he was going to be her next victim. She told him to make himself comfortable while she made drinks.

"I pegged you for a Scotch drinker," said Marilyn over her shoulder, as she went through the doors into the house. He knew he shouldn't, but he watched her hips sway as she walked to the door. She reappeared a few minutes later with a drink in each hand. She handed him one of them. "My late husband was a Johnnie Walker Black drinker. I hope that's all right."

"That's fine," said Ronnie, as he accepted the drink. *Eddie is not going to believe this, thought Ronnie. I'm sitting here with a beautiful woman by the ocean and she hands me a Johnnie Walker. And from the looks of her house, she has a lot of dough. Careful, Grip, don't let your aging hormones get the best of you. You're not a teenager anymore. Let's be thinking with the head between your shoulders and not with the one between your legs.*

"So," said Marilyn, "tell me what a guy who plays golf, but not professionally, really does for a living. I hope I'm not being too nosey, but you sound like an interesting guy."

Ronnie raised his glass to his lips, and before he took his first sip, alarms went off in his head. Something wasn't right with this scenario. A good-looking middle-aged woman appears out of nowhere in a bathing suit, and they walk down the beach to her beautiful home. Then she invites him, a total stranger, onto the patio for a drink. He knew that he appeared somewhat vulnerable, sitting out there on the sand sobbing like a little kid. He was wearing cargo shorts with lots of pockets in them—pockets that could hold something of value, like cash or credit cards. The Chicago hustler was somewhat embarrassed that he didn't catch on sooner. He deftly put his finger between the glass and his lips, pretending to take a drink. He set the drink down on the patio tile and bent over to retie his shoe. Before he picked it back up, he discreetly dumped about half of his drink off to the side into the sand. The sun had disappeared below the water line and it was just light enough to see two shadowy figures jogging out by the water.

They made small talk for a few more minutes, while Ronnie searched her face for some small sign of deceit. Maybe he was being too careful. Naw, with his looks, this sort of thing just didn't happen—maybe to Eddie, but not to him. He decided to make his move.

"Uh, I'm not feeling so good, Marilyn. I'm going to walk out on the beach for a minute."

"I hope your drink wasn't too strong, love," said the woman, feigning concern.

Ronnie walked through the open gate and pretended to stumble, knocking a hurricane lamp full of oil onto the white patio floor. When he was about ten yards from the gate, out of the corner of his eye, he saw Marilyn get up from her chair and go into the house. He immediately started jogging at a fast pace toward the public lot where his car was parked.

Marilyn stepped into the house and addressed the man that was standing there. "He went back out to the beach. Go get him. He won't get far. Make it look like he's had too much to drink if anyone sees you. Just get him back here."

For a guy that was 55, Ronnie was in great shape. He jogged a few miles three times a week in the summer and, like Eddie, he got out of the cart and walked another couple of miles when they played. The guy coming up behind him was no early evening jogger. Ronnie glanced over his shoulder and got a shadowy glimpse of his pursuer. The man's shirt and long pants looked out of place where the dress of choice was almost no dress at all. When Ronnie gauged the younger man to be two strides behind, he stopped abruptly and dropped to one knee. Before the pursuer could come to a complete stop, Ronnie slammed his fist into the man's stomach. Then he caught the guy in an uppercut to the jaw as he sprung back to his feet. The punch was backed by his legs as they straightened, which gave it tremendous power. He heard something crack, like maybe the guy's jaw was broken. It should be, because his hand hurt like hell. Ronnie looked around in the semi-darkness and didn't see anyone else on the beach. He quickly searched the man, who appeared to be out cold. He found a gun in a side holster and after checking that the safety was on, stuffed it into one of the lower pockets of his shorts. Next, he found the man's wallet and took out his driver's license and put that in a pocket as well.

"Southside Chicago, asshole," said Ronnie, looking over his shoulder, as he started to run back to his car.

Ronnie parked his borrowed car and went into the house where he had been staying for the past few weeks. The owner was an old friend and the Chicago native had a standing invitation to stay any time and as long as he wanted to. Sometimes he didn't see his host for days. The house had eight bedrooms, with a cook, a maid and a gardener. *Help a guy out with his golf game and you shall be rewarded*, thought Ronnie, the first time he stayed there. Ronnie packed his clothes, left a thank you note explaining that he had urgent business back home and called a cab for the airport. He had no idea who those people on the beach were, but he didn't want to take any chances. It was about time to head home anyway.

Fifteen hours later he was sitting in Herman's office drinking coffee.

* * *

"I called a guy I know in the San Diego Police Department," said Herman, looking up from his cluttered desk.

"There have been some strange disappearances in the beach area that you were at. Hopefully this will give them something to go on. The red oil stain from the lamp on the patio should be helpful, since we don't have an actual address. That was quick thinking. The driver's license might not be legit, but you did your part. I think if you had taken that drink, you would be on that missing persons list. It was probably Rufalin, or what's commonly called the date rape drug, and it's powerful stuff. What made you suspicious?"

"It all just seemed too good to be true," said Ronnie. "And it didn't hit me until I was about to take my first sip. What a rotten lady. I hope they catch her and the punks working with her."

"So, you want some more coffee?" asked Herman, as he leaned back in his chair.

"Naw, I'm good," said Ronnie, standing and offering his hand. "Hey, thanks for making the calls. I'm heading back to Michigan. Give the family my best. Keep me informed on the particulars of this year's tourney. I'm sure Eddie and I will be the senior favorite, so the odds on us will suck. But, thirty grand up front is nothing to sneeze at."

Herman took Ronnie's hand and then pulled him in close for a quick hug. When Ronnie was half way to the door, Herman laid a serious question on him.

"So, have you told Wilson that he's your grandson?"

Ronnie did an about face and came slowly back to the chair he was sitting in before. Herman signaled to his secretary that they both needed another cup of coffee. Nothing was said until it arrived. Ronnie held his cup with both hands and took a sip, collecting his thoughts.

"Okay," he started. "I thought about telling him the second time I saw him. But then I changed my mind. It's obvious that his mother still hates me with a passion. As you know, we never got along all that well, and I know she held me responsible for Rob's last tour in Iraq. I guess she felt that I was supposed to talk him out of it, and when I didn't, she put all the blame on me. She wouldn't even talk to me at the funeral. If there were any pictures in their house of Rob and me or of Wilson and me when he was a baby, he would have recognized me, but he didn't. I'm two sizes more in the waist than I was twelve years ago, but other than that, I look pretty much the same. He was not even two the last time he saw me up close, so I was like any other stranger to him when we ran into each other on the course last summer. He has turned out to be a really neat kid."

"Did you expect anything different from Robbie Green's son?" asked Herman.

"No, I guess I didn't. A few years ago when you located him and his mother for me, I knew exactly what I wanted to do. I just wanted to be close by so I could see him on a regular basis. You know, be in the crowd at his basketball games—that sort of stuff. I went to a few games this past winter and sat in the corner of the bleachers. I never saw Carol. She works the evening shift waiting tables at a nice restaurant in Battle Creek. He doesn't look like the athlete that Rob was, but he sure can swing the golf club. He's heard Eddie call me by my first name a couple of times, but the kid has always called me Grip. I'm sure that's what he told his mother my name was. She has no idea that's what some people call me, so that has worked out in my favor."

"When are you going to face up to this little 100-pound woman?" asked Herman.

"If I do, and she still harbors all this hate for me, even after all these years, she could forbid him to see me. I think we'll just cruise along the way we've been doing. We told him we would play at least once a week with him this summer. I'll stop by every week at the range to work with him on his game, too. She doesn't need to know that it's me. When the time is right, I'll tell him. I just hope he will understand my reasons for not letting him know sooner."

"All right, Ronnie," said Herman, shaking his head. "I hope it works out the way you want it to. The kid needs a father figure, that's for sure. Statistics show that it's one of the main factors in keeping young boys out of trouble."

"I'll be there for him, Herm," said Ronnie. "This way, he'll have a friend and a grandfather."

CHAPTER FIFTEEN

Horseplayer

> *Unlike the casino suits, racetrack management doesn't get mad or suspicious when you win a few bucks. It's the undesirable element that often congregates at the track that you have to watch out for. I used to carry one of those bubble wrap envelopes addressed to me folded up in my pocket when I went to the track. Sure enough, one day I won twelve grand, and some unsavory types were giving me the stink eye. I stuffed all of it into the envelope and dropped it into the mailbox that stood just outside the clubhouse door. It was risky, mailing all that cash, but I wasn't going to get caught carrying it across the parking lot. Then I turned my pockets inside out and pulled out my shirttail. It was obvious that I had nothing on me. I strolled right on by them like I had just lost every dime I had.*
>
> —Ronnie Costas, horseplayer

Eddie rolled back into Battle Creek on May 1st. The sky was filled with dark threatening clouds, indicating that a spring rain was imminent. Southern Michigan was the ideal environment for growing grass—
plenty of rain, warm days and cool nights. He had spent the night with an old friend and his wife in Indiana only a few hours from home. He went way back with the pro, Ralph Whalen, who was now at a small muni course north of Indianapolis. They teamed up and took a couple of locals for $100 each.

Eddie didn't like to give strokes away, preferring a different set-up like the one with the St. Louis boys last year at his home course, but their opponents said that was the only way they would play. Since they were playing a scramble, they agreed that to even things up, Eddie would have to sit out two holes each nine and the pro would sit out one hole. The hustler and his partner responded by each birdieing a hole while the other was sitting and enjoying the scenery.

The day's winners grilled steaks on the patio that evening and regaled Ralph's wife, Lee Ann, with stories of working together at a big country club in Detroit. Who cheated at golf and who was cheating on his woman, were just a few of the topics they covered. Ralph sometimes worked with the course maintenance crew when they were shorthanded, while Eddie was strictly a pro shop guy. Ralph said the strangest thing he ever saw there was when he was mowing a fairway and a prominent club member stopped his car on the shoulder of the road and walked over to him. He put Ralph's tractor between him and his real estate clients, who were sitting in the back of his car, and did a line of cocaine on the tractor's fender.

"What did you do?" asked his wife.

"I just sat there, stunned," said Ralph. "Then he looked up and gave me a stupid grin and asked if I wanted some. You know, assuming a young kid like me did drugs all the time. He was a creep. I think his wife divorced him later. You remember him, Eddie. I honestly can't remember his name, but he was a big real estate guy that thought he knew everything about everything."

"Devin Renner," said Eddie. He had a few of his own stories, but didn't bring up the one about the poker game and the death later that evening.

"Yup, that's the guy. He had a gorgeous wife too. What a schmuck! As you can see, I went for beauty and brains."

"Let's eat, guys," said Lee Ann giggling.

* * *

The steaks were better at Ralph's, but the food was secondary when you were dining with the people that mattered the most to you.

"So what do you think this strange lady and her partner had in mind, Ronnie?" asked Kathy, as the four of them sat around the table at a Kalamazoo steakhouse. It was the first time they had all gotten together since the guys came back from their winter trips.

"Seriously, I think they were going to kill me, rob me, and then take me out into the Pacific and dump my body," he explained. "Herm said there were several unsolved disappearances in the area over the last few years. This could be the break that the cops are looking for."

"What tipped you off?" asked Eddie.

"The whole strangeness of the situation, I guess," answered Ronnie, waving his fork for emphasis. "You know what they say about when something is too good to be true?"

Ronnie caught Kathy's pensive look and immediately attempted to explain his statement.

"Hey, Sweetie, a quick drink was all I was looking for. It's not like I was on the prowl or anything. I was drinkin' and walkin' and that's the truth."

Eddie, like most guys, was entertained when he saw his buddy trying to squirm out of a tense situation with his woman. He decided to do the gentlemanly thing, so he kept his mouth shut. There was no use in adding to Ronnie's discomfort. The guy did almost die.

"So what do you say, Suzanne?" asked Kathy. "Use your lawyer's intuition. Was my guy out sniffing around for some action or is his story legit?"

"I believe him," said Suzanne. "Except for taking liberties with the truth about who they were in the beginning, I think they have been honest with us. If he was looking for some action, he might not be with us here tonight."

With that last statement, Kathy teared up and left the table. Suzanne caught up with her as they approached the restroom door.

"Hey, are you all right?" asked Suzanne, once they were inside.

"Sorry about that," said Kathy, leaning against the sink counter dabbing her eyes with a handkerchief. "It's just that I missed him more than I thought I would these past weeks. And frankly, the thought of him not being around sent shivers through me. Now I've made a fool out of myself."

"He'll understand," said Suzanne. "To be honest, I've grown very fond of Eddie. It was tough with him being gone so long. I just threw myself into my work. Those people that Ronnie dealt with sounded pure evil. And believe me, I've seen some evil people in the courtroom. There are people out there that would kill others for a nickel. They're the dregs of society, that's for sure."

Kathy laughed, which surprised Suzanne, after the statement she had just made about the criminal element in society.

"I'm not laughing at what you just alluded to," explained Kathy. "It was something Ronnie said to me one time when we were…when we were talking late one night. He said people like Eddie and him were always on their guard. 'Never show your ass' is how he put it. He was referring to keeping things to yourself and not letting the other guy know what you're thinking or what you're up to. They consider that a sign of weakness. I guess in their business, that's important. I'm sure they've dealt with their share of low-lifes in the past."

"Well, were not in their business," said Suzanne. "And showing your ass once in a while isn't all bad, if you know what I mean." Her last comment got the response she was looking for.

"You're right. I'm going back to Ronnie's and I'm sure there will be some of that. I guess I'm just glad to have him back."

"That's the ticket," said Suzanne. "These two do play it close to the vest, but it doesn't bother me. I'm not really looking for a guy who needs to get emotional from time to time. I like Street just the way he is."

"Can I share something with you?" asked Kathy in a serious tone. "You can't let Eddie know about it, okay?"

"Sure."

"Well, that young boy that our guys have been helping out at the golf course," said Kathy, as she started to tear up again. "He's Ronnie's grandson. I was also thinking about that boy, who lost his father when he was very young, not being able to spend time with his grandfather. Ronnie hasn't told him yet, but I think he will soon. His mother and Ronnie had some sort of run-in years ago and she won't get over it."

"Don't worry about me telling Eddie. He already knows about Ronnie and Wilson, even though Ronnie hasn't said anything. Remember, Eddie is good at reading people. Not much gets by him. I feel like if I ever tried to deceive him, he would see right through me in a minute. Okay, let's put smiles back on our faces and let our guys know how much we appreciate them. Are you in?"

"Oh yeah, I'm definitely in."

* * *

"See what you did," said Eddie, as the girls left the table. "You got her all worked up for nothing. You should have downplayed the danger thing. Women take that kind of stuff to heart."

"Thanks for the hindsight advice," said a dejected Ronnie. "I wasn't going for the sympathy vote. I was just explaining what happened, that's all."

The girls walked up with bright smiles on their faces.

"Let's go, guys," said Suzanne. "It's time for your official welcome home party."

Eddie flipped a coin to see who would get the check and his partner lost. Ronnie gave him a disgusted look and put several bills in the waitress's envelope.

"Don't worry, love," whispered Kathy in his ear. "I'll make that dinner check well worth it. Let's get in your babe-mobile and head north to your place."

Ronnie looked over at Eddie and saw him flash a thumbs up. Suzanne caught the gesture and frowned at him.

"I see the boy doesn't stray too far from the man," said Suzanne, as they got into Eddies '57 Chevy.

"Would you have it any other way?" asked Eddie. Before she could answer, he pulled out onto the main road, dumped the clutch and broke the back tires loose. Ronnie and Kathy both cheered from Ronnie's convertible. "Listen to them. I'm sorry my friend and his woman are so immature."

"Right," said Suzanne. "Home, oh wise one. I'm anxious to experience what you, in all your maturity, have learned."

* * *

The two Divot Dogs sat in their cart and waited for the guys ahead of them to hit. They were playing the South course at Stonehedge on a picture perfect late May afternoon. They both preferred to play in the afternoon, when the sun was high in the sky and the grass was dry. A lot of the old boys liked to play around 8:00 or 9:00. The high rollers that they associated with in the past were late night people, which meant an early round for them started somewhere around noon.

"So tell me what it takes to win at the track," said Eddie.

"Well," said Ronnie, as he walked onto the tee on the par three third hole. "A lot of people believe that successful players have some sort of secret system. In reality, there's no such thing. You need to know horses, races and money." Ronnie hit a smooth 4-iron twelve feet right of the flag. "Twenty says you can't get inside it," challenged Ronnie.

"No way," said Eddie. "It's about 190 to the hole and you're in there pretty tight. Give me three-to-one."

"I'll go five-to-two," countered Ronnie. "Twenty gets you fifty. And it's only because I'm feeling charitable."

Eddie hit his 4-iron straight at the flag. He didn't hit it as pure as he would have liked to, and he paid the price. The ball landed six feet in front of the hole and rolled about twenty more, putting him a few feet outside of Ronnie's shot. Eddie paid up after they both made their pars. They drove to the par five fourth hole and saw the guys ahead of them looking for a ball. They settled in for a long wait. If these guys didn't let them through in the next two holes, they decided to head for the back nine.

"So, horses, races and money," said Eddie, coaxing his partner to elaborate.

"Okay," said Ronnie, as he watched the group messing around in front of them. "I remember a rare night when all three came into play. I bet a horse that was running his very first race at Maywood. At least, that's what most of the bettors thought. He was five years old, which isn't that old for a pacer. I happened to know that when he was three, he had a great record at Maywood's short track with its sharp turns. His past performances were only fair, but he was improving. At 4 to 1, I put $50 on him. Then I paired him up in a few perfecta bets. Sure enough, he wins and I pocket over four hundred. It helped to have and 8 to 1 long shot come in second. So you see, because I knew this horse, I had an edge."

"Sweet," said Eddie. "I like getting odds instead of giving them all the time."

"Here's an example of knowing how to size up a race," said Ronnie, as he teed up his ball. He settled into his stance and hit an arrow straight tee shot 275 yards down the center of the fairway. "On the very same night I'm looking at this race where the number five horse is going off at 8 to 1. Normally this would seem a little odd, because this was a quality horse, and he was coming off a winning performance his last time out. Tell you what—you tell me why a last time winner was an 8 to 1 long shot in his very next race, and I'll throw that twenty back to you. You've got until the end of this hole."

"One question," said Eddie, after he hit a similar drive and headed back to the cart. "Did the horse in question race the week before?"

"Good question. Yes, he had been racing steady for the last six weeks."

Eddie stopped the cart next to his ball. Ronnie's tee shot was only twenty feet away. This was often the case when they both hit solid drives. Eddie tended to be a little longer when he really munched one, but more often than not, you could throw a blanket out and cover both of their tee shots. He was deep in thought, trying to figure out why a horse that had just won would be going off at such long odds. They watched the guys up on the green as they putted out.

"Is there a super horse in the field that is going off at 1 to 5 or something?" he asked. "You know, sucking up all the money in the 'win' pool?"

"Nope. The favorite is at 2 to 1 and the next horse is at 3 to 1. So there's nothing weird like that going on."

Eddie put a slight draw on his 3-wood and made it to the front of the green. Ronnie's second shot with the same club stopped about ten yards short. When Ronnie got back into the cart Eddie was sitting there contemplating.

"Clock's ticking on that twenty, my man. The answer is very logical. I will tell you that's it's a high-end race with a substantial purse. It's the second largest purse of the evening, so they are all quality horses. There was this one horse that had no business being in the race, but he wasn't a factor."

Eddie drove up to the green and stopped. He watched Ronnie go over to his ball. *The answer is logical*, he thought. *I know one thing—I'm not seeing this race clearly. It's not a normal situation. There has to be something strange or at least out of the ordinary going on.*

"Last question," said Eddie, as he watched Ronnie's pitch shot settle in about three feet from the hole. "If I saw the program, would I be able to figure out why this horse had such high odds?"

"Anybody with half a brain would have been able to see it. So, let me think—yeah you would have figured it out."

Eddie rolled his ball up a foot right of the hole and tapped in for his birdie. As Ronnie took the putter back for his three-foot birdie attempt, it came to him. The Grip rolled his bird in and they strolled back to their cart.

"I've got it," said Eddie.

"Too late, the hole is over," said Ronnie.

"Not so, oh wise one," said Eddie. "This hole isn't over until we tee off on the next one. If either of us had made a mistake back there, like taking an improper drop, we could still go back and correct it."

"True. You've got me on a technicality. What's your answer?"

"He went off at 8 to 1 because he wasn't the only last time winner in the field."

"Smart ass," exclaimed Ronnie, pulling the twenty out that he had just taken off his partner. "You got it. There were actually three other last time winners in the field. There was big money on two of them, but he was overlooked by the bettors. I put $100 on him and paired him up in the perfecta with all other logical choices. I cleared over $1200 on that race. I remembered my teacher's advice on last time winners that go off at over 5 to 1—bet 'em. It's a solid angle and over the long run, it will give you a nice return. Problem is, there aren't many races like that that come along. I was lucky to be there that night. Here's your twenty."

"Man, betting horses is better than working," said Eddie, as he pocketed his twenty.

They drove to the next tee and saw that the guys ahead of them were only about 50 yards out. Eddie looked at his playing partner and nodded his head in the direction of the clubhouse. Ronnie shook his head in the affirmative, so Eddie steered them in that direction. After checking with the pro shop for the OK to go off the back, they played it in and hour and twenty minutes. They were both two under on the back side.

"All right," said Eddie, as they sat down in the Stonehedge grill for a sandwich and an ice tea. "You explained about horses and races. Now tell me about the money side."

"You won't believe it," explained Ronnie, "but guys that are real good at it, and there's very few of them around, can do calculations worthy of a mathematician. I'll give you a couple of examples. Let's say a horse is a 2 to 1 favorite. Now, I'm not big on betting favorites, but I will if I feel there's some value there. Anyway this favorite has a lot of money on it to win and to show. For some reason the place pool is low. It doesn't happen all that often, but if you're observant you catch it from time to time. It's like the guys that bet him to win hedge their bet and put some dough on him to finish in the money, so the show pool is bet heavily also. You obviously get a bigger payoff if the horse wins, but the best value in this instance, because of where the big money is, is to bet him to take second. That way, if he wins, or gets caught in the stretch, you still collect. Sure enough, on the same night I was telling you about, I ran into this situation. About a minute before post time a huge chunk of money was put down on the favorite to win and to show. I put a hundred down on him to place, and when he got beat at the wire, I collected $250—my $100 and $150 profit. A lot of guys were screaming for him to hold off the other horse in the stretch, but I didn't care if he won or not."

"Cool," said Eddie, as their sandwiches arrived. "What are you, the James Bond of horse racing?"

"Betting horses is not as glamorous as a lot of people think. The successful bettors are grinders, and they have to push a lot of money through the windows every year. More often than not, it's only a few big hits that define their whole season—a "pick six" or a trifecta that pays huge. Here's my other example on the money thing. Sometimes, if I think a horse is going to win I don't bet him to win if the perfecta payoffs will return more. Let's say a straight up bet is paying 2 to 1, but the lowest perfecta payoff is 10 to 1. It's not too tough to do the math on something like that. I usually throw out the two horses that I think don't have a chance at all when betting perfectas. So, in a nine-horse field, there are only six possibilities to pair with my horse. That's a twelve-dollar bet. When you win, you have to subtract the ten bucks you put down on the other horses. If the numbers are there, I go for it."

"What's the difference between a perfecta and an exacta?"

"Ha, nothin'. They're the same bet—you're just betting whoever comes in first and second. Some tracks call it an exacta and some call it a perfecta. Don't ask me why that is. I don't waste time trying to figure that trivial stuff out. I'm only interested in the numbers and the anomalies. You know, things that seem to be out of place. If you can spot 'em, it can be very profitable."

"You're a deep thinker, Grip. I think I'll stick to poker. When we're done here, let's go over and see the kid. He should be at the range by now."

"Exactly what I was thinking," said Ronnie.

* * *

Ronnie spent over an hour with his student explaining and demonstrating the importance of swing plane and a proper shoulder turn. He told Wilson that a lot of guys on the tour don't take the club back to parallel on their iron shots. This was because they create enough torque with their shoulder turn, and that gave them ample clubhead speed. It also helped to be in superb physical condition. He planted a seed in Wilson's mind when he said that most modern tour players worked out all the time. There was even a fitness trailer that followed them to all the tournaments.

Wilson knew that he had strong legs from riding his bike all the time. After hearing Grip explain the positives of being in good shape, he asked him if it was a good idea to lift weights. Grip told him that if he did it in moderation it would be beneficial. He told the kid he would write down the type of lifts he should do. For the last fifteen minutes, Grip went into the mental part of the game.

"Let's say that your basic shot is a draw. That's what Street and I recommend. But, for some reason, on any given day, your hands just won't cooperate and you're putting a little fade on your shots. An accomplished tour pro will make a few subtle adjustments and go about his business. If the adjustments don't work, he'll be sitting at home in front of the television watching the other guys play on that particular weekend. Until you get to that point, you need a plan 'B' to fall back on. Maybe you should just go with the fade if that's what your body is telling you. Or, you could lengthen your swing and concentrate on whipping your hands through a little more at impact. The bottom line is, you need to know what you need to do to get the best out of each round. One of the best rounds I ever shot in high school was the time I only hit three greens. Guess what I shot?"

"How about 78," said Wilson.

"Nope, 73. I made four bogeys and three birdies. I had a tap-in for one of my birds. Rolled in a fifteen footer from the fringe and chipped in for the other two birdies. I was leaking oil all over the place and was down to my 'C' game, but I made it work. It also helped to have a dynamite short game. When my girlfriend found out that I won the tournament she was all over…"

Grip looked up and saw Eddie standing behind Wilson shaking his head from side to side. He cut his celebration story short and continued with the lesson.

"The bottom line, kid, is to know your swing and your body. Sometimes you need another set of eyes to see what's going on, but most of the time you should be able to figure it out, and if it isn't anything major, fix it on the spot. The top players can do that. You got anything to add, Street?"

"Yeah, I do. When I was young I loved to play in bad weather. A lot of the guys you're competing with don't like the wind, the cold, or the rain. I'd say about half the guys in the field would give up before they hit their first shot if the weather was bad. Some, because they had a ready excuse if they didn't play well. Others, because they were pus, uh, sissies and just didn't like bad weather. If you can knock the ball down in the wind and draw and fade the ball when necessary, you've got a huge advantage. It helps to have all the shots, especially in bad weather."

Grip gave the kid a quick handshake and an even quicker hug. As they were leaving, they stopped at the end of the range and watched Wilson hit a few. The improvement in his swing was nothing short of remarkable. He was hitting five-irons that were dropping neatly behind the 175 yard marker. Each shot had a gentle draw as it landed softly.

"Let's see you fade one," hollered Eddie.

The kid adjusted his stance a little and attempted to fade one at the target. The result was a low slice the traveled about 150 yards and then dove to the ground.

"Keep working on it," said Eddie. "You'll get it."

The kid waved at them as they headed for their cars.

"I just had a thought," said Ronnie. "What do you think about teaching the kid a few hustling moves? You know, letting him in on a few trade secrets."

"You just had that thought," countered Eddie. "I've been thinking about that ever since I saw him swing the clubs that we bought him. He's a natural." Eddie almost said a 'chip off the old block', but he kept that to himself. He wondered why Ronnie didn't let on about him being the kid's grandfather. He must have his reasons. Guys like Ronnie and him had survived by keeping most things to themselves.

CHAPTER SIXTEEN

Wilson's Discovery

To a real golfer, golf is like a game of chess. You don't just go out there and bang it around. A lot of thought goes into it. That's why I'm so freakin' tired after a round. My mind just needs a break. That's why Scotch was invented.

—Peyton Guilinger, multiple tour winner

Wilson stood, doing stretches, on the practice tee at Stonehedge. He had everything looking shipshape, so it was time to hit balls. He was almost done stretching when Troy and a couple of his golf team buddies pulled up in Troy's car. Wilson sensed that this wouldn't be a good time to practice, so he put his clubs back in the storage building. He headed over to the range cart. Might as well go to the grill and get some lunch. Hopefully, the three of them would be gone by the time he got back. Troy was never much for putting in more than a half hour on the practice tee.

"Hey, range boy," hollered Troy, as he walked up on to the tee. "If you're going back to the clubhouse, bring us back a fountain soda. Here's five bucks. You can keep the change. And don't spit in our drinks."

Wilson took the five and got into his cart. He figured why start trouble with Troy? He was a guy that could make his life even more miserable if he wanted to. Besides, Street had once told him not to anger people that could hurt you. He wasn't wimping out. He was just doing his best to avoid a confrontation with one of the biggest jerks in school. The sodas would be $1.50 each and he would leave the rest for the waitress. Troy was obviously trying to be funny with his keep the change comment. It was just another way of keeping Wilson in his place.

After a quick lunch, Wilson made his way back to the range. Troy and his buddies were putting their clubs back into their bags. Wilson figured they had hit about five shots with each club—some practice session. He walked up and handed the drinks over.

"About time, Turtle Boy," said Troy. "We're dying of thirst out here while you were in the air conditioning sniffing around the waitresses. Don't worry, buddy, you'll get some one of these days—like when you're forty. Have you ever even had a girlfriend?"

Street's advice about not showing your ass flew out the window with Troy's last comment.

"Actually, I was thinking about taking Melissa away from you, Troy Boy. She's way too good for you anyway."

"You've got a smart mouth for a know-nothing sophomore," said Troy, as he threw his clubs in the trunk of is car. "Maybe I'll close it for you."

"C'mon, Troy," said one of his buddies, stepping between them. "This little punk isn't worth it. And I don't think the pro would like you beatin' on one of his employees."

"You watch your mouth, Randall," threatened Troy, as he got in the driver's seat. "It's going to get you in big trouble one of these days."

Wilson retrieved his clubs and pulled out his five-iron. He hit three draws and then three fades. Then he hit a couple of knock-downs, followed by a couple of high soft shots. He grinned to himself, knowing that at this point he was probably a better golfer than Troy The Magnificent. Someday Troy would get his come-uppance and he would love to be there when he did. He looked out at the range and noticed something. The only balls out by the yardage markers were the ones that he had just hit. It was obvious that Troy and his buddies had hit their practice shots into the trees off to the side of the range, which would take him a long time and a lot of effort to pick them up. He put his clubs back and grabbed a couple of shag bags from the storage area. With a laugh, he jogged out onto the range. He needed to get into shape anyway. When each bag was half full he started doing lateral raises and one arm presses. Nothing like working and working out at the same time. And, he was getting paid for it.

He wasn't sorry about making the comment about Melissa to Troy. He knew that their relationship was tenuous at best. She had broken up with him more than once, but for some unknown reason they always got back together. Why she kept coming back to him was anybody's guess. Oh well, he had more important things to attend to. Grip and Street were coming back tomorrow from their annual trip to Chicago. He knew they were there playing for big money. Those two guys were something. He had a few good friends at school, but he would have to admit, as weird as it looked, that those two old guys were his best friends. He couldn't wait to show them how much he had improved. Two days ago, just before sunset, he slipped out and played the front nine on the South course and had shot 39. It was the first time he had ever broken forty. Except for the Troy and Melissa thing, life was good.

Grip and Street showed up the next day at five o'clock, as promised. The first tee on the North course was open, so they headed through the tunnel under the highway. Wilson marveled at their smooth swings. They never took much time to line up their shots. Most of the time they just stepped up and smoked it. They were a little more attentive when they were around the green. Street showed Wilson how to read the grain. He told him if there was any question on which way the grain was running, that he should look at the cup. On one side the grass would be a little shaggy, while the other would be crisply cut. Wilson soaked up everything that his mentors had to say.

After a quick front nine, the kid popped up his drive on number ten and it landed about 50 yards out in front of the tee. He grabbed his 5-wood and took a mighty swing, trying to make up for the distance he lost on his tee shot. He jerked his second shot left and over a ridge. Things got worse from there. A triple bogey seven took him from five over to eight over. Wilson sat in the cart on the eleventh tee, disgusted with himself.

"Let's talk about that last hole," said Grip in a quiet tone. "Believe it or not, your second shot was worse than the drive you popped up."

The kid gave him a surprised look and then looked toward Street who was nodding his head in agreement.

"When you skied your tee shot, which will happen from time to time, you needed to set a realistic goal for the rest of the hole. Something like: after this poor tee shot, my goal is to have a putt for par under twenty feet, and uphill if possible. You swung from the heels with your 5-wood trying to make up the lost distance, and all it did was get you into more trouble. What would have been the smarter play?"

"The lie was pretty good, so I should have hit my 3-iron or hybrid with a little fade. Even if I didn't hit it great, I would still be close enough to hit my wedge for my third shot. Then, even if I didn't get my third shot inside twenty feet, a two-putt would still be a bogey."

"A golf round is like building a sand castle," added Street. "Starting on the first tee, you begin to build the foundation. Then you add a little more to it on each hole. If you're playing solid and having a good round, you don't want to jerk part of the foundation away with poor thinking. The whole thing might cave in. Look at it this way, kid. You're standing on eighteen two under par. If you played that hole with just irons, you could probably make an easy bogey. And if you bogey, you still break par. There's trouble left and right on that hole, so you don't want to swing the driver from the heels, hoping to hit your best drive of the day. Your swing thought is to keep it smooth and avoid the trouble. If you have any doubts, hit something other than driver off the tee. A good 3-wood and a hybrid second shot will put you within wedge distance of the green. A major part of this game is avoiding the trouble that the course designer has put out here for the golfers."

"He's right," said Grip. "There's a time to be aggressive and there's a time to protect what you've already accomplished. I can't tell you how many times I've heard a guy say he really had it going, then it all fell to pieces at the end. Well, there's usually a reason that everything went to hell. We're not saying that you shouldn't be aggressive out here, but you need to choose your spots carefully. Just play smart and trust your swing."

"By the way," said Street. "That swing of yours has really come along. We can tell that you're serious about this game and you've been putting in a lot of practice time."

"Yeah," said the kid, holding up his right hand. "Look at these calluses. I look like I'm a construction worker."

"Tell you what," said Eddie, "you play these last eight holes in three over or less, we'll buy you dinner over at GLV. You can throw your bike into the back of my car and I'll take you home."

The kid bore down after their little talk and hit some impressive shots. He played the last eight in two over. A birdie chip-in on sixteen took some of the pressure off. He was beaming when he put his clubs back in the range storage building. His score for the round was 82. It wouldn't be long before he was breaking 80 out there.

The three of them talked golf all through dinner. Pam waited on them, and for once, the dialogue between them didn't center around the usual back and forth banter. She knew the guys were behaving because they had Wilson with them. This was a side of them that she had never seen before. She was well aware of their humanitarian side when it came to her, and she was pleased to see that others were also the recipients of their good will. Wilson got a call from his mom right when they were finishing their meal. He left the table to talk to her on his cell phone, which showed excellent manners for someone his age. When he told them that she was coming by to pick him up in a few minutes, Ronnie came up with an excuse as to why he had to suddenly leave. Wilson looked at Street for an explanation, but all he got was a smile and an open hand gesture. Carol actually passed Ronnie at the highway intersection by the course, but it was too dark to see inside each other's car.

* * *

Wilson showed up for work at 8 a. m. the next morning. It was a beautiful mid-summer Michigan day. The high was forecasted to be a very comfortable 80 degrees and the humidity was tolerable.

The pro shop told him there would be a lot of golfers today, so he should expect a lot of business at the range. The first thing Wilson saw when he rode up on his bike was the door to the storage building. The overhead door wasn't all the way down in the locked position, the way he always left it. A quick inspection of the small building showed that only one thing was missing—his golf bag and clubs. The ball washing machine had not been tampered with and all the miscellaneous tools were still hanging from their hooks. If he didn't know any better, he would have thought that the sole reason for the break-in was to steal his clubs. Who would want to do something like that? It didn't take a genius to figure out who—Troy. He and his buddies were the only guys his age that knew about his clubs being in there. What was he going to tell Grip and Street?

* * *

The kid hadn't seen his two mentors for a couple of days, which was a good thing. He was still trying to figure out how to tell them the clubs they had bought for him were gone. Even with all the money he had given his mother, he still had about $800 in his savings. That would just about cover a new bag and a set of sticks like the ones that were stolen. Maybe the pro would give him a discount. He decided to talk to him about it. One thing, he wasn't going to do was feel sorry for himself. His two coaches had told him on more than one occasion that the world belonged to the mentally tough. And this was definitely a chance to show his mental toughness.

He was about to head out to pick up balls when Melissa walked up on the range tee. She had a few tokens in her hand. Wilson couldn't believe it. Here he was with the girl of his dreams—just the two of them. She said she was meeting her swing coach in a few minutes. He wanted to move their lessons to the Stonehedge range, because there were less distractions there. Wilson took her tokens and told her to go to the end of the range. He brought her two buckets and sat them gently on the ground. They talked for a minute while she went through her stretches, then he moved away so she could warm up.

Wilson pretended to busy himself with the range cart, but he was really watching Melissa. As she hit short wedges, he noticed two things. One, was her tan legs that were topped with a perfect figure. He caught himself staring with a wide-open mouth. He was glad he realized what he was doing, before he started drooling. She wasn't wearing those tight little shorts that girls her age usually wore. She had on cargo shorts with upper and lower pockets. They were more economical for a golfer. He assumed she had the same system that he did when he was playing: cell phone in lower left pocket, tees, green repairer and something to mark with in upper right, extra ball in upper left, and scorecard in lower right. It made sense to do it that way. He decided to give up on the covert looks and went over to watch her hit.

"What do you think?" she asked, surprising him.

"Seriously?" was all he could come up with.

"Yeah, seriously," she said, looking down at the ball she was about to hit.

His mind was racing. He wanted to give her some advice, but he didn't want to come off as a know-it-all. He chose his words carefully, which was hard for a hormone loaded fifteen year-old, who was talking to the most beautiful girl he had ever known.

"Melissa, your hands are too high."

She gave him an odd look. It wasn't a look that said she thought he didn't know what he was talking about. It was more of a "what makes you say that" look.

"I'll explain it the way a really good golfer explained it to me—with a story. That's probably why I remember it so well. Okay, if I were going to teach you to bowl, I would tell you to throw the ball out to the right. You, with your fingers stuck in the top of the ball would throw it into the right gutter. Then I would tell you to make the ball curve right-to-left."

With his finger, he showed her the spin the ball needs to have to make it hook. Then, he demonstrated the twisting motion that she would have to make, with his hand above the ball.

"Are you with me, so far?" he asked.

She gave him a strange smile, not knowing where he was going with all this talk about bowling.

"The next thing you need to do is to put them together. Throw the ball out to the right and then make it curve back to the left. That's the way all good bowlers throw the ball. They all throw a hook. Now, you throw a couple of balls trying to spin it just right to get the desired effect and you're all over the place. Finally, you look up and say that it's real hard to do what I'm asking. And my response is; it's real hard for you, because you've got the ball upside down. Good bowlers have their hand underneath the ball, not on top of it. It's a lot easier to throw a hook if your hand is in the lower position. It's a natural motion, like you're going to swing your arm up and put your thumb on your nose. With your hand underneath you don't have to falsely manipulate the ball to get the proper spin."

"What's this got to do with the golf swing?" she asked.

"I'm glad you asked," he said, as he took a club out of her bag and demonstrated. "When your hands are low they work more naturally, like this. You don't have to do something funny with your hands to get the club face in the proper position. That's hard to do consistently. I know you're going to ask why don't most bowlers throw a hook if it's so natural. It's simple—the ball is too heavy for them. It has to be to knock the pins over. But, if it were the weight of a beach ball, most bowlers would be throwing a big hook. Anyway, that's what I was told."

"So you think, that because my hands are too high, I'm having trouble getting them to work the way they should?"

"There you go. All you need to do is drop them down by your left thigh at address and then swing under your…uh. You know what I mean."

"How do you know this stuff?" she asked, helping him out of his predicament.

"I learned it from two really good golfers, and believe me, they know what they're talking about."

"Thanks, Wilson, I'll give it a try."

"I hope it works," he said, as he walked away.

"Hey, Wilson," said Melissa, as she rolled another ball over from the pile. "It's okay to say boobs to a girl, as long as you're being respectful."

"I'll remember that," he said.

Nice job, goof, he thought to himself.

* * *

A few days later, Wilson was sitting on the range bench contemplating whether he should buy a new set of clubs, and how he was going to tell his teachers that his clubs were gone. He was surprised when Grip pulled up by himself in his Corvette.

"Hey, kid," hollered Grip, "let's go spank a few."

Wilson walked slowly over to the car and just stood there admiring it. He had trouble looking Grip in the eye, and when he finally did his eyes teared up. He wasn't crying, but he was darn close. He got in and looked over at his mentor.

"Grip, my clubs are gone. Someone broke in the shed and stole them. I'm sorry."

To say Grip's response shocked Wilson would be an understatement.

"Stolen, huh? Hey, no worries," said Ronnie, as he turned onto the highway and went efficiently through the gears. "We'll just get another set. You can use mine until we get you some fresh sticks."

"Man, I thought you would be mad," said a relieved Wilson. "You and Street put out a lot of money for them. I've got enough to buy another set, and I'm sure the pro here will give me a good deal. I sure liked those clubs. I was getting real used to them."

"Don't worry about it, son, uh Street and I will spring for another set. You got any idea who took them?"

Wilson didn't seem to notice with the way Ronnie had just addressed him.

"Yeah, but I can't prove it. They're probably at the bottom of Gull Lake by now. I don't know if I can let you two buy me another set. You've done so much for me already."

"Listen," said Grip, as he pulled into the GLV parking lot. "Here's something just between you and me. Street and I are millionaires. Golf and other ventures have been very good to us, and we've been smart with our finances. We made all that money and we watched our expenses so we can live the way we do now. Did you see how much of a tip that Street left Pam the other night at dinner?"

"I did," said Wilson. "He left her twenty dollars. It was a huge tip."

"We always leave her that, because she needs the money. Having a lot of money doesn't make you any smarter or any more generous than you were before when you didn't have a lot of money. It does, however, give you certain freedoms. How you use those freedoms is up to you. You can buy a bunch of nice things for yourself or you can scale back a little and help out others that need a helping hand. Sorry, I didn't mean to lecture."

"That's okay. What you're saying makes sense. I hope I have a lot of money some day, so I can help out other people."

"You'll be rich some day, kid," said Grip chuckling. "I can pretty much guarantee it. Go in to the pro shop tomorrow and tell the pro what you need. Tell him Street and I will foot the bill."

"You guys are awesome," said Wilson, as he grabbed Grip's bag out of the trunk. "I'm not just saying that because you buy me things. You're like the uncles I never had. My mom and dad didn't have any brothers or sisters, so we're a pretty small family. Did you ever have any kids, Grip?"

Ronnie was about to spill everything, when the assistant pro stuck his head out the door and threw him the key to a cart. He said to get going, because league would be starting in ten minutes. They hurried over to the first tee. The Chicago hustler couldn't figure out why it was so hard to come clean with his grandson. Maybe it was because of the nightmare he had a few years ago. In his dream Wilson and his mom had moved again and this time it took Herman ten years to find them. When he did, the kid was all grown up and married with a family of his own. He had already missed out on a lot and didn't want to go through that again.

It didn't take long for Grip to figure out that there was something else bothering the kid. He appeared to be in a daze when he chunked and easy chip shot. And it wasn't because he was using clubs that were strange to him. They drove to the next tee and when Wilson started to get out, Grip put his hand on his shoulder signaling for him to stay in the cart.

"What else is bothering you?" he asked. "I can't read people as good as Street can, but it's pretty obvious that your head isn't in the game today."

Wilson gave Grip a wry smile.

"Yeah, you're right. There's this girl at school. She's pretty awesome. She's got this stupid boyfriend that acts like a jerk most of the time. At least he acts that way around me. I kinda like her and there's nothing I can do about it. Pretty weird, huh?"

"You're at a tough age, kid," said Grip. "If she's such a great girl, why does she go with this jerk?"

"One of my buddies at school has a theory on that. He says Troy always acts real nice when he's around her. I actually think she doesn't know what he's really like. He is one devious guy. Oh yeah, and I'm pretty sure he's the one who stole my clubs. He was at the range the other day and saw me put them away in the shed. I'm not sure why this guy hates me so much. I rarely see him at school and almost never talk to him."

"He sounds like a typical bully," observed Grip. "A lot of bullies act the way they do because they're on some sort of power trip. It's just their way of coping with things and their way of showing that they have power over you. I saw my share of them growing up in the city. Hey, let's forget this guy and focus on the game. There are a couple of things I've been meaning to show you…"

* * *

I can't believe how quickly Will is picking this up, thought Ronnie as he drove home to Richland.

He took to golf the way Rob took to football, basketball and baseball. All he had to do was show Rob one time and he would take it from there. He marveled at how well-balanced Wilson was for not having a father around. A lot of boys who grew up in households without a male figure tended to get into trouble. As Herman had reminded him on more than one occasion, having a dad, or at least an adult male around, helped to keep young guys in line and gave them someone to emulate.

Three days later Wilson was hanging around the house with nothing to do. It was Monday morning and the range was in good shape, so there was no reason to go in. Normally he would have spent a good part of the day practicing, but his new clubs hadn't arrived yet. He had all his chores done, so he called up his friend, Billy Kaminski, to see what he was up to.

"Bilbo, what's going on?" asked Wilson over the phone.

"Nothin' man," came the answer. "I'm bored. Let's do something."

"How about we ride our bikes into Richland?" asked Wilson. "We can scout the place for babes. Maybe we can pick up an old toothless woman for you."

"You're a funny guy. I don't know, Richland is pretty far. C'mon over to my place. I've got a couple of new video games we can play."

"You can only kill so many cartoon people. It's too nice to stay inside giving your thumbs a workout. Let's ride."

"OK, I'll be over in twenty."

Richland was a few miles west of GLV. The middle school and high school were both located there. The two friends rode around town looking for other guys or girls that they knew but came up empty, so they headed north out of town. Wilson turned down a country rode that he had never been on before. About half a mile off the main road he saw a guy on a four-wheeler pull into a pole barn. If he didn't know any better, he thought the guy looked just like Grip. He signaled for Billy to follow him. He rode part way down the driveway and sure enough, Grip was standing in the barn looking at his four-wheeler. Wilson stopped and waited for Grip to see them.

"Who's that?" asked Billy. "Do you know him?"

"Yeah, he's a friend of mine. Let's go say hello."

"He's pretty old to be just a friend," said Billy. "What if he's some kind of pervert dude that preys on cute guys like us? I'm serious. Why do you have old guys for friends?"

"Quit talking like a psycho. I told you he's a friend of mine."

"Well, go say hello then," said Billy. "I'll hang back here and go for help if he does anything weird."

"Suit yourself," said Wilson as he rode toward the building.

Ronnie heard the bike on the drive and lit up in a big smile when he saw Wilson.

"Hey, man, what are you doing way out here?" asked Ronnie.

"Billy and I are just riding around, Grip," said Wilson, looking at all the toys in Ronnie's barn. "You've got a pretty cool place here. Is all this stuff yours?"

"Yeah, I find that the older I get the more I get excited about toys. C'mon in and check out my boat."

Wilson was impressed with Ronnie's vehicles. They walked out of the barn and saw Billy sitting at the end of the drive.

"What's up with your friend?" asked Ronnie, nodding up the drive.

"He's sitting back there in case you turn out to be dangerous and he has to go for help. He's kinda weird sometimes, but he's a nice guy."

"Wave him in and we'll have something to drink," said Ronnie, as he headed for the patio.

Billy rode up and Wilson introduced him to Ronnie. Ronnie asked them if they wanted a soda and they both said yes. He told Wilson to go inside and grab some drinks out of the fridge for them. Thirty seconds later, Ronnie realized that he had just made a big mistake. He jumped up and raced inside. It was too late. Wilson was standing and staring at a picture on the wall of his dad and Grip. There was another picture of the two of them; only in this one Grip was holding a little baby. What was going on here? How did Grip know his dad? He turned when he saw Ronnie walk into the room.

"I just put all those up on the wall," said Ronnie, nodding toward the pictures. "Your dad was really something. He was one of the best high school athletes in the whole Chicago area. He could pretty much do it all. He talked about going to college and then maybe on to pro football. But then he got the idea to serve his country first."

"I don't understand," said Wilson in a shaky voice. "Are you telling me that you're…"

"Yeah, I'm your grandfather, Wilson," said Ronnie with misty eyes. He had finally told the kid and it felt pretty good.

"Where have you been all this time?" asked Wilson, trying to digest this new information.

"I've been here for a few years, once I found out where you and your mom were. It took me several years to find you. Actually a private eye found you. He's a friend of mine and he knew your dad real well. They served together. I'll introduce him to you someday. He was there when your dad died. They were real close."

"Why didn't you just come to the house when you found out where we lived?" asked Wilson.

"Your mom and I didn't get along very well in the beginning," explained Ronnie. "We both said things that we shouldn't have. Anyway, that's why she moved away from Chicago and changed her and your name to Randall."

"That doesn't make sense," said Wilson. "Why would my mom do something like that?"

"I guess she had her reasons. One of them was; she thought I should have talked your dad out of signing up for one more tour in Iraq. When I didn't, and he was killed over there, she held me partly responsible. We don't need to get into all the problems between us. The good part is, I'm here and I want to spend a lot of time with you. I can't stand in for a real dad, but I can be a hell of a grandfather if you want me to be."

Wilson looked his grandpa in the eye, then finally broke out in a big grin. He stepped forward and gave Ronnie a big hug.

"Hell yeah, I want you to be. I can't believe this."

"Hey, watch that language," said Ronnie still holding onto his only grandson. "I can't punish you, but I can make your life miserable, like embarrassing you in front of a certain girl."

They were still hugging when Billy stepped into the room. His eyes went wide when he saw the two of them.

"Pervert!" hollered Billy, pointing at Ronnie. "Get offa him."

Wilson and Ronnie separated themselves and started laughing.

"Relax, man," said Wilson. "Grip is my grandfather. I can't believe it. One of the best golfers in the whole world is my grandpa. This is awesome. Hey, does Street know?"

"Naw, I never told him," said Ronnie. "What are we going to do about your mom?"

"I don't know," said Wilson. "I guess I'll sit down and have a long talk with her tonight. Now that I've found you, I don't want either of us to go away. Hey, can I drive your Corvette? I've got my learner's permit."

"I can see it now, man," said Billy. "You pulling up to prom with Melissa in that fine piece of machinery—ha, not a chance. Maybe the car, but Melissa is out of your league."

"Let's go out on the patio and have a discussion about that," said Ronnie.

Ronnie talked for about fifteen minutes and touched on several topics. It was his first real heart to heart discussion with his grandson. He had thought about this moment for years and now it was here. He told the two boys that they shouldn't be afraid to take a chance once in a while. If people were afraid to take chances, a lot of great things wouldn't get done in this world. If you were beaten down because you tried something that was beyond your abilities, treat it like a learning situation. Get back up and solve your problems, but use what you've learned to get better.

"Tell me about my dad," said Wilson, when Ronnie paused to take a sip of soda.

"He was just as good a person as he was an athlete," said Ronnie. "He had several scholarship offers to play football in college. He also had a baseball offer, but football was his first love. When your mom got pregnant during their senior year, everything changed. Robbie knew he needed money to support his new family, and the service was the quickest way to start earning more than minimum wage. I told him his mother and I would help out, but he was the type of guy that wanted to make his own way. You were almost two when he was killed by a sniper in Iraq."

Ronnie didn't mention that Carol lied about being on birth control pills. If she got pregnant, she knew that Rob was the type of guy that wouldn't leave her and her child. That was one of the reasons that Ronnie disliked her. He had seen that strategy work before. The other reason was she had an arrest record for shoplifting. He had told his son on more than one occasion that he could do a lot better. Robbie just laughed and said that once his dad got to know her, he would like her.

"Anyway, like I said, your dad died when you were about two and your grandma died only a few months later. Shortly after that, your mom moved away and had your names changed. You were born Wilson Green. I guess your mom convinced a judge that it was a matter of safety for you and for her. If you want to know any more on that issue, you'll have to talk to Carol. Look, guys, I'd like to stay and talk, but I've got a date. I'm supposed to pick up Kathy in a half hour."

Billy had trouble processing this information. "You've got a girlfriend?"

"I'm not a hundred years old, Billy," said Ronnie.

"You should see her," said Wilson. "She's beautiful."

"I'll tell her you said that," said Ronnie. "You two will meet formally real soon. She's nice and real smart. I'm sure you will like her."

The two boys finished their drinks while Ronnie went in and took a shower. They said their goodbyes and started for home. The guys were about a mile down the road when Ronnie blew past them in his 'Vette.

"Dang," said Billy. "Your grandpa is pretty cool. I mean, for an old guy."

"You're right, Bilbo, he is pretty cool. I got a feeling that we are going to have some great times together. Right after I smooth everything over with my mom. I just hope she doesn't go ballistic when I tell her about him."

* * *

Wilson was waiting up for his mom when she returned home from a tough shift at the restaurant. Her customers had her running all over the place and they tipped like they were down to their last dollar. It only took her a minute to figure out there was something going on with her only son. When he was through explaining the events of the day, she broke down in tears. The look on his face and the enthusiasm in his voice told her that she had made another big mistake. Keeping Ronnie and his grandson apart was mean-spirited and it had hurt both of them dearly. She was trying to distance herself from her past errors in judgment, and now that Ronnie had introduced himself to Wilson, she realized that running was the wrong thing to do.

Wilson hugged his mom and told her everything would be all right. He forgave her for what she did, and then told her that he wanted a real family for once. He was thinking about all the cool stuff that he was going to do with his grandpa, in addition to playing golf with him.

"Hey, did you know that grandpa's loaded?" asked Wilson, as soon as his mother composed herself. "Before I left today, he said I can go to any college I want to and he would pay for it."

"No, I didn't know he was that well off," said Carol. "Willy, I promise I will do whatever it takes to have the real family that you deserve. I have been so stupid. I did some things as a young woman that weren't quite ethical and I blamed others for my bad decisions. Hopefully, it's not too late to fix some of the problems I have created. Do you think your grandfather will forgive me?"

"He's pretty cool, mom. I think he will give you another chance. Especially if he knows that's what I want too. We are going to have a great time—all three of us. I just know it."

CHAPTER SEVENTEEN

The Art of the Hustle

Jean-Baptiste Colbert once said, "The art of taxation consists of so plucking the goose as to obtain the largest amount of feathers with the least possible amount of hissing." I believe a proper hustle is similar. You want the guy to walk away feeling a little violated, but with the thought in his mind that it could have been much worse. And if he doesn't hate you for it, so much the better.

—Junior "Skids" Gustufson, Detroit hustler

The secret to a successful con is to get the "mark", or the guy that's being conned, to suggest a certain course of action. You make him think that he was the one that came up with the idea, even though, unbeknownst to him, he was put into a position where the choice was all too obvious. Quite often the mark was out to do a little conning himself. These are the guys that true professionals have no problem taking advantage of. There's a good chance that the guy would have done it to you if he had come up with the idea before you did. The ideal con is to have the mark walk away feeling grateful that he is still alive or that he didn't lose even more of his dough. The perfect con is when the mark didn't even know he had been set up. This is a rare occasion and worthy of admiration, only if you are not the one on the losing end when the smoke clears.

Actually, a hustle on the golf course is not a true "con".

It might be a distant cousin, but a true hustler would resent it if he were accused of actually conning someone. A hustle might involve some misdirection and maybe some smoke and mirrors, but any hustler worth his salt would not outright lie to his opponents. If he was a scratch golfer and he told his opponents at the beginning of a match that he was a seven—that would be dishonest and akin to cheating. It might also be an invitation for your opponent, or a close associate of his, to ask for his money back, and a maybe pound of flesh to go with it.

A legitimate hustler is not here to cheat you. He just wants a game—a game where the odds are monumentally in his favor. If he has a problem creating a scenario that reflects this, then maybe he should be in another line of work. The odds favoring them are so stacked that it's downright laughable (or pathetic, depending on which chair your ass is parked in). Creativity and the ability to come through in the clutch are what separates the true hustler from all the other wannabes out there.

Now, starting the round holding the club and swinging like a seven, then playing the last few holes like a plus two—well, that's just making a few adjustments during the round and playing a little smarter. You can't fault a fellow for trying to improve his game, can you?

The most effective strategy, when hustling other golfers, is to make the opponent think he has a decent chance of winning. Titanic Thompson used to beat his opponent playing righty, then feigning sympathy, offer to play him left-handed, giving the poor slob a decent chance to win his money back. Thompson was a lefty to begin with and could play at a high level no matter what side of the ball he was standing on. The mark figured that out well before he paid off the second bet.

Is it taking advantage of your opponent if you offer to play without teeing the ball up? How about using only irons or playing with nothing longer than a five iron in the bag? You don't always have to give strokes to give the impression that the match is somewhat even. A hustler can be extremely creative if he feels the situation is ripe for a big payoff. If a player feels that his opponent has a huge advantage because he is longer off the tee, the long ball hitter can offer to drive for the both of them. Both players will just hit their second shots from where big hitter's tee shot ends up.

Sound fair?

Not hardly.

All of a sudden Mr. Long Ball starts to slap the thing all over the place—trees, fairway bunkers and into the thick rough.

Whoops, he forgot to mention it, but in addition to being a big stick off the tee, he's extremely adept at getting out of trouble—much better at it than you are.

Cha-ching!

Grace under pressure can be a beautiful thing to watch. A successful hustler is usually unflappable when it comes to the crucial money shot. He might not pull it off all the time, but it won't be because he let his emotions get the best of him. His opponent is the one that's supposed to get flustered when he has to split the last tight fairway with his tee shot, or has to drop his wedge deftly over a trap to a pin placement that was put there by a raving lunatic who happened to be in charge of the hole cutter that day.

A successful hustler works his magic without any TV cameras around. He doesn't need, nor does he want, an audience. After collecting on his bets, he slinks off looking for another challenge to test his skills. He might even throw you a hundred to keep quiet about what you saw out on the course today. His business is a shadowy one and the less said about it the better. The main thing that sets him apart from tour players that are playing for big purses is the fact that he is putting up his own money. If he doesn't play well, he doesn't just miss out on a check. He has to dig down deep into his own pocket to make good on his losses.

Now that's kind of pressure that will cause even the most accomplished golfer to wake up screaming in the middle of the night.

* * *

"So you knew all along that the kid was my grandson?" asked Ronnie, as he and Eddie sat on the first tee at Bedford Valley. Bedford Valley was the fifth course that was also owned by the Scott family, and it was a beautiful layout. Part of the course wound through Michigan pine and other assorted trees. It was built over fifty years ago and had hosted some major amateur tournaments.

"It wasn't that hard to figure out," responded Eddie. "He's starting to swing like you and he has some of the same mannerisms, like your goofy laugh. Why didn't you tell me about him?"

"I don't know. I just didn't want to mess things up between him and me. Now that he knows, things are going to be great. He called me and asked me to come over for dinner some time next week. It sounds like his mother wants to make up. It should be interesting, but I'll go with an open mind. If she's legit, I won't hold a grudge. Life's too short for that. I was hoping you would come too."

"No problem, and I'm glad things are working out," said Eddie. "By the way, since you were keeping secrets from me, I've kept one from you."

"I knew it! You really are an IRS agent investigating me for underreporting my income."

"No, nothing that serious," said Eddie. "I am keeping that fact in the vault in case I ever need any leverage on you. Do you remember that high school girl that I told you about? The girl from Texas—Jimmy Smith's daughter."

"Yeah, you're like the keeper of her trust fund or something. Don't tell me you found a way to dip into that fund, and now she's broke. I knew you were living a little too high on the hog. I'm pretty much tapped out if you want to borrow some cash. I just told my grandson I'd pay for his college."

"Stay with me here," said Eddie. "Last month I hired Herman to go to Texas and ride the train with her and three other girls back here to Michigan. They spent a month at Western Michigan University. They were student coaches for a basketball and softball camp. I told you she was quite the athlete. Well, Suzanne and I ran across them at a pizza joint in Kalamazoo. This older guy, I think he was an uncle to one of them, came over to me and asked if I had some sort of a problem with the girls."

"Why would he do that? You're not on a sex offender list, are you?"

"Do you want to hear this or not?" asked Eddie.

"All right, but give me the short version. We're finally about to tee off."

"I think they recognized me from when I was at a few of their games back in Texas last spring. Anyway, in response to his question, I decided to do something dramatic, or in this case, overly dramatic. I wrote down a couple of lines to the song about me on a napkin and told the guy to give it to her."

"What happened then?"

"It was the wrong move. She broke into tears. I thought the other girls and the uncle were going to attack me. By the look Suzanne gave me, she would have joined right in. We got everything straightened out in the end. I took her aside and told her how proud her dad would be of her if he were here today. She's quite the young lady. It's too bad her and Wilson live so far apart. They might be a good match for each other."

"You kept that a secret from your best buddy and golf partner?"

"You didn't tell me about your grandson, so I figure we are even."

"It's not the same thing."

"Hey, fellas," came a voice from behind them.

The two hustlers didn't even hear the other cart pull up, as they were so engrossed in their conversation.

"The tee's open," said the guy that initially hailed them. "Do you mind if we join you?"

"Sure," said Eddie, as he walked back and introduced himself. "It looks like it will be slow going, so we might as well make it a foursome."

"You guys wouldn't want to play a little money game, would you?" asked the second guy. "Nothing too serious, but enough to make it a little more exciting."

"I don't know, what did you have in mind?" asked Eddie as he slid a Macanudo out of its tube.

* * *

"Hey Crandall," hollered Troy sarcastically. "We're gettin' low on balls over here."

It was late September and the golf team was putting in their weekly session at the range. Their season was in the spring, but the coach wanted them to be thinking golf all the time. A couple of the golfers were football players, so they were excused. Most of the time was spent trying to crush long drives and hitting shots that weren't conducive to improving their golf games. The coach rarely showed up, so practice was conducted using the honor system. Wilson brought them a huge bucket. Troy lined up about a dozen balls and hit them as fast as he could one right after another. The rest of the guys got a big kick out of his antics and followed suit. Wilson stayed out of their way, not wanting to start anything with his nemesis. He knew Troy and Melissa were on the outs, which didn't help Troy's disposition. He didn't fear Troy physically, because he had grown a few inches and had put on several pounds of muscle, but the bully had proven he would go to great lengths to get even with someone he didn't like.

Wilson had just finished picking up the balls that the high school team had scattered all over the place, when Eddie and Ronnie pulled up in two carts.

"Get your clubs, Will," said Ronnie. "Let's see how many holes we can get in before dark."

"So tell me again what happened in Chicago," said Wilson, as the three of them stood on the fourth tee on the North course at Stonehedge.

"It was our third year for that tourney," said Ronnie. "And since we were two-time defending champions, the odds on us were pathetic. On the pari-mutuel board, we were 2 to 1 to win. There was a lot more money involved, so our bet of five grand didn't change our odds. Any more than that and we would have risked running over our own money. It's a much better deal to get 2 to 1 on five grand than even money on ten grand. You win the same, but you only have to put up half the money with the first bet. Does that make sense?"

"Yeah, it does," answered Wilson, grasping his grandfather's math logic.

"Anyway," added Eddie, "we were five strokes up with four holes to go so we gave back three of them, and ended up winning by two shots. We figured, why ruin a good thing by running away from the rest of the field? Ronnie's guy, Herman, had some off-duty Chicago cops working security when we got paid, so there were no problems collecting our winnings and keeping them."

"I don't think we'll be going back there next year, if they decide to do it again," added Ronnie. "We've sort of worn out our welcome. In the last three years, I've won enough at that event alone to put you through college, and Street's won enough to keep Suzanne in diamonds and pearls for years. Not bad for a couple of old hackers, huh?"

"Pretty cool," said Wilson. "It's probably not that big of a deal to a couple of millionaires."

"Who said we were millionaires?" asked Eddie, with a surprised look on his face.

"Grandpa Ron said you both were."

"I think you've figured out by now that your grandpa tends to exaggerate from time to time," said Eddie.

"Let me ask you this, Street," said Ronnie, as he grinned at Wilson. "If you played a match today for two hundred grand and lost, would it change your lifestyle for one minute?"

"If I lost two hundred grand I'd be eating beans and weenies for a while, I'll tell you that."

"Ha, I happen to know you like beans and weenies and it's one of the only things you know how to cook. True?"

"All right, you've got me there," laughed Eddie. "Let's just say, like you, I wouldn't worry about where my next meal's coming from."

"I rest my case, Will," said Ronnie, with a look of triumph. "Okay, let's add some fun to this game. Will, what would you say if I gave you 3 to 1 odds on hitting this green for ten bucks?"

"Careful," said Eddie, indicating that Will should think it over in detail before he made a wager. "Talk it over out loud so we know what you're thinking."

"It's about 185 yards to the pin, with almost no breeze. That's about how far I can hit a smooth five iron. At 3 to 1 if I do it one time out of four, I break even. More than that, I make some money."

"That pin is sitting right behind that big old trap on the right," said Ronnie, trying to instill some doubt into his grandson's thinking.

"Now you've got me thinking," said Will, looking down at the green. "You're right, that pin is in a bad spot. It's a sucker pin, isn't it? A guy better have a darn good reason to hit at that thing from this distance."

"Hold it," said Eddie. "You've made two big mistakes and you haven't even pulled a club out of the bag."

"Two mistakes?" asked Will.

"Enlighten him, grandpa," said Eddie, deferring to his partner.

"Number one is your assessment of the yardage," said Ronnie. "It's about 185? You can do better than that. Exactly how far is it? Figure it out, don't guess, even if it's an educated guess. And, do you need make any adjustments because of playing conditions? And number two should be obvious. I threw that comment out about where the pin is to see if you were thinking. Who cares where the pin is? The bet is, you either hit the ball on the green or you don't. With that in mind, where is your target?"

"Okay, I guess I wasn't thinking. My target is left edge of the green with a little fade. If I aim for that spot, I have the biggest margin for error and it gives me the best chance of keeping the ball on the green, even if I'm a little short or a little long."

"That's the smart approach," said Ronnie. "Now execute the shot."

Will was a little pumped up, thinking about the thirty dollars he was about to win, and he nuked his five all the way to the back of the green where it took one hop and settled in the back fringe."

"Dang, I hit that solid," he said.

"A little too solid, my man," said Ronnie with his hand out.

Will dug out his money clip and handed over a ten-dollar bill. Both of the old-timers grinned when they saw the boy's money clip. How many sixteen-year-olds carried a money clip instead of a wallet? Four holes later, Eddie stood next to Will on the green as they watched Ronnie putt for a birdie.

"Hey," he whispered. "He's holding ten dollars of your money. Are you cool with that? If not, do something."

The ninth hole swept left to right and was playing about 500 yards. Will stepped up to the tee and assessed the situation.

"Grandpa, how about giving me 2 to 1 on parring this hole? I know you're feeling bad about holding some of my money."

"The sympathy angle is a nice touch, but it's falling on deaf ears," said Ronnie. "Tell you what; I'll give you 3 to 1." Ronnie looked over at Eddie and winked. "But you have to make par using your irons only."

"Talk it over," said Eddie, when he saw Will hesitate.

"Okay, if I hit my normal 3-iron, I'll have about three hundred left. From there it will be like playing a short par four. And short par fours usually have a lot of trouble you can get into, but the rest of this hole is pretty much wide open. All I need to do is avoid the traps. I'll take the bet. A par gets me thirty bucks and I lose ten if I don't. Right?"

"Right," agreed Ronnie.

Will hit a smooth 3-iron down the middle and watched it roll down the bent grass fairway. When they got to his ball, he jumped out of the cart still holding the club he had hit off the tee.

"Think before you hit this shot," cautioned Eddie. "What sort of lie do you have and exactly where do you want to hit it? Where's the pin at? This time it does matter."

"Man, there's a lot of thinking to this game, isn't there?" asked Will.

"You ever hear a tour pro interviewed on television?" asked Ronnie. "As a rule, they're pretty sharp. Hell, I don't think Trevino even finished high school, but he was so smooth that he did a little commentating when he was between the regular and the senior tour."

"Okay," said Will, looking toward the green. "The pin is back left, so it would be best to come in from the right side of the fairway. And, my lie isn't the best, so I'm going to hit a four instead of a three. How's that for sizing up the situation?"

"Good thinking," said Ronnie, after Will hit a nice 4-iron to the right center of the fairway.

Will stood behind his ball considering his third shot. According to his calculations, he was 101 yards to the pin. All he needed was a par, so his target was below the hole. There was no reason to try to stick it in there tight. If he hit it too hard, like he did back on the fourth hole, he would be left with a touchy downhill putt or maybe a chip. His mentors had taught him to hit his scoring irons, six through sand wedge, with four different swings. A "short" wedge would be taken back about three quarters with an aggressive swing. A "normal" wedge was his normal backswing with good tempo. The third swing, what he called his "big" wedge, was taken back a little farther than normal, but that was the only difference. The longer backswing would give him a little extra distance. He rarely hit the "big" wedge, as it was the hardest to control. The fourth swing was his favorite, the knockdown. That shot called for his hands to be way ahead of the clubface at impact. It took him a while to get that one down, but once he did, it was a valuable shot to have. In an eighteen-hole round, he would come across several situations where the knockdown shot was the smart play.

Will decided on the "short" wedge and hit it like he knew what he was doing. The ball came off the middle of the clubface and flew straight at the pin. It hit and stopped dead, ten feet under the hole. He looked at Ronnie and Eddie and gave them a big grin. He walked up to his putt, still excited about the way he had played the three previous shots. It was time to cash in. When it was his turn, he calmly rolled his putt in for a birdie four. When he looked over at Eddie and Ronnie, he saw strange expressions on their faces. Eddie turned away so he wouldn't have to look at him. As they walked back to the cart, Ronnie stuck his empty hand out. The thirty bucks that Will was expecting was nowhere to be seen. His bubble burst when Street spoke up.

"Sorry, kid," said Eddie. "You owe the old guy another ten bucks."

"But I birdied the hole," protested Will.

"Think back to just before you teed off," said Eddie. "You even said yourself, and I quote, 'A par gets me thirty bucks and I lose ten if I don't'. Well, you did not make the score that the bet was based on."

"But I did better than I said I would," said Will.

"Even though you played a hell of a hole, you didn't satisfy the bet," said Ronnie. "It's a hard lesson, but believe it or not, a cheap one. I know a lot of guys, and I bet Street does too, who have had to cough up a lot more dough than ten bucks to learn what you just did. A man, even a guy as young as you are, should come away a little smarter when something like this happens to them. So, pay up without complaining, and we'll both tell you a little story."

Will pulled out his money clip and slapped another ten in his grandfather's hand. He hoped the stories that were promised were worth the twenty dollars that he had so far forked over.

"I'll go first," said Ronnie, after he hit a beautiful drive up the tenth fairway. "I know you think that Eddie and I are just two guys with movie star looks that can swing a golf club better than most. The truth is, we have both hustled marks, for over thirty years."

"Marks?" asked Will.

"Guys that didn't know they were in over their head until it was too late," explained Ronnie. "Not only were we good players, we had something extra that gave us an advantage. We're both the type of player that didn't let the pressure of a money game throw us off. And we were savvy enough to come up with exotic bets to keep the money flowing into our pockets."

"You're not talking about cheating, are you?" asked Will.

"Nope, we were always honest with the guys we were playing, at least on the golf side of things," said Ronnie. "Let me give you an example. One of the things I would do was hit a big slice off the first tee. I would use a real strong grip and would hold the clubface open at impact.

My opponents got the impression that that was the way I was going to play every shot. It would be lying, and a low class thing to do, if I told them that I always had a big slice, or if I told them I just couldn't find a cure for my big banana ball. I just played that way until I needed to hit it straight. The funny thing is, sometimes I didn't have to change my ball flight. I actually beat some pretty good players slicing the hell out of it for eighteen holes."

"So that's how you got 'The Grip' nickname?" asked Will.

"Yup. The guys that knew me, and played with me regularly back in Chicago, started calling me that."

"Cool," said Will. "What about you. Eddie?"

"I always tried to structure a bet to my advantage," said Eddie. "I hated to give a guy strokes, so one thing I would do was to offer to let him play four or five shots over during the course of the match. Most of the guys that took that deal didn't know when to take the extra shot. Let's say I stripe one on a par five and my opponent hits his tee shot O. B. or into the woods. If it's not too long of a hole he should know that there's a real good chance I'll get home in two, which means I'll probably make birdie. So he jacks out another drive and hits his second shot fifty yards short of the green. Then, and this actually happened more than once, he hits his third shot about twenty feet from the hole. I chip to three feet. He misses the putt and decides to replay the shot, figuring that he can make the second putt. He misses it and I drain my three-footer. He has used up two of his replays and still loses the hole. That's just poor course management."

"Didn't you tell the guy you were playing what your handicap was?" asked Will.

"Ha, I didn't have a legitimate one," said Eddie. "If anyone asked, I just said I was a single digit player, which was true. Your grandpa was right about not lying to our opponents, when it came to our golf abilities. That would be a low-class thing to do. A couple of years ago I took a couple of St. Louis dandies for a few grand over on the West course at GLV. Standing on the tenth tee I told them that I was better than what I showed them on the front side. I didn't say how much better, but I did tell them I was better."

"So you both made millions hustling golf," said Will, with a look of respect in his eyes.

"Not me," said Ronnie. "I made a lot of money playing golf, but most of my money came from buying and selling houses on the side. My golf winnings were just the seed money. The first year I did it, I made eighteen grand on one home and twenty-two on another. I just had a knack for it, and a good contractor who knew what he was doing. What about you, Street?"

"One word, guys," said Street, as he headed for his cart just off the tenth green. Grandfather and grandson walked back to their cart and sat there looking at Eddie.

"Well, we're waiting," said Ronnie, doing best imitation of Judge Schmails from *Caddyshack*. Eddie took off and looked back over his shoulder. "Microsoft," he hollered.

Darkness was setting in, so the guys skipped sixteen and seventeen and drove on to the eighteenth tee. Will teed up and looked over at his grandpa.

"Grandpa, how about giving me 2 to 1 for a par and 3 to 1 for a birdie on this hole?"

"Not a chance," said Ronnie. "What I will do, is give your twenty back if you can answer a question."

"If I get it wrong, I don't lose anything, do I?" asked Will.

"Now you're thinking like a hustler," said Ronnie. "No, you don't owe me anything for a wrong answer. Eddie tells me one of his most successful gigs was to play the whole round with his 4-iron and a putter. Sometimes he would get odds to beat a certain score and sometimes he would play guys even up. My question to you is: If he had to play this hole with just his 4-iron and a putter, what would be his strategy?"

"This is gonna take some thinking," said Will. "Eddie hits his four about 190 to 195, and this hole plays about 520, with some of it downhill. So, two solid shots eats up about 400 yards, which means he has around 120 left to the green. I can't believe he would want to hit his four that distance for his third shot. He would have trouble stopping it, so he would be doing a lot of guessing on what the ball was going to do once it got to the green. And there's plenty of greenside trouble, so he would want to keep the guesswork and the chance that he would get an unlucky bounce to a minimum."

"Give us an answer, kid," said Eddie. "It's getting dark and I'm getting hungry."

"I got it. You play a normal tee shot. Then you figure out how far you have to hit your second shot to give you a full 4-iron into the green. You then hit a choke-down four to get the yardage you want on your third shot. Once you do that, it's like playing a 180 or 190-yard par three. I also happen to know that you love your 4-iron and are pretty much like a magician with it. Do I get my dough back, grandpa?"

"You earned it, Will," said Ronnie, handing him back his two tens. "What do you say skip this hole and go find us some food?"

The guys decided to go over to the GLV grill, because it was close and Pam was working. They knew she was frustrated with her job and her love life. She told them she had taken a course in restaurant management recently, but getting an interview for a management position was just about impossible. Her big drawback was she didn't know anybody with some clout. As in most businesses, knowing someone gave you a huge advantage when it came to opening doors. Eddie and Ronnie could tell from her body language that she was not happy with her situation and it was really getting her down.

All through dinner, Will peppered his mentors with questions on the art of winning golf and how to set up bets that were advantageous to him. He loved being around the two old guys—the way they talked and the stuff they talked about reminded him of some of his favorite golf movies.

"Most of it has to do with dealing from a position of strength," said Eddie. "If you pretty much know the outcome of a future event, you have the advantage. For example, would you bet Grip or me $50 that we couldn't break 75 on any of the five courses in the GLV complex?"

"No, I don't think I'd take that bet," answered Will.

"How about shooting 68 or better?" asked Ronnie.

"I'd bet you $50 you couldn't beat 68, but not $1000."

"He's learning," said Street, leaning back in his chair. "He knows for $50 we'd be yukking it up and having a good time. A grand, however, would get our attention."

"How about this?" asked Ronnie. "Would you bet me $20 that I couldn't throw a tee completely across eighteen green on the West course?"

"Meaning, you would stand in the fringe on one side and throw a normal length tee over the middle part of the green, and it would at least land in the fringe on the other side?" asked Will, as he pictured the event in his mind. "Oh, and who gets to decide where you stand?"

"I get to decide," said Ronnie. "It's a long green, so obviously I would throw the width and not the length. And that was good thinking about making sure the tee has to pass over the middle part of the green."

"Careful," cautioned Eddie. "This is an old bit—like when Don Johnson fooled Kevin Costner in the movie, *Tin Cup*. You remember, when they hit 7-irons for distance?"

"Yeah, Johnson hit his down the road," said Will. "Costner should have stipulated exactly where they had to hit their shots. Okay, I give up. I don't know how you would do it, but I still wouldn't bet against you."

"Good thinking," said Ronnie. "I would simply put the tee into the little bag where I keep my change and other small golf stuff, then I would add about six balls for weight. It wouldn't be too tough to throw the whole thing across the green. I only did that once, because I felt that I had been cheated during the round. That sort of circus stuff is for amateurs, if you ask me."

"Did you ever do anything like that, Street?" asked Will.

"Yeah, but not very often," said Eddie. "Like your grandpa said, it's a gimmick and not for guys that are legit. I did bet a guy that I could chip a ball from just in front of the green and keep it above the hole. The back half of this particular green had such a severe slope that on a normal day a ball wouldn't sit there. They always trickled back at least to the middle of the green. It was definitely a design flaw by the course architect or the guys with the bulldozers that actually built the green. He was no dummy, so he quizzed me on the type of ball that I would use for the shot. He wanted to know if I had altered it in any way so it wouldn't roll like a normal ball. I told him that I had done nothing to the ball and it was one that you could buy over the counter at any pro shop. When he agreed to the bet, I pulled a ball out of my bag that I had found on the edge of a pond a couple of days earlier. It had chunks of dried mud all over it. You could barely tell that it was a golf ball. I bumped the ball to the back of the green with a 4-iron, and then it started to trickle back. Ten feet short of the hole, one of the big mud chunks kept the ball from rolling any further. He wasn't happy, but he paid up. I'll admit, I wasn't too proud of that little wager, but the guy deserved it."

"Forget that stuff, kid," said Ronnie, looking over at Eddie for approval. "Here's what you need to know in addition to dealing from a position of strength. Bet on what is, not what you want things to be. Given the situation, if my normal round can beat your good round, we have a bet. I'm willing to lose if you play out of your head or if I just tank it—that's only fair. Look, two thirds of the time, Eddie and I will play our normal round. One sixth of the time we will play a great round and the other sixth of the time we will play worse than normal. When playing for money, emotion should not be part of the equation. Right, Street?"

"He's right," said Eddie. "Let me ask you this, could you beat your grandpa if he gave you five a side?"

"Let's see," said Will, as he mulled over the facts. "I know he wouldn't take it easy on me. I learned that the hard way earlier today. Okay, on a normal day he will shoot close to 70, or even a little better, which means I will probably have to break 80 to beat him. I haven't done that yet, so no, I wouldn't take that bet."

"What if he would let you hit four shots over, anywhere you want in addition to the five a side?"

"So now the question is, can I break 80 if I get to replay four shots? Yeah, I'd do that."

Eddie gave Ronnie a look of surprise. They liked the kid's confidence, but were worried that he might be a little too cocky. Ronnie looked his grandson in the eye and said in a serious tone.

"Would you play for $50?"

"Yup."

"How about $500?"

"No," answered Will. "Five hundred is out of my comfort zone, and you two always told me to stay within my zone. Let the other guy worry about losing the grocery or the rent money."

"The kid's got potential," said Eddie, throwing his napkin on the table and signaling to Pam for their bill. When she brought it over, the two old hustlers pulled out a coin to flip for the bill. Will surprised them when he pulled out his own coin.

"Odd man pays," he said.

The first time they all showed tails. On the second toss, Ronnie had a tail while the other two showed heads. He acted disgusted, but inside he was filled with pride. His grandson was learning fast, and not just on the golf course. He was becoming a man right before his eyes and Ronnie liked what he was seeing. The kid threw a ten on the table for a tip and got a nod of satisfaction from Eddie. What Will didn't see as he they walked away was Eddie throw another ten-spot down on top of his.

Outside, Ronnie put Will's bike in the trunk of his old beater and they headed for Will's house. Eddie had a sudden thought and turned back toward the clubhouse. He went up to the pro, who was closing up the shop for the evening, and asked if one of the owners was around. The pro led him to the owner's office and knocked on the door. John Scott was sitting in his office catching up on his paperwork.

"Hey, John," said Eddie extending his hand. "Name's Eddie Ferguson. Do you have a minute?"

"I know who you are, Eddie" said John, taking Eddie's hand. "I appreciate you and your partner keeping a low profile here. I don't think it would hurt business if my golfers knew about you two, and shall we say your exploits out on the short grass, but I think you'll agree that a few unsavory types might start showing up if they knew you were here."

"Yeah," agreed Eddie. "I know some guys that aren't what you would call 'members in good standing'."

"What's on your mind?" asked John.

"You've got a waitress, Pam, that needs a break, and I was hoping you might be able to help her. She's got restaurant manager training, but nowhere to show what she can do. Any chance she could take on some more responsibility here?"

John thought for a minute. He knew Eddie wouldn't have come to him unless he felt strongly about Pam. He also knew there was no romantic connection, because he had seen Eddie on the course and off with Suzanne, a prominent attorney, for at least a couple of years.

"Tell you what," said John. "I am in need of an event coordinator. The pro and his staff take care of the serious golf tournaments and outings, but it would be nice to have a woman in charge of the more social events. I'm always trying to get more ladies to play, so this might be the ticket. A week from Monday we're going to have a group of about 90 here from Lansing. They're senior couples that like to travel around and play different courses. I told them they had to come in the fall, during our slow time. We're going to shotgun them off the West course at ten. The pro shop personnel will put together a little gift bag for them, but Pam can take care of everything else, including lunch. If it goes off without any major problems, the job is hers."

"Fair enough," said Eddie standing. "I'm sure she'll be up to the task." He was confident about his last statement, because he and Ronnie were going to be there as volunteers. What could go wrong with two experienced guys like them giving advice?

Pam's emotions went from ecstatic to apprehensive to outright fear. When Mr. Scott offered her the opportunity for more money and more responsibility, she readily jumped at it. Now she wasn't so sure. What the heck did she know about running a golf outing? She stood under the West course pavilion and surveyed her set-up. The grounds crew had 49 carts staged and ready to go. She only needed 46 for the 92 golfers, but her two volunteers needed one and Eddie told her to have an extra one ready in case there were problems. Her sign-in table had 92 gift bags behind it. She had personally tied 46 pink ribbons around the ladies' bags. The womens' bags had lip balm and two low compression balls in them along with tees and assorted snacks. Ronnie told her that it would be a nice touch to add a few items just for the ladies.

When Pam asked how difficult it would be to check in 92 golfers, Eddie just chuckled. He said she didn't have to check in 92 golfers, she only had to check in 23—just the team captains. They would give them the instructions and then the captains would go back and tell their groups what was going on. She put her trust in him, because he seemed like he knew what he was doing. She had only checked in two groups when a tall 60ish man started to question her methods. He looked over the instructions and the hole assignments, as he walked away from her table. He only took a few steps before he turned back to her and asked why she had two groups starting on hole number six, a par three. Before she could answer, Eddie walked up behind her.

"Because number five is a tough par five," he explained. "Trust me, by the time the group on five walks off the green, the second group on six will be walking off their green."

"I don't like it," said the tall man. "We're going to be jammed up out there from the start."

"Here's what you need to do, chief," said Eddie, keeping his tone firm, but friendly. "It's a beautiful day. Go out, play this fantastic course and enjoy yourself. Everything else will take care of itself."

"Aggh," said the man, as he gave them a wave of dismissal and walked away.

"Wow," said Pam. "I hope there aren't many grumps like him in this group."

"He's the only one, dear," said Alice, a smiling gray-haired lady. "That's Rick Wayne. He's finished in the top five in the Senior Michigan Open twice, and because of that, he thinks he's God's gift to golf. The only thing we have to worry about now is if his team doesn't finish first. We're only playing for gag gifts, but he always takes it so seriously. We joke about paying the other three that draw him for the day for just playing with him."

Ronnie walked up and asked who the guy was that just slammed his bag on the back of a cart. Pam, Eddie and Alice just laughed. Another lady walked up and told Alice that they were short one golfer. One of the guys had to go back home for a family emergency. Alice looked at Pam.

"Young lady, I don't suppose you have a senior golfer hanging around that would like to fill in for us?"

Pam looked at Eddie and he nodded with a devious look in his eye. Before he went to retrieve his clubs from his car, he stopped and had a few words with Rick, the grump. It didn't take long to arrange a $100 bet between them. Eddie was taking a real chance without knowing the skill level of his teammates. He figured to shoot a few under on his own ball, and since they were playing a scramble, if one of his teammates could putt, they would probably shoot somewhere in the mid-sixties.

As it turned out, Alice was in his group, and the old girl could putt. She made two twenty-foot putts and a monster from thirty-five feet. Eddie chipped in for an eagle on the par five fifth, their last hole. He couldn't remember when he had had more fun playing in a couples format. They laughed and joked their way around the course, enjoying the weather, the scenery and each other's company. Eddie told them about some of the other courses in the area and they were impressed. Rick Wayne's grin faded when Alice, sporting a huge smile on her face, tossed their card on the table where Ronnie and Pam were tabulating the scores. He figured his team's 67 would easily win first place and $100 from the wise guy that challenged him. When Rick looked over Ronnie's shoulder and saw 63 on the card, he about lost it. He went straight to his cart and drove across the road to the pro shop. He hurried into the shop and confronted the assistant pro on duty.

"What's your name, son?" asked Rick.

"Name's Chris, sir. What can I do for you?"

"Do you have a pro about my age working here?"

"Nope. The head pro's younger than you and he's off today."

Rick was still not convinced that someone hadn't pulled a fast one on him. "Well, who is the guy that is helping out with our outing? Not the bald guy, the other one."

"You're probably talking about Eddie," said Chris. "He's just one of our members. He plays almost every day with the other guy that's helping out over there. Nice guy."

"Was he ever a tour player?" asked Rick, still not giving up on weaseling out of his bet with Eddie. He figured if he could prove that Eddie was some sort of ringer, and that he was set up, he would not have to pay up on the bet. Welching on golf bets was not new to him. He usually won most of his wagers, but when he didn't, he always looked for a reason not to pay.

"Not that I know of," said Chris. "Between you and me, I think he's a bit of a hack." It took Chris about one season to figure out that Eddie and Ronnie were not what they appeared to be. Ever since then, he had been instrumental in setting up a few gigs for them. He never lied on their behalf, but at times he pushed the truth to its limit. By calling Eddie a hack, he could have explained that, to golfers, the term 'hack' also meant a guy that liked to have fun during a round and wasn't opposed to goofing off a little just to lighten things up.

Rick started out the door only to see the rest of his group walking over for the buffet lunch that had been set up for them. When Eddie didn't show, expecting to be paid, Rick didn't know what to do, so he left the $100 with Pam. She was all aglow after receiving several compliments on her handling of the outing. Before Eddie left, he told her that Rick would come by with a bonus for her great organizational skills. That guy never ceased to amaze her. She wondered if Suzanne knew how lucky she was to have someone like him. Maybe someday a guy like that would wander into her life.

CHAPTER EIGHTEEN

Coming of Age

Wilson Randall is one of the nicest boys at school. It's too bad I didn't see it earlier. When I found out what my boyfriend for the better part of two years was really like, I felt pretty stupid for staying with him so long. I guess that's what being a teenager is all about—learning from your mistakes.

—Melissa Perkins, high school golfer/babe

Bullies. They're a constant source of stress for people of all ages. Some experts say bullies make other people's lives miserable because they have low self-esteem. Others say their behavior stems from too much self-esteem.

Whatever their skewed logic is, bullies are an enormous problem in our society. And this mindless stupidity is not just relegated to the younger crowd. People who should definitely know better also practice this form of cruelty toward their fellow man. Social media has given rise to a whole new class of bullies. In the old days, the bullies were the big guys or girls who walked around tormenting their peers. Today, anyone can get in on the act, no matter what his or her physical stature is. Through the Internet, words, pictures or videos can be used to demean someone else in front of a few or in front of thousands.

The question is: What do teen bullies think about their behavior when they are older and they look back on their formative years? Do they make excuses for themselves? Do they say the target of their abuse deserved it? Or do they just blow it off, quoting the ever popular, "everyone did that sort of thing back when we were kids".

Everyone, you say?

Let's ask for a show of hands at the next class reunion. "How many in the room were not bullies back in high school?" When the hands go up, the high school bully's little attempt at rationalization has been proven to be groundless. The problem is, these types will probably just shrug their shoulders and go about their business thinking that their actions were just part of growing up. It was no big deal. One thing is for certain; too many young people and even some who are well past their teens, can be very creative when it comes to being mean to others. It's too bad all that mean spiritedness can't be channeled into something more productive.

We desperately need more first-class problem solvers in this country. Bullies, we can do without.

It was mid-October and the air was starting to get nippy. Low sixties felt cool after five months of upper seventies and mid eighties.

Will stepped off the school bus and went straight to his bike in the garage. Thirty seconds later he was heading south pumping the pedals for all he was worth. He was now working out on the course, mowing or helping with special projects. The other guys liked his work ethic and the fact that he never complained no matter what job he was given. The grounds crew had gone home, and since they had left no instructions for him, he pulled his clubs from their hiding place in the range storage building.

Might as well see how many holes he could get in before dark.

The North Course looked to be completely empty, so he walked through the tunnel and over to the first tee. He liked starting out on a par five, because it was easier to make up for an early round poor swing. Sure enough, his first shot was an anemic fade that stopped about 180 yards out from the tee. He fired up his mp3 player and put his ear buds in. The music took most of the boredom out of playing by himself. It also helped to keep his mind off of Melissa. She wasn't with Troy any more, which was a good thing, but she seemed to be more interested in him as a friend than a girlfriend. Grip and Street both counseled him on what he should say to her, but they were old school. Times were different than when they were in high school.

Heck, weren't the girls wearing skirts with poodles on them back then?

A flushed 5-wood, followed by a crisp wedge, left him a fifteen-foot birdie putt. He left the putt hanging on the lip.

The kid was only one over as he stood on the eighth tee. His best score on this particular nine was a 40, so he was definitely pumped. He finished the front side with a bogey and a par for a 38. Then he played the next three holes in one under, leaving him at one over for the round.

Was this the day that it would finally happen?

His grandfather had told him that once he broke 80, he would start doing it with regularity. It was like breaking through a barrier, and once you got to the other side you tended to stay on the other side.

He walked up to the par three seventeenth tee. A dark shape shuffled along the cart path in front of him. The coon went about his business, oblivious to the human standing only thirty yards away. It was his time of day now, and he couldn't be bothered by something as silly as a boy playing a game. Will took a deep breath and reminded himself to relax before he took the club back. As he maneuvered his way around the course, Eddie's and Ronnie's voices were always in his head reminding him to think every shot through before he made his stroke—balance, tempo, swing plane, release. Every shot. Every time.

He could barely make out the green 165 yards away. He hit, but wasn't sure where the ball ended up. When he got to the green he saw that he was about ten feet short of the putting surface. A poor chip and an equally poor putt left him with a bogey. He was now three over for the round. Par eighteen for a 75, bogey for a 76. He would have gladly accepted either one.

The high school junior crushed his tee shot on eighteen. It was a remarkable feat, given the fact that he could barely see the ball as he addressed it. He spent ten minutes in the area where he assumed his drive ended up, but came up empty. It was too dark to finish so he hoofed it back to the range building. As he made his way through the tunnel separating the North and South courses he had delusions of grandeur running through his mind. He conjured up thoughts of huge quantities of cash all based on his ability to play the game. Playing for fifty grand or winning the U. S. Open—it was all heady stuff for a sixteen-year-old boy. He would have been humbled if he knew how many young guys around the world were fantasizing about the same glorious events. He put his clubs away and sat on a range bench for a minute taking in the dark silence all around him. He went over his round in his head. What was so different about it? He decided that the big difference was that he had made very few mistakes, and the ones he did make were minimal. Both of his mentors had told him on more than one occasion that 'a golfer was only as good as his bad shots'. Today's round was proof of that.

He put his hands behind his head, leaned back, and laughed out loud. It wasn't a loud "I knew it" laugh. It was more of a "I do love this game" laugh.

He stood and went over to his bike that was chained to a pipe on the back side of the building. A big grin adorned his face for the entire ride home. It was an amazing feeling. He was convinced that he was on his way to becoming more than just an accomplished golfer.

The bike ride home gave him time to reflect on his situation. He thought about what other high school juniors would do after they shot a career round. They would probably go around telling everybody how good they were, and their score should have been three or four shots lower due to bad breaks. That's what Troy always did. He didn't even like the guy and rarely talked to him, but he knew that Troy's best round on the North course was a 74. The cocky senior came to school the next day and told anyone that would listen about his great round, even his teachers. What would Grip and Street do? That was obvious. They would keep it to themselves until they could profit from it. He decided to take that course of action. Didn't they always say never to show your ass? He had the two best teachers a guy could have. A smart student would follow their lead and profit from their wisdom and experience. One thing he vowed not to do was forget who he was and where he came from, if and when he became successful at this game. With that thought in mind, he went in and did his chores, a little homework, and then fixed supper for his mom. She would be home around ten, and if she asked, all he would tell her he had a good round going, but it got too dark to finish.

Take that, Troy!

* * *

The next day at school was no different from any other day. Troy was on his case as soon as he saw him. He seemed to be a little worse since Melissa broke up with him.

"Hey, Willie Lump Lump," hollered Troy, when he saw Will coming toward him in the hallway. "You going out for golf this season? Wait, I forgot, you're awful. Forget about it. You just don't have the game, boy. Maybe you can caddie or wash our balls for us."

"Why don't you just punch that guy in the face, Will?" asked his friend Billy, as they headed down the hall in the opposite direction. "You're as big as he is and you're definitely a lot stronger. That jerkwad has been on your case big time ever since he found out you got the range job at The Hedge."

"I quit worrying about him a long time ago," answered Will. "He's the type of guy that my grandfather says he would like to buy him for what he's worth and then sell him for what he thinks he's worth."

"Wow, what are you, some sort of philosopher now? That's pretty good for a guy that's got no girlfriend and no prospects."

"I'm playing it cool, Bilbo. A lot of these guys are running around with their tongues out, drooling all over the place. They'd hook up with just about any female that can walk down the hall and not fall on her face. You want a cool babe, you have to be cool yourself. Opposites usually don't attract, when it comes to matters of romance."

"Okay, stop right there," said Bill, grabbing his friend by the shoulders. "Are you an alien that has taken over my friend's body? If you are, get out! There's no way the Wilson Randall I know is that smart."

"Stop it," said Will. "People are looking at us. Besides, I'm not that smart. There goes Rupert Wiffle with one of the hottest babes in school. That totally disproves my theory about how opposites don't usually attract."

"True that," snorted Billy. "That guy's even dumber than his name."

* * *

It was November and Eddie was getting ready to head south to visit his daughters and their families. Ronnie was out in San Diego testifying before a grand jury. It would only take him a day to answer questions, as a grand jury's responsibility is to conclude just one thing: Is there enough evidence to go to trial? From what Herman had told him, it looked like Marilyn, the temptress, and her accomplices were in big trouble. He would be only too happy to help put them away. He had decided to only spend a couple of weeks in Southern California this time around. Now that he had made up with his daughter-in-law, he wanted to spend more time with his little family. He and Kathy were also getting along very well. He had thought about asking her to move in with him, but couldn't bring himself to pose the question.

Eddie was planning on spending November in Dallas and December in Florida. Then he would be back in Michigan. He would have to endure the two remaining cold northern months until it started to warm up, but Suzanne said she would warm things up for him if he came back early. Besides, he had another project that he was mulling over. It had been somewhere in the back of his mind for a long time. One night, while relaxing in his tub, he started to toy with the idea of writing a book about his adventures on the golf course. Maybe he should get Ronnie to kick in some of his stories. Half of the book could be his, and Ronnie would get the other half. If they made a million bucks, they could donate it to charity. That would be a cool thing to do and it just might erase the memory of the two grand that he lifted from the poker game back when he was a kid. He knew he should let it go, but the memory of that night and the following day still haunted him.

* * *

Will was having a good day until he walked through the door closest to the school parking lot. He should have figured out that something was amiss when he saw the door was slightly open. Someone had stuck a doorstop in the way so the door wouldn't close completely. As soon as he opened the door a half can of Mountain Dew fell on his head, spilling most of its contents on his shirt. Someone, and he was pretty sure who that someone was, had set him up. He heard some snickers around the corner and then the sound of feet scuffling. When he rounded the hall corner the corridor was empty. He had an extra shirt in his locker, so he grabbed it and headed for the restroom. After cleaning up and changing his shirt, he walked into his first hour class and went right up to Melissa who was parked in a front row seat looking over her homework. He was inspired by the Dew can and decided to change his tactics to a full on frontal assault. Worshipping from afar was obviously not an effective strategy.

"Good morning, Melissa," he said, as Troy watched him from his seat in the back of the room. "It'll be golf weather pretty soon."

"Hi Will," said Melissa, returning his smile. "I know. I can't wait to get out there and smell the grass again. Winters around here seem to get longer and longer."

"That's probably because we don't go out and play in the snow like we did when we were little kids."

"You're right," agreed Melissa. "I used to stand at the window hoping it would snow. Now I dread it because it means I have to shovel the front walk. My dad refuses to buy a snow blower. He says shoveling builds character."

"And big muscles," said Will. "With all the shoveling you did this winter, you'll probably add ten yards to your drives."

"I could use another ten yards, that's for sure."

Will grinned like a fool all the way back to his seat. Troy sat at his desk staring at the range boy. It was obvious that he wasn't happy seeing Will act so friendly toward Melissa. Even though she had terminated their relationship, he hadn't given up hope. They had broken up once before, but two months later she decided to give him a second chance. He just assumed that since he would be commuting to Western Michigan University in Kalamazoo next year, that they would still be together. Now he had another reason to hate the Randall kid. Next time it would be something a little more treacherous than a soda can.

The kid was still beaming when lunch rolled around. He had taken a bad incident and had turned it into a positive thing. He still couldn't believe his conversation with the girl of his dreams. Dealing from a position of strength—wasn't that what Grip and Street had told him? Billy just sat there open-mouthed while Will went over his conversation with Melissa.

"Are you kidding me?' said Billy. "So what, by this time next week you'll be rolling around in the back seat with her? Oh, I forgot, you don't have a car."

"There you go again," said Will. "I'm not saying that being in the back seat with her would be a bad thing, but she's a classy girl. Maybe the girls you hang around with are back seat drama queens, but she's different."

"Really? How long did she go out with Troy Boy? If she's so classy, why would she hang around that dude, letting him lick all over her face and who knows where else? I'm not trying to bust your bubble here, but you need to be realistic."

"All right, all right. I don't have the answer to that. I'm sure it wasn't as nasty as you're making it out to be."

"Maybe you should just go up and ask her," volunteered Billy. "Hey, Lissa, did you like it when Troy use to slobber all over you with that big gross tongue of his?"

"Get away from me, man," said Will getting to his feet. "That's disgusting."

"You know it's true," hollered Billy, as his friend headed down the hall. "It's the way of all things. I think Einstein said that once, and that dude was never wrong."

For the rest of the day all Will could think about was Troy crawling all over Melissa. His first hour natural high had turned into a last hour bummer. Maybe Bilbo was right. Behind closed doors or in the back seat of a car, maybe she was like a lot of the other girls at school. He had to admit that he had put her up on some sort of mythical pedestal, and now Bilbo's comments made him think. One thing that his friend had said was true. He didn't have a car, so he decided to give Grandpa Ron a call that night.

It was time he grew up a little, and that meant not riding the bus to school every day like a little kid.

* * *

"Well, what do you think?" asked Will, standing in his driveway next to his first car. His mother walked around the five-year-old Toyota Camry, not really knowing what to look for. She checked out the tires and inspected it for rust.

"Does it have airbags?" she asked Ronnie. "It probably does, but I'm just making sure."

"Everything works on it, Carol," said Ronnie. "It's a safe car and the gas mileage isn't too bad either. I think it's a perfect vehicle for his first car. I actually bought it from the father of one of Will's classmates. He owns a small used car lot in Richland. He's a mechanic and works on the stuff he sells. He has a good reputation for selling reliable cars and taking care of them once they are sold. Used Toyotas are hard to find, because people tend to hang on to them."

"Grandpa says I only have to pay him back half of the cost," explained Will. "The other half will be part of my graduation present."

"That's very generous of you, Ron," said Carol.

"He's a great kid. A seventeen-year-old needs his own set of wheels. Now you won't have to worry about him riding his bike at night back from the golf course."

"That's true," said Carol. "And since he will get home so much faster, he will have more time for his studies."

"Sure, mom, whatever you say," said Will hugging her. "Wait until you see this machine in a couple of months. I'm putting in a lift kit, two huge bass speakers, and, oh yeah, neon light strips along the bottom of the doors. It should only cost me around four grand or so."

"You're kidding, right?" asked Carol, looking at Ronnie for support.

"Yeah, I'm kidding. You, grandpa and Eddie have brainwashed me into being responsible with my money. I should add Mr. Griswold, my economics teacher, to that list. He has been hammering us about making sure we don't live beyond our means since the first day of class. C'mon, grandpa, I'll take you back to your car at the course."

Carol stood in the driveway and watched her son and his grandfather drive off. He was growing up and there was nothing she could do about it. She was extremely proud of him for several reasons. He was responsible, respectful and a hard worker. What did she expect from Robbie Green's son? She decided to contact the courthouse the next day to see what it would take to have both their names changed back to Green. It was the right thing to do.

* * *

Will rolled into the parking lot the next day at school. Billy was in the passenger seat trying to reset the buttons on the radio.

"I'd believe it if Duke's dad said that this thing belonged to a little old lady," said Bill. "The stations that were programmed in are from like the eighteenth century. We need to get this machine out on the highway and blow some of the crap out of the engine and the exhaust."

"Do that with your own car," said Will. "This thing has to last, so I'll be taking great care of it. And I'm telling you right now, don't spill anything in here. You're sitting in the seat where Melissa might be sitting some day."

"C'mon, man, these wheels are pretty nice for a high school kid, but Troy drives his dad's Cadillac to school most of the time. If you're going to get her attention, you better come up with something better than a five-year-old Toyota. I'll admit, I'm a little jealous 'cause I don't even have a car."

The guys got out and were surprised when Melissa was waiting for them as they walked through the door—the same door that dumped a half can of soda on Will's head a few weeks earlier.

"Will, I need to talk to you," said Melissa, corralling him as soon as the two juniors stepped into the hallway.

"I'll catch up to you, Bilbo," said Will, as his friend headed off down the hall.

"Is that your car?" asked Melissa, nodding toward the lot.

"Yeah, I just got it."

"Good, I need you to do me a big favor," said Melissa, pulling Will off to the side out of the mainstream traffic. "You can say no if you want to, but I'm pretty sure you will say yes once I explain the circumstances."

Stop talking and ask me to go to prom with you, thought Will. *This is incredible! The first full day that I have my own car, and she wants to go to the big dance with me. This is better than winning the lottery.*

"So, will you ask her?" asked Melissa, with her head turned sideways and her eyes all sparkly.

"Uh, go over that again," he said, trying to get a grip on what she was saying.

"Will you ask Jane Pressly to the prom, because her date just came down with mono? I thought I just explained that. She's got a dress and everything. It would mean the world to her and to me. She's been my best friend ever since the third grade."

"Let me think about it," said Will, as he started to regain some of his cognitive thought processes.

"Fair enough," said Melissa, laying her hand on his. "I can't believe that you aren't already going with somebody."

Will watched Melissa as she turned and walked down the hall. After a few seconds, he looked around to see if anyone was watching him stare at her. He thought about what had just happened. He had to admit that he went into a fantasy world as soon as she started talking to him. What the heck! Taking her best friend to the prom was the next best thing to taking Melissa. Maybe he could even get a dance or two with her. Hopefully, she would be grateful for his humanitarian gesture. Didn't she say it would mean the world to her?

* * *

"So you're going to prom with the best friend of this girl that you've been sniffing around for the past two years?" asked Ronnie as he and Will stood on the range at The Hedge.

"I haven't been sniffing around her," said Will, defending himself. "She's just this really nice girl that I think about a lot."

"Why didn't you ask her to the dance?" asked Ronnie.

"I guess I was afraid she would say no," answered Will. "I heard the guy she's going to the dance with asked her about a month ago. And since I didn't have any wheels then, I would have had to borrow mom's car and you know what a piece of junk that is."

"That's a pretty lame excuse," said Ronnie. "Jeez, kid, you've got a grandfather with a '61 Corvette. It's a car that a lot of very rich dudes would like to have in their collection."

Will stopped right in the middle of his backswing and looked over at his grandfather.

"Are you telling me, that if I would have asked Melissa to the prom I could have taken the Vette?"

Ronnie stared at Will and tried hard to hold it together. Will was like Robbie in so many ways.

"Will, you're my only grandson. If you want anything from me, all you have to do is ask. I mean, it has to be within reason, of course."

"Okay, can I take Jane to the prom in your Vette?"

"Hell no! What are you thinking, man? I just said it's a collector car."

Will stood there and stared at his grandfather.

"I'm just messing with you, son," said Ronnie, slapping Will on the back. "Yeah, you can take the Vette. Stop over one of these nights and we'll go over everything you need to know about the car. You can drive a stick, can't you?"

* * *

The weather on prom night was right out of a storybook.

It was 80 degrees when Will picked Jane up at her house. She couldn't believe it when she saw the machine that Will was driving. The plan was to go out to dinner and then to the dance. He told her he could put the top up if she thought it would be too windy for her hair. She said she didn't care, because the car was so cool, and she wanted people to see her in it.

Billy and his date were sitting in his parents' car at the back of the school parking lot. Some of the students didn't like having prom and after-prom at the school, but the huge cost savings got the majority of the votes. That, and the fact that they could now afford better prizes during the after-prom festivities. They were about to get out of the car when they saw two guys run up behind Ronnie's Vette. Will had parked it under one of the lights in the lot, so it was easy to see what was going on. Troy and a buddy had something in a bag and it looked like they were tying a small rope to the car's rear bumper. Then they took out whatever was in the bag and tossed it under the car. The whole exercise looked well planned and it took only about thirty seconds to implement it. They high-fived each other and ran off laughing.

Billy looked over at the girl sitting next to him.

"What was that all about?" he asked, not expecting an answer.

"I don't know," said Mandy Jordan, "but it's probably something we should stay out of. That Troy Feltner is scary if you ask me."

"Let me think about this for a minute," said Billy, looking around the lot. He saw Duke Peterson get out of what looked like a '66 GTO. Duke's dad owned a car lot, so the classic car was no surprise. The surprise was that Duke was going to the dance and that he had a date. The guy spent a lot of time working on cars with his dad and not nearly enough time under the shower. From where Billy and Mandy were sitting, it looked like Duke cleaned up pretty good. Seeing Duke gave Billy and idea. He jumped out of the car and hustled up to the mechanic and his date.

"Hey, Duke, hey, Carrie," said Billy as he walked up with Mandy trailing behind him. "Can I talk to you for a minute? How would you like to earn a fast five bucks?"

"What do you want, Kaminski? If you haven't noticed, we're going to the dance."

"What do you think of Troy Feltner?" asked Billy.

"He's a puke," said Duke. "His dad comes in to the lot and orders my dad and me around, 'cause he's got a lot of money. Why?"

"Do you think you can open up his dad's Cadillac without setting off the car alarm? He just played a little joke on my friend and I want to pay him back. Like I said, there's five bucks in it if you can."

"The alarm's no problem," said Duke. "My dad disabled it a couple of months ago. Old man Feltner said it kept going off when it wasn't supposed to, so he had us disconnect it. Don't tell anybody, 'cause it's illegal to do that."

Duke walked over to the Feltner's Cadillac and looked through the window. He smiled and tried the door handle. The front door swung open. It wasn't even locked. Duke turned around and stuck his hand out. Billy slipped him a five and thanked him. Duke looked at his date.

"And they say mechanics are stupid," he laughed. "Wait until we're in the building before you do anything, Kaminski. We don't want to be in the vicinity in case you blow that thing up. You don't have any explosives, do you?"

"Nope," said Billy. "No one's going to get hurt here. But someone's going to be really pissed when he finds out his little joke backfired. Thanks, man. I hope you and Carrie have a wonderful evening."

It took only about a minute to untie and pull the dead coon out from under the Vette. Mandy held the back door open and Billy swung the smelly animal into the back seat. He then offered his arm to his date and they headed inside to the dance.

"You are such a rebel," whispered Mandy. "I like that in a man."

Billy didn't say a word, but he had the biggest grin on his face. One thing he was sure of, was this was going to be a memorable prom—one way or another.

* * *

"Where is that piece of crap, Randall?" hollered Troy, as he walked into the gym for the after-prom festivities. Apparently he felt that it was okay to prank someone else, but turnabout was not fair play. The dancers had to leave the building for one hour after the formal dance to give the after-prom committee time to set up the gym. Troy and his date spent the hour intermission scrubbing the back seat of his dad's Cadillac. The police were at the door when the prom goers returned, giving everyone a breathalyzer test. Safety was a main concern, given how many accidents and deaths occurred among teens on nights like this.

Billy had stationed himself just inside the door, waiting to intercept Troy before things got ugly. On Billy's suggestion, Will and Jane left the dance a little early so they could cruise through Kalamazoo in Ronnie's car. Billy told him about the coon and the switch, and they both agreed that Will shouldn't be in the vicinity when Troy opened his car door. After cruising, they went back to his house and parked the Vette in the garage. He decided that a vehicle like that shouldn't sit out all night in the school parking lot. Besides, the temperature was now in the mid-sixties and was supposed to hit fifty by dawn. He also didn't want to be driving his grandfather's car to Jane's house, and then back to his house after being up all night.

"Hey, Troy," said Billy, stepping in front of the fuming senior. "Before you get all excited, I've got something to tell you."

"Shut up, Kaminski," snarled Troy. "You little buddy is going to get an ass whupin' as soon as this thing is over." Troy's date gave Billy a big smile. She was one of the not-so-classy girls at school that Billy did his best to avoid.

"Shut up? Is that the way to talk to a guy that might be keeping you out of jail?"

"What are you talking about, dork?"

"Well," said Billy, holding up his phone. "I happen to have a few very clear pictures of you and Johnny Cantemeyer taking a dead coon out of a black garbage bag, tying a small rope to it, and then throwing it under that awesome 1961 Corvette that was parked out in the lot. Oh, by the way, did you know that Will's grandpa is from the south side of Chicago, and he loves that car more than anything? I'll bet he knows some real dangerous guys that will do most anything for a few bucks."

Troy was still breathing hard, but he was starting to calm down as Billy's words sank in. He reached for the phone that Billy was holding. Billy snatched it back out of reach.

"C'mon, man," he said. "Give me some credit, will ya. I already sent those pictures to my dad's phone and to two other phones. I'm not sure what I'm going to do with them yet. I guess it depends on how this conversation goes. Oh yeah, if it doesn't go well for Will or me, principal Jenkins will get a nice little e-mail explaining the whole scenario. I bet the golf coach would be interested in your little joke too. Did you two kill that coon or did you find him on the side of the road?"

Mandy moved forward and stood next to Billy as he was asking the last question. Troy stormed off without saying a word. Billy and Mandy got a nasty look from Troy's date. She was hoping for a little violence to bring some excitement to the evening.

"Wow, what are you, like Sherlock Holmes or something?" asked Mandy. "I never saw you take those pictures."

"Be quiet," cautioned Billy. "There are no pictures. I just thought of that a few minutes ago. But glamour boy doesn't know that. I don't think he'll be bothering us for a while. But with guys like that, you always need to be on your guard. That butthead just thinks he's better than everybody else. I'm not sure why, but he just does. C'mon, babe, let's go have some fun. I'm feeling lucky. Maybe one of us will win the flat screen that they're giving away."

* * *

"Hey, Kaminski," said Duke, as he walked up behind Billy. It was 4:00 a.m. and the after-prom participants were starting to feel the effects of no sleep. "Your boy just barfed in the can. Word is he and some other dicks snuck some booze in a few days ago and hid it in the locker room. He should be kicked off the golf team, but you can bet his dad will find a way for him to weasel out of it. Hey, the puke just puked. Ha!"

* * *

Everything was cleared up by lunchtime on Monday. Apparently Troy was the butt of a cruel joke played by some of his classmates. Someone had put vodka in the soft drinks he was drinking, and since he had never tasted alcohol before, he didn't know what was going on. At least that was the story that his dad was peddling and the principal decided to go along with it. His status on the golf team was secure and his WMU scholarship offer was not in any jeopardy.

"Can you believe that?" asked Billy during lunch. "Troy Boy was still smoking about the raccoon bit backfiring, so he gets hammered on school property. And his dad's money gets him out of the whole thing. Where's the justice in that?"

Will shook his head. "Yeah, you remember when Shirley Gunther got caught at that big drinking party last year?" asked Will. "Her mom argued before the school board that she had just stopped to pick up a friend and wasn't partying like everyone else in the house. She didn't get suspended for even one basketball game. It helps to have some pull—that's for sure. Hey, thanks again for everything you did on Saturday. You definitely turned disaster into victory."

"No problemo," said Billy. "Now Mandy thinks I'm some sort of superhero. The way I see it, it was a win/win situation. And to be honest, I don't think getting kicked off the golf team and losing a scholarship would have been the proper punishment for Troy's crime. Even if he is the biggest jerkwad in school."

"There's hope for you yet, Bilbo," said Will, as they headed for their fifth hour class.

CHAPTER NINETEEN

Slick

Crossroaders, mechanics and just plain old cheats. They're all over the place. Hell, the last time I played I had to deal "seconds" just to win a couple a hundred. What happened to all the honest card players?

—Louie "Hands" Michaelson, cardsharp

Eddie watched as she walked through the front door of the sports bar where he had been waiting for her. She had called him twice, an hour ago and a half hour ago, to tell him she was just about to leave the office. He had nursed his scotch and water for the last forty-five minutes and was getting hungry. A few baseball games were on the flat screens that were spaced around the room, but the Tiger game wasn't on, so he wasn't all that interested. The Cubs were getting shut out eight to nothing, which made him chuckle. Ronnie probably had the game on at home, as he played the horses on the Internet. Three twenty-something women in the next booth were going on and on about themselves, which made waiting for his date all the more irritating. He tried not to listen in on their conversation, but it was unavoidable due to their high volume, and the fact that there wasn't another open table to move to. Apparently they had been there a while and were bragging about all the drinks that they had hustled from the men at the bar.

Now the main topic of their conversation was a web site they could join that offered female companionship for a price. They were wondering how much their "companionship" was worth to guys that had money to spend on "hot" women like them.

Eddie stood when he saw his date come through the front door. Even though she was in her early fifties, she still turned a lot of heads when she walked into a room. Suzanne motioned that she would only be a minute and then headed for the ladies' room.

"Excuse me, sir," said one of the three women that had been annoying Eddie for the past half hour. "We were wondering if you could settle a little matter for us."

"What's that?" asked Eddie, not really wanting to talk to the booth's occupants.

"Well, you've been sitting there all alone for quite some time," said the blond one, as the other two in the booth tried to stifle their laughter. "Anyway, we assumed that you don't have a date, and we were wondering, just for conversation purposes, how much would you pay to have one of us spend the evening with you? And which one would you choose? I'm talking just dinner and drinks here. We're not hookers or anything. You could show one of us off to your friends and impress them."

"Let me think," said Eddie, as he watched the door to the ladies' room. The three women tried to suppress giggles as Eddie pretended to weigh the facts. Suzanne appeared and made her way through the crowd. She was her usual gorgeous self, wearing a black dress, black heels and an exquisite necklace that Eddie had recently given her. "To answer your questions, nothing and none of you. You appear to be lacking in the one essential quality that I require of female companions."

"Oh yeah," said the surprised blond. "What's that?"

"Class," said Eddie, as Suzanne came up and kissed him on the cheek.

"Sorry I'm late, Street," she said, looking at the three women in the booth. "It looks like you're making some new friends here."

"Not hardly," said Eddie, offering his arm to Suzanne.

"What was that all about?" asked the attorney, as they crossed the parking lot and got into Eddie's convertible.

"Just some young girls, who thought they were pretty special."

Suzanne gave him a quizzical look, but didn't ask what he meant. If he would have wanted her to know, he would have told her. That was one of the things she liked about Eddie. After working all day with other lawyers that liked to impress everyone with their rhetorical skills, it was refreshing to spend some time with a guy that wasn't in love with his own voice.

The three "special" ladies watched out the bar window as Eddie and Suzanne got into a beautiful blue and white classic automobile.

"Hey," said Eddie, looking over at his passenger. "Three twenty-something ladies walked into a bar."

"And?" asked Suzanne, as he held back the punch line.

"You'd think one of them would have ducked."

"Cute," said the attorney.

Eddie and his date had just finished a fabulous dinner of baked cod, red potatoes and fresh spinach, accompanied by an exceptional white wine. They chatted back and forth, telling each other about their activities for the past few days. Suzanne was working on a big case, but couldn't tell Eddie any of the details. He told her about Will taking the Vette to prom and the coon prank. He also told her that he was glad that Will's adversary didn't get kicked off the golf team. Kids are kids and that sort of stuff happens all the time. When he asked her what mischief she had pulled in high school, the only thing she could come up with was that she and some friends had t-peed the principal's house. She told him her high school years were filled mostly with work and studies. Her family didn't have a lot and her income was needed. Eddie admitted that he was pretty much in the same boat. He started out caddying at a public course and then ended up working in the pro shop.

They walked out into the cool Michigan air and started toward the lot.

"Hands up, Fast Eddie," said a threatening voice from behind them. Suzanne and Eddie both froze.

"I'm not carrying much money," said Eddie in a scared, whiney voice. "Take the woman. She's a smooth talker and not too hard on the eyes."

Suzanne gave him a shocked look. Eddie, recognizing Slick's voice turned around slowly and extended his hand. The black man shook his hand and waited to be introduced to Suzanne. Eddie got a punch in the arm for his little indiscretion. Slick said he needed to talk to Eddie, so they sat in his car out of the night air.

"Man, this is one sweet ride," observed Slick from the back seat. "I drive a Caddy, but there's something to be said for old time engineering. Listen, hey, she's not a cop is she?"

"Attorney," said Suzanne.

"Okay. Here's the deal. For the past few months me and some other guys have been playing poker in one of the back rooms at Big Daddy's. We're getting tired of the casino rake."

"What's that?" asked Suzanne.

"The casino takes so much out of every pot," explained Eddie. "That's their cut for providing the facility where players can get together and for dealing a legit game."

"I'm confident that there's some cheatin' going on, but I can't figure it out," explained Slick. "The same group of guys are consistently winning and they don't appear to be very good players. I mean, they make some of the dumbest moves, but still come out ahead at the end of the night. Any chance you would sit in and see if you can spot something?"

"Do you know all the guys in the game, or are there some unknowns?" asked Eddie.

"They're pretty much local guys," said Slick. "I can't vouch for all of them, but I do know that they're all from this area."

Eddie thought for a moment while Slick and Suzanne made small talk. Most of it was how did a smart lawyer type get hooked up with a poker-playing dude like Eddie? Slick was surprised when she told him they met at a golf course. He didn't even know that Eddie played golf.

"Okay," said Eddie. "I'll sit in and play a few hands. But, since I don't know these guys, I'll leave early and fill you in later if I see anything. That way they won't make the connection between me and getting caught at their little game. Trouble has a way of finding me, without me running around looking for it. Fair enough?"

"Fair enough," said Slick, as he opened the back door. "Suzanne, you ever been in the back seat of this fine machine? There's a lot of room in these older model cars."

"As far as you know, I haven't," laughed Suzanne. "Stay out of trouble, Slick. I don't want to see you in the courtroom."

"I hear that, lawyer lady. Next Tuesday, around 9:00, Eddie."

Eddie gave him a wave of acknowledgement and fired up the engine.

* * *

"I'll call," said Eddie, from his seat at the poker table in the back room at Big Daddy's. He followed up his statement by tossing a couple of chips into the pot.

Slick and four others sat around the green felted table. A couple of onlookers sat against the wall observing the action. Eddie was pretty sure that the larger of the two, who served as the banker, was also there to solve any disputes. When anyone entered he frisked them for weapons before he took their cash and converted it into chips.

The hustler knew what they were doing was mildly illegal, so the plan was to play for a few hours, get a feel for what the cheaters were doing, then politely excuse himself from the game. Hopefully, it wouldn't be too difficult to spot what was going on. The buy-in was $400 minimum, so no one would get burned real bad. The money made sense to Eddie. If a guy loses a few hundred, he goes away mad. Clip him for a couple grand, and he goes away devastated and maybe looking to get even.

After an hour, Eddie was down about $50 and Slick was up around $100. So far, he was coming up empty, as to what these guys, or maybe what just one guy was doing. If only one of them was cheating, he was very adept at disguising it. Two games were being played—Texas Hold 'em and Seven Card Stud. The deal went around the table, so the players didn't have to pay for that service. Big Daddy's take was a $20 fee from each player that was collected before play started. Of the guys he didn't know, three were black and one was white. The white guy, Brady, said he was from Marshal, a little town east of Battle Creek. He was the only one at the table wearing glasses, and he was about even for the night. At this point in the game, Slick was actually the big winner.

The three black players were friendly enough and they appeared to be mediocre players, like Slick said. They were the type of players that Eddie took regular money from at the Firekeepers Casino. They seldom won, but the lure of a big score kept them coming back. It was a little like golf. All a guy had to do was hit that one awesome shot, or birdie a tough hole, and it didn't matter what his performance was like in the long run. That one moment of glory was all it took to make him think he was close to actually being good at the game.

Eddie knew he had to do something unconventional if he was going to get a handle on what was going on. The current game was Hold 'Em and the guy to his left had the deal. Eddie cautiously looked down at his hole cards and saw a pair of kings. He called a modest bet by Slick and waited for the flop. When the first three cards were turned over, there was an ace, a king and a three, all diamonds. When Slick bet $20, the other four folded. Eddie felt that was odd, because if even one of the other players had a diamond, he would probably pay $20 for two shots at a flush. It was obvious that Slick was holding at least one diamond himself. Eddie looked at Slick and threw his cards in. Slick seemed a little disappointed, as he raked in the pot. Eddie expected that, but what surprised him was the reaction of the white guy with the glasses that he caught out of the corner of his eye. Eddie's peripheral vision was good and what he saw was intriguing. It was an inquisitive sort of look. If the Detroit gambler's vision would have been more acute, he would have also seen the same look on the other players' faces—but the look on Brady's face was enough.

The guy in the glasses knew what his hole cards were! That's why he had the surprised expression on his face when Eddie folded his pocket kings with another lying face up on the table. So that was it. Somehow the cards were marked and he was reading them with the glasses he was wearing. Eddie played for another hour to confirm his theory. When the hour passed, Eddie had the scam down pat. Brady and his buddies were slowly depleting Slick's and Eddie's chips. Brady must be signaling what Slick and Eddie were holding to his three partners. If the situation was right, they would build the pot, so the mark would stay in with inferior cards. On the last round of betting, they would all fold except for the guy with the strongest hand. Then he would go head-to-head with the guy with the second best hand—Eddie or Slick. They folded so they wouldn't have to show what cards they were holding. It wouldn't make sense to keep calling with absolutely nothing in their hand. They kept the bets modest, trying to bleed all they could from the two guys who weren't in on the bit. It didn't matter which one of them was winning or losing, as long as their two marks were down. When it was all over, they would end up splitting what the suckers lost.

Eddie verified his theory when, a few hands later, he hit trip sevens on the river, the last card turned up on the community hand, and everyone else folded. He had only thrown $20 into the pot and the cards all came flying in. A $20 bet on the last card shouldn't have elicited that sort of reaction. With an ace, a king and a jack showing, at least one of the three should have stayed. But since they all knew that Eddie had them beat, they folded. Eddie looked at his watch and excused himself from the table. He was down about $150, and another player was waiting to join the group, so there was no grumbling from the scammers. Fresh money was always welcome. He had the banker turn his chips back into cash and headed for the door. Just before he walked out he gave Slick a subtle thumbs up, indicating that he had something for him.

* * *

Two days later Ronnie and Eddie were having a late lunch at GLV.
The scorecard on the table read identical scores of 68. They had just played the North Course over at The Hedge and were $100 richer, thanks to Ronnie's baby driver scam on the second hole.

The group behind them all threw in $25, thinking the shot he proposed was all but impossible. Just like in practice, he lofted his driver barely over the front edge of the green and kept it on the surface. The guys they took the money from were good sports about it. They even asked Ronnie how long he had practiced that particular shot. As he and Eddie got in their cart, Ronnie asked them if they wanted to go double or nothing on him two-putting from about forty feet using his driver. The answer was a resounding "no".

"So," asked Eddie, in one of his philosophical moods, "if we polled 1000 guys, how many would agree with the saying that 'practice makes perfect'?"

"I'd say way over half of them," answered Ronnie, as he tied into his club sandwich.

"Just for discussion purposes," continued Eddie, "how many would pay, say $10, if I could prove that the saying is totally inaccurate? I'd offer two to one odds that I could absolutely convince them."

"Americans like to gamble," said Ronnie. "We're living proof of that. The odds would be tempting. How are you going to prove it to their satisfaction?"

"Pure logic. For example: I'm going to practice eight hours a day and in five years time, I'll be on the big stage singing opera. Or how about this? If your kid practices real hard every day he or she will make the Olympic gymnastics team. Anyone can see the false logic in that. Just practicing something for a long time does not necessarily mean you will be any good at whatever it is you are trying to do."

"I agree that you have to have solid fundamentals and a high degree of skill to do anything well," said Ronnie. "But I don't think people will pay you to crush their dreams, theirs or their kids'."

"I'm not crushing dreams. I'm just being realistic. Here's an example that proves my point. When I was about twenty, this member came into the shop I was working at and announced that he was on vacation for the next fourteen days. He said he was going to hit two or three large buckets every day, with the goal of lowering his handicap by at least five strokes. The pro and I watched him through the window for the first three days. The guy was a train wreck out there and finally the pro couldn't take it any more, so he went out to the practice tee and confronted him."

"What did he say to the guy?" asked Ronnie.

"He told the guy that hitting all those balls wasn't necessarily going to make him a better golfer. Then he ticked off about half a dozen major fundamental mistakes that the guy was making. The only thing that was getting better was the guy's timing, and because he was hitting more balls on the center of the club face, he would probably go out and shoot lower than he normally did. But as soon as he started back to work, his game would revert to the same sad state that it was in before he had started all the serious practicing."

"I'm guessing he didn't take it very well. What happened then?"

"The pro gave him three things to work on, and then he watched him for about ten minutes. He rolled about half of his shots. So, you're right. He didn't take it very well. When he was done, he walked by the big shop window and shook his fist at us."

"You're lucky it was only his fist," chuckled Ronnie.

"For the next ten days, he hit balls in the early evening when I was out playing and after the pro had gone home. I'm sure it was very frustrating for the first few days, 'cause he was probably hitting it worse than when he started. You know how guys are? They aren't usually willing to go through the pain period that you have to go through to get better at something. Give them a tip, and they'll hit two bad shots before claiming that your advice doesn't work for them. Two shots! That's all they're willing to commit to improving their game. If it doesn't work immediately, they drop it."

"Guys can be stubborn," said Ronnie. "I read in a magazine that the average nine-hole score for men across the country is 52. That's incredible considering how serious a lot of guys are about their game. What happened at the end of the guy's two-week vacation?"

"Believe it or not, he came into the shop and offered to buy the pro lunch. He said he had to stop his wife from coming in and giving the pro holy hell for ruining his vacation. Then with two days to go, during a late nine-hole round with her, he hit half a dozen shots better than he had ever hit a ball in his life. He admitted that hitting a bunch of balls without addressing his fundamental problems and expecting miracle results wasn't being very realistic."

"Speaking of being realistic," said Ronnie, changing the subject. "How good do you think Will is going to be? He's come a long way in such a short time. What I don't want is family pride getting in the way of what is. Remember, I told him to see what is, and not what he hopes things will be?"

"Truthfully," said Eddie, looking his partner in the eye. "I think the kid's got it. You know, the intangible qualities that can't be taught. They're starting to show up more and more. When he hits it flush, it comes off the club face like a bullet. There's no denying it. The kid's got tons of untapped talent."

"I see it," said Ronnie, as he watched a black man carrying a drink approach their table. "I was hoping you saw it too. Now, what are we going to do about it? He'll be breaking 80 soon and then who knows where it will end?"

What the two hustlers didn't know, was that Will's last two scores at The Hedge were 77 and 76. Apparently their teachings, in more ways than one, were all too effective. On their next round together, he was planning on getting odds from both of them and walking away with a few of their dollars in his pocket.

"What's up, guys?" said Slick, as he sat down at their table.

Eddie introduced his poker friend to Ronnie. Before Slick sat down, Ronnie picked up their scorecard and quietly slipped it into his pocket. Eddie asked Slick how he knew where to find him. Slick just smiled and said it wasn't too difficult. Eddie didn't show his displeasure, but if a non-golfer like Slick could ask a few questions about him and get the right answers, that might be something to worry about down the road. His "low key" existence here might be in jeopardy.

"Here's what I think is going on," explained Eddie. "The white guy with the glasses was 'painting' the cards with some sort of substance that he kept out of sight. He probably had a small container with some kind of dye in it stuck down between his legs. And some sort of cloth to wipe off his thumb, so he wasn't putting marks all over the place. The dye was something that we couldn't see with the naked eye. I'm guessing there was probably a spot on his glasses that, when he looked through it, the marks were visible. So, after he dealt eight or ten times, he had the opportunity to grease most of the cards. Then he would signal to the other guys as to what we were holding. I confirmed my suspicions when I folded pocket kings to you, with a king showing on the board, and got a funny look from Brady. I'm guessing that the other guys had strange looks on their faces too. I don't know if you remember, but there were three diamonds showing on the table—an ace, a king and a trey. Did you have the diamond flush?"

"No, but I was holding the queen, so I would have had the winning flush If another diamond had showed up," admitted Slick. "So, they make decent bets to build the pot and to keep us in, then all but the best hand among them folds. That's pretty sneaky. They slowly bleed you dry over the course of the evening. Thanks, man, I appreciate it. Let me get lunch for you two."

Slick dropped a twenty on the table. Both of them gave him a wave of thanks.

"What are you going to do?" asked Eddie, as Slick got up to leave.

"I'll have to think about it. These guys give legit players a bad name. Maybe I'll mention their little scam to some dangerous folks that I know. If these clowns are smart, they wouldn't hang around the area once these guys get the info on them. Hey, are you any good at this ball and stick game?"

"I can't even beat this guy on a regular basis," said Eddie, pointing across the table.

Slick gave a knowing smile and left the room. The guy that told him where Eddie could be found had also told him not to play Eddie for money. He had learned that the hard way. It wasn't a big deal to Slick. He had never swung a golf club in his life.

"Cheating at cards," said Ronnie. "Is nothing sacred anymore?"

"Apparently not," said Eddie. "Do you see a lot of cheating at the track?"

"Not as much now as there used to be. The cameras are so much better today, and they use more of them during the race. Drivers used to hold their horse back in the stretch or make him break stride if he was pacing too fast and looked like he might have a chance to finish better than he was supposed to. Now they have to be craftier. All in all, I think most races are legit."

"Let's go out to the practice green and putt for a while," suggested Eddie. "I'm working on a gig where we could use the kid, just to see if he has an aptitude for our line of work."

* * *

"Let me get this straight," said Ronnie, as they sat on his back patio with fresh drinks in their hands. There was a fire going in the fire pit and the crickets were playing their usual nighttime symphony. "You and I get into an argument and I storm off. Then Will happens to be in the area selling balls, and he takes my spot. That will be a tough sell, because it's been done before. I think the great Titanic Thompson used to do something similar."

"I think we can sell it if we choreograph it right" said Eddie. "It will take some theatre, but if we do it right, I don't think our opponents will question it. Do you think Will's ready?"

"There's only one way to find out," said Ronnie. "Explain the doubler game again."

"Okay. As you know, there is one die called the doubler in the game of Backgammon. It has a two, a four, an eight, a sixteen, a thirty-two and a sixty-four on it. Let's say at the start we agree on the stakes being $100. Any time after the first hole, if either team thinks they have the advantage, they can offer the doubler to their opponents. The opponents have two choices—they either take it and the game is now $200, or they refuse it and the game is over. If they refuse, they have to pay their opponents the original $100. If they take the doubler and the stakes are doubled, they are now in control of the die. They can just keep the money there for the rest of the match, or as the match progresses, if they think have a better chance of winning, they can offer it back to their opponents. Now their opponents have the same two choices as I mentioned before. Refuse and pay the $200, or accept it and the game continues, but we're now playing for $400."

"Doesn't sound all that difficult," said Ronnie. "What the best case scenario? Where do you want to be toward the end of the match?"

"We'll have to throw in the stipulation that the doubler can't be offered once there are three holes left. If one team is two or three up, and there are only three left to play, it wouldn't be right to jack up the bet when you've got your foot on their throats. It's done all the time in Backgammon, but we're playin' a different game here. And to answer your question, I want to be tied or even down one with four holes to go, and I want them to offer the doubler to us for $1600. Here's the beauty of the whole gig. I'll act like I'm working with Will throughout the match. And finally, on eighteen, he cranks out a big drive—big enough so I can get home in two. Then I'll let him hit his second shot first and he'll hook it or slice it real bad. This should dispel any notions that the kid is a whole lot better than he's been playing. Once our opponents see me get home in two, or at least close enough to chip it, it will put the pressure on them."

"I don't know," said Ronnie. "Are we going against the principles that we have been teaching him?"

"I don't think so," answered Eddie. "I'll have some questions prepared for him, and he will answer every one of them truthfully. And as far as hitting some bad shots on purpose, well, that just puts more pressure on me, and the whole thing could blow up in our faces if I don't come through."

"We should do a few practice runs, so he knows his part. Hey, somebody just turned down my drive."

Both hustlers were up and out of their chairs in an instant. They went around the far side of the house and peered around the corner. Suzanne and Kathy got out of Kathy's car and headed around the other side toward the back patio. Ronnie motioned for Eddie to follow him. He went around the corner and in the front door with Eddie close behind. Crouching behind the sofa, they could see the girls standing by the fire looking around for them.

"Follow my lead," said Ronnie as he stood up. "This could get interesting."

Ronnie stood and headed for the back door with Eddie in tow. Looking back over his shoulder at Eddie, he opened the door leading to the patio.

"See you later, babe," said Ronnie. "You two be careful on these back roads. I know you city college girls don't have much country road experience. Whoa, where did you two come from?"

Ronnie and Eddie acted like they were surprised to see their ladies sitting in their chairs.

"If there were four of you out here, where are their drinks?" asked the lawyer, pointing to the guys' drinks sitting on small tables next to their chairs.

"And why didn't we see a car beside Eddie's sitting out in the driveway?" asked Kathy.

"I don't hear one pulling away either," added Suzanne.

"Eddie can answer all your snoopy little questions," said Ronnie, deferring to his partner.

"Uh, there are only two drinks out here because the people we were with were too young to drink," explained Eddie. "And their car was parked along side of the house, out of sight. And, it's an electric car, so you didn't hear it pull away."

Ronnie just nodded in agreement.

"Can you believe this, Kathy?" asked Suzanne. "Most guys try to hide the fact that they were with other women. Our guys are trying to convince us that they were entertaining college girls back here on this beautiful patio by the fire. Quick, what were their names?"

"Buffy and Sheila," said Eddie.

"Amber and Chloe," said Ronnie.

"You two are such awful liars," said Kathy. "What were you going for, the jealousy angle?"

"Just keeping you on your toes," said Ronnie, as he slipped behind Kathy on the recliner. Eddie took up the same position behind Suzanne. "Hey," said Ronnie, looking over at the two of them. "That's the way you were sitting in the tub when I walked in on you. You remember, Suzanne. You were both naked and you asked me to join you and what's-his-name in his huge tub for some fun and games."

"No, I don't remember that," said Suzanne, making a face at Ronnie that he could barely discern. "That must have been something you were fantasizing about. What does a girl have to do to get a drink around here anyway?"

"All right," said Ronnie, as he got up and offered his hand to Kathy. "C'mon sweetie, I'll show you what I've got in the kitchen. We'll let these two pretend they're doing the tub buddy routine."

"What's a tub buddy?" asked Kathy, as she followed her guy into the house.

"It's somebody that you take long baths with," answered Ronnie.

"Why haven't you ever asked me to be your tub buddy?" asked Kathy, in her best seductive voice.

"Because my tub is so small," answered Ronnie. "Tell you what. Tomorrow morning I'll make a call and I will soon have a tub that will turn those two green with envy."

"You would do that for me?" asked Kathy.

"You know it," said Ronnie, holding up a bottle of white wine for her approval.

CHAPTER TWENTY

Breaking Eighty

Confidence that comes from experience is one thing. But cocky is just asking for trouble. A piece of advice: If you're starting to feel full of yourself, don't do it in front of guys that are more skilled and more experienced than you are. The result is inevitable—crash and burn!

—Wilson Randall, high school golfer

Will was hitting smooth drives with a slight draw well past the 250 yardage sign when Eddie and Ronnie pulled up in carts. He threw his clubs on his grandfather's cart and they headed for the first tee on the Hedge's South course. This was the day that he was going to dig deep into both of the old guys' pockets.

"What do you say, Mr. Street and Mr. Grip? Should we put a little something on this round?"

"What did you have in mind?" asked Eddie, as he lit up a Macanudo.

"How about you both give me five a side and we play a little ten dollar Nassau?" offered Will. "We can play for five if that's a little too stiff for you."

"He's getting cocky, Grip," said Eddie. "I say we take some of the punk's money."

"Deal," said Ronnie. "Ten for the front, ten for the back and ten for the total. Do you have $60 on you if you lose the whole shebang?"

"No legit player would make a bet that he can't cover," answered the kid, pulling out his money clip and waving it at them.

'The Grip' and 'The Street' just looked at each other and grinned. The kid was not only challenging them, it appeared he was also taunting them. They both loved it.

When the three of them walked off the eighteenth green at the South course, it was hard to tell who had won. Ronnie and Eddie couldn't have been happier if the kid had just told them he was the school valedictorian and was dating some rich guy's daughter. They both shot identical scores of 70, two under par. Will carded a 75 and took all the money.

"That wasn't the first time you've shot in the 70's, was it?" asked Ronnie.

"Nope," said Will. "And if you would have asked me what I shot the last time I played I would have told you."

"What was your last score?" asked Eddie.

"Seventy-five, just like today," said Will with a straight face. "I remember what you told me, grandpa. Bet on what is, not what you want things to be."

"I did say that," said Ronnie, still beaming. "Did I also mention a tradition among friends or relatives that gamble against one another?"

"What's that?"

"The winner buys," said Ronnie, slapping Will on the shoulder. "And in this case, it's steak dinners."

"I would be happy to buy dinner for two of the greatest teachers a guy could have," said an appreciative Will.

"I knew there was a reason I liked this kid," said Eddie.

* * *

After dinner, the three of them sat around discussing the doubler gig. Will was a little apprehensive, until Eddie reminded him that the only pressure shot he would have to hit would be the drive on eighteen.

"Think you can shoot in the 70's two days in a row?" asked Ronnie, smiling innocently across the table. "Tomorrow's Sunday and it slows down here around 4:00. Pick a course, and we'll play for $50. All you have to do is shoot 79 or better."

"Deal," said Will, deciding which course would give him his best chance of success. "Let's play the East course. It's only a par 70, so I'll be two strokes to the good before we even tee off. Not bad, huh?"

"Smart move," said Eddie as they got up from the table.

Will said he needed to use the restroom before they left. After the restroom door closed behind him, Eddie turned to Ronnie with a questioning look on his face. He knew Ronnie was up to something.

"You don't think he can do it two days in a row?"

"It aint gonna happen," was all Ronnie said, as he turned and walked over to Pam. She still waited tables a couple days a week in addition to her new duties as social events coordinator. Ronnie and her spoke for a few minutes. She frowned at him at first, but finally nodded her head in the affirmative. The three of them joined up, as Will came out of the restroom. Ronnie had a peculiar look on his face.

Will was coming along fast, maybe a bit too fast.

A little dose of reality would be good for him.

* * *

The next day was as good as it gets in southern Michigan. The temperature was around 80 degrees and there was just enough breeze to keep the bugs off. It was a perfect day to shoot a low number and take some cash from the old guys.

After finishing his duties on the Stonehedge practice range, Will hustled over to GLV with the intentions of fattening up his money clip. The way he was hitting the ball, barring a major disaster, breaking 80 would be a cinch. Like his grandfather had told him—once you figured out how to get past the seventies gatekeeper, what once was a huge snarling monster became a joy-filled puppy, excited to see you. The kid didn't know it, but the "major disaster" was waiting for him in Eddie's cart, only this time it didn't resemble any kind of monster.

Will grabbed his clubs out of the trunk of his Camry and headed for the East course first tee where Ronnie, Eddie and Pam were waiting. Pam was wearing a white blouse and a dark blue skirt that came to just above her knees. Her hair was done up in a bun to keep it off of her face. Will didn't think too much about Pam being along until they got to the second hole. Number two is a short par three over water. They had all parred the first hole and Will still had the honors. He nipped a nine iron just right and watched his shot settle in about ten feet left of the hole. Eddie hit last, and after his shot landed three feet from Will's, they all headed back to the carts. Will froze in his tracks, causing his grandfather to bump into him from behind.

Pam sat in the cart smiling at the three of them. She had divested herself of the white blouse and skirt, and her hair was down on her shoulders. She sat there in a bikini top and a pair Daisy Duke shorts that barely covered parts that the young teenager was totally unfamiliar with. The kid stood there with his mouth open. Pam had a terrific figure and very little of it was left to the imagination.

"I know this is against the club's dress code," she explained, "but there's no one else around and I wouldn't mind getting a little afternoon sun. You guys don't mind, do you?"

Eddie and Ronnie voiced no objections, while Will couldn't seem to find his voice at all. It didn't take long for the seventeen-year-old to figure out what was going on. He actually smiled to himself, thinking about his grandfather's creativity. Well, the old man's little plan was going to backfire on him. He held it together for the next two holes, making a par and a bogey.

Then, on number five, Pam got out of the cart and tended the flag for him. That was all it took. He absolutely hammered his thirty-foot putt and watched as it stopped about twelve feet past the hole. When he stepped up to hit his second putt, Pam had her back to them and was bending over by the side of the green. Will's next putt didn't even come close to the cup. He ended up four-putting the hole. When Ronnie asked what she was doing, she said she was looking at a strange bug that was crawling through the fringe. The kid was starting to sweat when he got back into the cart and it had nothing to do with the air temperature.

"Interesting scenario," said Eddie on the next hole, as he and Ronnie stood next to each other waiting for Will to hit his fourth shot out of a trap. "Do you think he'll even be able to finish the round?"

"I don't know," said Ronnie, trying to hold back his laughter. "By the end of the front nine, he won't know which stick to grab. She's leaving after nine, so his breathing should be back to normal—maybe by the time we putt out on fifteen."

"And you don't feel bad about setting him up like this?" asked Eddie.

"Hell, no. It's better that he go through this little exercise in concentration and focus with people he knows. You know what it feels like to go down in flames in front of a bunch of strangers. I can't think of a more humbling experience. It's all part of the educational process. Down the road, he'll thank me for this day."

"I'll have to admit," continued Eddie, "that he is handling it pretty well. She's putting on quite a show. If one of those melons comes spilling out over the top of her suit, he'll probably faint dead away. If I was seventeen and had to play under these conditions, I'd be slobbering all over myself."

"You and me both, pard," said Ronnie.

Pam put the rest of her clothes back on when they came to the ninth tee. She gave Will a sympathetic smile, but the damage was done. They drove back to the clubhouse to let Pam off and to get some drinks. She surprised the two old guys when she took Will aside for a few minutes and had a private conversation with him. He shook his head and they hugged. She felt wonderful. That hug was a reward for keeping his composure on the front nine. It was the only positive thing that came out of the last two hours. He carded a 48, the worst score he had shot in quite some time.

* * *

The golfers checked their cards as they walked off the eighteenth green. The two hustlers were grinning from ear to ear. Eddie had shot three under and Ronnie was minus one. The reason for the grins was Will's score. He had tied Ronnie on the back nine. It was the first time he had ever broken par for nine holes.

"Nice strategy out there, Grip," said Will. He seldom called his grandfather, Grip, ever since he had learned his true identify. "I'll have to admit, you got me on that one. I know you were sending a message, and I want to tell you that I heard, or saw it, loud and clear. There's a big difference between being cocky and being confident out there. That Pam is some babe. And she's real nice too. Why doesn't she have a boyfriend?"

"She's run into some hard luck in that department," said Ronnie. "What were you two talking about, right after we finished the front side?"

"She told me there was a reason for her being here today, and that she normally didn't dress like that in front of teenagers, and she didn't want me to think bad thoughts about her. She also said you two were great guys and that you both were real proud of me."

"Pam was right on both counts," said Eddie. "Now your grandpa's got a treat for you. He's got some sort of magical feast cooking in his crock pot at home, and he's asked your mom to join us for dinner."

"And now that you broke par on the back side, it's also going to be a celebration," said Ronnie. "So you need to go pick up your mom and bring her over. Street and I will hustle over to my place and set things up."

* * *

"That was an awesome meal, grandpa," said Will, as the four of them relaxed after supper on Ronnie's back patio. "So you never took any cooking classes, ever?"

"Nope, just picked it up on my own," answered Ronnie. "I don't know why I like it so much. Probably because we were so poor growing up. We ate a lot of corn fritters, rice and beans back then. My mom was pretty good at disguising it, but dad and I knew what it was. Hey, I've got something for you, Will."

Ronnie stood up and went back into the house. While he was gone, Carol asked how the golf game went.

"Well, there was this lady that rode along and ..."

Will stopped when he saw Eddie shaking his head, indicating he shouldn't tell his mother everything that happened on the course earlier—with Pam or about the gambling.

"Long story short, mom, I broke par on the back nine."

Carol gave Eddie a quizzical look. He just smiled and nodded his head in agreement. Before she could ask any questions, Ronnie came back outside with his hand behind his back. When he had everyone's attention he handed Will what looked like a dozen golf balls. Will took the box and opened it. There were only six Titleist NXT's in the box. That was because the other side was filled with $100 bills.

"I was saving that for a special occasion," said Ronnie. "And your first time breaking par is pretty special."

Will didn't know what to say. His mother was giving him a look that said, "don't accept it".

"I don't know, Grandpa, that looks like a lot of money. Are you sure you want to give me this? I'm still just a goofy kid."

"It's only two grand, Will. I like your response so far, but tell you what. I'll take it back if your next move isn't an honorable one. Fair enough?"

Will looked at Eddie, only to see his poker face. He would get no help on this one. Eddie didn't even tell him to talk it out, like he had done so often on the golf course. Will looked over at his mother. That's when it came to him. Offering it all to her would be the wrong move, so he settled on half of it. His choice should be sensible and with a touch of humility. That was in line with the lessons his teachers were always trying to pass on to him. He reached in and took out the bills.

"Thanks a lot, Grandpa," he said, choosing his words carefully. "This is incredibly generous of you. Mom, I want you to take $1000 and get your car fixed. And then take what's left over from that and buy yourself something really nice. I'm going to put $500 in savings and then I'm going to invest the other $500. Eddie, do you know any good stocks to buy? There isn't another Microsoft ready to take off is there?"

"No, but I know a couple of utility stocks that are paying great dividends. Maybe you should start there."

Will held the money up, offering to return it. Ronnie was never more proud of Will than he was at that moment. With his gesture, the kid was asking if he had passed the test. Ronnie also liked the fact that Will didn't get all googley-eyed when he saw that much cash. It showed that when it came to money, he had his priorities straight. He had learned his money handling skills early in life, and he was doing his best to pass on his financial knowledge to his only grandson.

Carol just sat there with tears in her eyes.

* * *

Carol left for home and Will stuck around to talk golf with his two mentors. Eddie offered to drop Will off on the way back to his place. The kid didn't want this evening to end too soon. He was having too good of a time, listening to the stories of the hustlers' early days.

"Here's one," said Ronnie. "We're playing with this real obnoxious guy for just a few bucks. When it came to arrogance, this guy was the crown prince. On the second hole, he's in a fairway trap with just a small lip on it. Well, he takes a mighty swing and kicks up a lot of sand. The ball hits the lip and goes straight up in the air. The wind was straight into him, so he's standing in the trap brushing the sand off his face, wondering where his shot went. Just as he gives us a questioning look, the ball comes back down and hits him on top of the head. We all started laughing, which made him mad. His cart partner actually fell out of the cart, he was laughing so hard. The guy got so pissed that he took his bag off the cart and started walking back toward the clubhouse. I think I lost ten or twenty bucks on the match, but it was worth it."

"I've got one for you," said Eddie. "This guy a couple of groups ahead of us hit a skanky little tee shot about ten yards out in front of the tee. So he jogs out to get it, you know, thinking he's just going to tee it up again. Well, on his way back, he steps in a hole and down he goes—broken leg. When we catch up to them there are seven guys, the rest of his group and the foursome that was right behind them, standing around arguing. The guy was moaning real loud, so you know that leg was hurting. The argument was, and you won't believe this, that the guys in the following group wanted the other guys to drag their injured buddy off the tee so they could hit. One guy even said, 'his leg's broke anyway, so what's the difference? You can't hurt it any more'. They refused to go up and play the forward tees, saying they had a big money match going. It got pretty heated. A couple of guys were hollering at each other, and the guy on the ground was lying there screaming. It was pretty crazy."

"What happened then?" asked Will.

"My group went around and teed off from the senior tees," explained Eddie. "We heard the ambulance coming as we were walking off the green."

"Let's talk serious golf," said Ronnie, changing the tone of the discussion. "Here's how I play my shots from 100 yards and in. If the pin is on the front of the green, I try to drop the ball in there with a high shot—usually a sand wedge or maybe a pitching wedge if the wind is in my face. Rarely ever will I try to land the ball short of the green. The ground there is too unpredictable. If at all possible, land it on the green. It's the truest surface out there, not counting the air. That's why the fee to play is called a 'greens fee'. You pay to use the greens. They get more attention than any other part of the course. Anyway, if the pin is in the middle of the green, I usually land the ball about ten to fifteen feet on the green with a highly lofted club. This is different than what a lot of good golfers would do. Most guys would just dial in the yardage and try to drop it on top of the hole if the greens are holding on that particular day. The young tour pros might even land it behind the hole, relying on the incredible spin they generate to bring it back."

"Why do you play it that way?" asked Will.

"I'm more comfortable hitting a lower shot in there and letting it feed toward the hole. Of course the type of lie you have and the wind conditions have to be taken in to account. Now, if the pin is back and I've got a lot of green to work with, I will hit it in there low, landing somewhere in the middle of the green. Heck, I'll punch an eight-iron from 100 yards if the pin is way back. There's nothing worse than misjudging an easy approach shot over the green, leaving yourself with a short downhill chip back at the hole. I've watched guys hit high shots that they thought were perfect distance, only to watch the ball hit on the back of the green and then bounce into the tall grass. I also don't try to hit every shot right next to the hole. I'd rather have a lot of decent birdie putts in a round than one or two gimmees. A big part of this game is avoiding the troubles out there. And I don't mean just the sand or the water. There are plenty of other things to avoid—trees, tall grass, slick downhill or sharp breaking putts, and so on."

"What Grip is saying," added Eddie, "is he maneuvers his way around the course—shot by shot, hole by hole. He just doesn't just go out and hit the ball. Each shot is played with a lot of thought and a certain degree of creativity. He sees the shot before he executes it. It's more like he's crafting a piece of art. Does that make sense?"

"Yeah, I guess it does," said Will, trying to digest what the guys were telling him. "So, is that why he laid up to about 100 yards on number ten today? If he would have hit more club, he might have been able to get home in two."

"Very observant," said Ronnie. "Did you see me put my 3-wood behind the ball, before I put it back and pulled out the iron?"

"Yeah, I did."

"Even though we were playing off of bent grass fairways, I didn't like the lie because of the downward slant of the fairway, so I decided to hit it to a spot where my third shot would be from the short grass and from a yardage that I'm confident I can handle. I also took care not to push the grass down behind the ball when I set the wood behind it. Some guys do that and it's just wrong. On bent grass it doesn't really help, but on bluegrass fairways or if you're in the rough, it can make a big difference. And, I know what you're thinking. Why do Eddie and I call them woods when they're made out of metal? Probably because we're old school and we miss the days when they actually were made out of wood. The new hi-tech drivers and fairway metals have changed the game, and I think Eddie will agree, not in a positive way. A 425-yard par four was considered long in its day, but when the big boys are pounding out 325 yard drives, it's just an easy sand or lob wedge for their second shot. That's not how the holes were originally designed to be played. On a normal course, the big hitters can give themselves a 100-yard shot to get on in regulation on pretty much all the par fours. And the par fives are a joke to them."

"You're the best from 100 yards that I've ever seen," remarked Will. "You stuck your third shot in there about eight feet under the hole. But Eddie played his second with a 3-wood and almost got home in two. And he ended up making birdie, just like you did."

"He's a hack, Will," said Ronnie. "I've been trying to teach him some of the finer points of the game for years, but he just won't listen. He's always trying to flex his muscles, pounding it out there like he's twenty years old again."

"Well, he does hit it pretty far for a …."

"For a what, Will?" interrupted Eddie. "You were going to say for an old guy."

"No, he was going to say for a guy with small equipment," laughed Ronnie. "Speaking of equipment, it's a good thing we had your clubs extended this winter. How tall are you now?"

"I'm six feet even," said Will with pride.

"I'll have you know that my equipment works just fine," said Eddie. "I'm getting no complaints in that department."

"Well, you're going to hear some complaining when I get my new tub installed. It's going to put yours to shame."

"What are you two talking about?" asked Will.

"It's an old guy thing, young lad," said Ronnie. "Your time will come soon enough. So, how's it going with Melissa? Any progress there, or are you still waiting for her to come to her senses?"

"She knows I'm alive, but that's about it," said a dejected Will.

"Why don't you just ask her out?" asked Eddie. "You told us she wasn't going with anybody. This is as good a time as any."

"She's coming to the range to practice this week. Maybe I'll say something to her then."

"Maybe," said Ronnie. "C'mon, man. This is no time for maybes. Get in there. You're a par-breaking stud that any decent girl would be glad to hook up with."

"Careful with that 'hook-up' talk, Grandpa," said Will. "It doesn't mean the same thing as it did when you were my age."

"All I know is this girl is making you miserable without even trying. What are you going to be like when they start making you miserable on purpose?"

"I'll talk to her when I see her this week."

"What, you don't have a phone?"

"He'll talk to her when he's ready, Grip," said Eddie. "At his age you were still scared to death of the opposite sex."

"You've got me confused with your youth," said Ronnie. "I will admit that I did make a fool of myself on a few occasions. Heh, there was this one time when I …"

The guys entertained Will for another hour with golf and dating stories. He loved listening to their exploits, on and off the golf course. Before he and Eddie left, he decided that he needed to do something about Melissa. He wasn't going to go through his senior year just thinking about her.

The old guys were right—it was time for action.

CHAPTER TWENTY-ONE

Caddy

I was once asked what kind of player I would most like to caddy for. The obvious answer would be one that makes a lot of money. But I thought about it for a while and decided to answer with a quote. The late Bruce Edwards, Tom Watson's caddy, once said of Tom, "Watch him when things go wrong. He gets better. Never whines or makes excuses. Just keeps playing." I guess that's the kind of guy I'd like to work for. A lot of guys out here can be real jerks when things go wrong, whether it's their fault or not.

—Johnny "Wing Man" Morgan, veteran tour caddy

Will stopped hitting balls at the end of the range when he saw Melissa taking her clubs from her car. She gave him a big smile as she walked onto the tee and acted like she was genuinely glad to see him. He didn't think the smile was an act, but one never knew. He brought over a bucket of balls and watched her warm up. Her excellent hand-eye coordination was evident by the way she nipped the ball off the turf.

"So, how long have you been playing, Will?" she asked, as she hit short wedges.

"About four years now," he answered.

"Why don't you go out for the golf team? They could use some help next year with Troy and a couple of the other seniors leaving."

"I guess I have my reasons," said Will. "I play a lot with my grandpa and his friend, Eddie. If I played on the team, I couldn't have my job here at the range—at least not during the season. I also work out on the course when they're shorthanded. I kinda like things the way they are."

"What do you usually shoot for eighteen holes?"

"My game's not important," said Will, dodging the question. "I hear you've got a big tournament coming up."

"Yeah," she said, stopping to look at him. He hadn't noticed before, but her eyes were almost bright green. "It's a junior qualifier for girls seventeen and under. It's going to be on the West course at GLV and I'm pretty nervous. If you finish in the top five, you get to move on. And now, my coach has deserted me. Well, he didn't really desert me. He took a better job at a big club down in Florida. He was an assistant pro over at a course in Kalamazoo. I remember most of the stuff he taught me, so for now, I guess I'll just go it on my own. He was going to caddy for me in the tournament next week, so I'm out of luck there. The rules say you can have a caddy and I was told that most of the girls bring one. I'd ask one of my parents, but they don't know much about golf. My uncle is a good golfer, but he's out of town on vacation."

"A caddy is a big help," said Will. His mind was working hard trying to come up with the right thing to say. "Not only do they take care of your equipment, they are part of your team."

"I was thinking of asking Troy," she said. "We're not going together anymore, but he does know a lot about golf."

"Melissa, if you asked him, he would take it as a sign that you want to get back together. I think that would be a dangerous move."

"You really don't like him, do you? Is it because he told you that you weren't good enough to play on the team?"

"No, that's not why," laughed Will. "It's probably because I see him the way he really is. You, on the other hand, at least when it comes to Troy, see things through a glass darkly."

"Wow, that's pretty deep. I will admit that he can be a jerk some of the time—especially around you. He really doesn't like you either. Well, you don't have to worry about him anymore. He's graduated and moving on to college. And, yeah, you're right. He did have me fooled for quite some time. I heard all about the dead raccoon prank he tried to pull. It was pretty cool the way Billy stuck up for you."

Will had to admit that it was getting easier to talk to her. He decided then and there to go for it. Besides, she was desperately in need of his services.

"Melissa, I'll caddy for you in next week's tournament. I think we'll make a great team. What do you say?"

She looked at him with a skeptical eye.

"Do you know anything about caddying or are you working some sort of angle here?"

"I know a lot about caddying. Tell you what. If I can help you with your swing, here and now, will you think about it?"

"Okay. What would you do to improve my swing?"

"I know you're working on keeping your hands low, like we talked about before, but your swing is still too loosey goosey," explained Will. "Girls are more flexible than guys. That's good in some sports, and obviously in golf too, but sometimes you can be too loose. When you come back into the ball, you're right elbow tends to get too far away from your body. It should be in your right pocket at impact. Here's your swing thought for that—'close is power'. If I was going to punch you, which one would you want—the one where my fist is way out here, or the one where my fist starts out right by my shoulder?"

He acted out what he was trying to tell her, first with his clenched fist way out to the side, then with it right next to his shoulder.

"I guess the one way out there. The one right next to your shoulder looks more powerful. You know, like your whole body is behind it."

"Not only is it more powerful, it's more athletic. When you keep your arms close, you are swinging more like an athlete. When your right elbow gets too far away, you're swinging mostly with hands and arms. The power from your hips and legs isn't being used as much. And the ball tends to go left of where you're aiming."

Melissa thought about what he was telling her. He was explaining it better than her coach used to. And when she tried to hit it a little harder than normal, she did hit it left.

"How do you know all this stuff?" she asked.

"I told you. I play a lot with my grandpa and Eddie. They're pretty good golfers and great teachers."

"How come they don't play in any of the club tournaments? My uncle has been club champion a couple of times and I've never seen your grandpa's or Eddie's name on the big score sheet after the tournament. The senior division is posted right next to the others."

"They don't play in those kinds of tournaments. If you asked them, they would tell you they're just social golfers. But believe me, they know what they're doing."

"Okay, you can be on my team for the tournament. What's the first thing we should do?"

"How about you meet me over at GLV tomorrow evening at 6:00? You play whatever nine is open on the West course and I'll caddy. If we're not compatible, like if you start screaming at me and blaming the hired help for your bad shots, at least we'll know it before the tournament."

"You're goofy," said Melissa. "I won't scream at you. By the way, what are your services going to cost me? Maybe I can't afford you."

"We'll talk about that later," said Will, as he walked over to the cart that pushed the ball picker.

My fee? What should I ask for? How about a thousand kisses? Yeah, that would be a nice start. And then maybe we could…c'mon, man, get those nasty thoughts out of your head. Right now I'd settle for just holding hands. One thing I do know about being a caddy is that I don't know much about being a caddy. It's lucky that I've got Grip and Street in my corner. I think both of them used to caddy.

* * *

Will drove over to his grandfather's house around nine o'clock that night. He was surprised when he saw his car gone and the house dark. He decided not to call him on his cell phone, because he was probably out with his girlfriend. He chuckled at the thought of his grandfather having a girlfriend.

He didn't have Street's phone number, but he knew where he lived. He had stopped by with Ronnie once on the way to the tire store in Battle Creek. The first thing they did when he bought his Camry was to put new tires on it. In addition to paying for half of the car, Ronnie offered to put new rubber on it all the way around. He said it was a safety thing, and his mother agreed.

It was 9:45 when he got to Eddie's house. From the curb he could see lights on inside. He walked up to the door and knocked. The porch light came on, but nothing else happened for a while. He was about to knock again when he saw Suzanne peek through the curtains. A few seconds later, the front door opened. Eddie stood there with a quizzical look on his face. Will smiled and Eddie responded with a smile of his own.

"What's up, Will?" asked Eddie, motioning for him the come inside.

"I made my move like you guys said I should," said Will, as he sat down at Eddie's dining room table. There were playing cards and a score sheet on the table. *So that's what adults do when they're not in bed together or watching TV,* he thought. "I sorta opened my mouth and offered to caddy for her next week. We're going to meet tomorrow evening at 6:00 for a trial run. You and grandpa have taught me a lot about how to play the game, but I don't know anything about being a caddy. This is my big chance, and I don't want to look like a goof in front of her. I'm sorry to bother you and Suzanne, but grandpa's not home."

"She must be a very special girl," said Suzanne, as she sat on the couch fiddling with the remote.

"She's pretty awesome," answered Will.

"All right, sport," said Eddie, as he walked over and opened the top drawer of a chest and took something out. "I'm going to give you a crash course on how to be a top notch caddie." Eddie threw a spiral notebook and a pencil across the table. "Here are the basics, so get to writing."

An hour later, Will looked down and saw that he had filled two and a half pages with the information that Eddie had given him. He used bullets, just like he did when he was taking notes in class.

"Did you know they did a survey of 100 successful people and the only thing they had in common was that they all took prodigious notes?" asked Eddie.

"So rich guys take a lot of notes?" asked Will.

"I didn't say rich guys. I said successful guys, and of course, gals too. If you just met a rich guy, the only thing you know about him is that he has a lot of money. Hence the term: rich. He might have earned it and he might not have, at least legally. Suzanne, how many different ways can a person be successful?"

She hit the mute on the remote and thought for a few seconds.

"Let's see, there's financial, social, spiritual, educational, professional and parental. How's that?"

"Not bad, babe," said Eddie. "The only thing I would have added would be personal satisfaction—a person who knows their capabilities and lives up to them. I'd call that person successful too, as long as they're accomplishing something worthwhile. All right, let's take a look at your notes."

Will turned the notebook around so Eddie could see what he had written:
- Get your stride to one yard—-know the exact yardage, don't guess
- Walk just behind her and off to the right—-keep up
- Keep clubs quiet—-use towels or hand to keep them from banging together—-show respect for her equipment—-it's annoying to hear them banging together
- Decide before the round how much she wants to talk and what is expected from me
- Clubs and grooves must be clean at all times
- Tell her it would be a big help if she threw her divots back to me—-if I have to get it myself, lay the bag down so it points at the spot where her divot came from—-be efficient
- Be encouraging—-mention things you see in her swing only if you agree on it ahead of time

- Tending flag—-pull it out and hold it at the back of the cup—-don't want any problems getting it out of the hole—-pebble from sand trap can get stuck between flag and hole—-don't step or stand behind hole when tending pin even if no one is putting from that direction—-if she hits her putt by she will have to putt back through your footprint
- Know the simple rules!—-ground under repair, lost ball, etc.—-if you have to pay for a drop, u get 2 club lengths—-if it's free u get 1 c. l.
- Remind her of simple stuff but don't overstate the obvious
- Do: you've got about a half club wind behind you Don't: it looks like the wind is at your back
- Sound confident—-don't want caddie's indecision to rub off on her
- Watch every shot until it stops—-it's my job to know exactly where her ball is and where everybody else's ball is
- Try to anticipate her every move—-she shouldn't have to ask me to do every little obvious thing—-her focus is on her golf game—-mine is on her game and everything else—-pay attention to the details, no matter how small
- Be aware of what the rest of the players in your group are doing
- Look over at other greens to check pin placements—-might get a pin sheet but on a long green the dif. between middle & back-middle could make a big difference
- If weather is good need a wet towel for clubs & a dry one for face and hands—-also need a few clean small bar towels to wet down—-good for cooling off—-if rain need more towels

"This looks good," said Eddie, tearing out Will's pages and handing them to him. "Remember, you're mostly taking care of your golfer out there, but if you want something more to come out of it, keep in mind that you're taking care of your woman too. And I don't need to tell you to use the head between your shoulders. I made a huge mistake when I was only a couple of years older than you are right now, and I paid dearly for it. The only part of your body that should do the thinking is your brain."

When Will gave him a look of confusion, Suzanne chimed in.

"He's saying; keep your hormones under control, young man. And I think he means that you should be compassionate and should be aware of Melissa's feelings. Girls, especially young girls, hear things differently than guys do. A smart comment that you think is funny, might not be taken that way—especially in stressful situations. The more you are with her, the more you will know what is acceptable conversation between the two of you."

"Wow, I'm going to be up all night studying this stuff."

"Most of it is just common sense," said Eddie. "Of course, a lot of golfers are lacking in that department."

Suzanne and Will both looked at him for an explanation.

"Have you ever noticed that most guys will stand right behind you on the tee while you're hitting? Why they don't stand over by the right-hand tee marker is beyond me. Wouldn't it be funny if Rory McIlroy went out and stood right behind Zach Johnson, as he was getting ready to hit his tee shot? He would get some funny looks from Zach and everyone else in the group. If a player has the tee, everybody else should be off the tee and over to the side. It's the safest place to stand out there and the guy hitting can't see your shoes or any other part of you. I once stopped my swing on its downward arc because the guy standing behind me started to walk over to his cart."

"What did you say to him?" asked Will.

"I told him if he was going to stand behind me, that he needed to stand still. I don't care if you do a backflip after I hit, but keep still until I do. A lot of guys have good peripheral vision, and they can see everything that goes on back there. All right, caddy. You've got most of the basics on that sheet of paper. I'm confident that you'll be a good team. One more thing—be patient with your golfer. She plays a totally different game than you do. Keep Ronnie and me posted as to how it goes. Who knows, there might be some…uh, never mind."

"Some what?" asked Suzanne, with an inquisitive smile on her face.

Eddie, with his back to Will, raised his eyebrows at her. When Will didn't hear him answer, he stood and gathered up his papers.

"Thanks for the advice guys. I'll study my notes. I know I'll have fun just spending a few hours with her."

"That boy's got it bad for this girl, doesn't he?" asked Suzanne, after Will left.

"You could say that," said Eddie, as he slipped his arms around his favorite attorney. "Hey, you wanna watch some golf on TV?"

"Sure. I'll get us another ice tea, and you can explain some of the finer points of the game to me. By the way, you owe me five bucks for the gin game. I was ahead when Will showed up and you quit playing."

"I'd argue the logic in that, but you being an attorney, I'm afraid it might cost me ten."

"That's one game that I know how to play," she said, heading for the kitchen.

* * *

Will drove into the GLV parking lot and saw Melissa hitting putts on the practice green across the road by the West course. He went in and asked the assistant pro if they could play the back nine on the West if it was open. The guy said to go ahead if no one was coming off of number nine.

Will crossed the road and went straight to her bag. He deposited some sun block and three clean bar towels in the big pocket. She walked over and hit him with a smile that immediately got his heart racing. He decided if he was to be effective, he had to calm down and see her as a golfer, and not as someone he wanted to be more intimate with. With a face and a figure like hers, this was not going to be a simple adjustment.

"Are you ready, caddy?" asked Melissa. She was wearing light green cargo shorts that came down to just above her knees and a yellow golf shirt. A white visor kept her hair out of her eyes.

"Ready. Let's go play the back nine. It's a lot tougher than the front, and I think it's where a lot of the other players will have problems."

The round went along smoothly for the first seven holes. They talked mostly golf, but a few personal items crept into the conversation. She seemed genuinely moved when Will told her his father was killed in Iraq, and that he had received the Silver Star for his brave actions. He found out that she was considering entering a nursing program after high school. Her mother was a nurse, so she already knew what the job entailed.

"Oh yeah," she said. "I'd also like to have two children—a girl and a boy."

"You've got very specific ideas about your future, don't you?" he said.

"I do. And one of them is I want to get better at golf!" she said. "It's an awesome game that my husband and I will be able to play with our children."

Will thought that line of thinking was pretty mature for a high school girl. That's one of the reasons he liked her. She wasn't into the girly drama that was so prevalent in the hallways at school.

They decided that Will could help her with her swing during the round, as long as he kept it simple. She had enough to worry about without trying to make any major swing changes in the heat of competition. This reminded Will of something Eddie told him once: "If you can't explain it simply, you don't understand it well enough." Eddie told him that it was an Einstein quote. He decided to keep his swing comments mostly in the form of encouragement. On seventeen, a downhill par four with a severe left-to-right slope, Melissa popped up her drive. They found it along the tree line on the right side of the hole.

"What do you think?" asked Melissa, as she surveyed her next shot.

"I think you should cut a 5-iron back into the fairway and let it run down the hill in front of the green. You won't get home with that club. It's strictly a position shot. The lie is a little dicey and you want to take six out of the equation. Even if you don't hit it solid, you should still have a short third shot to the green. If you keep your pitch under the hole, we have a shot at par, and should make no worse than bogey. You're only four over, so you're looking at shooting 40 or 41 back here. That's a decent score for this nine. You've done a good job of avoiding the water and the sand. Let's not go crazy and make a big number with only two holes to go."

Melissa looked at him in a totally different light. He sure seemed to know what he was talking about. She didn't realize that he was so perceptive when it came to golf. She thought back to how much fun they had at prom. Melissa and her date sat at the same table with Will and her best friend, Jane, when they weren't dancing. He was fun to be with and he had a nice sense of humor. And when she danced a couple of dances with him, he held her at a distance and didn't try to crush her up against him, like some of the other guys did. It was very respectful and she liked that. She smiled and he smiled back.

"What?" he asked. "Doesn't that sound like a good strategy? You've laid the foundation for a good round here. It's like you're building something out here. You don't want to rip part of the base out by taking chances and making a big number. If you do, all those good shots you hit earlier will be diminished. My grandpa's friend, Eddie, taught me that. I didn't come up with it on my own."

Now she gave him a look that he deciphered as a look of disgust. He didn't realize it, but it wasn't directed toward him. He backed off with her bag, putting some distance between them. He hoped he wasn't sounding like a know-it-all. That was not his intention. She just stood there looking down at her ball with her hands on her hips. When she didn't say anything, he thought of Suzanne's advice and softened his tone.

"What's the matter, Melissa? I hope I didn't say something out of line."

"No, everything you said makes sense. But there's one problem. I only know how to hit a draw. I can't fade it at all."

"Have you ever worked on it?"

"Not really. My coach was always concerned with me turning it over to get maximum distance on my shots."

"Okay, let's punch a 7-iron down the hill. That will be the one we put on the scorecard. Then we'll hit a few practice shots trying to fade it. Deal?"

She smiled at him and shook her head in the affirmative. After punching the seven, he handed her the five. She dropped a ball and hit a solid shot, only it curved to the left like all of her other shots and ended up way left of the green.

"I can't do it," she said.

"Just hit it with 'dead' hands," advised Will. "Keep them from releasing the clubhead until the shot is on its way."

She tried again and hit a carbon copy of the previous shot. Then she turned and handed him her club.

"You do it," was all she said. She walked over to the edge of the fairway and stood with her arms crossed in front of her. He had never seen her in this light before and he thought it was rather cute. She appeared to be pouting, but not like a little kid pout—just disappointed that things weren't going the way she wanted them to. She was frustrated that she couldn't do what he was asking. He hadn't realized it before, but one of the reasons he liked her so much was her serious attitude toward the game.

He took the club, dropped a ball, and after a couple of practice swings, hit a beautiful fade that came to rest ten feet under the hole. She looked at him with wide eyes. She couldn't believe what she just saw. Walking over to her bag, she took out another ball and tossed it to him.

"Hit another one," she ordered.

His next one didn't curve as much as the first one, and it landed on the front left of the green, about twenty-five feet from the flag. She tossed him another ball and motioned for him to come out to the fairway. He dropped the ball and reached into her bag for the 6-iron. From the fairway, he would hit his standard draw, so he didn't need as much club. They both stood and watched the flight of the ball to a green that was well below where they were standing. It hit about fifteen feet right of the flag and sat right down. He gave her a sheepish grin and cleaned the club with the wet towel.

"What's this all about, Will?" she asked, with a look of concern. "I don't understand. You just hit three exceptional shots with no warm-up and with my shorter clubs. Who are you?"

"I'm just a guy with two great teachers who loves this game. You're not mad are you?"

"I don't know what I am right now," she admitted. "What other secrets have you been hiding from me and the rest of the kids at school? You don't have a cape under that shirt, do you?"

"Not hardly. Listen, with some work, you should be able to fade the ball in no time. You've got skills, woman. I'll get Str, uh Eddie, or Ronnie to look at your swing and make some suggestions. They're great guys and real good teachers."

They picked up the extra balls, then Melissa played her third shot on to the green. After she two-putted for her bogey, she gave him her putter and motioned for him to putt the first ball that he had hit, which was still lying there, ten feet below the hole.

"I don't know," he said, thinking of a way to work the situation to his advantage. "When I play with the old guys we usually have something on the game. I work better under pressure."

"I don't have any money on me, wise guy."

Will decided to press the issue. The moment he had been dreaming about was finally at hand. They had been laughing and joking for the last hour and a half, and she appeared to like his company. If she said no, he decided then and there, to move on and to forget about a relationship with her. He was done fantasizing.

"Okay, since you don't have any money to bet, if I make this putt, I think I deserve a kiss. You know, for all my efforts and my awesome caddying skills."

"Your skills are worth a kiss, huh? I don't know. This is just a practice round. How about a practice kiss, with me over here and you over there?"

"Nope, a real kiss. And not a sympathy kiss either."

"Okay, a real kiss. Let's see what you've got."

Will's focus was laser sharp. As far as he was concerned the whole world had come to a complete stop. The breeze died down and the birds quit singing. Insects stopped buzzing around, and the trout in the pond nearby held deathly still, waiting for him to make the perfect stroke. Melissa was standing only a few feet away, waiting to give him his reward. There was no way he was going to miss this crucial ten-footer. There was more pressure on this stroke than on any one shot he had ever hit in his young life. He stroked it with calm hands and when it left the putter face he started to smile. He looked up and saw the ball tracking toward the cup at perfect speed. It got right to the hole, then unexpectedly, moved a little to the right. It rolled over the edge and stopped about six inches past the hole, directly behind it. Melissa smiled sweetly and he frowned. The world started back up and went about its business. He squatted down and looked the line over again. There was no way that should have happened!

"Stinking raised cups," he complained. "Whoever set this thing just cost me a kiss." He didn't realize it, but he sounded just like his grandfather when he made that comment.

Melissa walked slowly up to him and took his head in her hands. She pulled him down to her face and gave him a long slow kiss. His hear rated went from 60 to 160 in about two seconds. When they parted, she kept her face close to his.

"Wilson Randall, you are full of surprises," she whispered. With that, she turned and headed over to eighteen tee.

They walked up the eighteenth fairway shoulder to shoulder. Fifty yards short of her ball she reached out and took hold of his hand.

"I didn't kiss you and I'm not holding your hand just because you hit a few amazing golf shots back there," she explained.

"Melissa, I've got something to tell you."

She stopped and locked eyes with him. Her face looked serious, but her eyes were smiling. He wondered if that came naturally or did she have to work on it?

"My name is Wilson Green. My mom just had it changed back to what it should have been all along. It's a long story, but that's in the past. Oh yeah, and I've decided what my fee will be for my caddy services."

"What's this going to cost me, Mr. Green?" she asked.

"Whether you qualify to move on or not, you have to go out to dinner with me, and then we'll cruise a little around the lake. I promise you will have a great time." He was thinking about Eddie's offer of letting him use the '57 convertible.

"Ha," she laughed, as she turned and walked briskly toward her ball. "Then you're working for nothing, smart guy. I was thinking about doing that anyway."

Whatever, he thought, as she walked on ahead of him. It was a good day to be Willy Green.

CHAPTER TWENTY-TWO

The Challenge

When I first saw him hit balls, I thought Eddie was the greatest player in the world. Then Will came along and got so good so fast. He is phenomenal. Aint no doubt, the guy's blessed with some skills that very few have. And like his two teachers, he's somewhat of a character. I guess that's why I like to hang around with him.

—Mitch Winston, range manager/part-time caddie

"So, Will, have you, you know, with your new girlfriend yet?" asked Ronnie as they walked across the course parking lot together. He and Kathy were there to watch Melissa play a few holes, and to watch Will exhibit his newfound caddying expertise.

"Ronnie!" said Kathy. "That's personal. You don't ask that sort of stuff."

"Why not? He's family. It's not like I'm asking for details here. I just want to make sure he has taken all the necessary precautions."

"Keep your voice down, grandpa," cautioned Will. "Kathy's right. That's not the sort of thing you ask a guy. But since you asked, I will tell you that she's a decent girl and not a 'horn dog' like some of the others floating around school."

Ronnie looked at Kathy and silently mouthed 'horn dog', with a look of confusion.

"That would be like you when you where his age," she whispered in his ear. "And not much has changed since then, if you asked me." Then, with a louder voice, "Now, stop bothering him with questions like that. They've got a tournament to play."

"Exactly," said Will over his shoulder, as he spotted Melissa and her parents getting out of their car.

Melissa introduced him to her parents and Will did the same with Ronnie and Kathy. Then, golfer, caddy and support team all headed to the West course putting green.

Will was carrying two large towels and a small collapsible cooler with a cold pack and drinks that he managed to stuff into Melissa's golf bag. It was already getting hot and the forecast called for a high of around 87 degrees. Melissa stood off to the side of the green and did her stretches, and then hit some chip shots. She worked with three balls, which he rolled back to her. Then they putted for about twenty minutes. She had excellent touch and didn't seem to be overly nervous. That was a good sign. Melissa looked up and saw her dad signaling that there were two groups ahead of her.

Melissa's group sat on the fourth tee and waited for the girls ahead of them to play their second shots. One of them was in trouble in the trees on the left and it took some time for her to get it back into play. The other two girls in the group were from Portage, a city that adjoins Kalamazoo, so they didn't have to travel very far to get to the course. Neither one of them was very talkative. There was only one other caddie and it appeared that he was caddying for his girlfriend. Wilson didn't have a high opinion of him, as he had already violated several of the points that he had written down at Eddie's house. However, this goof was not his concern, Melissa was. The temperature was around 85 degrees and the air where they were sitting felt like a wet blanket had been thrown over them. He looked over at Melissa as she sat on the bench, and she looked miserable.

He unzipped her bag and dug into his cooler. There were two bottles of Gatorade and two bottles of water crammed in next to the cold pack. He took out one of the bar towels and wrapped the cold pack in it. Then he waved her over.

"Would you like something to cool you down?" he asked.

"Yeah," she responded, wiping her face on the dry towel. "There's no air moving back here."

"Here, put this on the back of your neck," he said, handing her the towel. "I've got cold Gatorade and more water in here if you need it."

Melissa took the towel with the ice pack inside and put it on the back of her neck.

"That feels wonderful," she said. "I could use a Gatorade. You didn't happen to bring an orange one did you?"

He pulled an orange Gatorade out of the bag and loosened the top for her. She gave him a look of appreciation. He had seen her drink a Gatorade at school lunch a few times, and when she did, it was always an orange one. He was glad that he had paid attention to the little things. Her appreciative smile was reward enough.

"Okay, what's my favorite color?" she asked, after taking a large gulp of the cool liquid.

"Uh, orange?"

"Ha, some caddy you are. It's green."

They both laughed. She gave him back the towel and proceeded to the tee with her 3-metal. After the other two girls had hit, they all started down the fairway. Melissa put the towel back on her neck.

"Put it on your wrists too," he said. "That's one of the best ways to get cooled down."

Llana Sovern, one of the other girls in the group, looked at her caddy.

"Where were you on that one? She's got a cold towel and drinks."

He just shrugged his shoulders. He was draining the last of his water bottle, so he stopped and offered her the last sip. She made a strange noise and stormed on ahead.

Will showed his worth on number nine, the long par five. Melissa hit a short drive up the right side and then followed it with a solid 5-metal that didn't draw back into the fairway. When they got to the ball it was dead against the trunk of a small tree in the short rough on the right side of the hole.

"Well, this stinks," she said in frustration. "If I take an unplayable and get my two club lengths, I'll still have tree trouble with no chance of getting it even close to the green. I'll have to punch it out sideways, and I'll be laying four, hitting five. After all that, I'll still be almost 200 yards out. What do you think I should do?"

Will thought for a minute. He ran through the three options when taking an unplayable lie. He looked behind them and had a flash of brilliance.

"Wait a minute," he said. "Remember, you can also go as far back as you want to take a drop, as long as you keep this little tree between you and the flag. If you go back about thirty yards or so, you'll be on the edge of number one fairway, back there by that trap. From there, if your lie is good enough, you can hit your 3-metal, and with your usual draw, you should be fairly close to the green. And you'll be laying four. Up and down from there gets you a bogey and a 39 if my math is correct."

Melissa made her best swing of the day and got her 3-metal close to the fringe. From there, she surprised herself by chipping in for a par. She wanted to jump into Will's arms and give him a big hug, but she settled for a small fist bump. Ronnie and Kathy were standing off to the side of the green with Melissa's parents, and they clapped along with a few of the other spectators. They waved their goodbyes as Melissa dropped her scorecard off at the scorer's table. The scorers quickly recorded the front nine scores on the big score sheet, so the spectators knew where the golfers stood. There was one other 38, so far. Standing on the tenth tee, Melissa was ecstatic.

They were both well aware that the back nine on the West course is much tougher than the front, and Melissa's scorecard showed it. She started out with three straight bogeys. Will tried to keep her calm, and so far, she was doing a good job of staying focused. One of their main goals was to make no worse than bogey on any given hole. However, the heat and the intensity of the situation were taking their toll on her. When they got to sixteen tee, she was four over par for the back and Will could see her shoulders starting to droop. She looked totally exhausted. He walked up behind her and put his hands on her shoulders.

"Want me to rub your shoulders?" he whispered. "Caddies can do that, you know."

"Okay," was all she said.

He worked his thumbs into her trapezius muscles, and even though it was hot, they felt tight. He worked his way down to her lower back and dug his thumbs in there trying to get her to loosen up. Melissa sighed and just stood there with a smile on her face. Llana looked over at them, then back to her boyfriend, Josh, who was sprawled out on the ground next to her bag.

"Where did you get this guy, Melissa? And do you rent him out, or are his services only for you?"

"Sorry, Llana, he's all mine," said Melissa, with a satisfied look on her face.

"I thought so. My guy's not much of a caddy, but he's a heck of a golfer. He could probably give your guy five a side and still spank him."

"Really?" asked Melissa, still enjoying the back rub. "Do you think Josh would play my caddy even up for $100?"

"You can't be serious," said Llana. "Josh plays number one for Portage Central. Does Will play for the high school team at Gull Lake?"

"No," said Melissa, trying to hide a smile. "He was told he wasn't good enough."

Josh, hearing the conversation, got to his feet and sauntered over.

"Let me know when you want to play, kid. I'll be glad to lighten your load by a hundred. I'm sure not making anything out here today."

"That's too bad," said Will. "I'm getting paid huge for my efforts."

"I figured that, by the way you're falling all over her," said Josh, as he walked back to Llana's bag.

* * *

Melissa finished par, bogey, bogey, for a six over, 41.

They stood by the scoreboard and watched the other scores come in. Will was right about the difficulty of the back nine. Almost every score on the back was higher than on the front. When it was all over, Melissa tied for second with her 79. It was the first time she had broken 80 in competition. Will received a huge hug, and it didn't matter to him if she was all sweaty. It was all good.

Will looked over and saw Josh and Llana loading up for the drive back to Portage. He jogged over and offered his condolences to Llana. Then he handed Josh a small piece of paper. Josh took it with a confused look on his face.

"My phone number, dude. Call me when you'd like to play. It will have to be later in the day, because I work mornings and early afternoons."

Josh and Llana just stood there staring, as he walked back to a beaming Melissa.

* * *

On the drive home, Will assessed his situation. His golf game was better than he ever thought it would be, and Melissa was fast on her way to becoming his girlfriend. He couldn't wait to tell Ronnie and Eddie. There was also the little matter of borrowing the '57 for their upcoming date.

Oh yeah, and he might have a $100 match set up with that Josh guy. Somewhere, way in the back of his mind, thoughts of his future were beginning to form. It was never too early to start planning.

* * *

Will was feeling on top of the world. He had a date later with Melissa and he was about to play a round with his two favorite golf partners. Eddie had driven the '57 over to the course for the big date. He was going to drive Will's car home and then they would switch tomorrow when Eddie and Ronnie played in the afternoon. As usual the two hustlers were inside getting ice teas and giving Pam the business. Will was swinging his driver off to the side of the first tee on the East course and wasn't really paying attention to his surroundings, when he saw a shadow come into view.

"If it isn't Will the Thrill," sneered Troy. "I hear you weaseled your way in to Melissa's good graces by caddying for her. Give it up, stud. She's can't be interested in a nobody like you. If you think you're going to tap that, you're dumber than I thought you were."

Will was inspired by his recent good fortune, and he was determined to not let a jerk like Troy put a damper on all the good things that he had going. But Troy's disrespectful comment aimed at Melissa was more than he could take. He decided it was time to stand up to Troy and his bullying.

"I don't know, man. We're going out later tonight, and something tells me that your name will never come up."

"You're lucky we're in a public place, punk," threatened Troy, as he closed the distance between them. "If we were anywhere else, I'd kick your sorry ass."

The kid fought to keep his adrenaline level from rising, but it was a losing battle. There was only one way to get Troy off his back. Actually there were two ways. One, was to actually fight him, and he had no experience in that area. Two, was to challenge him to a money match. If he couldn't smash his face, he might as well hit him in the wallet. There was no telling what it would do to Troy's ego. He would either slink away or he could come back looking for revenge. If he did come back, looking to get even in one way or another, he might as well be holding some of the jerk's money. Will stepped even closer and looked Troy straight in the eyes.

"I'll play you any time and for any amount of money."

"You can't be serious," said Troy, his voice dripping with arrogance. "You want to play me? And for real money?"

"I didn't stutter, chump," said Will, holding his ground. He didn't see Ronnie and Eddie watching the confrontation through the window. "Name the amount and the day. But make it soon. I don't want to give you the time to come up with an excuse to back out. How about within the next week?"

"Okay, a week from today, and we play for $200." With that statement, Troy expected Will to hem and haw around about that being a little out of his price range. The little toad did say that he'd play for any amount. When Will didn't answer right away, Troy felt the surge of confidence that comes when you think you've got the upper hand.

"I don't know," said Will, feigning indecision. Will looked around and saw the two old guys watching through the window. They knew something was going down and they wanted to give the kid his space to handle it on his own. This was one of the things they had been working on—turning the situation to your advantage, so you could deal from a position of strength.

Troy just stood there with a stupid grin on his face. He was shocked when Will came back with a counter offer.

"Gas prices have gone up lately," said Will. "Why don't we make it an even $300? Stroke play, and you can carry your own bag or bring a caddy. I'll get back with you on what course we're going to play."

Troy wasn't sure what to say to this turn of events. He figured his dad would back a sure thing like this, so he agreed. His old man would get a kick out of the whole thing, and he would have some extra money to spend on the big party that he was planning. He might even buy a keg all by himself, and then have everyone toast Will for his generous contribution.

"Done," said Troy, extending his hand.

Will shook it and then pulled his hand back quickly. Did that hand feel slimy, or was it his imagination? He was proud of himself for coming up with the caddy idea. He had just seen first hand how valuable a teammate could be out on the course. And he knew exactly whom he wanted to team up with.

His two playing partners came out of the building as soon as Troy walked away. Will took the ice tea that his grandfather offered him and went over to the cart. Eddie and Ronnie looked at each other, trying to get a read on the situation. They knew something big had just happened. There was no way the handshake they just saw was a peace offering between the two boys. There was too much bad blood between them for it to end with a simple shake.

Will went to the first tee and ripped his drive 285 yards down the middle. Ronnie and Eddie hit their standard drives, about fifteen yards behind Will's, and came back to their respective carts. They sat down and looked at the kid, waiting for an explanation.

"I might have just shown my ass a little," he said in a hushed voice. "I challenged that goon to a match for $300. Enough is enough. He needs to be put in his place."

Ronnie and Eddie looked at the kid with pride in their eyes. He was right. It was time to stand up to Troy.

"Are you up for it?" asked Ronnie.

"I don't know. Do you think I'm ready?"

"Damn straight, I think you're ready," said Ronnie, clapping him on the back. "What do you think, Street? Is our boy ready to play for more than just chump change?"

"Yeah," said Eddie through a haze of cigar smoke. "He's ready. Let's play some golf, fellas."

"One more thing," said Will, as they rode down the fairway side by side. "I think I've got another game set up for $100. The kid plays number one for Portage Central. I'm not in your league, but a guy's got to start somewhere, right?"

When they got to their drives the two old timers didn't get out of their carts. They just sat there staring at the youngster.

"What?" asked the kid smiling. "It's been a busy week. I can't let you two have all the fun."

Ronnie got out and addressed his ball.

"Five bucks for closest to the pin," he said.

"Done," said Eddie and Will in unison.

* * *

The match with Josh took place two days later. Will was surprised when Josh called him to set it up. The timing couldn't have been more perfect.

This was his chance to play for a few bucks without either of his two mentors looking over his shoulder.

It would be a good experience to see how he would perform with more than just fun money on the line. He placed a call to Mitch, the range guy at Cedar Creek, and asked him to go along. Mitch would be good moral support and he was pretty sure he had played the course where the match was going to take place. It was a public course between Richland and Kalamazoo called Eastern Hills. He also wanted to talk to Mitch about caddying for him when he played Troy.

Will got on the Internet and checked on Josh's scores for the past high school season. His best score for eighteen holes was a 75. Seeing this, he decided to spice things up a little. He got the impression from watching Josh caddy the other day that he was full of himself, just like Troy.

Mitch was surprised when Will changed his shirt just before they pulled out of the GLV parking lot on their way to Eastern Hills. The shirt he put on had a couple of holes in it and it looked like it hadn't seen the inside of a washing machine for some time. His shorts weren't in the best of condition either. Will looked over when he saw Mitch's questioning look.

"We're going to have a little fun with this guy," was all Will said.

"I thought whippin' his cocky ass and taking his money would be fun enough," said Mitch.

"Just go along and make sure no one sneaks up on me from behind with a wedge. I really don't know this guy very well, except he appears to be from the Troy Feltner school of 'look at me, aint I something'."

"All right, man. It's your show."

When they got to the Eastern Hills parking lot, Will pulled a ratty looking bag out of his trunk. It had a few holes in the side and the sweater pocket zipper was stuck in the down position. Someone had thrown it away at the Stonehedge range and he had retrieved it from the trashcan.

Mitch started laughing when he saw it.

* * *

"Man, was that dude pissed," said Mitch as they drove away from the course. "Your big slice on number one, and the way you carried that nasty bag by the handle had Josh and that Allan kid laughing behind your back. You looked like 'Hillbilly Will' out there. They quit laughing when you birdied number two and three. I will take some credit for the win, though. You'll have to admit, my course management advice was flawless. It was a smart thing for you to ask them if it was okay for me to give you advice, since you had never played the course before. Unless we're playing as a team, that's illegal. You're buying me dinner, right?"

"Your help was huge out there. And, yes, I'm buying dinner. I appreciate you coming over and watching my back—and for all the good advice. What do you think about caddying for me next week? I'm playing this psycho that just graduated from my school for three times what I played for today."

"Dang, you're getting into the big bucks. I see why, the way you played today. That Josh dude and his buddy were still in shock as we walked off eighteen. I was afraid he wasn't going to pay up. You were nukin' that thing out there. Sure, I'll caddy for you. It sounds like fun."

"Do you know anything about caddying?"

"No worries, man. You carry the clubs, clean them, and tend the pin. Oh yeah, and rake the traps."

Will gave Mitch an exasperated look and then reached into the glove compartment. He pulled out his caddy notes that he took at Eddie's house and handed them to his future caddy.

"Study these for the next few days. It's actually pretty cool. You won't be playing, but it will feel like you are. You'll live and die with every shot we hit. Believe me, it's going to get real intense."

* * *

Will lie in bed and crossed his hands behind his head, relishing the events of the last two days. His date with Melissa had been awesome.

They'd driven to Kalamazoo and had dinner, and then they cruised in the '57 for about two hours. When he walked her up to her door, she kissed him again. When he stepped back, he thought he saw the curtains in the house move. He turned and quickly headed back to the car, in case her mom or dad came out. When he called her to say good night, she told him that her little sister was spying on them.

He asked her why she brought up the idea of him playing Josh for $100. It seemed to be a little out of character for her. She said she didn't like his attitude, and she didn't like the way he had treated Llana. She also said that she knew Will could beat him. Will learned something from her answer—no matter what you were doing, the power of true belief was always a plus. One thing he didn't tell her was about his little act at Eastern Hills—the ratty clothes and bag. He wasn't even sure why he did it. Maybe it was to build his confidence for the match with Troy, and maybe because Josh acted like caddying for his girlfriend was beneath him.

* * *

Three days later, Will and his two mentors were about to head over to the West course when the pro stepped out of the shop and motioned to them.

"Hey, guys," he said when they drove over. "I heard a little rumor about a money match that's about to happen between a high school student and a recent graduate. Well, it can't happen here. Even though Will isn't on the high school team, he is an employee here. I think it would cause a whole lot of trouble, and I don't need that. So, the bottom line is, find somewhere else to play."

"Not a problem," said Ronnie. "We understand. Where would you suggest they play?"

"I'd go in to Battle Creek and play Riverside," said the pro. "It's public now and a great layout. Nobody knows you there, and if you don't mention that the boys are playing for money, no one would be the wiser. Let them think it's a grudge match, which I hear it is."

"Thanks for the advice, pro," said Ronnie. "I think that's what we'll do. In fact, we should go over there right now for a practice round."

"One more thing," said the pro, looking around to make sure no one was eavesdropping on their conversation. "What are Will's chances?"

"I'd give him 80/20 to win," said Ronnie.

"Good enough for me," he said, reaching into his pocket and pulling out a hundred dollar bill. "Can you get this down for me, without mentioning my name?"

Ronnie snatched the bill out of his hand and gave him a two-fingered salute. They three of them laughed as they headed back to the parking lot.

* * *

"Wow," said Will, after they had finished their round at the Riverside Golf Course. "This is an awesome layout. I can't think of one thing that I didn't like about this course."

"It used to be a private club," said Eddie. "The owner at Cedar Creek bought it a while back and turned it into a public course. We liked it the first time we played it too. Now let's get something to eat and talk strategy. I've got a feeling that this is going to be a very profitable week for you, my man. If you hit it the way you hit it today, you'll walk right through this guy."

Ronnie just sat there and grinned. Will was fast becoming a chip off the old blocks.

Robbie would have loved it.

CHAPTER TWENTY-THREE

Grudge Match

Setting the hook is as important as your performance out on the course. If you can get the money and the game where you want it to be, it isn't even gambling. It's short-term investing at its finest.

—Eddie Ferguson Davis, investor

No one likes a weasel. Weasels are guys that won't pay up when they lose a bet. They're the guys who are serious about the arrangement until they come out on the losing end. At that point they break out into a stupid grin and try to laugh it off. "You knew we weren't serious, right? I mean, I was just messing around when I said I'd bet you $100 that you couldn't chug that beer in ten seconds. C'mon, man. I don't have that kind of money to throw around." The question is: Would his hand be out expecting to get paid if the beer chugger had failed? You know it. Their total lack of integrity doesn't seem to be a problem to them. They probably got the idea watching mom or dad weasel their way out of their commitments. Non-weaselers tend to follow a simple creed: do what you say you are going to do, with no excuses. How simple is that? Apparently it is more difficult for some than for others.

The guy behind the counter at Riverside said he would allow a couple of carts to follow the group, since it was a serious grudge match and the course wasn't all that busy. If the manager at Cedar Creek had mentioned Eddie or Ronnie to him, or the nature of their business, he didn't let on.

Ronnie figured they could get a side bet with Troy's old man for a few hundred. It wouldn't be a problem if he were anything like his obnoxious kid. Nothing too outrageous, but enough to make it interesting.

Will was on the putting green when Troy and his dad pulled up in a Cadillac. He was surprised when Melissa got out of the car too. She smiled and walked over to him. As usual, she looked fabulous.

"Mr. Feltner called and invited me," she said. "You don't mind, do you? I can't wait to see you take him down. Good luck, Will." She gave him a quick kiss and walked over to Mr. Feltner's cart. Troy gave him a steely-eyed look and then drew his finger across his neck. Will smiled and waved at his opponent. He was way past letting gestures like that intimidate him.

"This is perfect," said Ronnie, as he stood watching his grandson roll putts on the practice green. "Remember our round with Pam? I told Eddie that you would thank me for it later. Well, later is here, my man. With your girl being here, it will put extra pressure on Troy, as he tries to impress her. You, however, will play your game, not trying to impress anyone. It's just you, Mother Nature, and the course designer. You can't play defense in this game. It's all offense, and there are no teammates to rely on or to blame. In case you didn't know it, it's the greatest game in the world. Now, go out and play it, the way we taught you. Remember to think your way around the course. Don't just go out there and hit the ball—play the game. Oh yeah, one more thing. Remember your grip pressure. Don't squeeze it too hard. In a tense situation, a lot of golfers, even good ones, tend to hold the club like they're trying to strangle it."

Man, I love that old guy, thought Will as he watched Ronnie walk back to his cart.

The two players and their caddies stood on the first tee. Ronnie and Eddie were in one cart and Carl Feltner and Melissa occupied the other. Ronnie decided that they needed drinks, so he jumped out and hustled back inside to get refreshments. He asked the occupants of the other cart if they wanted anything. Melissa said an orange Gatorade would be nice.

The first hole at Riverside is a unique design. It's a sharp dogleg from right-to-left. The play off the tee is a big hook around the corner if you want a decent second shot at the green. If the player can't hook it, or at least draw the ball, he is at a huge disadvantage. Will stepped up, and much to the chagrin of his opponent and the two caddies standing there, aimed at the trees on the left corner of the fairway, and hit a big slice with his 3-iron. It was the total opposite of the shot required. The ball curved across the fairway and ended up in the right rough. He walked back to his bag and gently put away his club. Then he did something that would have brought tears to his grandfather's eyes. Ronnie didn't see it because he had not yet come back from his drink run. But 'The Street' was there, and as always, he was taking in everything around him. Will stood by his caddy, staring intently at Eddie with an expressionless look on his face.

The kid's message was as plain as if he was holding up a sign. *I don't believe it*, thought Eddie. *The kid is trying to set the hook. Where the hell is Ronnie? He should be here to see this. C'mon, Carl, do your part. Take the bait. It's right there in front of you.*

"Damn," said Carl Feltner, looking at Melissa. "With a swing like that, Troy should be playing this guy for $3000, not $300."

The comment reminded Eddie of old times back in Detroit. He slowly got up out of his cart and waited for Troy to hit his tee shot. Troy hit a nice little draw that ended up on the right side of the fairway. Then he tossed his driver to his caddy and strolled off the tee.

Eddie continued back to Feltner's cart and stuck out his hand. Carl stared at him, not quite sure what Eddie was up to. The Detroit hustler looked over his shoulder and saw Ronnie coming towards them carrying their drinks. He needed to get this done before his partner made it back to the cart.

"What?" asked Carl.

"I thought I just heard you say you wanted to up the bet," said Eddie smiling. "Or were you just making conversation for the young lady's benefit? I believe the number mentioned was three grand."

Melissa's eyes went wide as she looked at Mr. Feltner. She knew he was a big cement contractor, so the money probably wasn't that big of a deal to him. She was also sharp enough to know that Eddie was serious, and he was making Mr. F. very nervous, standing there with his hand out like that. Did Will hit that big slice, hoping that Troy's dad would say something about increasing the bet? This was crazy. When Carl didn't move, Eddie used the same tactic that had been successful for him in the past.

"I'm sorry, Carl. I just thought you were a man of action and not just a talker. Forget it."

Carl didn't know it at the time, but his strategy of bringing Melissa along to unnerve Will, had just backfired on him. His son's ex-girlfriend was still looking at him, and this Eddie guy was making him look like a loudmouth. He reluctantly stuck his hand out. Eddie took it, winked at Melissa, and walked back to his cart.

"What was that all about?" asked Ronnie, as they sat on the left side of the hole watching Will decide what club to hit for his second shot. Will looked over at them and Eddie gave him a two-fingered salute. The kid returned the gesture. He didn't know for how much, but he did know the game just got more exciting!

"The stakes just got a little higher," said Eddie, as he took a sip of tea.

"How much higher?" whispered Ronnie, as they both watched Will hit his second shot with a fairway metal. The ball rocketed off the clubface straight toward the green. Troy and his caddy, Chad Sims, just stood there with their mouths open. Will's shot came to rest on the front fringe, where it looked like he would have and easy chip to the hole.

"Times ten," answered Eddie, looking straight ahead.

"How in the hell did you do that?"

"I don't get the credit. Will set him up and Curt took the bait like a baby reaching for his bottle. Well, maybe he hesitated a little, but Melissa's presence was the deciding factor."

"Will set him up?"

"Let's just say, being the grandson of 'The Grip' has taught him a few things. Just a few. The rest he learned from me. You should have seen it. It was classic."

On the second tee, Eddie walked over and gave Melissa her drink.

"Hey," said Carl in a low voice, so the players couldn't hear him. "I don't have that sort of cash on me. Do you?"

Eddie nodded his head in the affirmative.

"I'm sure your check's good, Mr. Feltner."

Melissa turned away so Carl couldn't see the expression on her face. She had already figured out what was going on. A few holes later, it also dawned on Carl. There's an old saying: 'After ten minutes at the poker table, if you can't figure out which player is in over his head—you're that player'. This time, Carl was the guy looking around the table.

* * *

Will was one over at the turn.

His had not putted particularly well, but his irons were crisp and accurate. He had missed three greens and got it up and down on two of them. Troy was four over and not taking it very well. It was apparent that he and his caddy were no longer working as a team. That will happen when the golfer tends to blame every poor swing and every bad bounce on the guy carrying his clubs.

Troy sunk a long birdie putt on ten to cut Will's lead to two. When the ball fell he pumped his fist and let out with a loud scream. Will tipped his cap in recognition of a well-played shot.

Troy stood by his bag on the eleventh tee. It was a tricky par four that normally called for a lay-up about 200 yards out. A tree on the left side of the fairway could be a problem if your tee shot was left of center. In a scramble format, if you had a safe one in play, the rest of the players in the group could bomb away. Troy looked over and saw that Will already had his driver out. Fueled by his birdie on the last hole, and the desire to not look like a wimp in front of Melissa, he pulled out the big stick. He hit a solid drive, but it drew a little too much, ending up down the hill on the left and in the trees. Will walked onto the tee with his 3-iron in his hand. He was going to hit the iron all along. He didn't feel bad about the ploy with the driver. It was an old bit that has been around since the beginning of the game. His mentors had taught him to focus on his own game and not worry about what the other guy was doing. It did help to know what the other guy was hitting, but only after he hit his shot. Apparently Troy was unaware of that little bit of golf knowledge. When the hole was over, Will's lead had doubled to four strokes. Still fuming, Troy then bogeyed the next hole, a par three, to go five down.

Melissa looked over at Mr. Feltner. Normally a talkative guy, he hadn't said anything for the last two holes. It was hard to tell if he was just mad or disappointed. Either way, she felt a little sorry for him.

Mitch and Will worked well together. Mitch had studied Will's notes like he was studying for a final exam at school. They were relaxed between shots, walking side by side discussing their favorite sports teams and the kids they went to school with. He was impressed when Will told him that the girl riding with Troy's dad was his new girlfriend. Will had only looked at her a couple of times during the round, and when he did, she lit up with a big smile. If that wasn't inspirational, he didn't know what was.

Number fourteen was a par five that both golfers were capable of reaching in two. Will hit a 5-metal for his second shot and caught it a little fat. Troy was only a few yards off the green with his second. Will made a nice pitch to about ten feet and Troy chipped two feet closer on the same line. Will asked Troy to move his mark so he wouldn't have to putt over it. His birdie putt rolled almost entirely around the cup, but didn't fall. He tapped in and went over and stood by Mitch. Troy replaced his ball and got ready for his birdie attempt. Will looked at him and sensed something was wrong. His opponent was hunched over the ball, eyeing the line.

"Uh, Troy," said Will.

Troy's head snapped up and he glared at Will.

"I might be wrong, but did you move your mark back to its original position?"

It was the first time that Will or Melissa had ever seen what appeared to be the look of gratitude on Troy's face.

"Thanks, man. You're right. I was so focused on making this putt that I forgot to put it back."

After re-marking and then moving the coin back to its original position, Troy rolled the putt in, cutting Will's lead to four. The lead came down two more when Will bogeyed and Troy birdied the next hole.

They went to sixteen with Will leading by two shots. Troy felt a small ray of hope, as he prepared to hit his tee shot. He stepped up and pounded his driver down the middle. Will followed with an identical tee shot. Troy hit first and groaned when his wedge found the trap in front of the green on the right. Will watched his own wedge sail the green, landing in the tall grass just short of some thick bushes. He was actually aiming for the middle of the green. With the pin on the right front just behind the trap, that was the smart play. He was learning that it was hard to dial back with so much adrenaline pumping through your system.

Troy blasted out of the trap with a shot that ended up about fifteen feet past the hole. Will stood next to Mitch and surveyed his options. He looked at his downhill shot to the flag. If he hit at the pin and went too far, he might hit it right off the green and down the hill, leaving an incredibly tight pitch shot back to the flag area. There was also the possibility of hitting it in the trap that Troy had just extricated himself from. The kid pulled the wedge from his bag. He took a couple of practice swings well away from his ball, and then he addressed it, aiming right at the flag. This could be the big turning point of the match. He looked up at his caddy and saw the concern on Mitch's face. Mitch also knew this shot could be a round changer. His two mentors were sitting in their cart about thirty yards away, apparently in a deep discussion. They could be talking about sports or cigars, or who had the coolest car.

At that moment, Will felt he was just about the luckiest guy in the world. His father wasn't around to teach him what he needed to know about becoming a man, but he had two pretty good substitutes. The kid stared at them until they stopped their discussion and returned the look. Will gave them both a two-fingered salute, then he realigned his stance. He was now aiming thirty feet right of the flag, toward a much safer part of the green. 'The Grip' and 'The Street' watched the kid execute the shot, nodding with satisfaction. He flipped his wedge out, landing the ball just short of the green. It hopped onto the putting surface and trickled downhill, stopping about thirty-five feet from the hole. He tossed his wedge to a relieved caddy and took his putter in return. Eddie and Ronnie gave each other a knowing look. The kid was a dedicated student of the game and their teachings had not fallen on deaf ears. It was obvious that Will was thinking about the "ripping part of the foundation out of your round" story. If the kid was three strokes or more behind, with only a couple of holes left to play, he would have had to go for the flag. In his present situation, it made sense to play away from the hole and to just get the ball onto the green. Now he was in a position to make five, possible four. If he would have gone right at the hole he was looking at four, possible six, or even worse.

They both two-putted for a bogey. Will dashed Troy's hopes by making birdies on the par five seventeenth and the downhill par four eighteenth. The last hole was a thing of beauty. He hit his drive fifteen yards past Troy's ball, then he hit a knock-down wedge two feet from the hole. His opponent came over and shook his hand. Will took off his cap and shook Troy's and Chad's hand, while Mitch did the same. Troy's hat remained on his head. Apparently he didn't know that, like in the old days, removing your cap was a sign of respect for your opponent.

"That was a pretty good round of golf, young man," said Mr. Feltner, as they were all loading up in the Riverside parking lot. "Wilson Randall, I don't recall Troy ever talking about your golf abilities. Why didn't you play on the high school team?"

"I have a job, and it would have been difficult to do both," answered Wilson. "And it's Wilson Green, sir."

"I thought you name was Randall."

"It used to be, but it's Green now."

"Well, I don't like this one bit," said Mr. Feltner, retreating to his "weasel" mode. "What did you do, Eddie, bring in some ringer to take our money? Some hot-shot golfer from the big city?"

"Dad," said Troy. "Will has been going to the same school as me for years."

"Three grand is a lot of money, and if you ask me, I don't think things were on the level here."

"What's the big deal, dad. It was 300, not 3000."

"It was 3000, Troy. Now shut up and get in the car. Mr. Ferguson, or whatever your name is, I'm going to have to think about this. I don't like being taken advantage of any more than the next guy. Here's the original $300. I'll let you know what my decision is on the rest of it."

Carl got into his Cadillac with Troy and Melissa and pulled out of the lot. Ronnie, Eddie and Will sat in Ronnie's car and laughed for five minutes straight. What a weasel! It's no wonder Troy turned out the way he did with a dad like that.

"That just goes to show you, kid," said Eddie. "In this business, you don't always win."

"And even when you do win," added Ronnie, "it doesn't always mean you'll get paid. Well, Street, the kid's three hundred to the good. What do you say he treats us to dinner?"

"Drive on, grandpa," said Will. "I'm buying. And I'm not up $300. I gave Mitch $50 for caddying. After feeding you two, I'll be lucky to break even for the day."

That statement brought on another chorus of laughter.

Will wondered what Mr. Feltner and Troy would think if they saw how they all reacted to being stiffed. He couldn't wait to call Melissa tonight to get the inside info on the Feltners' ride home.

Knowing her, she probably wouldn't say much. That's what a classy girl would do, and he was extremely fortunate to have a classy girl in his corner.

CHAPTER TWENTY-FOUR

The Doubler

Warren Buffet once said, "It's only when the tide goes out that you learn who has been swimming naked." I'm sure that most of the marks that I've taken money off of in the past have never heard of that saying. I like to keep things simple by not taking chances outside my area of expertise. If you want to know about golf, horses or money, I'm your guy. When it comes to women, I'm bluffing, just like the next guy.

—Ronnie Costas, simple man

Two days later, Eddie and Ronnie sat at their usual table in the GLV bar and grill. Pam was working, and she was all smiles. She had just informed them that she now had a decent boyfriend, and she couldn't wait to introduce him. He was a dentist that played the local courses occasionally. She explained it was only once in a while, because he was a member of a private club in Kalamazoo. And, he was a pretty good golfer.

"He even said he enjoyed playing for a few dollars if he doesn't have to give the other guy too many strokes," Pam laughed. "Do me a favor and don't take too much money off of him, okay?"

The two hustlers just grinned at each other across the table when she made that comment. Eddie had just shot 67 on the East course, and $50 of his money was now in Ronnie's pocket. They clicked their glasses acknowledging the compliment and sipped their whiskey.

"Do you think we should get Herman involved with the 2700 that Feltner stills owes us?" asked Ronnie.

"I say let it go," answered Eddie. "He's a local and it could mean trouble for us and our operation here. Getting humiliated in front of his son was bad enough. I've been stiffed before and for more than three grand. I'm sure the guy was thinking about a way to weasel out of paying as we played up eighteen. When it was over, he stormed off claiming I was playing with illegal clubs. That ever happen to you?"

"Two large was the most I ever lost on a deal like that," said Ronnie. "Come to think of it, the guy looked something like that Carl dude. What are the odds?"

"So how's the new tub working out?" asked Eddie, changing the subject.

"You won't believe this," said Ronnie, lowering his voice. "I came home the other day and I see Kathy's car in the drive. I figure she's stopped over to make dinner for us and maybe watch a ball game. But when I get in the house, she's in the tub waiting for me."

"Whoa, back this story up a little. How did she get into your house?"

"I gave her a key a while back."

"Now that she's got a key, you know she's going to be coming over all the time, checking up on you," said Eddie. "It will almost be like you're married."

"That wouldn't be all bad, would it? I've been thinking about it lately. What about you and Suzanne? You can't tell me the thought of marrying her hasn't crossed your mind before."

"Dude, think about what you're saying," cautioned Eddie. "There could be ramifications all over the place. If you propose to Kathy, it will put me in a heck of a spot. I'm going to look like schmuck of the year if I don't follow suit. You are holding the keys to our future here."

"Naw, Suzanne is a smart woman. All she'll be is happy for us."

"Maybe on the surface, but down deep she'll be thinking I'm the bad guy in this whole deal. Like you said, she's a woman, and a lawyer to boot."

"Well, you'll have to figure out a way to stay in her good graces," said Ronnie with conviction, "because I'm going to do it."

"All right, man, I'll guess we'll get married too," said Eddie, raising his glass to his fellow hustler.

"Just like that?" chuckled Ronnie, holding up his glass.

"Yup, just like that. I married for looks once, but this time I'm going for intelligence and character. The fact that she is a beautiful woman is just a bonus."

"I hear ya, Street. I hear ya."

"Hey, maybe we'll both get lucky and they'll turn us down," grinned Eddie, as he started to get up from the table.

"One more thing, pard," said Ronnie, motioning for Eddie to sit back down.

Eddie eased himself back into his chair and looked across the table. His ability to read people told him that Ronnie had something other than golf, women or Chicago sports teams on his mind. It was time to assume the role of friend and confidant.

"It's crossed my mind, and I'm sure you have thought about it too," said Ronnie in a measured voice. "Are we setting Will up for a big fall? You know. We fill his head with our stories of crazy gigs and money won on the course. In my early years I lost more than I won. I paid dearly to learn the ropes. I'm worried that my grandson thinks he can just go out, shoot close to par, and clean up. It's a lot different when you aren't playing your home course and are sleeping in a strange bed."

Eddie swirled what little ice and liquid remained in his glass. He knew what his partner was asking—were they putting delusions of grandeur in Will's head—leading him to believe that he could do what they had done in the sport? Finally he looked up at his friend and smiled.

"My honest opinion of the kid is this: I think he has all the ingredients to be a great golfer—college, tour, hustler, whatever he decides to do. The last time we played Bedford Valley he got more bad breaks than we get in a month. He hit the stick and rolled back off the green into the rough on one hole. He hit a sprinkler head and almost went O. B. on another. And what did he say when he had to play a sand shot sideways, just to get it out? He came out of the trap talking about how Walter Payton and Bronko Nagurski would be the greatest Bear backfield ever. How many seventeen-year-old kids display that kind of attitude when things aren't going their way? Did you see him play that shot out from under the overhanging branches on number fourteen? He had the ball positioned way back behind his right foot. And what did he end up shooting after all those bad breaks, 71? Grip, the kid's got it. What he does with it is up to him."

"I was thinking the same thing," grinned Ronnie. "But I'm too close, and I thought my assessment of his abilities might be a little overly biased. Okay, let's just do what we can for him and let him sort it out."

'The Grip' and 'The Street' stood and shook hands across the table. They both wondered how far the kid was going to go in the sport they had dedicated a large portion of their life to. Truth be known, they had no idea.

* * *

Later that evening, both parties were in their respective tubs. When the question was asked, both ladies said "yes" and got all misty about it. Ronnie explained that playing golf and playing the horses was his job, and once they were married, he shouldn't be expected to quit working. Eddie's explanation was similar, except playing the horses was replaced by playing poker. Both women agreed that they didn't want their guys to change in any way. It sounded like a win/win situation all the way around.

Ten minutes after Ronnie popped the question to Kathy, he picked up his phone on the side of the tub and saw that Will was calling.

"Grandpa, what are you doing?" asked Will.

"I'm taking a bath, if you must know," said Ronnie.

Kathy snickered at the thought of Ronnie explaining himself to his grandson.

"Is someone else there? I thought I heard someone laughing?"

"Will, you don't ask a guy that sort of thing," said Ronnie, feigning indignation.

"It's not like I'm asking for details," returned Will, mimicking his grandfather.

"Alright, alright. What's up?"

"I've been thinking about the doubler gig, and I have a few questions," said Will, with a bit of concern in his voice. "You and Street once told me that you were always straight with your opponents. You know, you never lied to them when it came to the golf part, like fake handicaps."

"True. Hell, I haven't had a legitimate handicap for thirty years and neither has Street. Listen, we're not going to lie to them."

"What if they ask what I shoot for eighteen holes? I can't lie about it. It wouldn't be right. And he wants me to hit some bad shots on purpose. Isn't that sort of lying?"

"Will, there's a reason Eddie is called 'The Street'," explained Ronnie. "He's got it all figured out. I will ask you this? Do you want to play me tomorrow for ten grand, even up?"

Kathy turned and looked over her shoulder at Ronnie. She had never heard or seen this side of him. She knew he played golf for money, but apparently she didn't realize the extent of it.

"No, you're better than me," answered Will. "I'd probably lose four out of five times, so you would have to give me four-to-one odds, and if I win once, there would be no blood."

Ronnie was amazed at Will's quick ability to figure out odds. If they played five times, like Will said, and if he won four, he would be up four units. For his one win, Will would need those four units just to break even.

"So, are we not replacing a better golfer with a less accomplished one?"

"Yeah, that's true."

"And if you hit some bad shots on purpose," continued Ronnie, "as far as the score is concerned, it's a risky strategy. You and Eddie would do better if you just played your normal game, right?"

"True," answered Will, as he started to bring things into focus. "If Eddie and I played a legit two-man scramble, we oughta be able to shoot seven or eight under on the West course. We wouldn't do that well if I spray a few shots."

"Exactly. Don't worry about it. Just leave it up to Eddie. It's his gig."

"What are you two cooking up?" asked Kathy, after Ronnie had hung up.

"It's Eddie's bit, tub buddy," said Ronnie.

"We're about to be more than tub buddies," said Kathy leaning back into him. "Where and when should we take the plunge?"

"I say, Vegas in a couple months," responded Ronnie. "I've got a friend that practically runs the MGM Grand. I'll give him a call and he can set the whole thing up. We'll get the VIP treatment and maybe he can get us a few gigs on the side to help cover expenses. You'll like him. He's one of the most interesting guys you'll ever meet—present company excepted."

"Get us a few gigs? I don't play golf."

"We can't do this without Eddie and Suzanne," said Ronnie, attempting to cover up his surprise of it possibly being a double wedding. He felt that Suzanne should break that news. He also didn't think it would be prudent to let on that his offer of marriage to her was a part of a package deal between Eddie and him.

"It would be nice to have them there to stand up for us," said Kathy. "I'll call her tomorrow. Hopefully she can get away from her practice for a few days."

"Something tells me, she'll have no problem with that," said Ronnie. "Now, let's get out of here. The Cubs are on the west coast playing a late game, and they should be starting just about now."

* * *

The next day Eddie was walking through the GLV pro shop. His partner was mowing the grass and doing other household chores, so he decided to put in a couple of hours practicing his short game.

"Hey, Eddie," said the assistant, motioning him over to the end of the counter. "A couple of guys named Hayes and Hansen, from somewhere down south, just teed off on the West course.

I think they might be worth talking to. They asked if anyone around here liked to play for a few dollars. I stepped outside and watched them hit their tee shots. Nice swings. One guy had a Rolex on, so I'm guessing they're not talking about a $50 Nassau. They're staying in the condos, and they said they will be here for the whole week. One other thing—those two acted like they owned the place the minute they walked in here. You know, the 'I'm better than you, because I make a lot of money' type. It's just my opinion, but I'm thinking these are the kind of guys that you like to take down."

"Thanks, man," said Eddie. "I'll check into it. Hey, can I borrow a cart? It wouldn't hurt to get a look at them."

Eddie retrieved his binoculars from his bag and headed over to the West course. Mostly keeping to the trees, to the untrained eye it looked like he was looking for balls. He kept his distance and stayed out of sight, like a hawk circling his prey. The binoculars came out only when the two new guys had their backs or sides to him. Watching head-on was too risky. They might catch a reflection or maybe one of them had exceptional eyesight, or had some binoculars in his bag and was curious about the guy that was checking them out. It didn't take him long to assess the potential competition. They both appeared to be around thirty-five to forty years old, with handicaps ranging from two to four. Being old school, Eddie always judged golfers using the old handicapping system and not the newer Equitable Stroke Control method. The taller of the two appeared to be the most skilled. On one hole, he attempted to hook a shot out of the trees and overcooked it a little, ending up in a greenside trap. His normal shot was a slight fade, so that shot showed Eddie that he was capable of moving the ball the other way if the situation called for it.

Sitting in the parking lot, Eddie went over his notes. Like he told Will during their caddy session, successful people made it a habit to write things down. Both of the guys were decent off the tee—270 to 275. That's about how far he and Ronnie hit it, so there was no advantage there. Will was now longer than both of them—darn kids and their young muscles. Eddie liked the situation and gave Ronnie a call.

* * *

The following day the three of them stood on the first tee of the West course. It was time to lay out Eddie's strategy. Will and Ronnie were surprised when Eddie told them they would be playing with their 4-irons and putters only. Neither of them asked why. Like Ronnie had told Kathy, it was Street's gig and he knew what he was doing. Eddie had checked earlier and the assistant pro told him the two visitors had just left for Stonehedge. It wouldn't do to run into them. If they saw the three of them playing together it might ruin the gig before it had a chance to materialize.

Eddie spiced up the game with a little wager. Since this was his forte, he gave Ronnie two a side and Will five a side. He played Ronnie for fifty and Will for five. They talked course strategy, sports, and even a little politics. Will loved every minute of it. The small plan in the back of his head grew a little more every time he went out with his two mentors. Will decided to test his grandfather on his knowledge of economics. He had recently received an 'A' in the class and was eager to discuss the subject.

"So Grandpa, are you a conservative or a liberal when it comes to the national economy?" asked Will.

"I'll tell you, kid," responded Ronnie. "I'm a conservative most of the time. I don't think the government should be the answer to people's personal problems. They should help out with the big-ticket items, like natural disasters and foreign problems, but in a country like this, a guy should be able to make it on his own. Of course, there are exceptions. If a guy's not physically or mentally capable, that's a different story. I believe that if the government gets involved in the small stuff, it should only be temporary. No one is guaranteed a level playing field when they are born. It's definitely tougher on some, but we've got all the resources necessary for a productive life. The problem is, once some people figure out they can get something for nothing, they think they're putting it over on the people that are actually doing the work and contributing to the economy."

"You sound just like my economics teacher," said Will. "He's big on people pulling their own weight and not being a drag on the system. One day drew this huge blimp on the board and said the people on board were the workers, working to keep the blimp afloat. Then he drew a bunch of ropes hanging over the side with stick figures holding on to them. He said some of the people on the ropes were trying to climb up into the blimp, which was a good thing, because they want to join the working people, and they want to be productive. But others were just holding on for the free ride. He explained that if the number of free riders gets too high, the blimp is in danger of crashing. It was pretty cool the way he described it."

"I hope he cautioned you about not being a close-minded conservative or liberal," added Ronnie. "I told you where I stand, and I think Eddie agrees, that capitalism is the greatest system ever devised. It rewards creative thinking and hard work, and it gives people the incentive to do their best. But, the system needs regulation. If we don't keep an eye on the big money people, like some bankers and politicians, and insurance company executives, they will try to manipulate the system to their advantage. It's happened before in this country, more than once, and it leads to disaster. Like I said, it's a great system and it works, unless the cheaters try to ruin it. It's amazing how low some people will stoop for money or power."

* * *

On the eighteenth tee, it was obvious who had the one-club game mastered. Eddie was so far ahead, he would have had to score double digits on the last hole for it to be even close.

"Here's where we win the dough," said Eddie, looking up the fairway. "We need to be even or one up standing here. Will, you need to bomb one out there so I can hit our second shot on. To make it look good, you will hit your second shot first. Put a big hook on it, so far over that we don't even bother looking for it. I'm guaranteed a good lie because I can place the ball on the turf. I'll hit driver or 3-wood, and will hopefully find the green. That will put a lot of pressure on our opponents, knowing that we will be putting for an eagle."

"What are we hoping for with the doubler?" asked Ronnie.

"I'm hoping it will go down like this: It would be nice to win one of the first two holes, but I'll give it to them for $200, regardless. On number three, we get into a little argument and you walk off. I will admit that I got that idea from our mafia friends that we threw the match to a while back. However, our act will be a lot classier than theirs. Will and I will convince Hayes and

Hansen to let him take your place. After a few holes, they give the doubler back for $400. A few holes later, I give it back for $800, and then we'll be exactly where we want to be. Ideally, and it probably won't happen this way, they will be one up, and will offer it back with four holes to go. That's when we'll have to go to work."

"That means we will be playing for $1600," said Will.

"Each," added Eddie. "I'm going to tell them that when we get down to three holes, the doubler is off the table. It wouldn't be right for either team to be two holes up with three to play, to want to double the bet. That's cranking the screws down a little too hard. Whatever the money is with three to play, that's where it stays. How's that sound?"

"I like it," said Ronnie. "Even if they don't offer it back for $1600, the $800 payoff is decent. Especially for the kid's first venture into high stakes play."

"That's why we're doing it," said Eddie. "We want Will to get some experience, and I need some cash to buy Suzanne an engagement ring. Will, I've got bad news, in addition to the fact that you owe me ten bucks. You're walking in from here, after Ronnie and I finish. Our opponents might be coming back from Stonehedge, and we don't need to be seen together. Hold it, I've got another idea to sell this thing. We'll even tell them that the kid is your grandson, Ronnie. That will be a nice touch. One more thing—Will's clubs need to be on the cart, but in Ronnie's bag."

"Let me guess," said the kid. "I've got a carry bag with legs, and it would look a little strange for an old, uh…a sophisticated gentleman like Grandpa to be playing out of a small carry bag like mine."

"You're catching on," said Eddie.

* * *

"Man, that was brutal," said Will, sitting on Ronnie's patio watching his grandfather grill steaks after the one-club round. "I must have shot a hundred. Sand traps are no place to be when your only weapon is a 4-iron. It took me three swings to get out on number two."

"Ninety-six," said Eddie, looking at the card. "Remember that figure, kid."

"Okay," said Will, looking at his grandfather for an explanation.

Ronnie just grinned and shrugged his shoulders.

* * *

Later that evening, Will picked Melissa up for a little cruise. She had been extremely busy lately, as she was now working at Kathy's store and babysitting around the neighborhood. As soon as Will pulled up in his Camry, she came bounding out the front door.

"What, no convertible?" she asked, smiling and kissing Will on the cheek.

"That's only for special occasions," answered Will. "That's not the reason you go out with me is it? The fact that I can borrow a couple of really cool cars once in a while."

"Well….maybe. Naw, I go out with you because of the type of guy you are. I can't believe it took me so long to figure it out. And since you asked, I'll tell you. I know I made the right choice right after you beat Troy in your big match. You didn't gloat or brag about it, like Troy would have done. The strange part is, Troy didn't say much in the car on the way home. His dad was too mad to talk, but Troy seemed to have something else on his mind. You know, besides losing a golf match to a guy that he had been picking on for all these years. Yeah, Billy told me all about the way Troy acted toward you when I wasn't around."

"That's all history now," remarked Will, as he steered his car down the short road that led to Gull Lake. "Troy's going off to college, and you and I have our whole senior year ahead of us. By the way, do you need a caddy for your upcoming tournament in East Lansing?"

"I know you'll understand, Will," said Melissa, in a serious tone. "My dad really wants to caddy for me this time. He doesn't know much about caddying, but it will mean a lot to him. I hope that's okay with you."

"I don't know," said Will as if he was pouting. "I'm pretty much devastated. The only thing that you can do to make it up to me is to give me a couple of kisses like you did on the seventeenth green that day."

"Ha, I win again," she said. "I was planning on giving you several kisses. But if you only want two…"

Will smiled to himself. He knew how incredibly lucky he had been the past few months. His grandfather was now in his life, and with Eddie, it was like he had two grandfathers. And Melissa was now his girlfriend. What more could a guy ask for! Oh, yeah, he was fast becoming a scratch golfer, before he started his senior year in high school.

*   *   *

"Are you fellas interested in playing something a little different?" asked Eddie, as they stood on the first tee on the West course. It was 84 degrees out, with a slight breeze blowing in from the west.

"Nothing too complicated," said Jon Hansen, a beady-eyed business owner from South Carolina. Eddie found out later that Hansen owned a string of tune-up shops throughout the Carolinas. "We're simple folk here."

"Either of you ever play backgammon?"

Dill Hayes, an insurance executive from Davenport, Iowa, said he had played the game when he was a kid.

"It doesn't get any simpler," explained Eddie. "We play a scramble and we start out playing for $100 per man. Then we use the doubler, the same way it's used in a backgammon game. The cool thing about it is if the doubler is offered and accepted for $200, the guys holding it can keep the money right there. Some games with automatic presses and such can get out of hand, but this can't, unless both sides agree to up the ante."

"So, if you give it to us for $200, and we take it, it won't go any higher than that unless we decide we want to play for more?" asked Dill.

"Yup, it stays right there unless you want to make it more exciting."

"We're good with that," said Hansen, pulling out his driver. "Let's do this."

Hayes and Hansen might have been greedy executive types, like the assistant pro said, but their golf games were top notch. They birdied one, while the home team countered with a deuce on number two. On the third tee, Eddie offered the doubler, raising the stakes to $200 per man. He explained that his birdie putt on two was an indicator of a good day for him on the greens. Ronnie argued, saying it was too early in the match and he didn't want the stakes to get too high.

Eddie told him to relax and just play the game. Ronnie hit first and still looked a little miffed when he hooked his tee shot into the trees on the left. Eddie followed with a well-placed ball about 265 yards out. After their opponents hit, Eddie started ribbing Ronnie about choking so early in the match.

By the time they got to the vicinity of Ronnie's ball, the argument had started. Hayes and Hansen were somewhat amused by the barbs flowing back and forth. They smiled at each other; with the knowledge that team dissention at any time during the round was not a good sign. When the conversation got really heated, Will, right on cue, came walking through the trees with a ball in his hand.

"Hey, Grandpa, is this your ball?" asked Will, holding a Titleist ProV1 in his hand. In his other hand he had a plastic shopping bag full of balls.

"Yeah, and you can keep it, Will. I'm not playing any more with Mr. Moneybags today."

Ronnie started to walk back up the fairway. He only covered a few yards before he turned around and addressed their opponents.

"Sorry guys," he said, walking toward their cart and digging into his front left pocket. "My big mouth partner is such a great golfer, that he will take you on all by himself. I don't renege on bets, so here's my hundred bucks for the original amount."

They watched Ronnie walk through the trees past number one green and back toward the clubhouse.

"Wow, what a sorehead," said Eddie. "I make a couple comments to try and loosen him up and he up and quits. Have you ever seen your grandpa do that before, Will?"

"Can't say that I have," answered the kid.

"Well, I'm not going to play you fellas all by myself," said Eddie. "How about Will taking his grandpa's place? I'll cover you Will."

"You've got to be kidding," said a skeptical Hansen. "That's one of the oldest bits around, Eddie. The old guy walks off and you bring in a ringer on us. What's your handicap, kid?"

"I don't have one," said Will.

"Do you play on the high school golf team?" asked Eddie, jumping in and setting the hook.

"No."

"Why not?" asked Eddie.

"I was told I wasn't good enough, and I have a job anyway."

"One more question," offered Eddie. "What's the last score you shot for eighteen holes?"

"The last round I played, I shot a 96," answered Will truthfully. Now he knew why Eddie had them play with 4-irons and putters the day before. Like Ronnie said, they don't call him 'The Street' for nothing.

"Is that good enough for you guys?" asked Eddie. "I still think it could be a good match. Even though the kid isn't the golfer his temperamental grandfather is. You guys are holding the doubler. I just need the kid to putt first to show me the line and maybe crank out a few drives. Tell you what, if you think anything fishy is going on, like we brought in a seventeen-year-old pro, you can call it off after the ninth hole. If you decide to go on and play the back, we finish it. No hard feelings if you back out. I'm just looking for a little action out here and, after the little tantrum we just saw, maybe a new partner."

The two visitors discussed it and decided that since they held the doubler, they would play on. The clincher was that they could call the whole thing off after they finished the front nine if they didn't like what they saw. Two holes later, Hayes and Hansen were one up, thanks to a forty-footer that came to a stop on the edge of the cup, rested there as if it was deciding what to do, then unceremoniously disappeared into the hole. They gave the doubler to Eddie and he took it. They were now playing for $400 each. Will was doing his part by overswinging and spraying the ball all over the place. He did hit a couple of respectable shots, but his acting was good enough to throw off any suspicions that their opponents might have. He and Eddie were both hoping it would look like dumb luck when it came to the crucial drive on eighteen. Before every shot, Eddie constantly coached him on what he was doing wrong—grip, stance, and tempo. Hayes and Hansen got a kick out of Eddie trying to fix the young man's game while they were playing for more than just pocket money.

On number nine, Eddie hit driver-driver to get to within twenty yards of the green. He and Will got it up and down for a birdie, which was his cue to offer up the doubler, as they stood in front of the soda machine under the pavilion—the same pavilion where Eddie first saw Ronnie several years earlier. Hayes was on his phone, so Hansen had to wait to confer with him.

"I told you," said Hayes, to the guy on the other end of the line. "Deny the claim. We're not running a charitable organization here. Keep stalling with the paperwork and whatever else you can come up with. Just wear him down. He's got a good job. He can afford to pay for it out of his own pocket."

Dill gave the three of them a sinister expression after he hung up.

"How am I supposed to pay for the Porsche I just ordered if the company is handing out money left and right? It's a dog-eat-dog world, kid. And in my business, you want to be one of the big dogs."

While the kid digested Dill's comment, Eddie just grinned inwardly. It was going to be a beautiful thing to see this self-proclaimed big dog get eaten up by an even bigger dog. He remembered the time when he was standing on a dock in Florida, watching the fish swim in and out from under a large boat. It was at night, but a floodlight under the water let him see what was going on down to about six feet. A few good-sized fish were just milling around, and then suddenly they quickly vacated the premises. Two seconds later, Eddie saw why they darted off. A huge fish, at least four feet long, swam into view. Then that fish got spooked and left. Eddie waited and watched. Sure enough, a fish longer than Eddie was tall, slowly swam out from under the boat. He laughed out loud, recalling something Lee Trevino had reportedly said at the end of a tournament, as Nicklaus was coming up the eighteenth fairway. If he remembered correctly it was, "Step aside, boys, and let the big dog eat." Well this big dog, or fish, was starting to get hungry.

"Hell yes, we'll take it," exclaimed Dill. "My Porsche should arrive in a couple of weeks, and $800 will just about pay the first two months of insurance on it."

The other three just stared at him.

"That's an insurance joke, boys. None of the execs in my company have to pay for any type of insurance. Kid, if you're smart, you might want to consider going into the business. I can't think of a sweeter setup."

"Thanks, but I'm thinking of another line of work," said Will, as he opened his soda.

* * *

The back nine on the West course, as usual, was a bear for the two guys that didn't play it on a regular basis. Eddie was doing his best to give the other guys the chance to go one up, but they were just scraping along making pars. On thirteen, the short par three, Eddie left his shot on the hillside short of the green. He gave Will an almost imperceptible headshake, indicating that he didn't want Will to hit the green either. The kid lined up on one of the trees that was well to the right of the green. When his ball hit the tree dead center he turned with wide eyes and looked at his partner. Eddie had his back to him and acted like he didn't see the shot.

"Nice shot," said Eddie as they followed their opponents' cart down the path.

"I learned from the best."

Hayes and Hansen went one up with a par. After a long discussion on the next tee, they offered the doubler to Eddie and Will. This was exactly the position that Eddie wanted to be in. They were now playing for $1600 per man. Eddie birdied fifteen on his own to draw the match even. Something in the back of his mind told him that things were going a little too smoothly. The whole thing was going according to his script with no glitches and that usually didn't happen. Maybe Will and he were the ones getting hustled.

As planned, it all came down to the eighteenth hole. The two teams were dead even. Will, after listening to Eddie tell him for the umpteenth time, to relax and let his hands work the way they were supposed to, cranked out the drive they were hoping for. He flew it 275, right down the middle. On a normal hole the ball might have rolled at least fifteen more yards, but eighteen was always a very soft fairway, and most balls ended up sitting within a few feet of their pitch mark. The best Hayes and Hansen could do was fifteen yards behind Will's ball, leaving them 240 to the middle—up a steep hill. Hansen hit his shot a touch fat and ended up 50 yards short of the green. Hayes fared a little better getting his ball to about 25 yards short of the putting surface.

"Man," said Will, as they rode to his tee shot. "That's got to be one of the best drives I've ever hit." He made sure he was just loud enough for their opponents to hear his comment.

Eddie was impressed with the kid's demeanor and, of course, his ability to come through with the crucial shot. Will hit before Eddie and did his part. He put a big whopping hook on it. He dropped his head and trudged back to the cart.

Street looked up the hill toward the green. It was time to do what he had done so well throughout most of his golf career—come up with the money shot when it mattered the most. He and Ronnie had explained to Will, on more than one occasion, that there were literally thousands of very good golfers in the country. But when it came to hitting a precise shot that meant the difference between winning and losing a tournament, or a bundle of cash, that number was reduced substantially. The pin was way back on the huge green. He knew this because he looked at it when they were teeing off on number ten. He calculated that it was 225 to get all the way back to the cup area. He also knew that he had about fifteen to seventeen feet behind the hole. That didn't leave him much margin for error with the 3-wood that he was holding.

The hill made the shot play more like 240 yards—all carry. Eddie made his swing and watched the ball as it flew toward the middle of the green. He had caught it flush and knew that it was the right distance. Tour players, and some top amateurs, can usually tell you exactly how far they hit a particular shot, even with the longer clubs. Eddie told Will, before they could even see his ball on the green, that he was about ten feet below the hole. They drove up next to the green and saw that Eddie was wrong—by two feet. He was eight feet, dead short of the flag. Will ran out to mark the ball while Hayes and Hansen waited. Hansen hit first and left his pitch about twenty-five feet short of the flag. Eddie knew that would probably happen. The sharp incline of the green made it very difficult to get the ball all the way back to the cup, even after you thought you had hit it hard enough.

Hayes needed to get it close or the match was over, and he and his partner would be going home $1600 lighter. He bent over his shot and then backed off. He finally settled in and skulled his sand wedge toward the hole. All eyes were looking past the hole to see how far the shot would clear the green—only the ball didn't fly the green. The flag was fluttering in the breeze and it grabbed the errant shot like it was a big catcher's mitt. The ball stayed in the flag for a few seconds, then it dropped out, straight down and into the cup for an eagle! Hayes and Hansen were jumping up and down like they had just won the U. S. Open. Eddie just shook his head in disbelief. Will didn't know what to think. Eddie grabbed his putter and motioned for Will to do the same.

'The Street' was standing behind his partner and a little off to the side, as the kid took the putter back. He took a deep breath as Will smoothly rolled in the eight-footer, matching their opponent's eagle. He was glad he didn't have to putt. What a way to finish!

"Don't that beat all," said Hansen. "A couple of years ago this lucky sumbitch won a BMW out in Vegas. I guess it's better to be lucky than good."

Eddie and Will took off their hats and extended their hands. It was a great match, but no money was going to exchange hands, except for Ronnie's hundred that Hansen had discretely pocketed. Eddie thought that was a chincy thing to do since the match went on as planned, only with a substitute.

"It was fun," said Eddie, as they shook hands all the way around. Not winning any money was secondary to giving Will the chance to perform under pressure, playing for decent money against total strangers. This was different than when he played Josh or Troy. He knew those two guys and they were roughly the same age. Playing against two strange adults was a little more daunting.

"Y'all aren't quitting, are you?" asked Hayes, remembering that his team had birdied the first hole to start the match. "Let's go back to number one—sudden death."

"Sounds good to me," said Eddie, looking at his partner. "The tee's open. Let's do it."

They headed back to number one. Just before they got to the tee, Eddie leaned over and whispered to Will.

"They're about to find out how stupid that little saying is. People don't practice being lucky, they practice to be good, or at least better than they were when they started."

Will was impressed with the confidence in Street's voice. He was doubly impressed when Eddie backed it up with some action. Eddie hit his drive down the middle, then into the breeze, he hit a knock-down 9- iron that took one hop, released and rolled about ten feet, ending up right next to the hole. Their opponents could get it no closer than twenty feet. When they failed to convert, Eddie walked up and tapped his ball in for the victory.

Money was exchanged right there on the green. Hansen said the price of a tune-up would have to go up for a few months to cover his losses. They weren't sure if he was kidding or not. Hayes just paid up and didn't say a word. Apparently the "rather be lucky than good" thing only worked on an intermittent basis. Eddie had trouble keeping a straight face when Will, seeing all the hundred dollar bills come out, commented that he thought they were playing for $16, not $1600. Like they had said before, the kid had potential.

Standing next to the car, Eddie explained to Will how he had played that last shot. He was only about 105 yards out, which was normally a full sand wedge or a short pitching wedge for him, even with the wind blowing in his face. He surprised Will when he said he had hit a 9-iron, choking it down and hitting it to the middle of the green. The ball didn't have as much spin as a hard struck wedge, so it hit and released a little toward the flag. He said if he would have tried to stick it in there against the breeze, there was a chance he would have hit it over into the long grass behind the green. Hayes and Hansen both hit wedges from a few yards farther out and both of their shots came in on a higher trajectory and consequently got caught up in the breeze.

"So you played it the way Grandpa would have played it?" asked Will.

"Yeah, but don't tell him that. He's got too big of a head anyway. Hey, let's call him."

Eddie dialed Ronnie's cell and when he answered they both sang, *"Who let the dogs out?"* and barked into the phone. Ronnie laughed and told them to hurry over to his place. A celebration was in order.

When they walked around the side of Ronnie's house to the back patio, Melissa, Suzanne, and Kathy were all sitting there. Ronnie had the grill fired up and promised them a meal to remember. He grilled up rib eyes and salmon for his guests, while Will went through the entire match hole-by-hole.

* * *

When Will was done entertaining the group with Eddie's golf wizardry, Eddie pulled their winnings out of his pocket. The kid was so excited about his first real gig, he had forgotten about the money.

"The way I see it," said Eddie, as he spread out thirty-two one hundred dollar bills on the table. "The kid should get half, because it was his first gig. Ronnie's acting job, was barely worth $800 and I'll take the other $800. A few more jobs like this, babe, and I'll be able to buy you a decent zirconium ring."

Suzanne smiled and lifted her wine glass in acknowledgement. She didn't know it, but Eddie had her engagement ring in his pocket. He had planned on giving it to her before the night was over. He was pretty sure it was bigger than the one Ronnie had picked out for Kathy. It was his way of going one-up on the guy that forced his hand on the marriage thing. Although, he did admit to himself that it was the right thing to do.

"I don't like the split, Street," said Will, with his hand out motioning for the bills. Eddie handed them over and the kid made two piles of $1500 and one small pile with the remaining $200.

"I like that," said Eddie reaching for the cash. "Ronnie should get the smallest cut, since his acting job wasn't as good as I let on. I was just trying not to hurt his feelings. Good move, kid."

"I was thinking more like the $200 was mine, and you two get the big piles," explained Will. "You guys were backing the whole thing, which means I didn't have anything at risk. A guy should have something at stake if he expects a major share of the spoils."

"What do you think, counselor?" asked Ronnie. "Care to arbitrate here?"

Suzanne walked over and made three piles with $1000 each and one small pile of $200.

"It was an equal partnership, so why not split it equal?" said Suzanne. "Even though Will had no cash to lose, he did have a lot of pressure on him, wanting to prove himself to his two mentors. The remaining $200 should go to a good cause. Sound fair?"

"Will?" asked Eddie.

"That's more than fair," said Will, looking at his grandfather, who was nodding his approval. "Let's donate the extra $200 to Disabled American Veterans."

Ronnie turned away from the group, so as not to expose the tearful look on his face. Robbie would be more than proud of his son today—for several reasons.

CHAPTER TWENTY-FIVE

Life Lessons

I'll admit it. I was a jerk in high school, and I've got no one to blame but myself. At least I figured out my shortcomings at an early age. Some guys never do.

—Troy Feltner, reformed bully

Doing the right thing. How often does a guy get the chance to do the right thing, and then he decides to look the other way? Sometimes it's tough to step in and help out someone in need, but when it's over it can give one a tremendous feeling of self-satisfaction. If the opportunity to do the right thing doesn't present itself, then create one. Try to do one nice thing for someone else every day. It doesn't have to be someone you know. Walk up to a stranger with a veteran's hat on at the mall and thank him for his service. Tell someone in law enforcement how much you appreciate what they do. It's a small gesture that will no doubt bring a smile to a fellow citizen's face. Besides, we're all in this thing together. It's better to have more teammates than opponents.

What does it take to be a good citizen of this country? Here's a short, and by no means complete, list: 1. Keep your property in order 2. Provide the necessary care that your children require 3. Pay your taxes 4. Vote 5. Obey the law 6. Be respectful to others 7. Be truthful 8. Don't take more than your fair share (for economic students, this is known as the 'Tragedy of the Commons') 9. Show some compassion toward your fellow man 10. Live within your means and don't incur expenses that you cannot pay!

If your mom and dad did not teach you the above as you were growing up it will be tougher on you, but adhering to the above list is not an impossible task. Take a look around and figure it out for yourself. Your fellow citizens will be grateful that you are part of the solution and not part of the problem.

* * *

It was mid-August and the guys had just finished a highly contested match on the East course. They were celebrating, as usual, at their regular table. In deference to Will, Eddie and Ronnie were drinking ice tea most of the time now—a fact that made Kathy and Suzanne very happy. They were in a congenial mood, as it was the first time all three of them had broken 70 together. Will's 67 topped the old guys' 68 and won him $50 from each of them. They did everything they could to rattle him down the stretch, but it was to no avail. He knew the razzing was all part of his education.

* * *

The Vegas wedding a month prior was a big success. Ronnie's guy at the MGM Grand was everything Ronnie said he was. Eddie finally admitted that Hott Mernanen was indeed an interesting guy—starting with is name. He seemed to know everyone, from big time celebrities to the laundry girls working at the hotel. The guy got more sultry looks from the women around him than any one guy deserved. Eddie thought that he knew a lot of characters, but Ronnie's list of interesting people seemed to be as long as his. Herman and his wife flew out to stand up for both couples. Eddie won a few hundred at the poker tables and Ronnie cleaned up betting the horses at the MGM Grand Sports Book. When the women complained, the guys threw them another grand and told them to go shopping. Their golf clubs stayed home.

* * *

Eddie was about to regale them with a story from his past when Will tapped on the table and nodded toward the doors. Troy Feltner was standing in the doorway looking around. When he spotted their table, he actually broke out in a smile. Troy had made himself scarce after their match earlier in the summer. Will had only seen him couple of times and that was only when they had passed each other on the road. Troy was not frequenting the Stonehedge range any more, because he was practicing with the WMU team in Kalamazoo. Rumor also had it that he was working for his dad on one of his crews pouring concrete. They watched as Troy approached their table. Before he got there all three of them noticed something different about the way he carried himself. His cocky attitude looked to have been replaced by something approaching humility.

"Uh, Mr. Ferguson," said Troy, reaching into his pocket. "I didn't think it was very cool when my dad refused to pay up after my match with Will. So, I'd like to settle up, if that's okay with you. I've been working for my dad this summer and we've been real busy. Anyhow, here's the $2700 he owes you." Troy laid a stack of hundred dollar bills on the table in front of Eddie.

Eddie, with elbows on the table, had his hands clasped under his chin while Troy was speaking to him. He looked down at the money and then slowly back up at Troy. It was obvious that the young man had grown over the past couple of months—both physically and mentally. His arms and shoulders looked more muscular and most of the baby fat he had been carrying was gone. Eddie slowly picked up the bills.

"It took guts for you to come over here and to be willing to pay a debt that really isn't yours to pay. If you had won the match, I would have paid your dad on the spot. So, I'm going to split it with you, and we'll consider the matter closed. College is expensive and I'm sure you can use it. Fair enough?"

Eddie counted out $1400 and sat it on the edge of the table.

"That's more than fair," said Troy, picking up Eddie's offering, then looked at Will. "Good luck on your senior year, Will. I'll tell the Western coach about you. I mean, if you're interested in playing college golf next year. You really should go out for the high school team. Most of the good players have graduated and they could use you."

"Thanks," said Will. "I'll think about it."

"Well, thanks again," said Troy, turning to leave.

"Hey, Troy," said Will. "Any chance you could introduce me to some of the college golfers on the team, once you get to know them?"

Troy turned with a confused look on his face. Then it slowly dawned on him as to what Will was getting at. College golfers on scholarship probably had some coin in their pockets and might not be averse to playing for a little something now and then. Troy smiled and nodded his head.

"Always thinking, hey kid," said Eddie, as they watched Troy leave the room.

"Hey, I'm learning from the best," said Will.

Eddie counted out three piles. One had $500 in it and the other two had $400. He slid the pile with the most bills in it across the table to Will.

"That's yours for playing so well," he said. "Ronnie and I will split the remaining $800, because we were fronting the money if you lost."

Will took his bills and put them in his money clip.

"Thanks, Eddie. Why did you take Troy's money? You did say it wasn't his debt to pay."

"For a couple of reasons: First, Troy was trying to save face in front of us and a few others, like Melissa and the kid that caddied for him. And if I had turned him down, it would have been disrespectful to his family name. Second, it's a cheap lesson for him to learn. It's all about paying your dues. Something tells me that up until a few months ago, Troy has pretty much gotten everything he's ever asked for. I think your match with him was an eye-opener, in more ways than one."

"I do feel kind of sorry for him," said Will.

"Don't," continued Eddie. "I've read a few books by this Larry Winget guy. He gives financial advice along with what I would call life lessons. In one of his books he wrote something like this: 'Up until you're thirteen, you are a product of your environment. Once you hit that age, you should be able to look around and figure a few things out by yourself'. Troy was about five years late doing this, and he certainly made life miserable for some people, while he was in the process of figuring things out. I hope he's on the right track. He still has to deal with the likes of his dad, who appears to be clueless when it comes to dealing with failure. I'll admit I was a little shocked when the old man refused to pay up."

"Hey, speaking of paying up," said Will. "Did you guys pay me? I was three under, you know?"

"We paid you, kid," said Ronnie. "Here comes the bill. Nice round today, Will, and thanks for dinner. Kathy and I are going to be vacationing for about ten days, so you two will have to hold down the fort. Don't get in over your heads and expect me to bail you out when I get back."

"No worries," said Eddie. "I think Pam's new boyfriend wants me to come over to Kalamazoo for a round. While I'm there, I'll check out the prospects for some future gigs."

"You do that, partner," said Ronnie, clapping Eddie on the back. He gave Will a hug and told him to stay out of high stakes games until he got back. The kid said he could make no guarantees.

* * *

Two days later Eddie was sitting at his usual table playing gin rummy with Butch Stone, one of the guys from the Tuesday afternoon game. Carl Feltner, who hadn't spoken to Eddie since the big match, was sitting at another table with a big guy that Eddie didn't recognize. The hustler could sense their eyes on him, even though he didn't look in their direction. From the volume of their voices, it was a safe bet that they already had several rounds under their belts. Eddie was dealing the cards when he noticed that Butch was looking up and over his shoulder. He turned slowly to see Carl's drinking companion standing directly behind him.

"Name's Eddie, right?" asked the stranger. Before Street could answer, the guy continued. "Name's Jim, but most people call me Pearl. Carl over there tells me you're some hot-shot golfer from Detroit. Says you tried to con him out of a couple grand a while back. Care to play me for a few dollars, Mr. Golf Hustler?"

"Naw," said Eddie, turning back to the card game. "Carl must have confused me with another good-looking guy. I'm just a recreational golfer, waiting for social security to kick in."

"You're a funny guy."

"I get that all the time," said Eddie, refusing to be baited by a guy he didn't even know. "My wife thinks I'm hilarious."

"I'll play you even up—any game and for any amount."

"Maybe some other time," said Eddie, without looking up.

"Yeah, Carl must have been confused. You don't look like much of a golfer."

"Like I said," responded Eddie, wheels beginning to spin his head. "I like to play for the scenery and all the fresh air out there."

"Don't kid me, buddy. I know fear in a guy's eyes when I see it. If you change your mind, I'll be around for a few more days. But something tells me you don't have it anymore and are happy just sitting around thinking about how good you used to be. Hell, you were probably never that good in the first place. Pretty pathetic, if you ask me."

The guy went back to his table and said a few words to Carl. Their laughter could be heard throughout the bar and grill area. Butch raised an eyebrow at Eddie, hoping to get an explanation for what had just transpired. Street just smiled and gave him a wave, indicating that the guy's challenge was no big deal.

"Do you know that guy?" asked Eddie.

"He's been here before," answered Butch. "He's a friend of Feltner's. He's a real good player. Big hitter. Won some amateur tournaments a few years ago. I heard he once qualified to play in the U. S. Open."

Twenty minutes later, Eddie paid off his gin losses and got up to leave. He had to walk by Carl and his buddy to get to the door. They watched him approach and snickered when he went by. 'The Street' turned quickly and leaned down between the two of them. He spoke softly so no one else could hear.

"Hey, Pearl. Any game for any amount, right?" asked Eddie.

"That's what I said," came the hesitant response.

"Tomorrow, at noon, we'll play the East course here for $1000 a hole. We'll each give six large to the pro to hold until after the match. That way no one can weasel out of paying when it's over."

Eddie was staring directly at Carl when he made his last statement.

"You're on," said Pearl, grinning.

"One more thing," said Eddie. "The game is 4-iron and a putter. Those are the only clubs you'll need to bring. See you tomorrow at noon. Don't forget the six large. It should be fun."

Before Pearl or Carl could respond, Eddie walked briskly across the hall to the pro shop. He wasn't sure what the pro would say about this little arrangement. Surprisingly, the pro said he would have no problem holding the stakes, and he would block off the tee sheet on the East layout for a half hour to give them some space. Eddie had explained earlier why the pro didn't win any money on Will's match. Since Carl didn't pay off, Eddie just gave him his hundred back. The pro said it didn't surprise him in the least. Now he asked if he could get a piece of Eddie's $1000 a hole wager. Street said he would give him $50 of the action.

Pearl had no idea how to play with just one club and a putter. On most of the holes he stepped up and hit his tee shot as hard as he could without putting any thought into it. As a result, he was constantly out of position, which forced him to attempt shots that a 4-iron wasn't designed to do. He knew he was in big trouble when, early in the match, Eddie blasted out of a trap and onto the green. He didn't get it close, but just extracting himself from the buried lie seemed like a miracle to his opponent. Eddie then two-putted for a bogey and halved the hole. Carl rode along for the first twelve holes. When it looked hopeless for his boy, he headed back to the clubhouse and started drinking. The sad thing was he didn't learn a thing after Troy's match with Will. He was too wrapped up in himself to see the improvement in his son's attitude and work ethic—something Troy should have learned from his father.

When it was over, Eddie collected $5000 of Pearl's money from the pro. He had won seven holes, while losing only two. After paying the pro his $250, he headed home, showered and waited for Suzanne to get home from work. After the wedding, they decided to live at Eddie's place. Suzanne's house, north of town, was still on the market.

"So, should I ask what you did today, while your wife was slaving away at work?" asked Suzanne, as they relaxed on the sofa watching the evening news. "Let me guess, you played golf and then a few hands of gin with one of the guys."

"Close," said Eddie. "Today I gave a golf lesson. And maybe a lesson in another area."

"What other area would that be?" asked Suzanne.

"Humility," answered Eddie. "Just when you think you're really good at something, someone else comes along and shows you that you aren't as good as you thought you were. It can be a very humbling experience. I've been on both sides of the issue."

"Can I ask what this lesson cost somebody today?"

"Five grand. And believe me, it was worth every penny to the guy that had to pay."

"This someone that had to pay—could he afford to lose $5000?"

"Sweetheart, it should save him money in the long run," said Eddie. "If he decides to learn from it. I did my part. How he reacts is up to him. Hey, let's go out for pizza. You're buying."

"Why should I buy when you just won $5000?"

"Because it took me about three hours to make that kind of money. A good attorney can earn that much while she's standing out by the back door burning one with the rest of the suits."

"You're a funny guy, Street," said Suzanne. "I'll buy, but I'm going to make you earn your supper later."

"I hope I'm up to the task," said Eddie, standing and offering her his hand.

"You will be by the time I'm done with you," she smiled.

* * *

Will's senior year was the most fun he had ever had in high school. He and Melissa were getting more comfortable with each other all the time. She played number one on the girls' golf team and had an exciting season. She missed going to the state tournament by one stroke. It only took her a day to get over it, then she was back to her old perky self. That was another thing that Will liked about her.

Once the range slowed down in the fall, Will went back to work out on the course, mowing roughs. He continued to practice at every available opportunity. His game was improving on a monthly basis. The pro told him he wanted Will to work in the shop next year.

One night at the dinner table, Kathy asked Ronnie how good he thought Will could be. He put down his fork and gave her a serious look.

"I think he will be better than Eddie or me. He's got an incredible swing with almost perfect tempo. He can hit all the shots, and the ball comes off the club face like a bullet. The only thing he is lacking at this point is experience. The pressure of playing for his own money doesn't bother him in the least. It doesn't surprise me. He's Robbie Green's son."

"And Ronnie Green's grandson," said Kathy, reaching across the table and taking her husband's hand in hers. "I'm glad you found him and I'm glad you made up with his mother."

"Following him here also led me to you, so it was a win/win deal all the way around."

"That's true," agreed Kathy. "By the way, when we visited my parents, what did you tell them that you did for a living before you retired?"

"I told them I worked with numbers a lot," said Ronnie with a sheepish grin. "You know, like an accountant. I figure with your dad being a minister, it was the smart thing to do."

"Well, if the subject comes up again, I'm going to tell them the truth," said Kathy. "My husband is a golf hustler and a horse player. If I can live with the shame of it, they'll just have to accept it."

"Yeah, yeah. Let's go in to the horse room. I want to show you this race that's coming up. There's something about it that just doesn't make sense…"

* * *

By the end of the summer, the head pros at GLV and Stonehedge were well aware of Will's golf ability. They got together and wrote to the Michigan State University golf coach and all but guaranteed that the kid would be an All-American. The coach questioned why Will had not played any high school golf or in any junior tournaments. They said there were extenuating circumstances, and that he should come down to look at the kid. Both of the pros had mentioned the possibility of playing college golf to Will, but he seemed only mildly interested in the idea.

The kid definitely traveled to the beat of his own drum.

The MSU coach came down in the fall and rode around with a member of the grounds crew. He kept his distance as he watched Will play with Eddie and Ronnie. The Stonehedge pro was surprised when the coach told him he knew who Eddie was. A legend was playing his course on a regular basis and the pro didn't even realize it. He figured 'The Street' deserved his lofty status if he could keep something like that a secret from him and most of the locals. He wondered if the GLV pro knew who he was.

Will started getting letters from the coach in November. He finally paid a visit to the East Lansing campus in February. It was more to get out of school for a day than to look the place over. He did think the guys on the golf team were pretty cool. A couple of them were yuppies, like Troy, but most of them were okay. His mom and Melissa were both in favor of his attending MSU. It wasn't so far away that he couldn't come home on weekends. Ronnie and Eddie said he should follow his heart as well as his mind, when making his decision. His grades were fair, but were his study and organizational skills good enough to be a success in college? He wasn't sure if they were, but his mother and his girlfriend would be awfully proud if he were an MSU Spartan.

Spring rolled around and the weather started to warm up. Most of the top athletes all over the country had signed their letters of intent in February. Will sat at a table next to Holly Shill, the highly recruited volleyball player from his high school. This was a special situation, because Holly had broken her leg the first week of the season, and wasn't sure it would heal in time for her to play ball at WMU. She had made remarkable progress, so a press conference was called for her to declare her intentions. Will was coerced into attending also. Two newspaper reporters and a television reporter were there to get both their stories. While they were waiting, Holly leaned over and whispered to Will that she didn't even know that he played golf. He just laughed and looked over his shoulder at his mother and Ronnie. Eddie was standing way in the back of the room with a passive look on his face. It was the same face that left other poker players wondering if he was holding bad cards or pocket kings.

Holly signed her letter first and answered a few questions from the media. When it came to Will's turn, he looked down at the paper in front of him. He held the pen above the document, but couldn't bring himself to lower it to the paper. He glanced up at Eddie and received a blank stare. The guy that had always been so helpful was offering nothing. He took it as a sign that he was totally on his own. He looked over his shoulder at his mother and his grandfather. His mother had a concerned look on her face. She nodded toward the paper, indicating that he should go ahead and sign it. Ronnie's face resembled Eddie's. He stared down at the paper and refused to make eye contact with his grandson. *Follow your head and your heart.* Wasn't that what they both had always said? He slowly laid the pen on the table and looked up at the people in the room.

"I'm sorry, everybody. Coach, it's nothing against you, the university, or the golf program. I just don't think this is the best course of action for me."

A bit of a smile started to spread across Ronnie's face, and Eddie gave the kid a two-fingered salute from the back of the room.

"I've decided to go into the family business."

"What business is that, Will?" asked one of the reporters.

"Investments," said the kid, breaking out in a big grin. "Short-term investments."

EPILOGUE

Three Years Later

A fresh gig for big money is kinda like the first time you made love to your woman. You're thinkin', man, it doesn't get any better than this.

—Will Green, future unknown

"What do you think?" asked Melissa. She was playing in a practice round for the Womens' State Amateur Tournament that would be held in Battle Creek in two days.

Will Green, now twenty-one, stood next to his wife in the middle of the tenth fairway at the Battle Creek Country Club.

Will set her bag down and looked the shot over.

"You're 195 yards out into a light breeze," he said. "I think you'll have to hit a strong hybrid to get home. Look over there. Shawna's only a yard behind you and she's got hers out."

"Hey, Shawna," hollered Melissa, as her playing partner stood there making practice swings with the club she intended to hit. "How about a little wager? I'll bet you $50 that my caddie can get it inside of your shot from right here."

"It's a bet," said Shawna. "Let's see what he's got."

"She's ranked in the top three in the state, sweetie," said Melissa. "Don't let me down."

Will took out Melissa's 5-iron and took a few practice swings. He threw a ball down and hit a nice little draw that ended up twelve feet below and a little left of the hole. The shot drew an applause from Shawna and her caddy. Then she lined up her shot and stuck it in there two feet inside of Will's.

"You hack," laughed Melissa. "I told you she was ranked in the top three in the state. The pressure's on and you chunk it? You just lost your caddy fee."

"I'll find another way to collect what I've earned," said Will, as he pulled out his money clip and walked over to pay Shawna. As usual, there were eight hundreds and a few fifties in the clip. He learned early on from 'The Grip' and 'The Street' that you should always be prepared, because you never knew when an opportunity would present itself. And, like his two mentors, his golf bag contained five grand and a pair of binoculars. He also had a notepad and a pen stashed away in the sweater pocket. Eddie's lesson on how successful people often took notes was not lost on him. The nine-millimeter was something he would have to think about.

* * *

Eddie, Ronnie, and Will sat at a restaurant in the Lakeview Mall in Battle Creek. Their wives were shopping, which meant they would be there a while. All three sipped on beers while Eddie and Ronnie entertained the group with stories of past victories and losses. Eddie recalled the time he was playing in Detroit and the guy he was playing against had a heart attack in the middle of the seventeenth fairway. Eddie knew that he had high blood pressure, because his face was always red. He said there was a doctor playing an adjacent fairway and that probably saved the guy's life.

"How much were you playing for?" asked Will.

"Five bucks a hole, and I was playing with only three clubs—driver, seven and putter," said Eddie. "And get this, the guy was a millionaire. He had offered to sponsor me on tour on several occasions. A week later he was out of the hospital, but I never saw my winnings. I didn't ask for them. The guy did almost die. You ever see anybody die on the course, Grip?"

"No, but we were playing this public course in Chicago one day when we heard gunshots. We immediately ducked behind our carts and looked around. When things quieted down, one of the guys in the group said he felt something in his eye. He started rubbing it and he pulled out what looked like a small piece of bark. We went back to the tree he was standing by when the action started, and sure enough, there was a bullet hole right next to where his head was—with the bullet still lodged in there. Golf can be a dangerous game, kid. You have to keep your wits about you at all times."

"You've got all the skills necessary," said Eddie. "The swing, the temperament, and you handle yourself well under pressure. What are your plans?"

"Well," said Will, setting his bottle down on the table. "Melissa gets her nursing degree in a few months and she's got a job offer at the big hospital in Kalamazoo. So we're going to stick around here. Besides, if I left the area, you two wouldn't have anybody to make fun of. That, and I need the lunch money that I take from you guys on a regular basis."

"With your communication skills, maybe you should look into a club manager's job at a big resort," added Ronnie. "Then Eddie and I can visit and play for nothing. And maybe some of the old boys there would like to donate to our retirement fund."

"Speaking of communication skills," said Eddie, "I've got a story for you. I wasn't there, but the guy that told me this swore it was true. This old boy was a member at a prestigious club in Detroit, and he was on the rules committee. The other three in his regular foursome were fed up with him bending the rules all the time. You know, mismarking his ball, teeing up a few inches ahead of the tee markers—that sort of stuff. So one day they walk into the club's bar and grill, and they see a member named Frank. Now Frank is an attorney with a real smooth delivery. I mean, his eloquence in the courtroom was the stuff of legend. They decide that Frank was the perfect guy to tactfully remind the rules fudger, that the rules of golf should be followed at all times, not just when it's convenient. They figured that Frank could make it sound so smooth that the guy would actually thank him for bringing it to his attention. What the guys didn't know was that the attorney had just finished off his fifth scotch and water, so he was more than half in the bag. Apparently he had been arguing with his wife and he wasn't in a very good mood. Well, the three of them explained the situation to him and he agrees to talk to the guy in question. He gets up from the bar and wobbles over to the guy's table and just stands there, looking down at him. The whole room went quiet, waiting for Frank to display the courtroom skills that he was famous for. When the guy looks up at him, Frank hollers, "Quit cheating, bitch!" Then he stumbles back to the bar and orders another drink. Five seconds later the whole place erupted. Rumor was that Frank didn't have to buy another round for the rest of the golf season.

Ronnie looked at Will and grinned.

"What are the odds he told that story to his wife, the attorney?"

"I did," laughed Eddie. "But I said the guy was an accountant instead of a lawyer. I know how to play the game. She thought it was semi-funny."

Will laughed and then a serious expression came over his face. It was obvious that he had something on his mind, and he was having trouble expressing himself. He looked over his shoulder at the waitress and signaled for another round. Then he turned and faced the two guys who had taught him everything he knew about the game he loved. In addition to golf, they also helped him to develop a solid set of principles.

"I've been kicking something around in my mind lately," he said in a pensive voice.

Eddie glanced at Ronnie, looking for some indication of what Will was talking about. Ronnie just shrugged his shoulders. The waitress sat three more beers in front of them. Will picked his up and took a slow drink. He sat the bottle gently back on the table.

"Grip, Street, I've been thinking about trying to qualify for the U. S. Open next year."

There, it was out. For the past week, he and Melissa had been discussing the pros and cons of entering the qualifier. If he did make it, he would no longer be an unknown entity, at least in the state of Michigan. His hustling days would definitely have to take a new direction, and it was undecided whether that direction would be good or bad. It was already hard for him to get a decent money game in the area, which meant he would have to branch out and do some traveling or get a real job that paid a decent wage with benefits. The GLV area wasn't like Chicago or Detroit.

"Why in the hell would you want to do that?" asked a shocked Ronnie.

"Now wait a minute, Grip," said Eddie, turning Will's revelation over in his mind. "What do you think the odds would be on the kid to, say, make the cut? Or finishing in the top twenty or even the top ten? Think about it. They would be…"

"Astronomical," said Ronnie, raising his bottle, signaling his companions to do the same. "The numbers on him at the Vegas Sports Books would be completely off the charts. This could be an opportunity to make a lot of dough."

They all clicked bottles and then leaned forward for some serious discussion. The three wives observed the toast, and the subsequent huddle, from the doorway of the restaurant.

"What do you think that's all about?" asked Melissa, nodding toward the guys' table.

"I don't know," answered Kathy. "My guess is they're planning another gig, as Ronnie calls it."

"Call it women's intuition," observed Suzanne. "For some reason I've got a feeling that life's going to get a little more exciting for all of us."

"I wouldn't have it any other way," said Melissa, as she led the way to their table.

In the works:
Links Lizards: The Continuing Adventures of 'The Grip', 'The Street' and The Kid

The action heats up when the two old guys, with the help from their favorite private detective, head overseas to solve a major problem. Will, not to be out done, stays home and does the unthinkable.

CHAPTER ONE

Setting the Hook

Wayne bobbed his head backwards and appeared to have trouble focusing on his cards. Making his decision to call, he tossed a twenty on the small pile of bills in the center of the table. He looked up at the other players.

"I'm calling," he said in a slightly slurred voice as he turned over his hole cards. "Three kings, gents."

The man across from him grinned and exposed his diamond flush. Wayne nodded his head slowly in acceptance and leaned back in his chair.

"You know that old song about if it weren't for bad luck, I'd have no luck at all?" he asked no one in particular. "Well, tonight I think that tune was written with me in mind."

"I'm surprised a kid like you would know that old blues tune," responded Curley, a bald executive type in his late fifties.

"There's a couple of old guys that I play golf with once in a while," said Wayne, as he took the last sip from the flask he'd been nursing for the past few hours, "and they love that old blues stuff. I probably heard about it from them." The flask he was drinking from had just enough whiskey in it to give off the familiar smell of alcohol.

"Well you certainly didn't learn anything about card playing from them," said his brother, Mack, as he sat across the table with a modest pile of bills sitting in front of him. "How much have you donated tonight, a couple a hundred?"

"Closer to three, but it aint no big thing. I've been working a lot of overtime lately. Like I said, old Lady Luck is puttin' the hammer on me tonight. Now if we were playing golf, that would be a different story. There's a little luck playing small-ball, but it's mostly skill, not like cards. Can't do much when all you're dealt is junk, hand after hand."

"Don't start in with that golf crap," said Mack, with more than a little agitation in his voice. "Every time you get a little drunk you start talking like you're God's gift to the sport."

The rest of the guys around the table were getting a kick out of the two young brothers that were sitting in on their weekly card game in the back of Bernie LaDuke's pro shop at a prestigious country club in Lansing, Michigan. The brothers heard that the pro ran an honest game where the stakes didn't get out of hand. Besides, poker wasn't their main objective when they wrangled and invitation to the game—an invitation that was two months in the making. Three of the players at the table were affluent members of the club and the other, in addition to the head pro, was one of his assistants.

"C'mon, bro, you're just pissed 'cause I can give you three a side and still beat you like the proverbial red-headed step-child," teased Wayne.

"You two don't look like brothers," commented Shaun, the assistant pro.

"Same mom, different dad," explained Mack. "I'm legit, he's the bastard."

Wayne stood up from the table and stared daggers at his half brother. "So that makes you better than me? There's nothing you can do that I can't do better. I make more money than you do and you know damn well that I'm a better golfer."

"All right," said the pro, attempting to diffuse the situation. "Easy, you two. Don't bring any family problems to my game. We're just here for a good time."

"Yeah," added Paul Champion, one of the club members. "A good time where there are no women involved. Hell, my wife thinks I'm at a Lion's Club meeting."

This little admission brought a round of chuckles from the players at the table.

"Mine thinks I'm meeting with the investment club I belong to," added Allan Spane. "Actually my time was invested wisely tonight, because I'm holding some of young Wayne's dough."

"Like I said, if we were playing golf, it would be a different story," said Wayne, sitting back down and digging into his left front pocket for some more bills.

Mack wouldn't let it go. "Can it, Wayno. There are probably three guys at this table alone that can kick your butt out on the course. The last time you played you barely broke eighty. I'm sure the pro, his assistant there, and at least one of these members would have no trouble with what you call a golf game."

Apparently fueled by the combination of the whiskey and being embarrassed in front of strangers, Wayne got up and quickly came around the table toward his sneering half brother. To everyone's surprise, he threw an open-handed slap that grazed the side of Mack's head. Before any of the stunned observers could react, Mack jumped up and retaliated with a shove that nearly put Wayne on the floor. The pro and his assistant stepped in and separated the two of them before things got out of hand.

"Sorry you guys had to see that," said Mack as he stood facing his brother. "He gets a little crazy when he's drinking the hard stuff. Beer isn't a problem, but once he gets a little whiskey in him he's a different person."

The assistant let Mack go, as it seemed he had no intention of continuing the altercation. Bernie still held on to Wayne, who was still breathing hard, and gave no indication of what he was going to do next.

"You know I don't like being called a bastard," wailed Wayne. "And you also know that I can beat any man in this room. I've got two grand to put up if there are any takers."

The pro, sensing an opportunity, let go of Wayne and stepped back.

"Let me get this straight. You're saying that you're willing to play Shaun here for two grand? Is that what you're saying?"

"That's what I'm saying," replied Wayne in a somewhat calmer voice. He reached into his pocket and pulled out a wad of bills. "And I aint just talking either. My money and my golf swing do my talking for me."

"Don't do it, brother. It's the booze talking and you know it. Shaun played college golf and he's won a few tournaments. You've never won a tournament in your life. Just because you work at a golf course doesn't make you an expert on the game."

"I don't care," said Wayne as he took his jacket off the back of his chair preparing to leave. "I meant what I said. So what, now you're all concerned on my behalf, brother?"

"I just don't want Angie to get all upset again because you've done something stupid. As soon as you do, she calls my wife and then we're all involved in one of your delusional escapades. He's not going to play, Bernie—at least not for even money. That would be pure suicide."

"What are you saying?" asked Shaun. "He wants some sort of odds?"

"I'm saying he's not playing you even up for two G's, that's all," explained Mack. "C'mon, hothead, let's go. You can fantasize about winning the U. S. Open on the way home—if you can stay awake that long. Sorry about the argument, guys. Y'all seem like a bunch of square fellas."

"Hold on a sec," said Bernie, taking Shaun by the arm and guiding him off to the side, where he spoke quietly to his assistant. "Look, Shaun. Let's assume you can beat this guy three out of four times. If you do, you would be two units up. You know, you're holding three and he's holding one. So, if you give him two-to-one, the odds say you will still come out ahead. If you pay him two units on his one win, you're still one unit to the good. And in this case, one unit is two grand."

"I hear what you're saying, but what if he's some kind of hustler trying to set us up?" asked Shaun, still not convinced.

"Could be, but I doubt it," reasoned Bernie, looking over his assistant's shoulder at the two brothers. "What did you shoot yesterday?"

"I was four under, a 68."

"Does that kid over there look like he can come in to your back yard and shoot a number like that?"

"No, but I don't have that kind of money to bet, even if it looks like a sure thing."

"Don't worry about that. I'm sure a couple of the members here would want some of the action. Let's offer him three-to-two. Maybe that will make his brother happy. Hell, he probably won't show anyway."

CPSIA information can be obtained at www.ICGtesting.com
Printed in the USA
LVOW03s1248040914

402221LV00002B/2/P